Living to the Praise of God's Glory

Australian College of Theology Monograph Series

SERIES EDITOR GRAEME R. CHATFIELD

The ACT Monograph Series, generously supported by the Board of Directors of the Australian College of Theology, provides a forum for publishing quality research theses and studies by its graduates and affiliated college staff in the broad fields of Biblical Studies, Christian Thought and History, and Practical Theology with Wipf and Stock Publishers of Eugene, Oregon. The ACT selects the best of its doctoral and research masters theses as well as monographs that offer the academic community, scholars, church leaders and the wider community uniquely Australian and New Zealand perspectives on significant research topics and topics of current debate. The ACT also provides opportunity for contributors beyond its graduates and affiliated college staff to publish monographs which support the mission and values of the ACT.

Rev. Dr. Graeme Chatfield
Series Editor and Associate Dean

Living to the Praise of God's Glory

A Missional Reading of Ephesians

MARK A. SIMON

WIPF & STOCK · Eugene, Oregon

LIVING TO THE PRAISE OF GOD'S GLORY
A Missional Reading of Ephesians

Australian College of Theology Monograph Series

Copyright © 2021 Mark A. Simon. All rights reserved. Except for brief quotations in critical publications or reviews, no part of this book may be reproduced in any manner without prior written permission from the publisher. Write: Permissions, Wipf and Stock Publishers, 199 W. 8th Ave., Suite 3, Eugene, OR 97401.

Wipf & Stock
An Imprint of Wipf and Stock Publishers
199 W. 8th Ave., Suite 3
Eugene, OR 97401

www.wipfandstock.com

PAPERBACK ISBN: 978-1-7252-9966-5
HARDCOVER ISBN: 978-1-7252-9967-2
EBOOK ISBN: 978-1-7252-9968-9

05/05/21

Scripture quotations (unless otherwise indicated) are from *New Revised Standard Version Bible*, copyright © 1989 National Council of the Churches of Christ in the United States of America. Used by permission. All rights reserved worldwide.

Scripture quotations are from the ESV® Bible (The Holy Bible, English Standard Version®), copyright © 2001 by Crossway, a publishing ministry of Good News Publishers. Used by permission. All rights reserved.

Scripture quotations have been taken from the New American Standard Bible®, copyright © 1960, 1962, 1963, 1968, 1971, 1972, 1973, 1975, 1977, 1995 by The Lockman Foundation. Used by permission.

Scripture quotations have been taken from the Holy Bible, New International Version®, NIV®, copyright © 1973, 1978, 1984, 2011 by Biblica, Inc.™ Used by permission of Zondervan. All rights reserved worldwide. www.zondervan.com. The "NIV" and "New International Version" are trademarks registered in the United States Patent and Trademark Office by Biblica, Inc.™

Scripture quotations marked CSB have been taken from the Christian Standard Bible®, copyright © 2017 by Holman Bible Publishers. Used by permission. Christian Standard Bible, and CSB® are federally registered trademarks of Holman Bible Publishers.

To my colleagues in ministry in Indonesia,
especially the faculty and students of
Aletheia Theological Seminary.

Contents

List of Tables | xii
Preface | xiii
Acknowledgments | xvii
List of Abbreviations | xix

1 Introduction | 1
   1.1 Background 1
   1.2 Research Questions 2
   1.3 Hypothesis 3
   1.4 Literature Review 1—Mission in Ephesians in Biblical Scholarship 3
   1.5 Literature Review 2—Missiological Works that Discuss Ephesians 15
   1.6 Theoretical Framework—Missional Hermeneutics 27
   1.7 Methodology 35
   1.8 Plan of the Present Study 44

2 Ephesians 1:1–14 | 45
   2.1 Introduction 45
   2.2 Portrayal of God's Intentions, Actions, and Purposes (the *missio Dei*) 46
   2.3 Portrayal of God's Person and Character 49

- 2.4 Intertextuality—Literary and Thematic Links to the Wider Biblical Narrative   51
- 2.5 Portrayal of Humanity and the World in Relation to God's Mission   61
- 2.6 Evidence of a Missional Context in the Problems, Crises, or Issues Addressed   61
- 2.7 The Portrayal of Paul and His Involvement in Mission   63
- 2.8 Conclusion   63

3 Ephesians 1:15–23 | 65
- 3.1 Introduction   65
- 3.2 Portrayal of God's Intentions, Actions, and Purposes (the *missio Dei*)   65
- 3.3 Portrayal of God's Person and Character   67
- 3.4 Intertextuality—Literary and Thematic Links to the Wider Biblical Narrative   68
- 3.5 Portrayal of Humanity and the World in Relation to God's Mission   71
- 3.6 Evidence of a Missional Context in the Problems, Crises, or Issues Addressed   72
- 3.7 Portrayal of the Character and Mission of God's People in the World   74
- 3.8 Conclusion   76

4 Ephesians 2:1–10 | 77
- 4.1 Introduction   77
- 4.2 Portrayal of God's Intentions, Actions, and Purposes (the *missio Dei*)   78
- 4.3 Portrayal of God's Person and Character   80
- 4.4 Intertextuality—Literary and Thematic Links to the Wider Biblical Narrative   81
- 4.5 Portrayal of Humanity and the World in Relation to God's Mission   86
- 4.6 Evidence of a Missional Context in the Problems, Crises, or Issues Addressed   89
- 4.7 Character and Mission of God's People   92
- 4.8 Conclusion   93

5 Ephesians 2:11–22 | 94
  5.1 Introduction   94
  5.2 Portrayal of God's Intentions, Actions, and Purposes
      (the *missio Dei*)   95
  5.3 Portrayal of God's Person and Character   99
  5.4 Intertextuality—Literary and Thematic Links to
      the Wider Biblical Narrative   101
  5.5 Portrayal of Humanity and the World in Relation
      to God's Mission   117
  5.6 Evidence of a Missional Context in the Problems, Crises,
      or Issues Addressed   119
  5.7 The Character and Mission of God's People   121
  5.8 Conclusion   123

6 Ephesians 3:1–13 | 124
  6.1 Introduction   124
  6.2 Portrayal of God's Intentions, Actions, and Purposes
      (the *missio Dei*)   124
  6.3 Portrayal of God's Person and Character   129
  6.4 Intertextuality—Literary and Thematic Links to
      the Wider Biblical Narrative   131
  6.5 Evidence of a Missional Context in the Problems, Crises,
      or Issues Addressed   135
  6.6 Character of the People of God in God's Mission   137
  6.7 Portrayal of Paul and His Involvement in God's Mission   140
  6.8 Conclusion   142

7 Ephesians 3:14–21 | 144
  7.1 Introduction   144
  7.2 Portrayal of God's Intentions, Actions, and Purposes
      (the *missio Dei*)   144
  7.3 Portrayal of God's Person and Character   146
  7.4 Intertextuality—Literary and Thematic Links to
      the Wider Biblical Narrative   148
  7.5 Evidence of a Missional Context in the Problems, Crises,
      or Issues Addressed   150
  7.6 Portrayal of the Character and Mission of God's People
      in the World   151
  7.7 Conclusion   151

8 Ephesians 4:1–16 | 153
   8.1 Introduction   153
   8.2 Portrayal of God's Intentions, Actions, and Purposes (the *missio Dei*)   153
   8.3 Portrayal of God's Person and Character   155
   8.4 Intertextuality—Literary and Thematic Links to the Wider Biblical Narrative   157
   8.5 Portrayal of Humanity and the World in Relation to God's Mission   160
   8.6 Evidence of a Missional Context in the Problems, Crises, or Issues Addressed   160
   8.7 Portrayal of the Character and Mission of God's People in the World   162
   8.8 Conclusion   164

9 Ephesians 4:17—5:20 | 166
   9.1 Introduction   166
   9.2 Portrayal of God's Intentions, Actions, and Purposes (the *missio Dei*)   166
   9.3 Portrayal of God's Person and Character   168
   9.4 Intertextuality—Literary and Thematic Links to the Wider Biblical Narrative   169
   9.5 Portrayal of Humanity and the World in Relation to God's Mission   178
   9.6 Evidence of a Missional Context in the Problems, Crises, or Issues Addressed   179
   9.7 Character and Mission of God's People in the World   181
   9.8 Conclusion   184

10 Ephesians 5:21—6:9 | 186
   10.1 Introduction   186
   10.2 Portrayal of God's Intentions, Actions, and Purposes (the *missio Dei*)   186
   10.3 Portrayal of God's Person and Character   188
   10.4 Intertextuality—Literary and Thematic Links to the Wider Biblical Narrative   189
   10.5 Evidence of a Missional Context in the Problems, Crises, or Issues Addressed   192
   10.6 Character and Mission of God's People in the World   195
   10.7 Conclusion   195

11 Ephesians 6:10–24 | 197
    11.1 Introduction   197
    11.2 Portrayal of God's Intentions, Actions, and Purposes
          (the *missio Dei*)   198
    11.3 Portrayal of God's Person and Character   199
    11.4 Intertextuality—Literary and Thematic Links to
          the Wider Biblical Narrative   200
    11.5 Portrayal of Humanity and the World in Relation
          to God's Mission   210
    11.6 Evidence of a Missional Context in the Problems, Crises,
          or Issues Addressed   211
    11.7 Portrayal of the Character and Mission of God's People
          in the World   213
    11.8 Portrayal of Paul and His Involvement in God's Mission   214
    11.9 Conclusion   216

12 Missional Context of Ephesians | 217
    12.1 Introduction   217
    12.2 Summary of Missional Context Observations
          from Preceding Chapters   219
    12.3 Historical Context of Ephesus and Asia Minor   221
    12.4 Conclusion   227

13 The Purpose of Ephesians | 229
    13.1 Introduction   229
    13.2 Review of Existing Proposals   230
    13.3 Ephesians as a Missional Document   237
    13.4 Conclusion   243

14 Conclusion | 244
    14.1 The Research Question   244
    14.2 Summary of Arguments   245
    14.3 Evaluation   251
    14.4 Contribution to Scholarship   252
    14.5 Conclusion   252

    Bibliography | 255

List of Tables

Table 1: Missiological and Biblical Works' Engagement with Particular Passages in Ephesians | 25

Table 2: Parallel Terms in Romans 3 and Ephesians 2 | 85

Table 3: Parallel Terms in Ezekiel 36–37 and Ephesians 2 | 101

Table 4: Parallels between Isaiah 9, 52, 57 and Ephesians 2 | 106

Table 5: Parallels between Daniel 2, 7 and Ephesians 3:3–10 | 133

Table 6: Parallel Terms in Isaiah 59–60 and Ephesians 5:6–14 | 175

Table 7: Parallel Terms in Isaiah 52 and Ephesians 6 | 203

Preface

READING THE BIBLE *WELL* should matter to every Christian and every biblical scholar. This is because the way we read the Bible has a direct impact on how people live and what they believe about God, the world, and their place in it. The questions, assumptions, and methodologies that drive any particular individual's or community's engagement with Scripture are not neutral, but they are shaped by their own cultural and theological heritage. I realized this at an early point in my Christian journey as I butted heads with sincere believers who had rigid ideas about what certain passages meant, but who weren't willing to explore how they arrived at those interpretive conclusions. All this is to say that hermeneutics (the theory and methodology of interpreting texts) is a vital discipline that should matter to all Bible readers.

This thesis is a case study in interpreting a book of the Bible (Ephesians) using a relatively new hermeneutical framework: missional hermeneutics. This framework is not adopted merely because of its novelty, but because the *missio Dei* (God's mission) is a prominent theme throughout the biblical narrative and is arguably significant in every book. Missional hermeneutics poses a set of illuminating questions that deliberately explore how the biblical text might be shaping its recipients for *involvement* in mission—a focus that is largely absent from historical-grammatical exegesis and various critical interpretive methodologies. Missional hermeneutics offers a corrective to the discipline of biblical studies that can be too narrow, too abstract, and too culturally blinkered.

I also embarked on this study as a missiologist and former missionary. I have been involved in mission organizations and mission endeavours in Asia for more than two decades. Living in Indonesia for six years as a

New Testament lecturer, in particular, has shaped my understanding of non-Western approaches to reading the Bible. Christians in non-Western contexts are interested in what the Bible has to say about ethnic tension, the spiritual world, hostile religious and cultural forces that oppose Christianity, evangelism, Christian identity, and ethics. These are all issues addressed by Ephesians but sometimes neglected by commentaries on Ephesians. On the other hand, works in the field of missiology are prone to cherry-pick a handful of verses or themes from Ephesians, like unity, reconciliation, Spirit-gifted ministry and spiritual warfare, and plug them into a section on Pauline mission theology and practice. Such an approach fails to respect Ephesians as a coherent, occasional document that has a unique voice and contribution to make to a Christian understanding of mission.

In this study I was therefore deliberately working to bridge the gap between the disciplines of biblical studies and missiology, and to bring to light insights from Ephesians that may have been missed by existing interpretations of the letter. This methodology also allows for an inductive approach to discerning the meaning of mission as it emerges from a careful and systematic reading of Ephesians. Such an investigation had not been done previously, and therefore was a prime reason to embark on this thesis. This thesis, then, is an attempt to read Ephesians *well*; to read Ephesians attuned to it as a missional document pointing to the work of a missional God.

Using missional hermeneutics as the interpretive approach, this thesis analyzes every passage in Ephesians for its portrayal of the *missio Dei*, the characterization of God, intertextual links to mission in the wider biblical narrative, the portrayal of humanity and the world in relation to God's mission, evidence for a missional context, the character and mission of God's people, and the portrayal of Paul and his involvement in mission. The adoption of a missional hermeneutic yields multiple insights into the theological message, context, and purpose of Ephesians. The study concludes that Ephesians is a missional document, written to inform, encourage, and shape its recipients for participation in the *missio Dei*.

Few works on Ephesians proceed without some comment on the issue of authorship. Ephesians is categorized by biblical scholars as a disputed Pauline letter; that is, some critical scholars have argued it was not written by the apostle Paul himself. In this study I adopted the neutral terminology "the author of Ephesians" rather than "Paul" so as not to make any prejudgment about authorship, which was not within the scope of my research. Nevertheless, in the course of my research and carrying out a systematic missional reading of Ephesians, I found nothing to exclude the possibility that Paul himself was the letter's author.

Finally, in choosing the title for this published version of my thesis, "Living to the Praise of God's Glory," I am alluding to Ephesians 1:6, 12 and 14. Reading and studying Ephesians is transformative. As we explore the call in the letter to understand and respond to the *missio Dei*, readers should not remain passive spectators to a historical phenomenon (a letter written to an early church community in Asia Minor). Rather, readers are invited to see God's purposes as universal and enduring, and to respond personally and wholeheartedly to God's work in the world by becoming witnesses to and agents of his reconciliation and salvation, and in so doing, they will live "to the praise of his glory." I pray that this study will assist its readers to join in that missional movement.

Acknowledgements

I wish to express my sincere appreciation to my principal supervisor, Dr. Brian Rosner, for his advice, encouragement, and critiques throughout my course of study. I also wish to thank my adjunct supervisor, Dr. Timothy Davy, for his guidance, input, and critique at critical junctures over the past three years. Ridley College has provided a fruitful environment in which to undertake doctoral research. I thank the library staff, other research students, and the faculty for their input and encouragement. Frank Duerrmeier kindly assisted me with the German translations. Thanks are also due to Greta Morris for her editorial work readying the manuscript for publication.

I am grateful to the Leon and Mildred Morris Foundation and the Australian College of Theology for providing grants during my studies. I also wish to thank the members of St. John's Blackburn for their understanding and support as I balanced study and the privilege of leading the parish during 2016 to 2019.

I wish to thank the examiners of the thesis, Michael J. Gorman, of St. Mary's Seminary and University, and George Wieland, of Carey Baptist College, for their helpful critique of the work. Mark D. Owens, of Cedarville University, also provided input, some of which has been incorporated into the final shape of the thesis.

My deepest thanks go to my wife Louise for her patient encouragement and constant support throughout the course of this research. I also thank my two boys for their patience and understanding during those times when this research necessitated my absence or absentmindedness.

This project is testament to the power of God to "accomplish abundantly far more than we can ask or imagine," and I pray its contribution to the missional reading of Scripture brings glory to God.

Abbreviations

All Bible quotations are from NRSV unless otherwise noted.

All English translations of the LXX are from LES unless otherwise noted.

AB	Anchor Bible
ACCS	Ancient Christian Commentary on Scripture
ANRW	*Aufstieg und Niedergang der römischen Welt: Geschichte und Kultur Roms im Spiegel der neueren Forschung.* Part 2, *Principat.* Edited by Hildegard Temporini and Wolfgang Haase. Berlin: de Gruyter, 1972–
ANTC	Abingdon New Testament Commentaries
ASMMS	American Society of Missiology Monograph Series
AUS	American University Studies
AUSS	*Andrews University Seminary Studies*
BBC	Believers Church Bible Commentary
BBR	*Bulletin for Biblical Research*
BDAG	Danker, Frederick W., Walter Bauer, William F. Arndt, and F. Wilbur Gingrich. *Greek-English Lexicon of the New Testament and Other Early Christian Literature.* 3rd ed. Chicago: University of Chicago Press, 2000 (Danker-Bauer-Arndt-Gingrich)

BibInt	Biblical Interpretation Series
BNTC	Black's New Testament Commentaries
BTB	*Biblical Theology Bulletin*
BZNW	Beihefte zur Zeitschrift für die neutestamentliche Wissenschaft
CBQ	*Catholic Biblical Quarterly*
COQG	Christian Origins and the Question of God
CSB	Christian Standard Bible
CurBR	*Currents in Biblical Research*
EGGNT	Exegetical Guide to the Greek New Testament
EMS	Evangelical Missiological Society
ESV	English Standard Version
EvQ	*Evangelical Quarterly*
ExpTim	*Expository Times*
FRLANT	Forschungen zur Religion und Literatur des Alten und Neuen Testaments
HTR	*Harvard Theological Review*
HTS	Harvard Theological Studies
IBC	Interpretation: A Bible Commentary for Teaching and Preaching
IBS	*Irish Biblical Studies*
ICC	International Critical Commentary
IEph	*Die Inschriften von Ephesos*. Edited by Hermann Wankel. 8 vols. Inschriften griechischer Städte aus Kleinasien 11–17. Bonn: Habelt, 1979–1984
Int	*Interpretation*
JAC	*Jahrbuch für Antike und Christentum*
JEPTA	*Journal of the European Pentecostal Theological Association*
JETS	*Journal of the Evangelical Theological Society*

JGRChJ	*Journal of Greco-Roman Christianity and Judaism*
JPT	*Journal of Pentecostal Theology*
JSNT	*Journal for the Study of the New Testament*
JSNTSup	Journal for the Study of the New Testament Supplement Series
JSOTSup	Journal for the Study of the Old Testament Supplement Series
JTS	*Journal of Theological Studies*
KEK	Kritisch-exegetischer Kommentar über das Neue Testament (Meyer-Kommentar)
L&N	Louw, Johannes P., and Eugene A. Nida, eds. *Greek-English Lexicon of the New Testament: Based on Semantic Domains.* New York: United Bible Societies, 1988
LES	Brannan, Rick, Ken M. Penner, Israel Loken, Michael Aubrey, and Isaiah Hoogendyk, eds. *The Lexham English Septuagint.* Bellingham, WA: Lexham, 2012
LNTS	The Library of New Testament Studies
LSJ	Liddell, Henry George, Robert Scott, and Henry Stuart Jones. *A Greek-English Lexicon.* 9th ed. Oxford: Clarendon, 1996
NA28	Nestle, Eberhard, Erwin Nestle, Barbara Aland, and Kurt Aland, eds. *Novum Testamentum Graece: Based on the Work of Eberhard and Erwin Nestle.* 28th ed. Stuttgart: Deutsche Bibelgesellschaft, 2012
NAC	New American Commentary
NASB	New American Standard Bible
NETS	International Organization for Septuagint and Cognate Studies. *New English Translation of the Septuagint.* Oxford: Oxford University Press, 2009
NewDocs	*New Documents Illustrating Early Christianity.* Edited by Greg H. R. Horsley and Stephen Llewelyn. North Ryde, NSW: The Ancient History Documentary Research Centre, Macquarie University, 1981–
NIBC	New International Biblical Commentary

NICNT	New International Commentary on the New Testament
NICOT	New International Commentary on the Old Testament
NIV	New International Version
NovT	*Novum Testamentum*
NovTSup	Supplements to Novum Testamentum
NRSV	New Revised Standard Version
NSBT	New Studies in Biblical Theology
NTL	New Testament Library
NTS	*New Testament Studies*
OTL	Old Testament Library
PNTC	Pillar New Testament Commentary
ResQ	*Restoration Quarterly*
RevExp	*Review and Expositor*
SBLMS	Society of Biblical Literature Monograph Series
SBS	Stuttgarter Bibelstudien
SNTSMS	Society for New Testament Studies Monograph Series
SOTBT	Studies in Old Testament Biblical Theology
StBibLit	Studies in Biblical Literature (Lang)
TDNT	*Theological Dictionary of the New Testament.* Edited by Gerhard Kittel and Gerhard Friedrich. Translated by Geoffrey W. Bromiley. 10 vols. Grand Rapids: Eerdmans, 1964–1976
TLG	*Thesaurus Linguae Graecae: A Digital Library of Greek Literature.* http://www.tlg.uci.edu/
TynBul	*Tyndale Bulletin*
UBS5	*The Greek New Testament.* 5th ed. Edited by Barbara Aland, Kurt Aland, Iōan D. Karavidopoulos, Carlo Maria Martini, Bruce M Metzger, and Holger Strutwolf. Stuttgart: United Bible Societies, 2014

USQR	*Union Seminary Quarterly Review*
VT	*Vetus Testamentum*
WBC	Word Biblical Commentary
WGRWSup	Writings from the Greco-Roman World Supplement Series
WTJ	*Westminster Theological Journal*
WUNT	Wissenschaftliche Untersuchungen zum Neuen Testament
ZBK	Zürcher Bibelkommentare
ZECNT	Zondervan Exegetical Commentary on the New Testament
ZNW	*Zeitschrift für die neutestamentliche Wissenschaft und die Kunde der älteren Kirche*

1

Introduction

1.1 Background

I. Howard Marshall claimed that the documents of the NT are "documents of a mission" and that NT theology is essentially "missionary theology."[1] Christopher Wright similarly claims that the whole Bible is "the product of and witness to the ultimate mission of God."[2] For Wright, the overarching theme and hermeneutical key to the Bible is the *missio Dei*.[3] These claims warrant testing at the level of individual books in the canon.

Although Ephesians is routinely portrayed by missionary writers and popular Christian writers as supportive of priorities including church growth, gospel witness, evangelism, and spiritual warfare aimed at extending God's kingdom on earth, it is construed by some critical biblical scholars (such as Margaret MacDonald) as a letter that eschews such activities and instead reflects an "introversionist" impulse and withdrawal from the world.[4] For example, Ernest Best states: "It was [the author's] intention to deal with the internal life of Christian communities."[5] Best further comments that "Ephesians . . . has no interest in mission activity."[6] Amongst

---

1. Marshall, *New Testament Theology*, 34–35.
2. Wright, *Mission of God*, 22.
3. Wright, *Mission of God*, 30–32.
4. E.g. Hedlund, *Mission of the Church*, 199–242 (missiological work); Stott, *Message of Ephesians*, esp. 24–28 (popular-level evangelical work); MacDonald, *Colossians and Ephesians* (representative critical scholarly treatment of Ephesians).
5. Best, *Ephesians*, 4.
6. Best, *Ephesians*, 56.

scholars, Clinton Arnold voices a dissenting opinion, claiming that "Paul strongly emphasizes in Ephesians taking the good news of God's redemptive message to a world that has not heard it."[7] These sharply contrasting interpretations invite investigation and resolution.

Not only is the extent of Ephesians' interest in mission debated, there are more fundamental uncertainties in the scholarly treatment of Ephesians. Historically, Ephesians held a position close to Romans as one of the most influential Pauline letters in Christian theology. However, in modern critical biblical scholarship, the combination of doubts about its authenticity, original destination, occasion, and purpose have led to the letter being marginalized in some quarters of NT scholarship.[8] The variety of opinions regarding its setting and purpose are diverse. It has been seen, inter alia, as wisdom discourse, a summation of Pauline theology, a response to emergent Gnosticism, a baptismal homily, a liturgical work, a response to tension between Jewish and gentile believers, and an attempt to strengthen believers to withstand the spiritual and cultural pressures from their pagan surroundings.[9] Most of these proposals share a bias towards internal ecclesiological concerns, rather than a focus outwards. The lack of scholarly consensus regarding purpose and setting, together with the divergent views regarding mission in the letter all indicate that a reappraisal of Ephesians is warranted. The present study will test whether a missional reading of Ephesians yields a more coherent and satisfying account of the purpose and context of the letter than existing proposals.

1.2 Research Questions

Firstly, in the light of existing works in both biblical studies and missiology, does the consistent and comprehensive adoption of a reading using missional hermeneutics yield new insights into the theological message, context, and purpose of Ephesians? Secondly, is the characterization of Ephesians as introversionist and uninterested in mission (as claimed by scholars including Best and MacDonald) supported by the text or not?

---

7. Arnold, *Ephesians*, 506.

8. E.g. Dunn, *Theology of Paul*, 13; Wright, *Faithfulness of God*, 59 speaks of a prejudice against Ephesians; Muddiman, *Ephesians*, 20 expresses skepticism about the possibility of determining the letter's setting or purpose.

9. Schlier, *Brief*, 21; Bruce, *Epistles*, 229–46; Pokorný, "Epheserbrief," 160–94; Dahl, "Einleitungsfragen," 3–106; Kirby, *Ephesians, Baptism and Pentecost*; Käsemann, "Ephesians and Acts," 288–97; Arnold, *Ephesians, Power and Magic*.

In order to situate these research questions within the relevant scholarly context, the remainder of this introduction will present, firstly, a literature review of how the topic of mission has been treated in commentaries on Ephesians, then, a literature review of missiological works and thematic biblical studies that discuss an element of mission in Ephesians, and thirdly, an introduction to missional hermeneutics as the theoretical framework employed for this study. Flowing from these three sections, the methodology adopted in this study will be presented.

1.3 Hypothesis

Ephesians is a missional document, written to inform, encourage and shape its recipients for participation in the *missio Dei*.

1.4 Literature Review 1—Mission in Ephesians in Biblical Scholarship

The following review examines what has been said about mission in Ephesians in fourteen representative biblical commentaries and studies. Although works on Ephesians begin in the patristic period and continue through to the modern era of biblical scholarship, these works from the last half century capture the most significant ideas on mission specifically in Ephesians within the field of contemporary biblical studies. Although Pauline and NT theologies generally treat Ephesians, these have not been included in this survey as they rarely comment explicitly or in any great detail on mission in Ephesians.[10]

1.4.1 Fischer (1973)

Karl Fischer interprets Ephesians through the hypothesis that it reflects a period of transition after the first apostles died. Accordingly, the charismatic ministries associated with the first generation of Christians are replaced by institutional offices and the missionary work of the apostles is repressed.[11]

---

10. E.g. Schreiner, *New Testament Theology*, 724–26 discusses mission in Pauline letters in three pages, citing only Eph 2:11–12; 6:15, 17; Stuhlmacher, *Biblical Theology*, 462–64, focuses on ecclesiology (esp 3:10), 469–40, comments briefly on the role of apostles, prophets, and evangelists (Eph 4:11–12) in mission.

11. Fischer, *Tendenz und Absicht*, 201.

He identifies the picture of Paul in Eph 3:8–9 as indicative of a changed approach to mission:

> Paul appears less as a missionary than as a mystagoge. The words sound strangely as if the gentiles were already Christians, and as if Paul's task was no longer to convert the gentiles in the first place, but to additionally communicate to them the mystery of the church.
>
> It is precisely at this point that the fundamental difference between Paul and Ephesians becomes clear and reveals the diversity of the starting points. The problem of Ephesians is no longer primarily mission, but the preservation of the unity of the church.
>
> ... There is also no mention of mission. Their problems lie elsewhere. The episcopal church is in the process of consolidation and invokes Paul and the revelation he has been given by Christ himself.[12]

Fischer's view succinctly captures the trajectory of German scholarship regarding Ephesians that prevailed in the early- to mid-twentieth century beginning with Rudolph Bultmann and continued by Ernst Käsemann.[13]

1.4.2 Barth (1974)

Markus Barth's Anchor Bible volumes on Ephesians contain numerous observations explicitly addressing mission. In his preface he rejects the view of scholars that Ephesians, as a post-apostolic document, is:

> an introverted glorification of the church, which forgets the centrality of the Messiah Jesus, neglects the church's mission to the world, and falls victim to those thought-patterns of nascent Gnosticism which teach that individual souls are saved by a flight out of this world.[14]

Accordingly, at various points in his commentary he argues for a missionary character in concepts like knowledge/knowing/making known (e.g. at Eph 3:8–10; 6:19); the seal of the Holy Spirit (1:13); new creation/

---

12. Fischer, *Tendenz und Absicht*, 99, 101, my translation.

13. E.g. Bultmann, *Theology*, 1:178–79; Käsemann, "Ephesians and Acts," 296. "The church has become an independent theme vis-a-vis cosmology, just as it became one with respect to Christology. Intra-church problems press to the fore and cause, at the same time, the idea of mission to recede."

14. Barth, *Ephesians 1–3*, ix.

new humanity (2:10, 15); marriage (5:21–33); and the broader ethical material of 4:25—6:20.[15]

Barth consistently portrays the ecclesiology of Ephesians as missional.[16] For example, in commenting on the body of Christ image at 1:23, he approves the formulation of E. Schweizer that, "the church is the manifestation of Christ to the world."[17] Regarding 4:11–12, he argues that:

> All the saints (and among them, each saint) are enabled by the four or five types of servants enumerated in 4:11 to fulfill the ministry given to them, so that the whole church is taken into Christ's service and given missionary substance, purpose, and structure.[18]

Ministry gifts are given precisely in order to enable mission. Unity is similarly understood by Barth to serve the goal of mission.[19] Barth refuses to isolate or idealize Paul's gentile mission as a past-tense phase or a task restricted to the apostle. Instead, based on Eph 6:18–20, he argues that through intercession, the believers addressed by Ephesians do not just provide "merely emotional, verbal, or moral support; [their prayers] manifests that an "apostolic" mission is theirs, too (3:7–10; cf. 2:7; 5:8–14; 6:15)."[20]

Barth's commentary represents the most affirmative and comprehensive engagement with mission in Ephesians in the last half century. Accordingly, we will refer to Barth's work frequently, while still testing his exegesis and seeking to extend his insights where possible.

1.4.3 Gnilka (1977)

In his excursus concerning ecclesiology, Joachim Gnilka states that the church in Ephesians is conceived both as the body (σῶμα) of Christ and fullness (πλήρωμα) of Christ.[21] The impact of this equation is to spiritualize the nature and functions of the church, with a consequent diminishment of practical engagement with the world.

---

15. Barth, *Ephesians 1–3*, 14, 44, 56, 120–21, 143–44, 270, n. 72; Barth, *Ephesians 4–6*, 596, 711, 736.

16. Barth, *Ephesians 1–3*, 119, 176, 206 (at 60 he states that the "Comments" sections will discuss the "relationship of the church to Israel, to her mission, to theological thought").

17. Barth, *Ephesians 1–3*, 198, citing Schweizer, "Church as Missionary Body," 1–11.

18. Barth, *Ephesians 1–3*, 479, cf. 314–17.

19. Barth, *Ephesians 1–3*, 466 (commenting on 4:4–6).

20. Barth, *Ephesians 4–6*, 808, cf. 784.

21. Gnilka, *Epheserbrief*, 109.

> The dynamic and organic understanding of the church as a body is intensified by *pleroma* and directed inwards. In the background there is no expansive missionary process, but a process in which the church acts as the mediator of salvation and peace in the world, just as Christ is mediator of God. Considering this, the consequence is that *pleroma* must first be interpreted passively as that which has been filled, namely with divine life power.[22]

Similarly, in discussing the hymn of Eph 5:14, Gnilka says this is not a missionary invitation to belief, but an address to believers only. When discussing Eph 6:15, Gnilka rejects the idea that there was institutionalized missionary activity, but upholds a general obligation for all Christians to be active in spoken and lived witness to the gospel:

> In the horizon of the letter, the expansive missionary aspect of the gospel is not in view, and that is why it cannot be read from this passage either. No member of the church can be relieved of his or her mission to stand up for the gospel, testify to it, and to live a life that testifies to it.[23]

1.4.4 Lincoln (1990)

The vast majority of occurrences of "mission" in Andrew Lincoln's commentary relate to the Pauline mission, primarily as a period in the past which had resulted in the existence of Pauline churches.[24] Lincoln rejects the interpretation of Ephesians as a turn inwards, insisting instead that the overarching goal of the letter is to foster unity in the church, as a paradigm and witness of the cosmic unity that is God's ultimate salvific goal.[25] He affirms that the church's calling includes, "demonstrations of cooperation and unity in worship, witness, and social action."[26]

In discussing Eph 4:11 Lincoln states: "it is likely that here 'evangelists' are to be seen as those engaged in mission and the founding of churches and, therefore, as having responsibilities beyond the local congregation."[27] But a little later, in summing up the force of 4:1–16, Lincoln places the

---

22. Gnilka, *Epheserbrief*, 109, my translation.
23. Gnilka, *Epheserbrief*, 312, my translation; cf. 262–63 regarding Eph 5:14.
24. Lincoln, *Ephesians*, lxi, lxix, lxx, lxxii, lxxx, lxxxi, lxxxv, 192–94, 233, 453.
25. Lincoln, *Ephesians*, xciv.
26. Lincoln, *Ephesians*, xcvi.
27. Lincoln, *Ephesians*, 250.

emphasis on the promotion of unity and maturity rather than expansion of the church:

> Evangelists, pastors, and teachers produce unity and maturity as they proclaim, preserve, and apply the apostolic tradition ... The *focus of the passage is on the Church's inner growth rather than on its mission*, but the quality of its corporate life has everything to do with the Church's fulfilling its role in the world.[28]

Lincoln's reading of the letter retains a very ecclesiocentric flavor but nuances it by insisting that the church should be concerned with "the whole of created reality."[29] The recipients are "not to think of themselves as a little group that needs to hide away. Rather, they have a gospel that is to be announced freely and openly in the midst of the surrounding world."[30] So we see in Lincoln a more nuanced position than those who describe Ephesians as reflecting a turn away from the world.

1.4.5 Schnackenburg (1991)

Rudolf Schnackenburg touches on mission in his discussion of the church and the world. He sees that in Ephesians:

> (c) The church in the world has the God-given task of overcoming in herself those corrupting forces which rule in the world. This takes place through the powers graciously bestowed upon her, the filling with the Holy Spirit, in concrete terms by the love received from Christ and passed on. In that she grows in love and gains strength in unity, she also has an influence outside herself on the world which is still separate from Christ and repels the influence of evil. She also achieves a task of mission to the world.
>
> (d) The church and world are not separated areas. The Church should not retreat into her internal life nor should the world remain separated from God ... God's power ... "fills" world and Church, each in a special way; but it is the goal of its work of salvation to penetrate the world ever more deeply through the Church with the healing, liberating power of his love.[31]

---

28. Lincoln, *Ephesians*, 268 (italics added).
29. Lincoln, *Ephesians*, 80–81.
30. Lincoln, *Ephesians*, 455.
31. Schnackenburg, *Ephesians*, 308.

Schnackenburg sees both internal and external dimensions to the church's task. Moreover, he rejects the notion that Ephesians countenances the church retreating into its internal life. Although mission is not defined, in Schnackenburg's view it clearly involves the church manifesting God's healing and liberating power in the world in order to overcome the corrupting force of evil. The mission of the church is to bring salvation to the world by proclaiming the "inexhaustible riches of Christ" to the nations.[32]

1.4.6 Pokorný (1993)

Petr Pokorný recognizes that the ethical imperatives of Eph 4–5 create a distinction between the church and the world. There is a tension between exclusivity and universality. For the sake of the universal mission, the church should not turn away from the world, but it must nevertheless remain distinct ethically from the world.

> Through its growth, to which the individual charisms and ministries serve (4:11), the Church can influence its environment, even the cosmos (→ 4:15–16). Apart from traditional references (6:19–20), there is no talk of a missionary beginning. The Christianization of society obviously belongs in the realm of eschatology. The Church is present in the world and for the world as the diaspora that proclaims and warns, representing the goal and meaning of all creation.[33]

1.4.7 Best (1998)

Best stands firmly in the tradition so strongly criticized by Barth of viewing Ephesians as a post-apostolic turn inwards by the church. In Best's view the overarching concern or main theme of Ephesians is "the inner life of the communities to which he writes."[34] The majority of times that Best speaks of mission, it is with reference to Paul's mission.[35]

He explicitly denies any concern for mission in the text on two occasions. Firstly, in his introduction, he states: "The Spirit is not, as in Acts, a guide in travel and mission work, but then Ephesians is not narrative and has

---

32. Schnackenburg, *Ephesians*, 344.
33. Pokorný, *Brief*, 33–34, my translation.
34. Best, *Ephesians*, 45, cf. 5, 64, 74–75, 88, 354, 407, 621.
35. Best, *Ephesians*, 42, 43, 45, 136, 295–98, 317, 608.

no interest in mission activity."[36] Secondly, in an essay on the church, Best takes a position contra George Caird who affirms the importance of training church members for their role in mission in his discussion of Eph 4:12. Best states, "[The author of Ephesians] has however concentrated on the interior life of the church; it is to this his paraenesis is directed and not to training for mission."[37] Even when discussing related activities like evangelism, Best is insistent that the evangelists of 4:11 are not, "those who travel as missionaries taking the gospel into fresh areas," rather they carry out a ministry to build up believers.[38] Although not explicitly defined, Best's conception of mission appears to be limited to verbal proclamation of the gospel.

1.4.8 MacDonald (2000)

MacDonald includes numerous explicit comments about mission in her commentary. Apart from its regular usage to describe Paul's mission as a foundational but now past phase in church life,[39] two main themes emerge in MacDonald's discussion of mission. Firstly, she claims that the church has largely abandoned mission, and become defensive towards the outside world and essentially introverted:

> Ephesians reveals a stronger introversionist sectarian response than the other Pauline epistles, including Colossians . . . [in Ephesians believers are urged] to turn into the church and away from the nonbelieving world. Despite an awareness of the goal of church expansion and the importance of universal mission, Ephesians displays very little interest in dialogue between believers and non-believers.[40]

Secondly, MacDonald argues on the basis of 3:10 that the church is ultimately escaping the world, not penetrating it. MacDonald states that the goal of Paul's mission is the demonstration of God's wisdom and superior power over all other spiritual forces. The realities of "earthly evangelization" have been left behind with the shift in focus towards heavenly beings and realities.[41] MacDonald finds only a few hints that there is still scope

---

36. Best, *Ephesians*, 56.
37. Best, *Ephesians*, 638, referring to Caird, *Paul's Letters*, 76.
38. Best, *Ephesians*, 390.
39. MacDonald, *Colossians and Ephesians*, 223, 260, 264, 265.
40. MacDonald, *Colossians and Ephesians*, 21, see also 321 for virtually identical comment.
41. MacDonald, *Colossians and Ephesians*, 266, 269–70.

for evangelistic activity in the church addressed by the post-Pauline author (e.g. at 5:8–14 and in the household code 5:21—6:9).[42]

1.4.9 Muddiman (2001)

John Muddiman regards Ephesians as a composite letter, comprising authentic material from Paul himself, edited and expanded by a later editor. Consequently, he says it lacks a coherent theology, and he makes very few claims about the purpose of Ephesians. Nevertheless, at two points he states some possibilities. In the introduction he says: "The appeal for unity among Christians is the overarching theme of Ephesians in its final form and provides the chief motive for its composition."[43] He argues that the ethical section of 4:17—5:20 is largely focused on "inner-ecclesial concerns," but that there is a goal evident in 1:10, where achieving the summing up of all things in Christ, "involves the overcoming of all barriers of injustice, enmity and inhumanity that obstruct the peace of Christ (2:14–16, 18)."[44]

The majority of instances where Muddiman explicitly mentions mission are restricted to comments on Paul's particular mission to the gentiles.[45] However, in one isolated comment, he voices a surprisingly clear rationale for the letter:

> The different strands in post-apostolic Christianity in Asia, whether Pauline, Petrine or Johannine, need to be fitted together for the sake of more effective mission and greater holiness of life. This is the overriding aim of the letter to the Ephesians.[46]

Muddiman also sees a missional element to some of the church ministries of 4:11–12, stating "evangelists are the missionary successors of the apostles, just as pastors and teachers are the local successors of the prophets."[47] Finally, Muddiman sees the armor of God in Eph 6:10–18 incorporating at v. 15 a readiness on the part of believers to witness to others.[48]

---

42. MacDonald, *Colossians and Ephesians*, 238, 321.
43. Muddiman, *Ephesians*, 49.
44. Muddiman, *Ephesians*, 50.
45. Muddiman, *Ephesians*, 99, 120, 145–50, 302.
46. Muddiman, *Ephesians*, 144.
47. Muddiman, *Ephesians*, 199, citing MacDonald, *Pauline Churches*, 133.
48. Muddiman, *Ephesians*, 285–86.

1.4.10 Hoehner (2002)

Harold Hoehner's substantial commentary on Ephesians mentions mission only in relation to Paul's special mission to the gentiles.[49] He does not, even implicitly, identify a strongly missional ecclesiology; instead he describes the purpose of the letter as encouraging love for God and for fellow believers.[50] The closest theological idea to mission in Ephesians highlighted by Hoehner is reconciliation, which he sees as underlying God's eternal plan for humanity (Eph 1–3), and the role of the church (Eph 4–6).[51]

1.4.11 Sellin (2008)

Gerhard Sellin mentions mission only occasionally, largely in association with the Pauline mission. For example, he argues that Ephesians presents Paul as the normative figure of Christianity (from the late first century onwards); the apostle having a soteriological function analogous to Christ.[52] He characterizes the vocabulary of 1:13 (believe, hear, word, truth, save) as "Missionssprache" (missional language), but does not elaborate this idea further.[53] For Sellin, the dominant theological motifs of the letter are the universal reign of Christ (both spatially and temporally) and unity.[54] However, he does not explicitly elaborate how God's mission or the church's mission create and further these key ideas.

1.4.12 Thielman (2010)

Frank Thielman does not use the word mission to discuss any element of the church's activities or nature in his commentary. There are a couple of occurrences of the word "mission" relating to the activities of apostles and the role of Tychicus (6:21–22) as the courier of the letter.[55] Thielman comes close to discussing mission in a comment regarding the ministries of 4:11–12:

> Christians in Ephesus needed to work together harmoniously to bear an effective witness to the inimical powers that their

---

49. Hoehner, *Ephesians*, 135–36, 420, 423, 424, 432, 455.
50. Hoehner, *Ephesians*, 106.
51. Hoehner, *Ephesians*, 112–13.
52. Sellin, *Brief*, 62.
53. Sellin, *Brief*, 116.
54. Sellin, *Brief*, 61–62.
55. Thielman, *Ephesians*, 32, 391, 440.

efforts to frustrate God's work were doomed to failure (3:10). They also needed to work together to bear effective witness to the wider society that its hopeless way of life (4:17–19) could be transformed by the gospel (5:11–14).[56]

Apart from these incidental mentions, Thielman is silent about the topic of mission in Ephesians.

1.4.13 Arnold (2010)

Arnold addresses mission primarily in a thematic section on the theology of Ephesians. Prior to that synthesis, he identifies Eph 1:22–23 as a paradigmatic text, establishing the mission of Christ, through the church, as "filling all things" (also 4:10). According to Arnold, "The principal goal of that mission is to reach the entire world . . . with the redemptive message of the gospel."[57] The apostles of Eph 4:11 are those who continue the mission of Jesus and the Twelve as they "go and proclaim the good news, establish churches, and teach them to observe all that the Lord commands (Matt 28:19–20)."[58] The armor of God (6:10–20) is given to strengthen believers so that they can fulfill the mission of the church, being equipped with the traits and virtues of the Messiah.[59]

In his summary essay, Arnold reiterates the key points just outlined, adding that the readiness of the gospel in 6:15 and the sword of the Spirit in 6:17 indicate that there is an obligation for all believers to aggressively spread the gospel.[60] In a final comment on the nature of the church's mission, Arnold draws on Eph 2, saying:

> Paul's goal is for the new covenant temple to increase and grow by seeing more and more living stones added to this organic structure (2:21). The growth of this temple is thus not only intensive (growth in virtue), but extensive (growth in numbers) until it fills the whole world.[61]

Arnold readily adopts an interpretation of mission as verbal gospel proclamation complemented by the ethical witness of good works (at both the individual and communal level). This interpretive stance pervades his

---

56. Thielman, *Ephesians*, 28; see also 209, 285.
57. Arnold, *Ephesians*, 121, cf. 466.
58. Arnold, *Ephesians*, 257.
59. Arnold, *Ephesians*, 451, 466.
60. Arnold, *Ephesians*, 506.
61. Arnold, *Ephesians*, 507.

commentary, setting his commentary as the most explicitly *evangelistic* commentary on Ephesians even among similarly conservative works like Thielman's volume.

1.4.14 Windsor (2017)

Lionel Windsor's evangelical post-supersessionist reading of Ephesians refers to mission at several points, but never defines what is meant by the term. While seeking to correct supersessionist "overreadings" of Ephesians, Windsor himself ultimately reads into Ephesians a larger place for ethnic Israel in the apostolic mission than is warranted by the text, since Israel is explicitly cited only at 2:12, and the letter is ostensibly addressed to gentiles (2:11; 3:1). Windsor's explicitly evangelical orientation also seemingly leads him to equate mission with gospel proclamation, with a consequent inattention to other expressions of mission.[62]

1.4.15 Roels (1962)

Before concluding this literature review, we will consider a work that from its title is clearly relevant but is neither a commentary nor a straightforward work of biblical theology. Edwin Roels's monograph, which reflects his ThD dissertation from the Free University, Amsterdam, addresses the topic of the present study—mission in Ephesians. It contains sections on the church as the goal and instrument of mission (incorporating the images of church in Ephesians: body, bride, and temple).[63] It also relates fullness to eschatology and begins with a theological framework for mission.[64] While it contains many helpful discussions of key verses or interpretive possibilities, the work falls far short of a comprehensive treatment of mission in Ephesians, since it does not systematically work through the letter, allowing exegesis to determine theology. Instead, at times, it begins from a topic of concern in Reformed theology (such as election in chapter 1), and proceeds from topic to pertinent verses.[65] Roels does not define mission, but summarizes his findings about the church's role in God's mission as follows:

---

62. Windsor, *Reading Ephesians*, 192, 224, 230.

63. Roels, *God's Mission*, 84–151.

64. Roels, *God's Mission*, 13–82 (it is noteworthy the extent to which this section depends on J. H. Bavinck's missiological works; see 297 for the multiple references).

65. Roels, *God's Mission*, 25–77, for examples of dogmatically driven exegesis; cf. 45, 77.

> by her very existence in the world [the church is] a demonstration of the victory of the power of God over the powers of destruction and evil. For this reason the church is enjoined to maintain a way of living, a manner of life, consistent with and indicative of her new life in Christ Jesus . . . [the church] is called and elected also to a present demonstrable holiness of decisive mission significance.[66]

These conclusions, it will be seen, are essentially sound, but the methodology used to reach them can be improved. For example, at a few points, Roels begs the question of whether Ephesians comprehends mission as verbal witness to the gospel in addition to good works.[67] Rather than imposing the theological categories of election, universalism, ecclesiology, and eschatology on the text (as Roels does), the present study will work inductively and systematically through each pericope in Ephesians, allowing the grammatical, historical and literary contours of each pericope to shape the conclusions drawn before engaging in the task of synthesis.

1.4.16 Conclusion

Having discussed each work in turn, we can see that there is a clear division between those scholars who see Ephesians as a post-Pauline work in which the church is turning away from engaging with the world (Fischer, Gnilka, Pokorný, Best, MacDonald) and those who see it as advocating a missional role for the church in the world (Barth, Schnackenburg, Arnold, Roels). The passages that most frequently are discussed in relation to mission are 1:10, 22–23; 3:8–10; 4:11; 6:15–17. Some commentators relate the ethical material of 4:17—6:9 to the mission of the church in the world (e.g. Barth), while others see this as proof of the inward focus of the letter's ecclesiology (e.g. Best).

This survey reveals a number of areas warranting further research: the relationship of Paul's gentile mission to the ongoing role (if any) for the church in mission; the definition of mission assumed by biblical scholars; the relationship of mission to ecclesiology; and whether missional concepts are to be found outside the passages most frequently mentioned by scholars (namely, 1:10, 22–23; 3:8–10; 4:11; 6:15–17).

---

66. Roels, *God's Mission*, 227.
67. E.g. Roels, *God's Mission*, 227, 282.

1.5 Literature Review 2—Missiological Works that Discuss Ephesians

1.5.1 Introduction

This section will explore a representative (but not exhaustive) set of missiological works that draw on Ephesians and works of biblical scholarship that treat the theme of mission in Ephesians. The goals are, firstly, to determine those passages within Ephesians that are most frequently cited as relevant to mission, secondly, to ascertain what particular themes are deemed missionally significant by scholars, and thirdly, what methodological patterns emerge in the way such themes are derived from the biblical text. The works have been selected as relatively recent (generally within the last forty years) and inclusive of evangelical, ecumenical, and Catholic perspectives.

The literature surveyed is grouped according to the nature of the work. The first group comprises biblical theologies of mission, or survey works in missiology which refer to Ephesians. The second group consists of thematic studies exploring one aspect of mission in Ephesians. The third and final grouping comprises articles or book chapters that discuss mission in Ephesians in its entirety.

1.5.2 Missiological Works that Cite Ephesians as Part of Developing a Composite Picture of Pauline Mission

The predominant way in which many biblical theologies of mission refer to Ephesians is as a proof text for a particular theme such as reconciliation or spiritual powers. We see this in works by Arthur Glasser, Eckhard Schnabel, Craig Ott, and others.

Don Howell, "Mission in Paul's Epistles," sees the Pauline mission as anchored in Paul's status as an apostle, one sent with authority and responsibility to extend and establish the church, particularly through gospel proclamation (1:1; 2:20; 3:1–6; 4:11; 6:17–19).[68] The universal scope of Paul's mission, encompassing gentiles as well as Jews, was authenticated by the activity of the Holy Spirit (Eph 1:13–14).[69] Howell concludes his portrait of the Pauline mission by emphasizing the importance of prayer to persevere and proclaim the gospel (6:18–20).[70] Howell's treatment of Ephesians texts

---

68. Howell, "Mission," 64–65, 70–71.
69. Howell, "Mission," 84.
70. Howell, "Mission," 81, 90.

is sound, but abstracted from OT background and interacts with biblical scholarship only to a limited extent, mainly in the footnotes.

Christopher Little, *Mission in The Way of Paul*, argues that God's glory is the biblical goal of mission, and is evident in Paul's writings including Ephesians, where δόξα appears eight times (Eph 1:6, 12, 14, 17, 18; 3:13, 16, 21).[71] In Ephesians glory is both a goal and a means of sustaining God's people for their missional life (Eph 3:16).[72] Further missional themes identified by Little include the removal of the Torah as a barrier between Jews and gentiles (Eph 2:14–15); apostolic ministry as the foundation of mission (2:20); and the concept of the revealed mystery (that gentiles are fellow heirs and joint members of Christ's body, Eph 3:4–6).[73] Little's treatment of Ephesians is more nuanced than many other missiological works, since it consistently draws on biblical scholarship to underpin the author's thesis and argument.

Glasser, *Announcing the Kingdom*, highlights the principle of unity in diversity as a key characteristic of Paul's mission reflected in Ephesians. Diverse Jews and gentiles are united as fellow heirs by Christ's work, as co-workers in the Pauline mission, and the church fosters unity as it exercises diverse ministry gifts (Eph 2:14–16; 3:9; 4:5–7).[74] Glasser's methodology seeks to present core missiological themes that emerge across the Pauline writings, and elaborate them in some detail drawing on particular passages in Pauline letters. Glasser does not develop the OT background of Ephesians, nor does he interact with the insights of biblical scholarship to support his conclusions.

John Mark Terry's edited volume *Missiology* incorporates chapters authored by a range of missiologists. John Massey argues that the church has a specific task within God's sovereign purpose of sharing the gospel "to the ends of the earth and, thereby, be the showcase of God's glory and the living temple to which living stones are continually added (Eph 2:21; 6:14; 1 Pet 2:5)."[75] Massey also notes the significance of Eph 2:13–17 which states that in the cross of Christ "all vertical and horizontal barriers to fellowship with God and man" are eliminated.[76]

In the same volume Ed Stetzer argues that ecclesiology and missiology are inseparable, and both are balanced by Ephesians' Christocentric

---

71. Little, *Way of Paul*, 53.
72. Little, *Way of Paul*, 54, citing Newman, *Paul's Glory-Christology*, 4–6, 246.
73. Little, *Way of Paul*, 69, 106.
74. Glasser et al., *Announcing the Kingdom*, 285, 294–96, 309, 319–20.
75. Massey, "Missionary Mandate," 89.
76. Massey, "Missionary Mandate," 91.

perspective: "The church joins God's work to place all things under the reign and rule of his son, Jesus (Eph 1:9–10, 21–22)."[77] Gerald Wright develops the idea that God's people are the light of the world. As children of light, they are called to encourage and strengthen one another (Eph 5:8, 15–20), and to pursue their mission of opposing the powers of darkness (Eph 1:18–2:7) with spiritual weapons (Eph 6:13–18).[78] Terry's book also contains a chapter specifically on spiritual warfare in which Charles Lawless discusses Satan (2:2; 4:17–32) as well as the panoply of 6:11–18, and prayer for mission 6:19–20.[79] Throughout Terry's volume we find Ephesians treated as a source of timeless mission principles which emerge independently of their original context and are applicable without particular regard to the diversity of contemporary contexts.

In *The Mission of the Church in the World*, Roger Hedlund affirms that many themes within Pauline theology arise from his missional context. Ephesians is particularly concerned with the implications of new life in Christ: reconciliation, gentile salvation, and the function of the church (1:22–23; 2:1, 10–22; 3:6, 10; 4:4–14, 22–24; 5:23–30).[80] Hedlund pays particular attention to Eph 4:11–16 as a particularly significant passage. All gifted ministries contribute to the work of mission: apostles are particularly active in founding churches; prophets to edify and stir the church to action; evangelists to stir up the evangelistic vision of churches; and pastor-teachers to "lead God's people on to maturity (Eph 4:13–14) and active participation in ministry (Eph 4:15–16)."[81] Hedlund's engagement with Ephesians concludes with a discussion of spiritual warfare in 6:10–20. His approach is particularly shaped by Heinrich Schlier's work on "the powers" which can be understood as evil spiritual beings and forces that possess individuals, institutions, historical circumstances, and religious trends.[82] The items of spiritual armor (truth, righteousness, preparedness, faith, salvation, the word of God, and prayer) are character virtues that enable mission.[83]

The ecumenical movement has frequently drawn on Ephesians to support its emphasis on unity. In the WCC paper *The Nature and Mission of the Church: A Stage on the Way to a Common Statement*, several

77. Stetzer, "Missional Church," 103.
78. Wright, "Purpose of Missions," 24–26.
79. Lawless, "Spiritual Warfare and Missions," 541–42, 553.
80. Hedlund, *Mission of the Church*, 220–21.
81. Hedlund, *Mission of the Church*, 210–11, 241–42; drawing substantially on Murphy, *Spiritual Gifts*.
82. Hedlund, *Mission of the Church*, 227–28, citing Schlier, *Principalities and Powers*, 67.
83. Hedlund, *Mission of the Church*, 236–39.

18 LIVING TO THE PRAISE OF GOD'S GLORY

paragraphs cite Eph 4:1–6 to underpin the goal of unity.[84] Other missional themes that emerge in the paper are images of the church (body of Christ, temple, bride, 1:23; 2:21–22; 5:25–32); ethnic reconciliation (2:13–16); the cosmic scope of the church's mission (1:10); and the role of ministers in strengthening the church's witness in the world (4:12–13).[85] The paper gives no context to the citations, and does not interact with scholarship to nuance the claims made regarding mission.

Schnabel presents a detailed historical account of mission in *Early Christian Mission*. He notes the imperial and social context of Jewish-gentile reconciliation in Eph 2:8–17.[86] He mentions the importance of teams in mission (Eph 4:11; 6:21), and states that in Ephesians, gospel proclamation is carried out by evangelists (4:11–12), apostles (6:17), and churches (6:10–20).[87] Christian behavior within the family and in church assemblies had missionary significance as a second evangelistic function (Eph 5:14; 6:4, 23).[88] Schnabel's treatments of Ephesians texts marks an advance from many earlier biblical theologies of mission because he respects the historical particularity of Ephesians as a reflection of early Christian mission thought and practice.

Craig Ott, Stephen Strauss, and Timothy Tennent, *Encountering Theology of Mission*, is a more recent missiology text which follows a well-worn path in associating a number of missional themes with passages from Ephesians: ethnic and social reconciliation as the dynamic and outcome of mission (Eph 2:11–22; 4:32); doxology as the purpose of mission (Eph 1:5–14; 3:10); redemption from the power of Satan as the foundation of mission (Eph 2:1–2); the church as agent and goal of mission (Eph 5:25–27); the gifts of the Spirit given to equip the church for mission (Eph 4:7–16); ethical living as spiritual warfare (Eph 4:2, 32); and prayer as vital to mission (Eph 6:18–20).[89] Ott's descriptions are summary statements only; there is no engagement with the historical or literary context for the verses cited.

This survey highlights a common deficiency with most biblical theologies of mission. Their use of Scripture is largely acontextual and homogenizing, extracting individual proof texts from their literary contexts and consolidating them into portraits of broader mission principles or themes.

84. Commission on Faith and Order, *Nature and Mission*, paras. 12, 16, 53.

85. Commission on Faith and Order, *Nature and Mission*, paras. 12, 19, 20, 23, 33, 34, 118.

86. Schnabel, *Early Christian Mission*, 1409, 1414.

87. Schnabel, *Early Christian Mission*, 1425, 1463–65, 1471–72, 1548.

88. Schnabel, *Early Christian Mission*, 1453, 1526.

89. Ott et. al., *Encountering Theology*, 30, 49, 80–81, 85–86, 95–96, 119, 147, 159, 195–96, 242, 247–48.

The danger with this methodology is of course that when historical-grammatical considerations are ignored, the resultant theology may reflect more of the contemporary author's presumptions and framework than the original author's context, concerns, and thought-world. H. D. Beeby criticized the tendency of some churches to support their version of mission by an arbitrary and biased selection of texts, shaped more by "fashion, prejudice, or ideology" than the full canon of Scripture.[90] David Bosch's criticism of much Protestant missiological writing is still pertinent. He characterized a prevailing method as mining through the "rocks and rubble" of the OT and NT to isolate "nuggets of pure 'missionary' gold" that legitimated the contemporary missionary enterprise.[91] Bosch proposes that a more suitable foundation for building a biblical theology of mission is to pay attention to "four cardinal missionary motifs in Scripture": compassion, witness/martyria, God's mission, and history.[92] Bosch himself barely mentions Ephesians, and while we will not employ Bosch's four motifs, the missional hermeneutic pursued in this project does seek to consistently explore the *missio Dei*, the role of the people of God in mission, and missional context.

We turn now to a work which self-consciously attempts to redress the tendency to proof text missional principles evident in many biblical theologies of mission. Wright in *The Mission of God* employs a missional hermeneutic in pursuit of his thesis that mission is the grand narrative of the Bible.[93] Wright seeks to construct an exegetically and theologically sound treatment of mission in the Bible, with monotheism, idolatry, election, covenant, ethics, and the nations as key subthemes.

The majority of Wright's references to Ephesians come in his exploration of the identity and role of God's people in mission. He argues firstly that the identity markers mentioned in Eph 2:11—3:13 (citizens of God's people, members of his household, God's dwelling place) generate "an ethical and missional responsibility in the church and the world."[94] In discussing covenants in biblical theology, Wright observes that Christ's reconciling work on the cross overturns gentile exclusion from citizenship and from the covenants of promise (Eph 2:12). Not just access, but full inclusion of former outsiders (gentiles) without becoming Jewish proselytes, in the multinational dwelling place for God, the temple, is the fruit

90. Beeby, *Canon and Mission*, 6.
91. Bosch, "Biblical Models," 175–76.
92. Bosch, "Biblical Models," 180–87. In Bosch, *Transforming Mission*, 157, 172, 378, 518, he refers to Eph 2:14–15 in regard to the removal of Jewish exclusivism, and 2:20–22 to support the pneumatic nature of the church.
93. Wright, *Mission of God*, 21–23, 33–38.
94. Wright, *Mission of God*, 58.

of mission.[95] The "covenant privilege [of access to God's dwelling place] has been universalized through Jesus (cf. Eph 3:6)."[96] God's election and calling has in view an ethical purpose: to make God's people holy and blameless (Eph 1:4), living a life worthy of their calling (Eph 4:1). Ethics are thus part and parcel of God's universal plan for the restoration of the whole creation. His purpose is to bring all things "together in reconciled harmony with God through the cross of Christ (Eph 1:10)."[97]

Wright's work marked a significant advance in how a biblical theology of mission was conceived and executed. Methodologically, the strength of Wright's treatment of Ephesians is that he consistently interprets passages in the letter against their OT precursor texts (especially Isaiah and Psalms). A significant limitation in his treatment of Ephesians, however, is that it lacks balance, being disproportionally focused on 2:11–22.[98]

The next set of works we will review adopt a thematic focus in order to provide greater depth in their exposition of mission in Ephesians.

1.5.3 Works that Explore a Particular Thematic Focus in Ephesians

Having surveyed works that incorporate various verses from Ephesians into a composite picture of Pauline mission, we now move to consider works that focus on one aspect of mission only. These authors are better classed as biblical scholars commenting on mission rather than missiologists.

Peter O'Brien, *Gospel and Mission in the Writings of Paul*, focuses on Paul's self-understanding as a missionary in Eph 3:1–13 and Paul's call for believers to be active in gospel proclamation in Eph 6:10–20. In Eph 3:1–13, O'Brien identifies the following elements as vital aspects of Paul's missionary self-understanding: his calling by grace (3:2, 7, 8), his role as revealer of the mystery that is gentile incorporation as equals into God's people in the church (3:4, 5, 9), his contribution to God's wisdom being made known to the cosmos (3:10), which occurs as his preaching to gentiles hastens the consummation of God's redemptive plan for the world.[99] O'Brien presents Eph 6:10–20 as paraenesis that urges believers to stand firm against Satan through resisting temptations to immorality (cf. 4:27)

---

95. Wright, *Mission of God*, 354, 518.
96. Wright, *Mission of God*, 340, cf. 528.
97. Wright, *Mission of God*, 388.
98. Ten of the fourteen times Wright cites and discusses a passage from Ephesians relate to Eph 2:11–22: Wright, *Mission of God*, 58, 186, 313, 340, 354, 495, 518, 523–24, 528.
99. O'Brien, *Gospel and Mission*, 15, 17–18, 21.

and secondly, through gospel proclamation (6:15, 17, 19).[100] O'Brien's work is exegetically more defensible than the missiological works surveyed above since it respects the particularity of Ephesians as conveying a distinct missional message, best understood through deliberate exegetical analysis, underpinned by sound biblical scholarship.[101]

Another robust discussion of Eph 6:10-20 is found in Craig Keener, "Paul and Spiritual Warfare." Spiritual warfare encompasses believers acting as God's agents in his mission to promote righteousness and justice in the world. Such warfare is undergirded by prayer, and includes character formation and gospel proclamation (Eph 4:24; 5:9; 6:15, 17).[102] Keener attends to the worldview envisaged by Ephesians, in which spiritual and political powers oppose Christ, who nevertheless is exalted above all other powers (1:20-22; 2:1-2, 6; 4:27; 6:12).[103] Keener engages with the historical and OT literary background of the passages he analyzes, and so methodologically is a sound approach to follow.

Michael Goheen, *A Light to the Nations*, explores missional images of the church found in Ephesians. The "body of Christ" image is missional since the church manifests the authority and salvation of Christ (the church's head) in the world (Eph 1:20-23; 2:15-16; 4:7-16; 4:17—6:20).[104] Secondly, "The imagery of the temple [Eph 2:18-22] signifies the expansion and enlargement of the knowledge of God's presence throughout the world."[105] A third image, the church as diaspora, enables Goheen to discuss the church in tension with its surrounding culture, which is ruled by the powers of darkness (Eph 2:1-3). Noting the ever-present temptation of believers to live their lives under the influence of these economic, cultural, social, and political powers that dominated life in Ephesus, Goheen draws mainly on 1 Peter to argue for a stance of critical or transformational engagement with society.[106] Goheen's work models a missionally focused use of intertextuality that is lacking in the surveys and biblical theologies of mission discussed above.

Roger Gehring, *House Church and Mission*, studies in considerable detail the role households played in the Pauline mission. In addition to the

---

100. O'Brien, *Gospel and Mission*, 109, 119-26, 131.

101. O'Brien cites, inter alia, Bruce, *Epistles*; Caragounis, *Ephesian Mysterion*; Arnold, *Ephesians, Power and Magic*.

102. Keener, "Paul and Spiritual Warfare," 107, 111-12.

103. Keener, "Paul and Spiritual Warfare," 114-17.

104. Goheen, *Light to the Nations*, 171-73.

105. Goheen, *Light to the Nations*, 180.

106. Goheen, *Light to the Nations*, 181, 185.

household code of 5:21—6:9 with its explicit concern for all members of the ancient household, Gehring notes the prominence of οἶκος vocabulary in Eph 2:19–24; 4:12, 16.[107] For Gehring, this household material in Ephesians reflects the early Christians' concern to have an apologetic and evangelistic impact that reached every class of society.[108] Gehring constructs his conclusions accounting for theology, sociology, and history, and so are methodologically sound.[109]

There have been a number of articles in recent years that explore an aspect of mission in Ephesians. Max Turner explored the significance of unity in Ephesians for mission.[110] Andrew Walls discussed the implications of ethnic reconciliation in Eph 2:11–22 for contemporary mission.[111] Roy Ciampa accounted well for both the theology and ethics of Ephesians through a dual focus on *missio Dei* and the exhortation to imitate God at the heart of the paraenetic section of the letter (5:1).[112] Timothy van Aarde, in three articles, has argued that οἰκονομία in Eph 1:10; 3:2, 9 should be understood as specifically connoting God's mission, and that together with πλήρωμα, the terms delineate the relationship of the church's mission to God's mission.[113] In another article Van Aarde explores church structure and the ministries of Eph 4:7–16 as enablers of mission.[114] Mark Owens analyzes Eph 6:10–17 as the summation of the letter, exhorting its readers to continue Christ's mission as divine warriors informed by the prophetic vision of Isa 11, 52, and 59 to extend the new creation through gospel proclamation.[115]

1.5.4 Works Elucidating the Theme of Mission in Ephesians as a Whole

The third set of missiological and biblical works considered in this review includes works that treat Ephesians (or multiple passages within Ephesians) in their own right, not subsuming them into a generalized portrait of

---

107. Gehring, *House Church*, 256–59.
108. Gehring, *House Church*, 243–49, 254.
109. Gehring, *House Church*, 23.
110. Turner, "Mission and Meaning," 138–66.
111. Walls, *Cross-Cultural Process*, 72–81, discussed in §5.6, below.
112. Ciampa, "*Missio Dei*," 229–43.
113. Van Aarde, "Οἰκονομία in Ephesians," 45–62; Van Aarde, "Οἰκονομία for Missions," 1–10; Van Aarde, "God's Mission," 284–300.
114. Lotter and Van Aarde, "Priesthood of Believers," 1–10.
115. Owens, "Spiritual Warfare," 87–103.

Pauline mission. These works also engage with works of biblical scholarship more consistently in their discussions.

Sherron George, "Holistic Mission in Ephesians," aims to clarify the role of the church as a participant in the *missio Dei*, based on a missiological reading of Ephesians. Key themes for him are: the gathering of all things in Christ (1:10), fullness πλήρωμα (1:22–23), grace (2:8; 3:7, 8), making known God's wisdom (3:10), reconciliation that creates unity (2:14–16; 4:1–3), and diversity (4:7–16).[116] Because Ephesians conceives the *missio Dei* as cosmic in scope, George argues that mission must be holistic in nature, integrating "evangelism, witness, compassionate service, social justice, and the integrity of creation."[117] George's points are supported by interaction with commentaries, and encompass current issues in missiology (such as holistic mission and ecumenicalism).[118] As such, George models a healthier methodology than the works surveyed in §1.5.2, above.

Regina Meyer's brief monograph, *Kirche und Mission im Epheserbrief*, is significant for its exploration of the concepts πλήρωμα (fullness) and σῶμα (body) as metaphors for the church in relation to mission (1:23). Meyer links the idea of the universal church to universal salvation, which necessitates a worldwide missionary obligation for the church.[119] The church's experience of the lordship and fullness of Christ propels it to be involved in the mission of extending that lordship and fullness throughout the world.[120] Meyer notes a number of other key ideas and passages such as Jewish-gentile reconciliation in 2:14–18; Paul's missionary example and the μυστήριον as the proclamation of the gospel to the nations (3:1–11); and the gifts of Christ as mission enablers (4:7–16).[121] Meyer's methodology attempts to relate systematic theology (specifically Karl Rahner's approach to universal salvation) to a biblical theological study of Ephesians.[122]

Donald Senior and Carroll Stuhlmueller's *The Biblical Foundations of Mission* provides an excellent treatment of mission in the letter. Rejecting the notion that Ephesians prioritizes ecclesiology over mission, they focus particularly on the cosmic scope of Christ's mission of salvation (1:9–10, 22–23), Jewish-gentile reconciliation (2:14–22), the church experiencing

116. George, "Joined and Knit Together," 398–405; republished and expanded in George, *Better Together*, 58–79.

117. George, "Joined and Knit Together," 399.

118. Namely, Barth, *Ephesians 1–3*; Martin, *Ephesians*; Caird, *Paul's Letters*; Stott, *Message of Ephesians*.

119. Meyer, *Kirche und Mission*, 78–79.

120. Meyer, *Kirche und Mission*, 33.

121. Meyer, *Kirche und Mission*, 11–17.

122. Meyer, *Kirche und Mission*, 5.

the fullness of Christ (1:23), and the church as God's servant for the whole cosmos (cf. 2:7; 3:10; 4:12; 6:10–20).[123] Senior and Stuhlmueller then present the remainder of Ephesians (Eph 3:10, 14–20; 4–6) as an elaboration of the "responsibility of a Missioned Church."[124] The unity and ethical conduct urged in Eph 4–6 is a "function of the church's world-serving mission."[125] More specifically, the gifts in 4:11 and the household codes of chapters 5–6 exist to build up the church so that it is able to become the fullness of Christ, with a mission that extends across the whole world.[126]

Senior and Stuhlmueller's exposition of mission in Ephesians is exceptional because it seeks to present the missional message of the entire letter and is developed by explicitly drawing on the insights of biblical scholarship (especially Barth, Caird, and Meyer). One weakness in their analysis is their tendency to subsume all aspects of mission in Ephesians against the cosmic scope of God's salvation plan announced in 1:10, 22–23; in so doing, they give minimal space to the ethical material in chapters 4–6 and no attention at all to the spiritual warfare discussion of 6:10–20.

Sunday Komolafe, "Christ, Church, and the Cosmos: A Missiological Reading of Paul's Epistle to the Ephesians" seeks to interpret the Christology and ecclesiology of Ephesians, particularly in light of Eph 1:10, 22–23, which declare the cosmic scope of Christ's lordship. He argues that in Ephesians ministry and mission have a revelatory, salvific and unifying dimension. Komolafe's argument builds on biblical scholarship, systematic theology, and missiology, and concludes that the church must not be understood in cultural or historical terms, but theologically as the servant-steward of God's economy of salvation by which God's power to heal and liberate penetrates the world.[127]

Michael Gorman's monograph, *Becoming the Gospel: Paul, Participation and Mission*, represents a thoroughgoing application of missional hermeneutics to key Pauline letters. It is important for this study both methodologically and for what it says about mission in Ephesians. Gorman argues that the overarching missional theme in Ephesians is peace (εἰρήνη), a term which occurs eight times (1:2; 2:14, 15, 17 twice; 4:3; 6:15, 23). Gorman traces the various ways in which the letter speaks of the *missio Dei*, the character of God, and the role of the church, particularly in terms of

---

123. Senior and Stuhlmueller, *Biblical Foundations*, 191, 199–203; their discussion is particularly indebted to Meyer, *Kirche und Mission*; and Barth, *Ephesians 1–3*.

124. Senior and Stuhlmueller, *Biblical Foundations*, 203–4, quote at 204.

125. Senior and Stuhlmueller, *Biblical Foundations*, 207.

126. Senior and Stuhlmueller, *Biblical Foundations*, 204–6.

127. Komolafe, "Christ, Church, and the Cosmos," 273–86.

peacemaking. The goal of God's mission is the reestablishment of *shalom*, understood as comprehensive salvation and wholeness, the recreation of humanity, human society, and all creation (1:10, 22–23; 2:15). The church is to walk worthily of its calling (4:1) by embodying the gospel of peace in its communal relations and in its stance towards the world (4:1—6:9) and the spiritual powers (6:10–22).[128]

Regarding methodology, Gorman's work models how missional hermeneutics builds on normal exegetical grammatical-historical and intertextual analysis in order to rightly interpret the text, but constantly moves to ask what implications the resultant insights have for the church in mission. Through the image of centripetal and centrifugal movement, Gorman relates the elements of Ephesians that seem largely inward-focused with the outward dynamic seen in Paul as missionary in God's universal salvific purposes, arguing that both movements are how the church participates in the *missio Dei*.[129] Gorman also includes several contemporary examples of peacemaking in varied cultural settings as indicative applications of his missional reading.[130]

1.5.5 Conclusion

Having reviewed a wide range of works that discuss mission in Ephesians, it is possible now to draw some conclusions concerning which passages are seen as most *missional* and what *missional themes* are judged to be present in the text.

The following table (Table 1) presents references to Ephesians by the scholars surveyed, grouped according to the pericope divisions found in the UBS5 Ephesians text.

	1:1-2	1:3-14	1:15-23	2:1-10	2:11-22	3:1-13	3:14-21	4:1-16	4:17-24	4:25—5:5	5:6-20	5:21—6:9	6:10-20	6:21-24
Gehring				x				x			x			
George		x	x	x	x	x		x						
Glasser		x			x	x		x						

---

128. Gorman, *Becoming the Gospel*, 186–207.
129. Gorman, *Becoming the Gospel*, 59–62, 182, 196.
130. Gorman, *Becoming the Gospel*, 207–11.

	1:1–2	1:3–14	1:15–23	2:1–10	2:11–22	3:1–13	3:14–21	4:1–16	4:17–24	4:25–5:5	5:6–20	5:21—6:9	6:10–20	6:21–24
Goheen			x	x	x	x		x				x		
Gorman	x	x	x		x			x					x	x
Hedlund					x			x					x	
Howell		x	x		x	x	x	x					x	
Keener			x	x						x			x	
Komolafe		x	x											
Little		x	x		x	x	x							
Meyer			x		x	x		x						
O'Brien						x								
Ott					x			x		x			x	
Owens													x	
Schnabel		x	x		x	x		x				x	x	x
Senior and Stuhlmueller		x	x		x	x	x	x				x		
Terry		x	x	x		x			x	x			x	
Van Aarde		x				x	x							
WCC					x			x				x		
Wright		x			x	x			x	x			x	
Total discussions	1	11	11	4	14	12	3	13	2	4	0	5	9	2

Table 1: Missiological and Biblical Works' Engagement with Particular Passages in Ephesians

Based on the works surveyed, the passages that are most frequently discussed are 1:3–14; 1:15–23; 2:11–22; 3:1–11; 4:1–16, and 6:10–20. Apart from the most commonly discussed passages, engagement with mission themes in Ephesians tends to be passing, relatively superficial, and set amidst a list of Pauline texts. As such, the distinctive voice of Ephesians is drowned out as it is subsumed into a homogenized portrait of Pauline mission principles and practices.

The most frequently recurring missional themes in Ephesians according to the surveyed works include: the doxological goal of mission (Little, Terry), reconciliation between Jews and gentiles (Hedlund, Ott, Schnabel, Wright, Goheen, WCC), reconciliation between humanity and God (Wright, Senior, and Stuhlmueller), the church as temple dwelling-place of God (Terry, Wright, Goheen, WCC), the witness of the united church to spiritual powers (Terry, O'Brien, Goheen, Keener), Paul as model missionary (Howell, Glasser, Schnabel, Ott, O'Brien), the gifts of the Spirit (Howell, Glasser, Hedlund, Ott, Goheen, Senior, and Stuhlmueller), a ministry of apostleship for founding churches (Hedlund), the ethical life of believers as missional (Ott, Gehring, Wright, Senior, and Stuhlmueller), spiritual warfare (Terry, Keener, Hedlund), and prayer (Howell, Terry, Hedlund, Ott, Keener). In the following chapters we will evaluate the extent to which these themes are validly derived from the particular passages of Ephesians in question. We will especially explore the OT background to themes such as divine warfare, temple, and glory, a step which is largely omitted in the works surveyed above. Beyond identifying various missional themes, this project in missional hermeneutics also seeks to discern how these themes relate together, and whether they address particular missional circumstances that shaped the production of the letter in the first place, that is, its purpose.

1.6 Theoretical Framework: Missional Hermeneutics

1.6.1 Introduction

Missional hermeneutics provides the theoretical framework for this study for the following reasons: (a) it is a lens specifically designed to investigate mission in the Bible; (b) it takes a broad view of what constitutes mission, not limiting it to initial evangelism through verbal proclamation; (c) it provides a set of questions that invites deeper investigation of mission from multiple perspectives; (d) it is oriented towards contemporary relevance in addition to historical analysis; and (e) it seeks to enrich biblical scholarship through incorporating insights and concerns from the field of missiology.[131] As a form of theological interpretation of Scripture, missional hermeneutics adopts approaches and dispositions to interpretation that are conditioned by explicit faith in the biblical narrative as God's word given to form the believing community for participation in God's mission in the world.[132] In this respect, it shares certain presuppositions with theological

---

131. Barram, "Social Location," 48–49.
132. McKinzie, "Missional Hermeneutics," 159–60, 177–79.

interpretation. Firstly, theological reading is regarded as necessary because, "Readings that remain on the historical, literary, or sociological levels cannot ultimately do justice to the subject matter of the texts."[133] Secondly, theological reading is concerned to serve the church by providing readings of canonical Scripture which highlight the triune God's word and works as they apply to the contemporary church and world.[134]

In this section, we will firstly review the emergence of missional hermeneutics as a distinctive interpretive approach, then briefly note the major emphases within missional hermeneutics practice, before ending with the set of questions that will be employed in the body of the present study to apply a missional hermeneutic to Ephesians.

1.6.2 The Emergence of Missional Hermeneutics

A range of scholars have argued the need for a missional hermeneutic for some time. In 1991, Bosch advocated reading the entire Bible missiologically. Having noted Martin Kähler's observation that mission is the "mother of theology," Bosch develops Martin Hengel's statement that "the history and the theology of early Christianity were, primarily, 'mission history' and 'mission theology.'"[135] Bosch affirms that "one of the main reasons for the existence of [the NT] is the missionary self-understanding and involvement of the people who gave birth to it." Marshall made a similar point in 2004: that the documents of the NT are "documents of a mission" and that NT theology is essentially "missionary theology."[136]

One of the earliest instances of a scholar using the phrase "missional hermeneutics" was James Brownson in 1994.[137] He argued that the interaction between biblical studies and missiology is a fruitful zone in which hermeneutical issues come to the fore. Both NT scholars and missiologists, said Brownson, are concerned with the interpretation of "the gospel in diverse cultural contexts and across cultural lines."[138] The character of the early Christian movement and the writings they produced was, according

---

133. Vanhoozer, "Theological Interpretation," 21.

134. Vanhoozer, "Theological Interpretation," 22.

135. Kähler, *Christologie und Mission*, 53, cited in; Bosch, *Transforming Mission*, 16; Bosch, "Biblical Models," 177, citing Hengel, *Between Jesus and Paul*, 53.

136. Marshall, *New Testament Theology*, 34–35.

137. Brownson, "Speaking the Truth," 479–504; expanded and later published as Brownson, *Speaking the Truth*.

138. Brownson, *Speaking the Truth*, 3.

to Brownson, *missionary* because it "crossed cultural boundaries and planted itself in new places."[139]

Another early work advocating a missional reading of the Bible was Beeby, *Canon and Mission*. He argued that "the scriptures are the account of the *missio dei*: that is, they arise out of mission and are intended for mission because they are the word of the missionary God."[140] For Beeby, a missionary hermeneutic is required because of the "continuing themes and ordering of the contents of the canon . . . creation to new creation . . . renewal, restoration, and redemption . . . through a sent nation, a sent son, and a sent community."[141] Beeby also mentions other factors which support the relevance of a missional hermeneutic such as the way the promises to Abraham shape the canon and the Christocentric arrangement of the canon.

We see from these early works establishing the field of missional hermeneutics that both the nature of the Bible and its function in the early Christian movement are described as missionary. Jumping forward a few years, in 2011 George Hunsberger sought to summarize the various ways in which practitioners of missional hermeneutics were approaching their task. He surveyed representative authors and developed a schema for missional hermeneutics which revolved around four recurrent emphases or streams of thought:

> [i] the *missio Dei* as the unitive narrative theme of the Bible, [ii] the purpose of biblical writings to equip the church for its witness, [iii] the contextual and missional locatedness of the Christian community, and [iv] the dynamic of the gospel's engagement with human cultures.[142]

Hunsberger's article and its analysis of the field of missional hermeneutics has been widely accepted as a watershed moment in the development of the field, and is routinely cited by practitioners of missional hermeneutics when discussing methodological approaches.[143] Nevertheless, it has some limitations, most notably that the first stream is too broad and that, to date, insufficient attention has been given to the third and fourth streams.[144] A fifth emphasis has also been incorporated in recent years: "the ways in which the biblical text discloses its fullest meaning only when read together with the

---

139. Brownson, *Speaking the Truth*, 14.
140. Beeby, *Canon and Mission*, 12–13 italics in original.
141. Beeby, *Canon and Mission*, 111.
142. Hunsberger, "Proposals," 309.
143. Flemming, *Why Mission?*, xviii.
144. Hunsberger, "Mapping," 66–67.

culturally and socially "other."[145] This emphasis extends the scope of the third stream, which already affirmed the significance of the reader's circumstances (interpretive horizon) for the hermeneutical process.[146]

In order to refine the methodology adopted in the present study, we will elaborate these four streams now in greater detail, drawing on the works of representative practitioners in each stream.

1.6.3 First Stream: Mission as the Theme of the Bible

The idea that the Bible is a product and reflection of mission was expressed and explored by Wright in *The Mission of God*. Wright's book crystallized an essential idea in missional hermeneutics—that the Bible as a canonical whole is "the product of and witness to the ultimate mission of God."[147] That is, God through self-revelation is engaged in a self-giving movement towards the creation and particularly towards humanity so that broken relationships can be restored.[148]

Another important writer in the field of missional hermeneutics, Gorman, focuses on what biblical texts say "about the polyvalent (complex and comprehensive) *missio Dei* and the missional character of God."[149] Many biblical writings, but especially the NT gospels, Acts, and letters, reflect events, struggles, or crises that arose as God's people sought to articulate and live out "their understanding of God's revelation and redemptive action in the world."[150] Or as Marshall puts it "The NT thus tells the story of the mission and lays especial emphasis on expounding the message proclaimed by the missionaries."[151] Michael Barram made a similar observation that the Bible functions as "the word of a missional God to a community defined by the divine mission."[152]

The methodological question therefore firstly is to ask: How does this particular writing speak of or witness to God's mission to redeem and restore humanity and sin-affected creation? The focus is on the impetus that led to the production of the particular text in the first place (i.e. purpose); the characterization of God in the text; the characterization of humanity in the text;

---

145. Hunsberger, "Mapping," 64.
146. Brownson, "Speaking the Truth," 481–82.
147. Wright, *Mission of God*, 48.
148. Wright, *Mission of God*, 48, referring to Taber, "Missiology," 229–45.
149. Gorman, *Becoming the Gospel*, 56.
150. Wright, *Mission of God*, 49.
151. Marshall, *New Testament Theology*, 35, cited by Wright, *Mission of God*, 50.
152. Barram, "Social Location," 43.

and the character and actions of those who are caught up in God's actions in the world because they understand themselves to be God's people, responding to God's revelation in the Scriptures and in Jesus.[153] These are historical questions, which can be answered satisfactorily only by employing the tools and techniques of historical-grammatical analysis.[154] Addressing these issues forms the largest proportion of the present study.

The nature of the Bible as a document in which mission is the overarching theme and a unifying narrative thread has a further implication for interpretation.[155] "Interpreting any specific biblical material requires attending to this pervading story of which it is a part. The parts must be read in light of the whole."[156] While respecting and indeed focusing on the particularity of Ephesians, a major element of the missional reading conducted in the present study will be an exploration of intertextual links and themes in biblical theology (such as covenant, temple, and the Divine Warrior motif) that enrich our appreciation of the message of the text. The goal of this intertextual reading is not merely to clarify the original meaning of particular verses or passages, but to explore how words, phrases, quotations, and imagery in Ephesians tap into and extend biblical theological motifs, and therefore convey a missional sense.[157] As will be discussed below, the literary phenomenon of metalepsis (the evocation of a precursor text's context by a later text through a quotation or allusion) is one way in which Ephesians reveals its missional purpose and character.

The focus of a missional hermeneutic on the missional purpose and character of the Bible is the first stream in what Hunsberger categorized as four streams or emphases in missional hermeneutics. We move now to consider the second stream.

1.6.4 Second Stream: Equipping for Mission

The second element of a missional hermeneutic arises from the first and brings into sharper focus one element already mentioned: the purpose of the biblical writings to equip or form the people of God to participate

---

153. Cf. Wright, *Mission of God*, 31; Barram, "Social Location," 49; Gorman, *Becoming the Gospel*, 56.
154. Wright, *Mission of God*, 40.
155. Wright, *Mission of God*, 22, 31, 51, 531.
156. Wright, *Mission of God*, 50.
157. This approach to biblical theology is expressed in Rosner, "Biblical Theology," 3, 6.

in God's mission.[158] Barram expresses it in this way: "the NT texts themselves are in some real sense missiological, inasmuch as they equip their original addressees for the community's vocation in the world."[159] Craig Bartholomew discusses how each distinct genre of the OT Scriptures functioned to form and equip Israel as "a faithful missional people."[160] The law ordered their national, liturgical, and moral life so that they might be a light to the nations; the historical books told the story of Israel's missional calling; the prophets warned Israel when it was diverging from God's missional plan for them; the psalms nourished Israel through worship to remember and remain true to their calling. The NT was the "literary expression of the apostolic preaching and teaching, which continued to make Christ present to form and nourish particular missional communities in different parts of the Roman Empire."[161]

Hunsberger focuses on Darrell Guder as the prime exemplar of this second stream. Guder, in pursuing this emphasis, asks: "How did this text equip and shape God's people for their missional witness then, and how does it shape us today?"[162] The key verbs used by proponents in this area are *equip*, *shape*, and *form*. The object of these verbs is the community of God's people who are called to participate as agents of God's mission. N.T. Wright uses analogous language in his discussion of reading the NT missionally:

> A NT hermeneutic must therefore be about learning to read the New Testament, not in order to cull from it the few verses that make us feel good; rather, a faithful NT hermeneutic will *sustain* and *energize* the church—from every possible angle—as it goes about its God-given, Jesus-shaped, Spirit-driven missionary task.[163]

Dean Flemming similarly speaks of how the text calls the recipients to "proclaim, enact, and embody the gospel."[164] Colin Yuckman contrasts this approach with traditional academic hermeneutics, saying, "While traditional biblical criticism asks, 'which hermeneutic is most qualified to understand

---

158. Guder, "Missional Hermeneutics," 107–8.

159. Barram, "Social Location," 49.

160. Bartholomew, "Manifesto," 17.

161. Bartholomew, "Manifesto," 17.

162. Guder, *Unlikely Ambassadors*, 5, cited in; Hunsberger, "Proposals," 313; cf. Guder and Barrett, *Missional Church*, 223.

163. Wright, "Reading," 181, emphasis added.

164. Flemming, *Why Mission?*, 16.

the Scriptures?' missional hermeneutics asks instead, 'what kind of community does a faithful hermeneutic foster?'"[165]

Whereas the first stream focuses on the nature of the Bible as a *product and record of mission*, the second stream focuses on the purpose of the Bible as a *tool to equip* God's people for mission. There are a number of indicators in Ephesians that its author intended his letter to effect the transformation of his audience. Most obviously, the paraenetic material urges the recipients to live in a particular way (e.g. 4:1–3, 14–15, 17, 25; 5:1, 21, 25; 6:1). More than explicit moral exhortation, the letter also urges particular spiritual actions: growth in knowledge and experience of God and Christ (3:16–19), reliance on God's power in spiritual conflict (6:10–17), and prayer (6:18–19). In the present study, we will test whether and how such exhortations (and other elements of the letter) contribute to forming believers for mission in particular.

1.6.5 Third Stream: The Missional Locatedness of the Readers

The third approach identified by Hunsberger in his schema of missional hermeneutics moves from a focus on the missional character of the text and how it functioned to equip its original recipients for mission, to consider the contemporary reader. Barram argues that a faithful interpretation of God's missional word is best arrived at by communities actively engaged in mission in the contemporary world.[166] This third stream in missional interpretation seeks to hear a wider diversity of voices than is often represented in Western academic settings, especially "the culturally and socially 'other.'"[167] It also pushes professional biblical scholars to be more self-aware and self-critical of the presumptions and blind spots created by their social location.[168]

As noted by Hunsberger, the third and fourth streams "are by nature local and communal practices that fall more naturally elsewhere than in the academy."[169] The present study will not explicitly pursue this aspect of missional hermeneutics, as the focus is on the nature of Ephesians in its

---

165. Yuckman, "Ulterior Gospel," 14.

166. Barram, "Social Location," 52.

167. GOCN Forum on Missional Hermeneutics 2011, quoted in Hunsberger, "Mapping," 64.

168. Guder, *Unlikely Ambassadors*, cited in Hunsberger, "Proposals," 316; Barram, "'Located' Questions"; Russell, *(Re)Aligning with God*, 110.

169. Hunsberger, "Mapping," 67.

original setting. At times, however, sources from majority world contexts will be incorporated into the discussion, in order to avoid a hermeneutically limiting reliance exclusively on Western academic voices.

1.6.6 Fourth Stream: Missional Engagement with Culture

Hunsberger's fourth stream is concerned with how the received biblical tradition is critically brought to bear on particular cultural contexts.[170] His main exemplar in this approach is Brownson who speaks of the way the NT writers applied the OT Scriptures to their contemporary situation as an interpretive matrix centered on the gospel of Christ.[171] Brownson defines the gospel as "the proclamation of God's soteriological purpose and claim on this world, a purpose and claim extended paradigmatically through the crucified and risen Christ."[172] Brownson's focus, however, is not only on the content of the gospel, but more on the way in which it dynamically interacts with context and tradition. He argues that the patterns of appropriating tradition in new contexts that are seen in the NT are a hermeneutical structure which contemporary Christians can and should employ. In practice, this means that missional hermeneutics welcomes the diversity of NT voices, as well as the diversity in the history of interpretation up to the modern day. For Brownson, the goal is not to make all the texts uniform, but to allow tradition and context to both inform and critique our own situation in the light of the gospel, just as they informed and critiqued the situation of the first generations of Christians.[173]

The present study will not seek to explore examples of the contemporary application of Ephesians in missional contexts. We will however, pay particular attention to how the author of Ephesians has creatively drawn on OT texts and themes in elaborating the nature of God's action in the world and intentions for the church. The intertextual analysis will reveal a consistent interest in texts that have been characterized variously as new creation, new exodus, and gentile pilgrimage.[174] These themes signal that salvation

---

170. Hunsberger, "Proposals," 316–17.

171. Brownson, *Speaking the Truth*, 39–41.

172. Brownson, *Speaking the Truth*, 51.

173. Brownson, *Speaking the Truth*, 78–82; cf. Guder, *Called to Witness*, 91, the NT texts aimed "to deal with the problems and the conflicts, the challenges and the doubts as they emerged in particular contexts, so that these communities could be faithful to their calling."

174. Owens, *As It Was*, 169–70, Gen 1, 2, 12; Ps 8; Isa 52; 57; 65–66; Cozart, *Present Triumph*, 252–59, Isa 11; 44; 49; 50; 52; 59; 61; Jeremias, *Jesus' Promise*, 56–62, Zech 8; Isa 2; 60.

history has entered a new phase with the death and resurrection of Jesus. Furthermore, in a concluding chapter (chapter 12) we will explore how the missional context implied by the text intersects with the probable historical context of Western Asia Minor in the first century CE. The extent of the fit between implied and probable historical context enables us to pinpoint particular ways in which Ephesians does offer a missional engagement with the culture of its original audience.

Having explored each of the streams or emphases apparent in the field of missional hermeneutics, Hunsberger concluded:

> These accents have made proposals regarding the *framework* for a missional hermeneutic (the narrative of the missio Dei), the *aim* of a missional hermeneutic (ecclesial formation for witness), the *approach* of a missional hermeneutic (socially located questions), and the interpretive *matrix* of a missional hermeneutic (the gospel as the interpretive key). In substance and girth, these conversations have provided foundations for the continuing development of a robust missional hermeneutic.[175]

As practitioners of missional hermeneutics have demonstrated in treatments of both OT and NT books, and overview studies, missional hermeneutics does indeed provide a broad and innovative approach to biblical interpretation.[176] It is for this reason that it has been selected as the theoretical framework for the present study.

1.7 Methodology

1.7.1 Gaps and Questions Arising from Literature Reviews

The review of literature has highlighted a number of gaps in existing scholarship on Ephesians. Some commentaries acknowledge the importance of Paul's gentile mission but deny or inadequately relate it to any ongoing role for the church. There is also a lack of consistency in how mission is understood, and the extent to which it is present throughout the letter, or only in key verses or in particular themes such as reconciliation, temple, or spiritual warfare. The review of missiological works revealed a tendency for biblical theologies of mission to engage in selective proof texting, ignoring historical and literary context.

---

175. Hunsberger, "Proposals," 319.
176. Goheen, *Reading the Bible*, 107–237; Gorman, *Becoming the Gospel*.

The methodological intent in this study is therefore to move beyond proof texting, and go deeper than thematic studies on individual missional ideas such as reconciliation (whether focused on one passage or the whole letter). We plan to explore: (a) how missional themes arise from and are integrated with their immediate literary context, (b) how missional themes develop across the whole of Ephesians, (c) how mission is uniquely conceived and portrayed in Ephesians, and (d) whether these various elements of mission in Ephesians converge such that mission can be claimed to constitute a meta-narrative in the letter. On the basis of these explorations, we will then be in a position to reassess the context and purpose of Ephesians in light of the missional reading.

In the following sections, we will outline the questions to be utilized in the body of the research, clarify the meaning of the key terms *missio Dei*, mission and intertextuality, and note limits on the research.

1.7.2 Seven Questions that Shape the Missional Reading

Hunsberger's taxonomy of four streams is helpful in establishing the breadth and distinctive approaches within the discipline of missional hermeneutics but lacks precision when it comes to implementation. The jump from theory to practice is facilitated by using carefully framed questions.[177] The following seven questions will be used in chapters 2–11 in order to provide a consistent and rigorous analysis of mission in each passage of Ephesians.

1. How does this text portray God's intentions, actions, and purposes for the world and humanity (the *missio Dei*)?

2. How does this text portray God's person and character? Is the Trinity in evidence and if so, how do the persons of the Trinity particularly function in relation to God's mission[178] (the missional character of God)?

---

177. Lists of questions posed by practitioners of missional hermeneutics can be found at Wright, "Reading," 122–23; Flemming, *Why Mission?*, xxi–xxii; Hunsberger, "Bible Study Questions," 7; Russell, *(Re)Aligning with God*, 131–33; Gorman, *Becoming the Gospel*, 56. The following questions are an amalgamation and paraphrase of these various formulations.

178. Many practitioners of missional hermeneutics adopt a Trinitarian understanding of the *missio Dei*, allowing that theological commitment to enrich their missiological reflections prompted by the text, McKinzie, "Missional Hermeneutics," 160–61, 164. Ephesians contains a number of "Trinitarian" passages (1:3–14, 17; 2:18, 22; 3:4–5, 14–17; 4:4–6; 5:18–20). In this project, such Trinitarian language will be highlighted and exegeted to see if and how it contributes to our understanding of God's mission. This attention to Trinitarian elements in the text does not necessitate that the author had a formalized understanding of the Trinity (Best, *Ephesians*, 56), but it does acknowledge

3. How does this text connect to the whole canon of Scripture? Are there thematic or literary linkages that reveal points of continuity with the wider narrative of the biblical story? How does this text contribute to the narrative of God's mission in the world?

4. How does this text portray humanity and the world in relation to God's mission?

5. What evidence is there in this text that Ephesians is a product of mission (i.e. a document that arose in a missional context)? What problems, crises, or issues are addressed by the text?

6. What does this text reveal about the character and mission of God's people in the world?

7. How does this text portray the character, motivations, and actions of the apostle Paul and his involvement in God's mission?

Practitioners of missional hermeneutics admit that there is considerable overlap between the streams, which together constitute a working hypothesis for the discipline.[179] The questions that will be used to shape the investigation of Ephesians in the present study reflect the streams in the following manner. Stream one, the framework for missional hermeneutics is prominent in questions 1–4 and 7. Stream two, the aim of the Bible as formation for mission is most clearly addressed by question 6. Stream three, concerning the context of the Christian community as the letter's audience, is only obliquely addressed in question 5. Stream four, the interpretive matrix of missional hermeneutics, is reflected in question 3 concerning intertextuality.

To date, the only published discussion of Ephesians explicitly adopting a missional hermeneutical approach is found in Gorman, *Becoming the Gospel* (noted above, §1.5.4).[180] The present study will seek to provide a more detailed and systematic missional reading of Ephesians than Gorman's chapter, not because of any fundamental flaw in Gorman's presentation of Ephesians, but because missional hermeneutics provides the scope to delve ever deeper into the missional dynamics of the biblical text.

---

the richness of Trinitarian thought throughout the letter (Arnold, *Ephesians*, 493–94; Hoehner, *Ephesians*, 106–10).

179. Hunsberger, "Proposals," 319; Guder, "Missional Hermeneutics," 110.

180. Gombis, *Drama of Ephesians*, while not claiming to adopt a missional hermeneutic, presents a reading of Ephesians that aligns in many respects with the focus of missional hermeneutics. Gombis states, at 181, "This is also a theological reading of Ephesians in that the drama is set within the wider context of the Christian narrative of creation, fall, and redemption. God is on a mission to reclaim his broken creation and is doing so through Jesus Christ and his people, the church."

In summary, the missional hermeneutic reading to be pursued in the present study will explore what Ephesians tells us about the *missio Dei*, the character of God, the broader scriptural context of mission in Ephesians, its view of humanity and the world, its missional context, the character and role of God's people, and of Paul in God's mission. Or more briefly, how *Ephesians functions as a record, product, and instrument of mission.*[181]

1.7.3 Definitions and Presuppositions

Rather than beginning with the debates about authorship, provenance, and dating of Ephesians, the present study deliberately leaves the range of possibilities in those areas open, concentrating on a close reading of the text as the most significant determinant of its probable context and purposes. Only following the readings of each pericope of the letter using the missional hermeneutics framework do we turn to draw out possible implications for the original context and purpose of the letter. The working assumption for the reading of Ephesians in chapters 2–11 here, is that it addresses and reflects real life circumstances of particular Christian communities in the second half of the first century CE. That is, whether or not it is pseudonymous, its life setting is not fictional.

1.7.3.1 MISSION

The definition of mission is contested by scholars. Writers adopting missional hermeneutics invariably see mission as a broad concept, encompassing proclamation, embodiment, social justice, and creation care. For example, at the conclusion of Flemming's missional reading of the NT, he describes the understanding of mission that emerges: "The church's mission, like the mission of Jesus, is all-embracing and integrated. It involves being, doing, and telling."[182] For Barram, mission is necessarily *holistic* (or *integral* to use the phrase preferred by UK missiologists): "issues of socio-cultural, political, economic, and environmental justice [are] essentially inseparable from the church's evangelistic outreach to unbelievers."[183] Similarly broad is Bosch's approach that identifies the key dynamic of mission as boundary or frontier crossing:

---

181. Goheen, "Continuing Steps," 61, 90–91.
182. Flemming, *Why Mission?*, 133.
183. Barram, "Social Location," 44.

These frontiers may be ethnic, cultural, geo-graphical, religious, ideological or social. Mission takes place where the Church, in her total involvement with the world and the comprehensiveness of her message, bears testimony in word and deed in the form of a servant, with reference to unbelief, exploitation, discrimination and violence, but also with reference to salvation, healing, liberation, reconciliation and righteousness.[184]

A more succinct definition is provided by Wright, who defines mission as: "our committed participation as God's people, at God's invitation and command, in God's own mission within the history of God's world for the redemption of God's creation."[185]

Drawing these varied emphases together, our tentative understanding of mission is that it should not be limited to proclamation, but holistically encompass the just actions, character and witness of God's people crossing diverse geographic, ethnic, and economic boundaries in order to further God's redemptive plan for all creation.

The set of questions that provide the methodological framework for the present study contain a presumption that the Bible does witness to mission. However, the presence and form of mission reflected in any given text is the question to be determined. This approach (more inductive than deductive) is adopted to minimize the risk of circularity or question-begging in this study of mission in Ephesians.

Missional is used adjectivally to characterize its complement as having "the qualities, attributes or dynamics of mission."[186]

1.7.3.2 *Missio Dei*

Missio Dei, literally, the "mission of God," is a foundational concept in modern missiology. It is beyond the scope of this study to detail the history of debates about *missio Dei*. In essence, the *missio Dei* concept rejects the conceptualization of mission as focused on individual salvation, Christianization, or church expansion. Instead, the phrase draws attention to the principle that God rather than the church is the initiator and source of mission, and that mission is an attribute of the triune God, particularly his sending love. The *missio Dei* has as its goal "the establishment of the lordship of Christ over the entire redeemed creation."[187] Acknowledging

---

184. Bosch, *Witness to the World*, 18.
185. Wright, *Mission of God*, 23.
186. Wright, *Mission of God*, 24.
187. Hartenstein, "Theologische Besinnung," 54; translation by Ott, *Mission of the*

flaws in the history of how *mission* and *missio Dei* have been understood does not necessitate their abandonment.[188] Indeed, the present study seeks to provide firm scriptural data that will ultimately enrich the picture of mission rather than constrain it.

1.7.3.2 Intertextuality

Question 3 of the seven guiding questions (§1.7.2, above) concerns the linkages between particular verses or passages in Ephesians and the wider biblical text, that is, the issue of intertextuality. More than half a century ago, C. H. Dodd argued that NT authors drew upon extended passages in Isaiah and other OT books as they wrote: "Particular verses or sentences were quoted from them rather as pointers to the whole context than as constituting testimonies in and for themselves."[189] Dodd continues, "the governing intention is to exploit whole contexts selected as the varying expression of certain fundamental and permanent elements in the biblical revelation."[190] He later elaborated, "The reader is invited to study the context as a whole, and to reflect upon the 'plot' there unfolded."[191]

More recently, the literary phenomenon of metalepsis was applied by Richard Hays to the study of Pauline letters, who defined it as follows: "When a literary echo links the text in which it occurs to an earlier text, the figurative effect of the echo can lie in the unstated or suppressed (transumed) points of resonance between the two texts."[192] Jeannine Brown describes metalepsis as "an author's reference to the larger literary context when offering a citation or allusion from an earlier text. In this sense, metalepsis is the use of a part of a precursor text to evoke the whole of it."[193]

Hays's proposal has been critiqued by a number of scholars. Stanley Porter claims that Hays's seven criteria to identify metalepsis are vague.[194] Christopher Stanley has argued that literacy levels and the poor availability of the LXX in written form meant that only a small group within early Christian audiences could have understood and appreciated any metaleptic

---

Church, xiv. For an overview of the history of *missio Dei*, see xiii–xvi and Bosch, *Transforming Mission*, 389–90.

188. Stroope, *Transcending Mission*; Flett, *Witness of God*, esp. 286–98.
189. Dodd, *According to the Scriptures*, 126.
190. Dodd, *According to the Scriptures*, 132.
191. Dodd, *Old Testament*, 20.
192. Hays, *Echoes of Scripture*, 20.
193. Brown, "Metalepsis," 30.
194. Porter, "Allusions and Echoes," 29–40.

effects in Pauline letters (he distinguishes informed, competent, and minimal audiences). He cautions against presuming too high a level of readerly competence when discussing Paul's use of Scripture.[195] Despite such criticism, most scholars generally do not doubt that the broader context of a quote or allusion from the OT in the NT should be considered as a relevant factor in interpretation.[196] The existence of intertextual features is not debated; what is at issue is the prevalence of subtle forms of intertextuality such as metalepsis, and the validity of claiming it is present in particular passages. The sophistication with which the author of Ephesians weaves OT quotes, allusions, and themes into his letter creates a prima facie presumption that he believed his audience did have a reasonably high level of readerly competence.[197]

With regard to the use of the OT in Ephesians, the main studies of previous decades were those by Lincoln, Barth, and Thorsten Moritz. Lincoln's study focused disproportionately on quotations, with insufficient regard paid to allusions and echoes.[198] Barth's study acknowledged the importance of allusions, but predominantly sought to disprove the then-prevailing view that Ephesians incorporated Gnostic influences.[199] Moritz's monograph was a more substantial engagement with both OT quotes and allusions than anything prior, including exploration of OT *Vorlagen* and the NT appropriations thereof.[200] Moritz only focused on very clear allusions, and so in more recent works, scholars have had scope to evaluate a wider set of possible allusions. Nevertheless, there has been a disproportionate emphasis in this area of study on Isaiah as the source of precursor texts in various passages of Ephesians.[201] In our investigation of intertextuality focused on missional texts and concepts, we will find that other OT books are also alluded to in Ephesians, and warrant further attention.

The starting position adopted in this study is that a number of passages in Ephesians are capable of being interpreted as metaleptic tropes. This was the explicit conclusion of Owens with regard to the use of Isa 11, 52, and 59 in Eph 6:10–17.[202] Other studies by Paula Qualls and John Watts, Thomas

195. Stanley, *Arguing with Scripture*, 47–48, 66–69.
196. Beale, "Conversion," 191.
197. Starling, *Not My People*, 184–86.
198. Lincoln, "Use of the OT," 16–57.
199. Barth, "Traditions in Ephesians," 3–25.
200. Moritz, *Profound Mystery*, 1–8.
201. Qualls and Watts, "Isaiah in Ephesians," 249–59; Lunde and Dunne, "Isaiah in Ephesians 5," 87–110; Cozart, *Present Triumph*.
202. Owens, "Spiritual Warfare," 103.

Yoder Neufeld, and Richard Cozart also saw evidence of conscious appropriation and creative transformation of the broader contexts of Isaianic citations in Ephesians, which can fairly be described as metalepsis.[203]

In the missional reading of Ephesians conducted in the present study, we will utilize Hays's tests for echoes of OT material in NT texts as the criteria to judge whether an intentional allusion or echo can reasonably be judged to be present. Hays bases his tests on the following principle:

> Claims about intertextual meaning effects are strongest where it can credibly be demonstrated that they occur within the literary structure of the text and that they can plausibly be ascribed to the intention of the author and the competence of the original readers.[204]

He then lists seven tests:

1. Availability. Was the proposed source of the echo available to the author and/or original readers?

2. Volume. The volume of an echo is determined primarily by the degree of explicit repetition of words or syntactical patterns, but other factors may also be relevant: How distinctive or prominent is the precursor text within Scripture and how much rhetorical stress does the echo receive in Paul's discourse?

3. Recurrence. How often does Paul elsewhere cite or allude to the same scriptural passage?

4. Thematic coherence. How well does the alleged echo fit into the line of argument that Paul is developing? Is its meaning effect consonant with other quotations in the same letter or elsewhere in the Pauline corpus?

5. Historical plausibility. Could Paul have intended the alleged meaning effect? Could his readers have understood it?

6. History of interpretation. Have other readers, both critical and pre-critical, heard the same echoes? The readings of our predecessors can both check and stimulate our perception of scriptural echoes in Paul.

7. Satisfaction. With or without clear confirmation from the other criteria listed here, does the proposed reading make sense? Does it illuminate

---

203. Qualls and Watts, "Isaiah in Ephesians," 256; Yoder Neufeld, "*Armour of God*," 155; Cozart, *Present Triumph*.

204. Hays, *Echoes of Scripture*, 28.

the surrounding discourse? Does it produce for the reader a satisfying account of the effect of the intertextual relation?[205]

In the following chapters, a *citation* is understood as a quotation with an introductory formula (the only example in Ephesians being 4:8) and a *quotation* is a phrase or sentence that largely replicates the vocabulary and syntax of the precursor text. An *allusion* is the use of particular vocabulary (though not necessarily syntax) that is sufficiently unique in the Scriptures to raise the possibility of authorially-intended reference, a possibility which may be confirmed or refuted through the application of Hays's criteria. An *echo* is a subtler reference (often because it consists of only one or two words, i.e. Hays's test of volume is insufficiently satisfied) which may or may not have been intended by the author to evoke reflection on a particular precursor text. Both quotations and allusions are evaluated on the basis of authorial intent and the competence of the original audience (that is, Hays's tests of recurrence and historical plausibility).[206]

In addition to applying Hays's criteria to potential allusions and echoes, the discussion of Ephesians' use of the OT will draw on the suggested interpretive approach of G. K. Beale. This will include (as appropriate): identifying the OT reference; noting the NT context where the OT reference occurs; analyzing the OT context of the quotation or allusion; noting particularly significant uses of the OT text in second temple Judaism; and analyzing the author's theological use of the OT.[207] Our particular focus will be the extent to which OT precursor texts and their contexts support the claim by missional hermeneutic writers (discussed above in §1.6.2–3) that mission is a meta-theme unifying the biblical narrative. If the precursor texts (and their contexts) utilized by Ephesians evince a consistent interest in mission, then this claim is validated. We will also explore whether particular aspects of mission (such as gentile pilgrimage to Zion, universal salvation or the renewal of creation) are present in Ephesians' use of the OT.

1.7.4 Limitations

There is insufficient scope in the present study to deal with the relationship of Ephesians with Colossians. Similarly, it is not necessary or possible to examine all the factors behind scholarly judgments concerning whether Ephesians is an authentic, composite or pseudepigraphal Pauline work. We

---

205. Hays, *Echoes of Scripture*, 29–31.
206. Hays, *Echoes of Scripture*, 23–29; Beetham, *Echoes of Scripture*, 11–24.
207. Beale, *Handbook*, 42–43.

will simply refer in this study to "the author of Ephesians" to indicate neutrality in this matter. Instead, in the final chapters, we will draw out some implications of a missional reading for the issue of the occasion, purpose, and context behind Ephesians in its canonical form.

1.8 Plan of the Present Study

As already foreshadowed, the body of the present study comprises a missional reading of each pericope within Ephesians (based on UBS divisions of the text), structured around the seven questions identified in §1.7.2, above (though not every question is relevant in each section). Following from that ground-up, exegetically driven discussion of Ephesians, two summary chapters seek to synthesize and apply the missional reading firstly to the context (occasion) of Ephesians (chapter 12), and then to the question of the purpose of Ephesians (chapter 13). A final concluding chapter will seek to synthesize the data from each of the guiding questions before returning to the research questions and hypothesis.

The next chapter treats the letter's opening *berakah* (blessing) and begins the systematic exploration of mission in each passage of Ephesians.

2

Ephesians 1:1–14

2.1 Introduction

EPHESIANS OPENS WITH A standard Pauline greeting (1:1–2), followed by a thanksgiving (*berakah*) (1:3–14). As outlined in the introduction, the missional reading of Ephesians will be structured around a set of questions (focal points) applied to each passage in turn. Here, we will investigate the following features of Eph 1:1–14: the portrayal of the *missio Dei*; the characterization of God; intertextuality; humanity in relation to the *missio Dei*; missional context; and the portrait of Paul. The character and mission of the people of God (question 6) is primarily revealed in vv. 6, 12, 14, and will not be discussed separately. Instead, it is covered in §2.4.1, where the intertextual analysis clarifies the meaning of living "to the praise of God's glory."

The passage introduces a number of key themes that will be developed more fully in the course of the letter. These include grace, peace, being *in Christ*, the cosmic scope of God's actions, and the holy lives of believers. While commentaries typically describe the opening *berakah* as encompassing salvation history,[1] they rarely note the implication that all believers who have received the numerous blessings poured out by God are thereby caught up in a missional project that is ongoing. Through intertextual links to 1 Chr 16 and Deut 7:6–8, the passage evokes an understanding of the covenant people of God as witnesses to God's sovereignty before the nations. As God's people live "to the praise of his glory" they become part of God's mission to see the whole cosmos reconciled to God in Christ.

---

1. E.g. Lincoln, *Ephesians*, 43.

2.2 Portrayal of God's Intentions, Actions, and Purposes (the *missio Dei*)

As with all Pauline letters, the letter's opening greeting not only introduces Paul as the author, but also foreshadows pastoral or theological issues that will be developed in the body of the letter. The greeting of v. 2, in typical Pauline style, specifies God the Father and the Lord Jesus Christ as the *source* of grace and peace for the recipients.[2] Grace is a characteristic of God in 1:6, 7; 2:7; 3:2, 7; and a way of expressing God's saving action for humanity in 2:5, 8. Moreover, grace drives Paul's mission (3:2, 7–8). As we will see below (in §2.7), Paul's description as an apostle "by God's will" (1:1) ties the Pauline mission to the *missio Dei*. The establishment of peace is central to God's purposes for the world (2:14–17). The prominence of peace vocabulary and themes in Ephesians prompts Gorman to characterize the letter as centering on "the gospel of peace" (6:15).[3]

The long single sentence of the *berakah* which stretches from v. 3 to v. 14 elaborates a series of divinely intended outcomes (blessings) in the lives of the recipients. The language of intention and purpose is particularly rich in this passage: v. 4 chose (ἐξελέξατο), v. 5 predestined (προορίσας), the good pleasure of his will (τὴν εὐδοκίαν τοῦ θελήματος αὐτοῦ); v. 8 wisdom and understanding (σοφίᾳ καὶ φρονήσει); v. 9 his will (τοῦ θελήματος αὐτοῦ); v. 9 his good pleasure (τὴν εὐδοκίαν αὐτοῦ); v. 9 purposed in Christ (προέθετο ἐν αὐτῷ); v. 10 plan (οἰκονομίαν); v. 11 predestined (προορισθέντες); v. 11 the purpose of his will (τὴν βουλὴν τοῦ θελήματος αὐτοῦ).[4] The extensive use of intention and purpose language makes it undeniably clear that the status of the letter's recipients as beneficiaries of God's will is neither a recent innovation nor accidental, but is central to God's mission in the world since before the foundation of the world (v. 4).

Verse 4 states that God's intention is that the recipients become established in a particular state (holy and blameless in love) before God (cf. 2:10, which indicates an element of missional witness to their ethical status and behavior).[5] In v. 5, God's actions are stated in familial terms, the recipients are predestined for "adoption as his children through Jesus

---

2. Best, *Ephesians*, 102.
3. Gorman, *Becoming the Gospel*, 181.
4. Qualls and Watts, "Isaiah in Ephesians," 250.
5. Taking ἐν ἀγάπῃ to modify "chosen to be holy and blameless" rather than God's foreordaining purpose, Lincoln, *Ephesians*, 17, 24; Thielman, *Ephesians*, 49–50; Hoehner, *Ephesians*, 182–85 (giving the most detailed exegetical reasons for this interpretation); cf. Graham, *Exegetical Summary*, 24, for a survey of which translations and commentaries support the various possible readings.

Christ." Linking predestination with adoption is also evident in Rom 8:29, a passage in which ethical conduct is also tied to the will of God and the work of God's Spirit (8:4, 14–17, 20, 27).

God's purpose for all his saving actions is stated three times in a thematic refrain that occurs with slight variations in vv. 6, 12 and 14. The letter's recipients are chosen, sanctified, adopted, redeemed, and sealed with the Holy Spirit, "to the praise of his glorious grace" or "to the praise of his glory." Verse 7 adds forgiveness of trespasses to the list of blessings bestowed on the recipients.

Then in vv. 9–10 we reach a significant statement of God's ultimate missional purposes and will for the entire cosmos: "to gather up [ἀνακεφαλαιώσασθαι] all things in him, things in heaven and things on earth." The meaning of ἀνακεφαλαιόω is debated. Barth and Schlier emphasize the aspect of headship, based on the root κεφαλή (*to be comprehended under one head*) and the language of 1:22.[6] Other commentators such as Lincoln, however, argue that the word's meaning in classical Greek and its only other NT occurrence at Rom 13:9 are determinative. The word derives from κεφάλαιον, and so means *to sum up*.[7] Relating ἀνακεφαλαιόω to headship is a flawed etymologizing interpretation.[8] The immediate context of the word at 1:10 is sufficient to determine its meaning, which is summation of a now-revealed divine plan (οἰκονομία 1:9), by which a final unification of all things (τὰ πάντα, 1:10) in the cosmos will be achieved (ESV "unite"; CSB "bring together"; NIV "bring unity").[9] This reading anticipates but is not anachronistically dependent on the ideas of unification and reconciliation which are elaborated in 2:14–16 and 4:3–6, 13, and which feature in the related verse, Col 1:20.[10] Prominent here is a centripetal vision of mission.

Meyer sees the verb ἀνακεφαλαιώσασθαι, *to sum up*, in v. 10 as a key word, encapsulating the process and result of the apostolic proclamation of the gospel. To the extent that the church is the result of God's thorough

---

6. Barth, *Ephesians 1–3*, 89–91; Schlier, "ἀνακεφαλαιόομαι," 681–82; cf. Arnold, *Ephesians*, 88–89.

7. Lincoln, *Ephesians*, 32–33. It occurs only one other time in the NT, at Rom 13:9, where it clearly means sum up.

8. Barr, *Semantics*, 237; Sellin, *Brief*, 106.

9. Cf. Irenaeus, who drew on Eph 1:10 for his theory of salvation as recapitulation: through Christ, humanity is able to be reunited with God, restoring the image of God and unity with God lost by Adam. Irenaeus, *Haer*, 3.16.6; 3.18.1; 5.20, 21; Kitchen, *Ephesians*, 36.

10. Best, *Ephesians*, 140–43; Muddiman, *Ephesians*, 75–76; Thielman, *Ephesians*, 65–67; L&N, §63.8.

saving works, it is also called to continue those saving works until all of creation is encompassed in God's salvation.

> Thus, the verb ἀνακεφαλαιώσασθαι [v. 10] ultimately means the event of the proclamation and hearing of the gospel, people becoming believers and being sealed with the Holy Spirit for inclusion among those who are predestined for sonship by grace, according to God's eternal decision of salvation. In other words, it [ἀνακεφαλαιώσασθαι] can be a description of God's general (universal) will for salvation, the goal of which is explicit lived Christianity and lived church through missionary proclamation.[11]

Verses 11–14, which Muddiman regards as an addition to the "preformed liturgical material"[12] of vv. 3–10, focuses on the concept of inheritance. Although many translations and some commentators interpret the passive verb (ἐκληρώθημεν, 1:11) as indicating what believers receive from God (final salvation),[13] it is better to understand that redeemed believers constitute God's inheritance, as Israel was said to be in the OT, Deut 9:29; Ps 33:12 [LXX 32:12].[14] God's seal of the Holy Spirit is, therefore, a mark of believers' ownership by God (v. 13), a down payment (ἀρραβών) which indicates the eschatological fulfillment of God's blessings will be even greater than those presently experienced.[15] God's mission therefore extends from prehistory to the eschatological future.

In summary, the *missio Dei* is to choose, redeem, adopt, and sanctify for himself a holy people, who are the firstfruits of his inheritance, sealed by the Spirit until the eschaton, at which time a reconciled and unified cosmos will exist to the praise of his glory. As is common in Pauline letters, the opening greeting and thanksgiving indicate major themes that will be developed in the body of the letter.

---

11. Meyer, *Kirche und Mission*, 32, my translation.
12. Muddiman, *Ephesians*, 65.
13. E.g. NRSV, ESV, CSB; Best, *Ephesians*, 146; Pokorný, *Brief*, 70.
14. Lincoln, *Ephesians*, 36; Hoehner, *Ephesians*, 225–27. The passive verb more naturally supports this meaning, rather than the first option, which would require it to be understood as a middle. Further, the noun form of the root κλῆρος (κληρονομία) occurs at 1:18 with the widely accepted meaning of "God's inheritance."
15. Arnold, *Ephesians*, 192–93.

2.3 Portrayal of God's Person and Character

This passage, through use of synonyms and redundant expressions, emphasizes God's sovereign intentionality in the plan of salvation and his loving, gracious motivation in this mission.

The introductory blessing of Eph 1:3–14 is an element also present in shorter form in 2 Cor 1:3–4. The "God and Father of our Lord Jesus Christ" has acted to bless the writer and recipients with "every spiritual blessing in the heavens in Christ." While *spiritual* (πνευματικῇ) may denote a contrast with worldly blessings, the context here, in which God's Spirit is explicitly linked to believer's experience of salvation (vv. 13–14), implies that the blessings are the work of the Spirit of God, (cf. Gal 3:14; 1 Cor 2:14–16).[16] Accordingly, this verse foreshadows a Trinitarian flavor which will become more pronounced as the role of God working in Christ (vv. 4–12) concludes with the role of the Spirit in vv. 13–14.[17]

As noted briefly above, the customary Pauline greeting employing χάρις *grace* (of which God is the source), foreshadows a concern with grace in the thanksgiving and body of the letter. God's grace towards the recipients is prominent in vv. 6–8. In particular, v. 7 describes the act of redemption, the forgiving of the recipients' trespasses as flowing from "the riches of God's grace," which "he richly poured out on us" (v. 8). This gracious act is then further specified in v. 8 as being characterized by "all wisdom and understanding." God is portrayed as powerful and sovereign over humanity and the cosmos, since his will and pleasure are effected according to his plan (vv. 9–10).

Verses 3–6 use verbs for God's actions on behalf of the recipients and the world which stress God's deliberate and favorable orientation towards the world, his concern for it, and his generosity in relating to the world: blessing the recipients (v. 3); choosing (v. 4); predestining and adopting (vv. 5, 11); lavishing grace on the recipients (v. 6); making known the mystery (v. 8). This combination of intention vocabulary with the themes of grace and love emphasizes that God's motivation for the grand plan of salvation was his "free good-pleasure . . . his gracious resolution to save."[18]

The portrayal of God's nature and character in vv. 1–14 has "a trinitarian character"[19] (noting that most commentators hold that the author of

---

16. Fee, *God's Empowering Presence*, 28–32; Hoehner, *Ephesians*, 167–68; Best, *Ephesians*, 113–14; contra Muddiman, *Ephesians*, 66.

17. Baugh, *Ephesians*, 75.

18. Schrenk, "εὐδοκέω, εὐδοκία," 747.

19. Thielman, *Ephesians*, 44.

Ephesians had no systematic doctrinal conception of the Trinity).[20] There is specific mention of "God our Father" (v. 2), "the God and Father" of Jesus (v. 3); Jesus/Jesus Christ/Christ (vv. 2, 3, 5, [v. 6 the Beloved One] 10, 12); and the Holy Spirit (v. 13).[21] As noted above, the spiritual blessings of v. 4 are likely those that derive from the work of the Holy Spirit.[22] God the Father is the implied subject of vv. 4, 5, 6, 7, 8, 9. Christ or "in Christ" is emphasized in vv. 9, 10, 11, 12, 13.[23]

A number of emphases within God's mission are discernible in vv. 3–14. God as Father is portrayed as the designer and instigator of the plan of salvation since before the foundation of the earth (v. 4). Predestination of "the faithful saints" (v. 1) is to inclusion in God's family to the praise of his glory (vv. 5–6). God's plan for cosmic unity as the goal of the *missio Dei* is the focus in vv. 9–10. Verse 7 mentions "his [Christ's] blood" to describe the means by which redemption and forgiveness are secured.[24] In Eph 2:13 Christ's blood is also specified in relation to salvation. Such usage is consistent with Paul's usage in Rom 3:25; 5:9 and Col 1:20 where "the blood of his cross" makes the connection with the crucifixion explicit. The coincidence in v. 7 of blood, redemption, and forgiveness suggest that the author was portraying Christ's death as a covenant-forming sacrifice (cf. Heb 9:15 where Christ's death as redemption from transgressions explicitly is stated to establish a new covenant).

In v. 13 the Holy Spirit is introduced as a seal applied at the time of first belief. Jacob Adai notes that the proclamation of the gospel by apostles and prophets (Eph 3:5), which leads to belief is a missional activity in which apostles and prophets become mediators of the Holy Spirit.[25] Verse 14 then specifies that the Spirit functions as an assurance that the eschatological redemption of believers as God's people is certain.

The qualities of God's character particularly emphasized in this passage are: his sovereign election of a people who are made holy through redemption, adoption, and sealing with the Spirit; God's gracious initiative in this plan for salvation; and God's love as the motivator of his actions. The author highlights in turn God the Father as sovereign over salvation history, Christ as agent of redemption, and the Spirit as eschatological seal in this rich passage. Mission is thus understood to be an intrinsic element

---

20. E.g. Best, *Ephesians*, 56.
21. Arnold, *Ephesians*, 97; Lincoln, *Ephesians*, 13.
22. Best, *Ephesians*, 113–14.
23. Lincoln, *Ephesians*, 43.
24. Thielman, *Ephesians*, 57–60.
25. Adai, *Heilige Geist*, 277.

of God's dealings with the world from the world's creation until final eschatological consummation.

2.4 Intertextuality—Literary and Thematic Links to the Wider Biblical Narrative

The next step in the missional hermeneutic framework adopted in this study focuses on whether literary and thematic linkages between this text and the wider biblical narrative contribute to our understanding of mission. Ephesians 1:3–14 has strong links to 1 Chr 16, in which Israel's role in relation to the nations is prominent. Therefore, the following intertextual analysis of Eph 1:3–14 seeks to highlight neglected or unobserved linkages with missional significance in the intertexts. We will also consider an allusion to Deut 7 and a number of echoes of other key texts.

2.4.1 1 Chronicles 16

2.4.1.1 FACTORS ESTABLISHING AN ALLUSION TO 1 CHRONICLES 16

The three variations on the refrain "to the praise of his glory" (εἰς ἔπαινον δόξης αὐτοῦ) in Eph 1:6, 12 and 14 share a rare word combination of ἔπαινος, δόξα and αὐτοῦ with 1 Chr 16:27, which reads δόξα καὶ ἔπαινος κατὰ πρόσωπον αὐτοῦ "glory and praise are in his presence."[26] In addition, a number of other distinctive words are found in Eph 1:3–14 and 1 Chr 16:8–36 (LXX), namely εὐδοκία *good pleasure* (Eph 1:5, 9; 1 Chr 16:10), οὐρανός *heaven* with γῆ *earth* in the same verse (Eph 1:10; 1 Chr 16:31), εὐλογέω *praise/bless* (Eph 1:3; 1 Chr 16:36), κληρονομία *inheritance* (Eph 1:14; 1 Chr 16:18), and σωτηρία *salvation* (Eph 1:13; 1 Chr 16:23, 35). The clustering of all these distinctive words is found nowhere else in the OT. This quantity of explicit lexical repetition satisfies Hays's criterion of *volume*.

Turning to the criterion of *thematic coherence*, we see that the literary form of both Eph 1:3–14 and 1 Chr 16:8–36 is a *berakah* (eulogy to God), in which God is praised for his works on behalf of his people. In 1 Chr 16 the audience is exhorted to praise God for his glorious works (1 Chr 16:9, 23–25, 28–29, 36), while Eph 1:3–14 expresses praise to God for his glorious plan of salvation worked out in Christ. Further thematic links emerge from

---

26. My translation. δόξα and ἔπαινος occur together only once in the LXX, at 1 Chr 16:27 (in the NT, aside from Eph 1:6, 12, 14 they also occur at Phil 1:11 and 1 Pet 1:7).

some of the shared vocabulary. For example, the idea that believers are chosen and adopted as God's children (Eph 1:5, 11) conceptually links to 1 Chr 16:13, "O offspring of his servant Israel, children of Jacob, his chosen ones." The theme of the whole created order joining in worshipful submission to Christ as Lord (Eph 1:10) coincides with 1 Chr 16:29–33, especially v. 31, "Let the heavens be glad, and let the earth rejoice, and let them say among the nations, 'The LORD is king!'"

The *historical plausibility* of Eph 1 alluding to 1 Chr 16 is reasonably high. Hays's discussion of this criterion specifically mentions the need for contemporary readings to acknowledge Paul's Jewish heritage. Isaac Kalimi reports that 1 Chr 16:8–36 "is cited completely in the Verses of Praise and Song (*Pesuqei deZimrah*), a part of the daily, Sabbath, and festival morning prayers/service (*Šaḥrit*)."[27] The *Pesuqei deZimrah* is a second-century CE source. Its adoption into Jewish liturgy makes it probable that this passage was familiar to synagogue congregations in the first century CE, and therefore Paul and early Christian communities with mixed Jewish and gentile membership could have recognized and readily drawn on its key themes or vocabulary.[28]

Although there is a strong case for seeing an allusion to 1 Chr 16 in Eph 1 based on *volume, thematic coherence* and *historical plausibility*, the other criteria noted by Hays are harder to satisfy in this case. *Availability*—while Hays judges that Paul "was acquainted with virtually the whole body of texts that were later acknowledged as canonical within Judaism,"[29] UBS5 does not list any allusions or echoes from 1 Chr in the Pauline letters. However, 2 Chr is alluded to in Rom, 1 Cor, Gal, and Col.[30] The weight of evidence for this criterion is modest and inferential only. Consequently, Hays's criterion of *recurrence*, which asks whether the precursor text is alluded to in other Pauline passages, is not present in the case of 1 Chr 16.[31] *History of interpretation*—the only major commentator to see a link to 1 Chr 16 in Eph 1 is Markus Barth.[32] Taken as a whole, although the proposed allusion has not been observed previously except by one commentator, the weight of

---

27. Kalimi, *Retelling of Chronicles*, 179.

28. Cf. Altink, "1 Chronicles 16:8–36," 187–96 argues for adoption of 1 Chr 16 in Rev 14 on the grounds of thematic, linguistic, and structural features.

29. Hays, *Echoes of Scripture*, 30.

30. 2 Chr 13:9 (in Gal 4:8); 2 Chr 15:7 (in 1 Cor 15:58); 2 Chr 19:7 (in Rom 2:11); 2 Chr 19:17 (in Eph 6:9, Col 3:25). Further, Ps 106 (verses of which are incorporated in 1 Chr 16:34–36) is echoed in Rom 1:23 (Ps 106:20) and 1 Cor 10:6, 20 (Ps 106:25–27, 37).

31. Cf. Aune, *Revelation 6–16*, 827 sees an allusion to 1 Chr 16:8–36 in Rev 14:7: "Fear God and give him glory."

32. Barth, *Ephesians 1–3*, 113.

evidence in the areas of verbal and *thematic coherence* is strong enough to warrant further exploration to test whether reading Eph 1:3–14 in the light of 1 Chr 16 is *satisfying* (Hays's final criterion).

2.4.1.2 OT Context

In order to explore the significance of the material in 1 Chr 16 as background to Eph 1:3–14, we will first examine the general structure and content of 1 Chr 16. First Chronicles 15–16 depicts the triumphal entry of the ark into Jerusalem, expanding the brief source in 2 Sam 6:17–19 especially by amalgamating and modifying the text of three Psalms (105, 96, and 106) which celebrate God's sovereignty and saving works on behalf of his people. First Chronicles 16:8–22 derives from Ps 105:1–15; 1 Chr 16:23–33 is a modified quotation from Ps 96:1–13; and 1 Chr 16:34–36 reflects Ps 106:1, 47–48. Howard Wallace summarizes the two primary themes in the composite psalm of 1 Chr 16: "Israel among the nations and the idea of YHWH's sovereignty over the other gods and nations."[33]

A more detailed account of the structure and themes in 1 Chr 16 is provided by Mark Throntveit, on the basis of three previous scholarly analyses.[34] He notes that John Kleinig develops a structure in which Yahweh's praise is offered in increasingly large spheres: Israel's praise (1 Chr 16:9–22), international praise (vv. 23–30), and finally, cosmic praise (vv. 31–33).[35] Eph 1 also expands from a focus on believers in 1:3–9 to a cosmic sphere of God's action in 1:10. Throntveit also refers to a study by James Watts in which several distinct movements of worship and response are evident: an invocation to worship (1 Chr 16:8–13), reminders of God's covenant faithfulness in the past (vv. 14–22), a declaration of Yahweh's superiority over foreign gods (vv. 23–29), nature's reverence now and into the future (vv. 30–33), thanksgiving (v. 34), salvation as the basis for worship (v. 35), and a concluding blessing (v. 36).[36] A number of parallel elements are discernible in Eph 1: God's faithfulness in election (1:4–5), the cosmic scope of Christ's lordship (1:10), God's sovereignty in all time periods (1:4, 10, 14; past, present, and future), "the praise of God's glory," which may be equated with thanksgiving, and salvation as the basis for worship (1:6–7, 13–14). These broad structural and thematic similarities support the proposition that an intentional allusion to 1 Chr 16 is present in Eph 1.

33. Wallace, "What Chronicles Has to Say," 275.
34. Throntveit, "New Key," 159–65.
35. Kleinig, *Lord's Song*, 143–44.
36. Watts, *Psalm and Story*, 156.

The core motivation for praise in 1 Chr 16:25–26 is Yahweh's sovereignty over the gods of the nations, who are mere idols, in contrast to Yahweh who made the heavens. The verses conclude with an affirmation that his presence with his people results in "strength and joy" (v. 27); that is, he will empower them and bring them good fortune in their endeavors.[37] This affirmation is pertinent to the audience of Ephesians. There are indicators throughout the letter that the audience felt threatened or insecure in their faith because of the apparent power of pagan gods. Ephesians 1:19–23 emphasizes that God's power and the enthroned Christ are greater than "all rule and authority and power and dominion" (v. 21). Accordingly, the church as Christ's body shares in that authority over all other powers (vv. 22–23). In Eph 3:16 the author prays for his readers to be "strengthened in your inner being with power through his Spirit." Similarly, God's enabling power for believers is mentioned in 3:20. The theme of power over spiritual forces reaches its climax in the final chapter, with the exhortation to "be strong in the Lord and in the strength of his power" (6:10 and vv. 11–20). Therefore, the refrain in Eph 1:6, 12 and 14 that believers live "to the praise of his glory" encompasses the truth that God is glorious because he is greater than the nations' gods, and that Christ's blood which brings redemption (v. 7) also brings victory over spiritual forces that threaten those who are "in Christ." God's glory is made increasingly manifest in the world and to the heavenly realms when believers boldly declare Christ as God's chosen King (cf. Eph 6:19–20).

Confirmation for this reading of Eph 1:3–14 is also available when we consider that the source text for 1 Chr 16:23–33 is Ps 96:1–13, a royal (enthronement) Psalm, in which Israel and the whole earth acknowledge Yahweh as the true sovereign over the earth. Ephesians 1:3–14 may be seen as a NT parallel, in which Christ is enthroned as the head of the cosmos, and believers assume the place of Israel, expressing their thankful praise to God for his works of redemption. In his discussion of the Psalm incorporated into vv. 24–27 of 1 Chr 16, Theodore Mascarenhas notes that a missionary role for Israel is clearly evident. In Ps 96, Israel is commanded to proclaim the name of Yahweh to the nations and to speak of Yahweh's glory. The nations are invited to respond by acknowledging that Yahweh is the only true God.[38] The word usually adopted for praise (*hll* הלל) in this passage (v. 10, 25, 35, 36) is usually rendered as αἰνέω in the LXX. However, in 1 Chr 16:35 (par. Ps 106:47), the LXX uses καυχάομαι. This verb is particularly linked in

---

37. Cf. Watts, *Psalm and Story*, 158; Throntveit, "New Key," 168 argues that there is a chiasm in 1 Chr 16, with vv. 23–29 as the center.

38. Mascarenhas, *Missionary Function*, 13–14.

the Psalms with exhortations for Israel to declare God's praises before the nations (Ps 117:1–2; 145:4, 10–13).

The implicit audience for the recipients' praise of God's glory in Eph 1:6, 12 and 14 is not God alone, but (in the era before "the fullness of time" is reached) the nations who are yet to submit to Christ's headship. In Ps 96:3–4, 7 (par. 1 Chr 16:24–25, 28) the nations are invited to acknowledge Yahweh's sovereignty and glory and to submit to him before final judgment (Ps 96:10, 13).[39] Psalm 96:3 (par. 1 Chr 16:24), in particular, challenges the psalm's hearers to explicit witness: "Declare his glory among the nations, his marvelous works among all the peoples." In Eph 1:12, the concept of "being" or "living" to the praise of God's glory therefore connotes an active witness to the nations, inviting them to faith in Christ as God's chosen king.

2.4.1.3 Missional Implications of the Intertextual Reading

The Psalm medley in 1 Chr 16 functions to emphasize Yahweh's faithfulness to Israel, control over nature and history, and superiority to foreign gods.[40] Trent Butler notes that the historical setting of 1 Chronicles is a new post-exilic generation, "few in number, wandering between world powers, but armed with God's eternal covenant and his warning to the nations not to harm his designated leaders."[41] Moving to the middle section which incorporates Psalm 96, Butler notes that in the midst of the "political and religious claims of many nations . . . the sovereignty and kingship of Yahweh is praised, while the nations are invited to join in that praise."[42] The allusion to 1 Chr 16 in Eph 1:3–14 may therefore be seen as a new application of that exhortation for a new era. To an audience conscious of their minority status amongst powerful political and religious forces (cf. Eph 6:10–12), the author of Ephesians highlights God's ultimate sovereignty, his control over nature and history, and his intent that ultimately all peoples will be enfolded in the worship of Yahweh as Savior, the one true God, now revealed in the person of Jesus and the work of the Spirit. Thus, the key vocabulary in common between Eph 1 and 1 Chr 16 underscores God as the source of salvation (Eph 1:13; 1 Chr 16:23, 35) and God's sovereignty in providing an inheritance to his chosen people (Eph 1:4, 11; 1 Chr 16:13, 14, 18).

---

39. Mascarenhas, *Missionary Function*, 14.
40. Watts, *Psalm and Story*, 161.
41. Butler, "Forgotten Passage," 144, cf. 1 Chr 16:19–20.
42. Butler, "Forgotten Passage," 144.

In 1 Chr 16:24 (cf. vv. 8–9) Israel is charged specifically with declaring (praising) God's glory among the nations. As Savior and Lord over the created world, he is worthy of praise (1 Chr 16:23–24, 30–33). The refrain in Eph 1:6, 12, 14 that God's people should exist "to the praise of his glory" therefore portrays the chosen, predestined people of God as the paradigmatic worshippers of God—who through their example of praise in word and life would lead all the peoples of the earth (indeed the whole creation) to acknowledge and praise God. Thus, v. 10 looks to the gathering up of "all things in heaven and earth" in Christ. The privileged position of those who become God's "children through Jesus Christ" (v. 5) is not to the exclusion of others, but is meant to be a sign, invitation, and connection to the world that has not yet submitted to the lordship of God in Christ and so been adopted into God's family. This dynamic movement of salvation from the elect "few" to a future "many" is, according to Richard Bauckham and Brownson, a recurrent motif in the Bible's portrayal of mission.[43] Accordingly, at v. 12, where the author identifies with the readers as those "who were the *first to set our hope* (προηλπικότας) on Christ," the meaning of προηλπικότας (although debated) can be understood here as anticipatory, looking forward to a future point when a greater number will also set their hope on Christ.[44] When combined with the reference to the Spirit in v. 13, this passage is reminiscent of the firstfruits language of Rom 8:23; 11:16; 1 Cor 15:20, 23; and 2 Thess 2:13. In commenting on 2 Thess 2:13, Gary Demarest states "it is the idea of the first fruits that best expresses the concept of divine election of some to bring His blessing to all. Those who are chosen are the first fruits. And the first fruits are always seen as the guarantee that a rich and full harvest will follow."[45]

The specific setting of 1 Chr 16, as it concerns the ark of the covenant coming to Jerusalem, also provides an interesting counterpoint to Ephesians. The post-exilic audience of 1 Chr 16 were being encouraged through the narrative of the ark to remember God's power, to give thanks for his sovereignty, and to ask for his deliverance.[46] The ark, as the symbol of national unity and God's presence with his people, coming to Jerusalem highlights the blessings and privileges enjoyed by God's chosen people and the ground of their confidence in his rescue (despite external threats and internal discord).[47] With

---

43. Bauckham, *Bible and Mission*, 27–49, citing e.g. Gen 12:1–3; Ps 67:1–3; Brownson, "Speaking the Truth," 484.

44. Hoehner, *Ephesians*, 231–33.

45. Demarest, *Thessalonians*, 129.

46. Shipp, "Remember His Covenant," 29–39.

47. Cf. Thompson, *1, 2 Chronicles*, 30–32.

the ark installed in the sanctuary in Jerusalem, the glory of God is visible to the nations. Or, in Kleinig's analysis, the proclamation of Yahweh's name in choral praise is a declaration of "his presence with his people."[48] In Eph 1:3–14, the dominant phrase concerning location is not a place, but a person. To be *in Christ* or *in him/in whom* occurs in every verse except for vv. 8 and 14. The locus of God's presence and hence his blessings and power to rescue, which previously was associated with the ark and Jerusalem, is now centered in Christ, and through him, extends to the saints and his faithful ones (Eph 1:1) who become the means by which God's glory is declared and displayed to the cosmos (Eph 1:3, 10, 12, 14). The mission of God's chosen people is therefore unbounded by geographic considerations.

God's mission is truly global. A strong tendency in the OT was to conceive of mission as the movement of the nations towards Jerusalem, which was the focal point of God's presence on earth.[49] However, with the advent of Christ as the focal point of God's presence on earth, Jerusalem loses its particular role, and believers assume the role of taking the light of God's glory/presence out to the world. In Eph 2:12–13 (to be discussed in chapter 5, below), those who were geographically far from Israel and spiritually separated from God and the blessings of his covenant, are said to have been brought near through Christ. The same passage goes on to adopt temple imagery to portray believers as the new locus of God's presence on earth (2:19–22). The use of the phrase *in Christ/in him* in Eph 1:13–14 therefore also has missional weight. This conferred identity is not a personal privilege to be kept secret, but a public demonstration of God's sovereignty and God's plan that his salvation be known and enjoyed throughout the earth by all nations.

2.4.2 *Deuteronomy 7*

In addition to the intertextual links with 1 Chr 16, Eph 1:3–14 has thematic linkages to a significant OT text, Deut 7:6–8. Israel is said to be chosen in love by God to be holy and to be his treasured possession, redeemed from slavery (Deut 7:6–8). The LXX uses ἐξελέξατο in Deut 7:7 for *choose*, the exact form also found in Eph 1:4, 5, and 9. The recipients of Ephesians are chosen to be *holy* (ἅγιος 1:4), and Deut 7:6 addresses the Israelites as "a *holy* people" (λαὸς ἅγιος). In Deut 7:8 the Lord *loves* (ἀγαπάω) Israel, and in Eph 1:4 the recipients are chosen to be *holy* and blameless *in love* (ἐν

---

48. Kleinig, *Lord's Song*, 145–48; cf. Klein and Krüger, *1 Chronicles*, 366, n. 55, "the ark symbolized Yahweh's presence (1 Chr 13:8, 10; 16:1)."

49. Jeremias, *Jesus' Promise*, 57–61.

ἀγάπῃ).⁵⁰ The Israelites were *redeemed* (λυτρόω Deut 7:8) from the house of slavery. The recipients of Ephesians have "*redemption* by his blood" (τὴν ἀπολύτρωσιν διὰ τοῦ αἵματος αὐτοῦ 1:7).⁵¹ The significance of the identity of Israel as God's chosen holy people is reiterated at Deut 14:2; 26:17–19.⁵² The concept of God choosing his people in love to be holy as found in Deut 7:6–8 is echoed in a few other OT texts (Deut 18:2; Ps 46:5 LXX), but nowhere in the NT as clearly as in Eph 1:4–9.

A number of commentators note Deut 7:6–8 as background to Eph 1 without developing the missional implications for the recipients of the letter.⁵³ One exception to this silence is Stephen Fowl, who draws the link from Deut 7 to Gen 12:1–3 and the Abrahamic covenant which promises blessing to the nations.⁵⁴ The choice of vocabulary in Eph 1 echoing Deut 7:6–8 suggests that the author of Ephesians views his audience as standing in continuity with Israel. Therefore, as the renewed people of God, they continue the ministry of Israel to the world as originally conceived by God. The chain of texts which emphasizes Israel's priestly identity in relation to God and the world is long, but certainly includes Exod 19:5–6 and Isa 43:20–21.⁵⁵ Peter Gentry and Stephen Wellum comment that as a kingdom of priests, Israel's function was:

> to make the ways of God known to the nations and also to bring the nations into a right relationship with God. Israel will display to the rest of the world within its covenant community the kind of relationships, first to God and then to one another and to the physical world, that God intended originally for all of humanity.

50. See note 5, above, regarding ἐν ἀγάπῃ as modifying 1:4 "to be holy and blameless."

51. Pauline letters consistently use ἀπολύτρωσις for redemption, while the LXX uses λύτρον (e.g. Exod 21:30; Num 3:12; Rom 3:24; 8:23; 1 Cor 1:30; Col 1:14).

52. Malone, *God's Mediators*, 134–35 argues that Deut 7:6, 14:2, and 26:18–19 intentionally develop Exod 19 vocabulary (see also references at n. 56, below).

53. Deut 7 is acknowledged in passing as background or an allusion by Best, *Ephesians*, 119, 153; Gnilka, *Epheserbrief*, 72; Hoehner, *Ephesians*, 185–86, 227; Lincoln, *Ephesians*, 23, 27; Muddiman, *Ephesians*, 71; Starling, "New Exodus," 142; Thielman, *Ephesians*, 48–50. However, these commentaries don't develop the implications of the allusion for the church's role in the world. Hays's test of *volume* is satisfied by virtue of the multiple shared terms surveyed in the preceding paragraph; *availability* and *recurrence* are demonstrated by the widespread use of Deut 7 in Pauline letters (e.g. Deut 7:6 at Rom 9:4); *history of interpretation* is clear from the works just cited; *thematic coherence* is argued in the following discussion.

54. Fowl, *Ephesians*, 39; Windsor, *Reading Ephesians*, 91–94 also sees Eph 1:3–14 as evoking the priestly function of Israel to the nations.

55. Another text which combines ideas of redemption, deliverance, calling, and inheritance is Col 1:12–14, which according to Beale likely draws on Deut 7:8; Ps 106:10; and Isa 43–44. Beale, "Colossians," 848–49.

In fact, through Abraham's family, God purposes and plans to bring blessing to all the nations of the world.[56]

As will become apparent as we move to consider the following chapters, the recipients of Ephesians are exhorted to walk in holiness according to their privileged covenantal status in contrast to those outside the covenant, *as a witness to the wider world*. In the NT, 1 Pet 2:9, 12 adopts the covenant terminology of Exod 19, applying it to Christians, before explicitly stating the missional consequences of their priestly, elected identity for their actions: "in order that you may proclaim the mighty acts of him who called you out of darkness . . . so that, though they malign you as evildoers, they may see your honorable deeds and glorify God when he comes to judge."[57] This revelatory and proclamatory function for the people of God anticipated in the OT priesthood is also alluded to by Eph 1; God has chosen and blessed believers in order for them to become witnesses to God's glory and grace before the nations.

2.4.3 Broader Links and Echoes

In addition to the metaleptic allusion to 1 Chr 16, and the allusion to Deut 7, there are more subtle echoes in Eph 1:3–14. F. F. Bruce detected an echo of Isa 43:20–21 in the terminology of declaring praise (Eph 1:6, 12, 14).[58] The language of chose (v. 4); adopted (v. 5); inheritance (vv. 11, 14); sealed (v. 13); and possession (v. 14) is covenantal.[59] David Starling sees a number of echoes of the exodus narrations of the OT, including adoption (Eph 1:5; Exod 4:22–23; Hos 11:1); redemption (Eph 1:7; Deut 7:8; 9:26; 13:5; 15:15; 21:8; 24:18); revelation (Eph 1:9; Ezek 20:11; Neh 9:14); and inheritance (1:14; Exod 15:17; Deut 32:9).[60] Chrys Caragounis has noted that μυστήριον is used in Eph 1:9 in a way reminiscent of Dan 2, where God's previously hidden salvific and eschatological will is made known to a gentile King.[61] Ephesians 2:12 explicitly describes gentiles as separated from the covenants of promise before Christ, and so the clustering

---

56. Gentry and Wellum, *Kingdom Through Covenant*, 303, and for the connection between Exod 19 and Deut 7:6–8 see 388; Malone, *God's Mediators*, 181; Blackburn, *God Makes Himself Known*, 90–92.

57. Bader-Saye, *Church and Israel*, 114.

58. Bruce, *Epistles*, 267.

59. Stirling, "Transformation and Growth," 34.

60. Starling, "New Exodus," 142.

61. Caragounis, *Ephesian Mysterion*, 123–26; Lincoln, *Ephesians*, 30; as highlighted by Owens, *As It Was*, 123.

of covenantal terminology in Eph 1 foreshadows the discussion in chapter 2. The nature of the covenants of promise alluded to in Eph 2 is debated, but at least encompass the Abrahamic covenant of blessing to all nations that will come through the promised offspring.[62] The theme of promise is also evident in 1:13 ("the promised Holy Spirit") which may echo Ezek 36:26–27 and 37:14 ("I will put my spirit within you"), precursor texts which come into prominence in Eph 2.[63]

The temporal markers in this text also link it to the broader biblical revelation of how God is at work in the world to redeem humanity and the cosmos. Lincoln notes that:

> The flow of thought spans past, present, and future . . . The blessings of salvation are related to the pretemporal ("before the foundation of the world," v. 4), to the past (what God has done in Christ, vv. 3, 7; and the believer's past appropriation of this, vv. 13, 14), to the present (the current enjoyment of redemption and forgiveness, v. 7), to the future (the believer's inheritance which coincides with God's complete possession of his people, v. 14), and to the overlap between the present and the future (as this is reflected in the summing up of all things in Christ, v. 10, and the experience of the Spirit as a guarantee, v. 14).[64]

This passage builds and extends the biblical narrative of God's mission in the world by envisaging salvation as encompassing the entire cosmos. The scope of God's mission is thus broader than both the particularity of Israel as God's chosen people in the OT and the universality of salvation extended to gentiles in the NT era. In common with Rom 8:22, 23, Phil 2:10, and Col 1:16, 20, Eph 1:10 envisages all things in heaven and on earth as the intended scope of God's redemptive mission in Christ (τὰ πάντα ἐν τῷ Χριστῷ, τὰ ἐπὶ τοῖς οὐρανοῖς καὶ τὰ ἐπὶ τῆς γῆς ἐν αὐτῷ).[65]

The strong links in Eph 1:3–14 to 1 Chr 16 and Deut 7 call to mind God's purpose that he is to be glorified among the nations through the praises and holy lives of his people. The believers addressed in this passage stand firmly within the trajectory of God's covenant dealings with Israel, who were called and redeemed in order to worship God not only

---

62. Thielman, *Ephesians*, 156 and cf. references in fn.16; see also the extensive discussion of covenantal themes in Eph 2 in Stirling, "Transformation and Growth," 109–21.

63. Starling, "New Exodus," 143. Other OT occurrences include Isa 32:15; 44:3; Ezek 39:29; Joel 2:28–29; see also Robinson, *Ephesians*, 33, who notes the links from Eph 1:10 to Gen 12:3 and Ezek 36:22–23.

64. Lincoln, *Ephesians*, 43.

65. Cf. Meyer, *Kirche und Mission*, 51–52.

for their own benefit, but for the sake of renewing creation and as a witness to all nations. The nature of this witness is not active proselytism. Indeed, the notion of a missionary role for Israel within the OT does not necessitate the conclusion that Israel understood or acted on that calling.[66] We are making a modest claim that the OT precursor texts discussed above contain indicators of a missional role for God's people that the author of Ephesians drew upon to undergird his elucidation of God's actions and purposes in salvation history.

2.5 Portrayal of Humanity and the World in Relation to God's Mission

Those people who are predestined to be chosen as part of God's people are the object of God's plans for redemption (he predestined us, v. 5; grace poured out on us, v. 8; we have received, v. 11; you were sealed, v. 13). In v. 10, there is a universalistic note to the idea that all things in heaven and on earth will ultimately be summed up (gathered up) in Christ, and as such no part of humanity is excluded from God's concern. There is no explicit statement about those who do not believe in Christ and their status in God's salvation plans.

This passage is significant because it connects the salvation of believers in the first century CE with the plan of God formed before the foundation of the world. Predestination is thus seen as a positive expression of God's commitment to the ultimate establishment of holiness and fellowship throughout the cosmos. God's deliberate actions in mission extend across all time "according to the plan of the one who works out everything in agreement with the purpose of his will" (v. 11).

2.6 Evidence of a Missional Context in the Problems, Crises, or Issues Addressed

Establishing the problems or issues addressed by a NT letter in the absence of explicit statements requires mirror-reading. In the case of the undisputed Pauline letters, this poses certain challenges, but even more so in a potentially pseudepigraphal letter.[67] Any historical background inferred

---

66. See the following works for introductions to the extensive literature and debate on Jewish missionary self-understanding and activity: Dickson, *Mission-Commitment*; Bird, *Crossing Over*; Goodman, *Mission and Conversion*; Carleton Paget, "Jewish Proselytism," 65–103; McKnight, *Light Among the Gentiles*.

67. Gupta, "Mirror-Reading," 361–81; Lincicum, "Mirror-Reading," 171–93.

from the mirror-reading is necessarily a tentative hypothesis, since it may instead be a rhetorical fiction or exaggeration. Acknowledging this risk, we will nevertheless treat the text of Ephesians as a realistic and coherent communication by which the author sought to address problems, crises, or issues facing his original audience. In chapter 13, below, we will assess whether the data from the letter aligns with a historical setting that can be established from other sources.

It may be inferred from the emphasis on God's loving and gracious choice of the recipients that they were feeling alienated or insignificant in their religious and perhaps social identity. The mention of heavenly places (v. 3) and all things in heaven (v. 10) perhaps indicates that the letter's recipients were concerned or particularly interested in the spiritual realm, because of their religious milieu. Arising from this emphasis, a number of scholars have speculated that Gnosticism constitutes the background to the letter,[68] while others have drawn on the Qumran literature to elucidate the possible context for the original audience.[69] In chapter 13, below, we will evaluate whether these proposals are convincing in the light of the evidence of the whole letter. With regard to Eph 1, a less speculative approach is found in Lincoln who suggests that the force of this passage is to counteract feelings of insecurity brought about by the dominant religions of the age.

> To be in Christ, therefore, is to be part of a program which is as broad as the universe, a movement which is rolling on toward a renewed cosmos where all is in harmony. Counteracting insecurity and insignificance in the face of the claims of syncretistic mystery religions or cosmic forces, the effect of this part of the blessing is to produce confidence in the God whose gracious decision embraces everything in heaven and on earth, and to inspire those who echo it to play their part in God's administration of the fullness of the times in Christ.[70]

Mystery religions were found throughout the Greco-Roman world, and so Lincoln's mention of them is not unreasonable, and a concern about cosmic forces is defensible given Ephesians' explicit statements about contending with spiritual powers in 2:2; 3:10, and 6:12. The note of reassurance in 1:13–14 about the effectiveness of God's work of salvation adds weight to the possibility that the recipients were feeling vulnerable or insecure in their faith. They were perhaps tempted to look to other religions as a means of

---

68. See Pokorný, *Brief*, 22, n. 11 for references to the relevant works. Schlier, *Brief*, 19–20.

69. Kuhn, "Light of Qumran," 115–31.

70. Lincoln, *Ephesians*, 44.

accessing God's blessings and power.[71] The passage emphasizes the future hope of being part of God's work in the world, despite the final realization of God's restoration being yet future (v. 14).

The opening pericope of Ephesians therefore functions to sensitize its audience to their privileged position in God's plans, and to counteract any thoughts that alternative religions or spiritual practices could grant them greater power, protection, or prospects.

2.7 The Portrayal of Paul and His Involvement in Mission

The opening greeting of Ephesians not only introduces Paul as the author (or as the source of claimed authority), but also particularly emphasizes his status as an apostle. In v. 1, Paul's calling to apostleship is "by God's will" (διὰ θελήματος θεοῦ). Vocabulary stressing God's *will* (θέλημα) as the driver of salvation history recurs in vv. 5, 9, 11. By this repetition of God's will, the author positions Paul as playing a central part in God's mission. Later, in 3:1–13, Paul's special commissioning as an apostle (3:5) to proclaim to the gentiles the "riches of Christ" is elaborated. As in Rom 1:1–5, the greeting of Eph 1:1 functions to emphasize apostleship, whereby a select group of delegates and eyewitnesses to the risen Christ announce and extend the universal reach of God's salvation plan (his mission), as developed in Eph 1:3–14.[72] Apostles are then mentioned at 2:20 where they are foundational in the household of God, at 3:5–6 where they are the first recipients of the mystery that is gentile incorporation into God's people, and in 4:11, where they play a role in building up the body of Christ. Paul's status as an apostle at 1:1 therefore introduces the importance of apostolic ministry as a pioneering vehicle of God's mission in the world.

2.8 Conclusion

The missional hermeneutics lens adopted in this reading of Eph 1:1–14 builds on existing scholarly awareness of the rich portrait of salvation history painted in the passage. It adds a sharper focus on 1:10, 22–23 as a statement indicating the end point of the *missio Dei*: cosmic unification

71. Brannon, *Heavenlies in Ephesians*, 113, "The fact that Paul stresses that God has granted every spiritual blessing ἐν τοῖς ἐπουρανίοις to those in Christ also implies that believers need not look elsewhere or outside Christ for God's rich spiritual blessing."

72. Windsor, *Reading Ephesians*, 79; Muddiman, *Ephesians*, 58; Talbert, *Ephesians and Colossians*, 32.

under the universally acknowledged lordship of Christ. The missional reading also highlights the important role of Paul the apostle as a pioneering agent of God's mission. Most significantly, the intertextual analysis has argued for 1 Chr 16 to be understood as a metaleptic precursor text, with the result that the call for believers to live to the praise of God's glory should be interpreted to incorporate witness to the nations. The intertextual analysis also underscored the priestly function of God's people with respect to the nations in the light of allusions to Deut 7.

3

Ephesians 1:15–23

3.1 Introduction

UNUSUALLY FOR A PAULINE letter, where there is normally an introductory thanksgiving or blessing, Ephesians contains both. In the light of the great blessings God has provided for the recipients and the insights the *berakah* contains into the *missio Dei*, the author now adopts a more pastoral tone, asking God to equip them for their missional life in the world by giving his readers knowledge of the hope, glory, and power that they enjoy as God's people. There is a personalization of God's work, intended to inform and ready believers for participation in God's mission as the body of Christ in the world. We will work through the missional hermeneutics questions that constitute our theoretical framework (*missio Dei*, characterization of God, intertextuality, humanity and the world, missional context, and mission of God's people), omitting question seven, concerning Paul's role in mission, since the portrayal of Paul here is purely as thankful intercessor for the church.

3.2 Portrayal of God's Intentions, Actions, and Purposes (the *missio Dei*)

Ephesians 1:15–23 builds up to a significant statement of God's intentions for the world in vv. 22–23. The goal towards which God is working is the subjection of all things to Christ (v. 22). Christ is made (given as) head of all things "for the church" (τῇ ἐκκλησίᾳ), that is, for the benefit of the church. This passage, with its strong christological thrust, underlines both the centrality of

Christ (and his resurrection) to God's purposes for the world and the significance of Christ's resurrection as a demonstration of God's power over all things (vv. 19-21). Prior to this climactic material, we encounter a thanksgiving in vv. 15-16, and an intercessory prayer report in vv. 17-19.[1]

The prayer report contains a number of ideas about God's intentions, actions, and purposes for believers. Verse 17 identifies God as the giver of wisdom and revelation (v. 17). Taken with vv. 18-19, where the goal of the wisdom is the strengthening of the recipients to grasp the hope and power they already possess, there is an implicit refutation of other sources of wisdom or revelation (cf. 1 Cor 3:18-20).

In v. 18, the use of calling terminology (κλῆσις) recalls the election language of 1:4, 5, and 11, and reminds the readers that God has acted concretely in history to bring people into relationship with himself.[2] Furthermore, God's action in calling believers is future oriented. His intention is for them to have hope and to realize the privilege of being part of God's inheritance (as God's people, they feature in God's eternal plans), v. 18.[3]

Verses 19-20 affirm that God is powerfully active in the world for the benefit of believers (v. 19 εἰς ἡμᾶς τοὺς πιστεύοντας). Three synonyms for power are used: δύναμις, κράτος, and ἰσχύς (power, might, strength), to underscore the unique empowerment undergirding believers. The specific actions in which that power was manifest are all concerned with Christ: his raising (ἐγείρας) from death, his seating (καθίσας) at God's right hand, the subjection (ὑπέταξεν) of all things under him, and his establishment (being given, ἔδωκεν) as head over all things for the church (vv. 20-22).[4] Thus God's power is most clearly evident in the key steps demonstrating God's victory over death and the establishment of his universal reign. The power terminology looks forward to Eph 2, esp. vv. 4-6, where the author speaks of God's action raising and delivering believers from sin and death.[5]

Verses 22-23 will be considered in more detail at §§3.4 and 3.7, below. At this point we note that the subjection of all things to Christ means that the scope of God's mission (consistently with 1:10) is all creation: humanity, all living beings (including spiritual entities) and the physical cosmos. God is acting in history in order to fill the cosmos with Christ's reigning presence (he is the head, κεφαλή) over all things (ὑπὲρ πάντα) through his body, the church (τῇ ἐκκλησίᾳ). The dative is best understood as a dative of advantage

---

1. Lincoln, *Ephesians*, 47.
2. Schlier, *Brief*, 82-84, cited in Lincoln, *Ephesians*, 59.
3. Lincoln, *Ephesians*, 60.
4. Arnold, *Ephesians*, 110.
5. Best, *Ephesians*, 170.

("for [the benefit of] the church" NRSV, NIV, CSB), rather than an indirect object (e.g. NASB), since the passage from v. 7 has been accumulating the benefits for believers of God's actions in Christ (esp. vv. 7, 10, 13–14, 18–19).[6] The description of the church in v. 23 as "the fullness of him who fills all in all" also points to the goal of God's mission: the complete revelation of God's glory throughout the world, as the church grows in its knowledge and experience of God's salvation and renewed life (cf. Eph 3:19; 4:13).[7]

In summary, this passage is strongly christological, with the resurrection featuring both as a central moment in salvation history and as a source of power for believers. Christ's present universal reign defines the nature of the church's involvement in God's mission; believers are filling that which is already claimed by Christ, and which will inevitably acknowledge Christ.

3.3 Portrayal of God's Person and Character

The dominant descriptors of God in this passage are glory and power: πατὴρ τῆς δόξης, "the father of glory" (v. 17), ὁ πλοῦτος τῆς δόξης τῆς κληρονομίας αὐτοῦ, "the riches of his glorious inheritance" (v. 18), ὑπερβάλλον μέγεθος τῆς δυνάμεως αὐτοῦ, "the immeasurable greatness of his power" (v. 19), τοῦ κράτους τῆς ἰσχύος αὐτοῦ, "his mighty strength" (v. 19), and ὑπεράνω πάσης ἀρχῆς καὶ ἐξουσίας καὶ δυνάμεως καὶ κυριότητος, [Christ enthroned] "above every rule, authority, power and dominion" (v. 21). The emphasis on glory carries over the thematic refrain of vv. 6, 12, 14, where believers live to the praise of God's glory. In this passage, God is glorious by virtue of his works of self-revelation and salvation. God's glory is therefore focused on believers knowing and enjoying the fruits of salvation—incorporation into God's family (his inheritance) and access to God's unparalleled power. The presence of power language introduces a significant theme that will recur throughout the letter (2:2; 3:10, 15; 4:8, 27; 6:11, 12, 16), and is crucial to establishing the circumstances of the original audience (discussed in chapters 12 and 13, below).

The Trinitarian tone of the passage is noted by many commentators.[8] In v. 17, God, the Father of glory, is differentiated from the Lord Jesus Christ, and it is God the Father who is the source of wisdom and revelation for

---

6. Barth, *Ephesians 1–3*, 198–99; Muddiman, *Ephesians*, 91–92; contra Hoehner, *Ephesians*, 289.

7. Barth, *Ephesians 1–3*, 209; πληρουμένου is understood as middle voice, with active meaning, as per the majority of translations (e.g. NASB, NRSV, NIV, ESV), Graham, *Exegetical Summary*, 100; cf. Arnold, *Ephesians*, 116–18.

8. Best, *Ephesians*, 163; Schlier, *Brief*, 77–79; Hoehner, *Ephesians*, 256–58.

personal knowledge of him. Wisdom is more than ethical understanding, but in the light of 3:8–10 is focused on the *mystery* now revealed, God's plan of salvation for all, including gentiles. Thus, wisdom is the understanding of how God's saving activity in Christ brings salvation and all the blessings enumerated in vv. 3–14 to believers.[9]

The reference to the *spirit* (πνεῦμα) of wisdom and revelation raises the question of whether this is a reference to the human spirit or to God's Spirit. A majority of interpreters take it as a reference to the Spirit of God, since the closely related passage in 1 Cor 2:6–16 is explicit that the Spirit of God reveals wisdom, and both passages derive from Isa 11:2, where the Spirit of the Lord is the source of wisdom and related qualities.[10] This verse therefore conveys the idea that God's Spirit, as a gift of God the Father of glory, is particularly active in revealing the trajectory of salvation history and enabling believers (individually and collectively) to comprehend their current status and future hope.[11]

In summary, we observe: (a) God as Father of glory sovereignly directing the events of salvation history (v. 18, 20–22); (b) God's Spirit bringing awareness of and personal appreciation of the works of salvation for the believer (v. 17); (c) Christ reigning as the authoritative leader of the created cosmos (consisting of both material and spiritual powers vv. 20–23); and (d) Christ present in the cosmos through his body, the church, which is progressively extending the sphere of Christ's reign throughout the cosmos.

3.4 Intertextuality—Literary and Thematic Links to the Wider Biblical Narrative

This thanksgiving and prayer report follows a pattern evident in a number of other Pauline letters, especially Philemon and Colossians.[12] Thanks for the faith of the recipients and love towards the saints (v. 15) is a similar phrase to that seen in Gal 5:6, Col 1:4, 1 Thess 1:3, 2 Thess 1:3, and Phlm 5. The transformation of lives due to the gospel is therefore both an outcome of mission and a foundation for the ongoing missional life of Christian communities (e.g. 1 Thess 1:3–10).

---

9. Lincoln, *Ephesians*, 56–57.

10. Arnold, *Ephesians*, 104; Best, *Ephesians*, 162–63; Lincoln, *Ephesians*, 56–57; Schlier, *Brief*, 78; Schnackenburg, *Ephesians*, 74; Fee, *God's Empowering Presence*, 674–76 details grammatical, contextual, and intertextual reasons for preferring "Spirit" (ESV, CSB, NIV) to "spirit" (NRSV, NASB).

11. Cf. Arnold, *Ephesians*, 105.

12. Lincoln, *Ephesians*, 49.

The wording of v. 17, πνεῦμα σοφίας καὶ ἀποκαλύψεως, "a spirit of wisdom and revelation," is not paralleled exactly elsewhere in the Bible, although Wis 7:7 is closest: "Therefore I prayed, and understanding was given me; I called on God, and the spirit of wisdom came to me." A number of commentators note the significant messianic text, Isa 11:2 (LXX) contains the phrase πνεῦμα σοφίας καὶ συνέσεως, πνεῦμα βουλῆς καὶ ἰσχύος, πνεῦμα γνώσεως καὶ εὐσεβείας, "a spirit of wisdom and intelligence, a spirit of counsel and strength, a spirit of knowledge and piety" (LES). Gordon Fee and Arnold see Eph 1:17 as dependent on Isa 11:2, in common with Col 1:9 and 1 Cor 2:6–16, while other commentators are more circumspect in their assessment.[13] There are other verbal connections between Eph 1:15–23 and Isa 11:2–10: strength (ἰσχύς), Eph 1:19 and Isa 11:2; fullness/fill (πλήρωμα/πληρόω), Eph 1:23, and filling (ἐμπίπλημι), Isa 11:9; knowledge (ἐπίγνωσις), Eph 1:17, and know (γιγνώσκω), Isa 11:9; hope (ἐλπίς), Eph 1:18, and to hope (ἐλπίζω), Isa 11:10. On the basis of these parallels, Hays's criterion of *volume* is tentatively satisfied. *Availability* and *recurrence* of this Isaiah text to a Pauline audience is readily demonstrated from Rom 15:12 where Paul explicitly cites Isa 11:1, 10 (not to mention the clear dependence of Eph 6:11 on Isa 11:4–5, discussed in §11.4.2, below). *Thematic coherence* is demonstrated because the messianic prophecy of Isa 11:1–10 together with Eph 1:15–23 share an eschatological orientation to the conditions that prevail in the new age, specifically how Spirit-mediated knowledge will lead to the establishment of God's reign on earth. Regarding the verse's *history of interpretation*, Tertullian linked Eph 1:17 with Isa 11:2.[14] The weight of these considerations supports seeing Isa 11:2 as background for Eph 1:17.

In the light of the intertextual link to Isa 11, we may infer that the author wanted his recipients to recognize that the special capabilities that the messiah receives through God's Spirit are now also available to believers. This means that all believers are equipped by the Spirit in order to continue the mission of the messiah, which in Isa 11 results in the whole land being filled with the knowledge of God and the nations putting their hope in the Lord, and in Eph 1:20–23 sees all powers brought under Christ's dominion, and the church filling all things.

The allusion to two Psalms (Ps 110:1, v. 20 and Ps 8:6, v. 22) is used in the early Christian community to support their understanding of Jesus as the messiah reinforces the above interpretation of v. 17.[15] The reference to

---

13. Fee, *God's Empowering Presence*, 675; see also Arnold, *Ephesians*, 104; cf. Best, *Ephesians*, 163 who sees it as an indirect reference.

14. Tertullian, *Marc.* 5.17

15. Best notes the similarity of language and likely same source tradition underlying 1 Cor 15:24–27; 1 Pet 3:22, and Phil 2:5–11, but rejects direct dependence on any of

raising Christ from the dead (v. 20) is close in wording to Acts 3:15; 4:10; 13:30; 26:8; Rom 4:24; 6:4, 9; 8:11; 10:9; Col 2:12; and 1 Pet 1:21. Christ seated at God's right hand is particularly prominent in Acts 2:34–35; Heb 8:1; 10:12; 12:2, verses which clearly depend on Ps 110:1, a favorite christological text for the early church.[16] Psalm 110 contains stark language of military victory over foes for God's chosen agent of judgment. This tone is appropriate considering the emphasis in 1:20–22 on the resurrection as the demonstration of God's victory over death (the ultimate foe of humanity, cf. Eph 2:1, 4; 1 Cor 15:26).

The usage of power, strength, and might language in v. 19 recalls the descriptors used of God in association with the exodus (e.g. Exod 15:4, 6, 13; 32:11; Deut 4:37; 9:29). Cozart has argued that the exodus motif is a major theme in Ephesians, coming to climactic prominence in Eph 6:10–20 via allusions to Isaiah's Divine Warrior (discussed in chapter 11, below).[17] In Eph 1, God's power to redeem is the basis for personal thanksgiving, but leads naturally to a broader confidence that God's power (after Christ's resurrection) is now available continually (v. 21 "in this age and the age to come") to extend God's triumph over "the powers."[18]

The subjection of all things in creation to Christ (v. 22), is drawn from Psalm 8:6.

Καὶ πάντα ὑπέταξεν ὑπὸ τοὺς πόδας αὐτοῦ. (Eph 1:22)

πάντα ὑπέταξας ὑποκάτω τῶν ποδῶν αὐτοῦ. (Ps 8:7 LXX)

Lincoln notes that "It is likely that Eph 1:20, 22 are dependent on 1 Cor 15, which in turn draws on a common exegetical tradition in the early church whereby Ps 8:6 had become linked to Ps 110:1 in drawing out the implications of Christ's resurrection and exaltation (cf. Heb 1:3, 13; 2:5–8; 1 Pet 3:22)."[19] The common tradition utilizing this text was also noted by C. E. Hill in his earlier study of Ps 110.[20] Noting that Ps 8 alludes to Gen 1:26–28, Lincoln concludes that the allusion portrays Christ as the last Adam, whose dominion over the cosmos restores what was lost by the first Adam in the fall.[21] Isaiah 11:1–10, which we have argued above is echoed

---

these texts, Best, *Ephesians*, 181.

16. Moritz, *Profound Mystery*, 9.
17. Cozart, *Present Triumph*, 231–51.
18. Longman and Reid, *God Is a Warrior*, 169.
19. Lincoln, *Ephesians*, 66.
20. Hill, "Paul's Understanding," 313; Hay, *Glory*, 109–10.
21. Lincoln, "Use of the OT," 41; cf. Arnold, *Ephesians*, 115; Owens, *As It Was*, 134, noting 1QS 11:20–22 also interprets Ps 8 in the light of Gen 1.

in this text, also evokes new creation imagery (livestock and wild animals feeding together), and this supports Lincoln's conclusion that Eph 1 is here portraying the new creation.

In the light of the intertextual links, we may conclude that Eph 1:22 therefore enfolds the sweep of biblical history from creation and fall to restoration and new dominion. Believers are encouraged and empowered to live in a hostile world because they know that the Lord of the cosmos has come, has risen, has been exalted, and is reigning at God's right hand, far above all other powers. As with the similar christological hymns found in Phil 2:6–11 and Col 1:15–20, the recitation of Christ's path to exaltation undergirds the practical exhortation in adjacent verses to live in a particular manner that reflects Christ's humility and victory as a witness to the world (Phil 2:12–16; Col 1:9–14).

Another significant OT text that may be echoed in Eph 1 is Hab 2:14, "the earth will be filled with the knowledge of the glory of the LORD, as the waters cover the sea." This phrasing which has the key ideas of *earth*, *fill*, and *glory* is also present in Isa 6:3 "the whole *earth* is *full* of his *glory*" and Isa 11:9 (discussed above). Ephesians 1:15–23 opens with a prayer for the recipients to have knowledge of God's glory (vv. 17–18) and closes with the declaration that the body of Christ (blessed with this knowledge of God's glory) is the fullness of God and will fill all things (vv. 22–23). Although there is not a sufficient basis in Hays's tests to suggest an echo here, the Habakkuk verse is remarkably pertinent to both chapters 1 and 2 of Ephesians. In Eph 2, the author's use of temple imagery to portray God's work in the world continues the ideas of 1:22–23, and the pattern of God's presence flowing to all parts of the world. These ideas operate at the broader level of themes that we will continue to point out as they recur in the rest of Ephesians.

This text therefore contributes to the broader biblical narrative of God's mission in the world by reiterating the centrality of Christ's resurrection and heavenly session in God's salvation plan. As believers grasp the significance of these acts of salvation, they are thereby encouraged and empowered to be part of Christ's continuing mission in the world, as his lordship expands and progressively encompasses more of the cosmos, through his body, the church.

3.5 Portrayal of Humanity and the World in Relation to God's Mission

This passage explicitly addresses "us who believe" (ἡμᾶς τοὺς πιστεύοντας, v. 18, equivalent to *saints* τοὺς ἁγίους, vv. 15, 18). Believers receive benefits of hope, knowledge, an inheritance, and power from God that are by implication unavailable to nonbelievers, vv. 18–19. All humans, as part of the world that is the sphere of God's redeeming work, are the potential beneficiaries of God's mission, who is working to bring about a reordered cosmos with all powers and authorities (which are as yet undefined) brought under Christ's headship (vv. 20–22).[22]

3.6 Evidence of a Missional Context in the Problems, Crises or Issues Addressed

The passage envisages a situation in which the recipients need reassurance that God's power is greater than other powers that affect the life of the recipients ("rule and authority and power and dominion, and above every name that is named," v. 21). In the light of subsequent passages in Ephesians, these powers are understood to control the lives of non-Christians (2:2) and must be resisted with spiritual armor (6:10–20). The missional context is therefore one in which loyalties and allegiances to spiritual powers are a contested space, and the author is writing (in part) to call his audience to unwavering commitment to the God he represents as apostle (1:1–2). The author's choice of OT sources that anticipate the reestablishment of divine authority on earth specifically address this context. Moritz states:

> Exaltation and subjection language taken from the Psalms is combined with power language which shows God's superiority over pagan deities and principalities. The implication is that the God of the Hebrew Scriptures is well in control over the powers whose grip on the inhabitants of Asia Minor leads to *widespread existential fear*.[23]

To this we might add that an echo from Isa 11:2, in which the Spirit's gifts of wisdom and revelation are conferred on the messiah, intimates that God's people are also endowed by the Spirit to understand God's immense power now at work in them.

A wide variety of possible meanings for "all rule and authority and power and dominion" (ἀρχῆς καὶ ἐξουσίας καὶ δυνάμεως καὶ κυριότητος, 1:21) have been proposed in the history of scholarship.[24] We note for now that

---

22. Meyer, *Kirche und Mission*, 62–63.
23. Moritz, *Profound Mystery*, 19; cf. Thielman, *Ephesians*, 106.
24. Arnold, *Powers of Darkness*; Asumang, "Powers of Darkness," 1–19; Berkhof, *Christ and the Powers*; Carr, *Angels and Principalities*; Walter Wink, *Naming the Powers*.

as well as personal spiritual beings opposed to God's purposes and people (Eph 6:12; cf. Rom 8:38), "the powers" may also connote:

> religious structures (especially the religious undergirdings of the stable societies), intellectual structures (e.g. -ologies and -isms), moral structures (codes and customs) and political structures (the tyrant, the market, the school, the courts, race and nation).[25]

Arnold gives an example of how the vocabulary employed in Ephesians could be recasting phrases employed in folk belief to assert God's victory over other spiritual forces.

> The term translated "incredible" (ὑπερβάλλον) is an adjectival participle that never appears in the Greek OT, but is used in a number of inscriptions from Ephesus and in the magical papyri. One of these magical texts invokes a god with the following invocation: "Greatest god, who exceeds all power (ὑπερβάλλει τὴν πᾶσαν δύναμιν), I call on you . . ." People in Western Asia Minor and in a context of folk belief were familiar with rival claims of local deities to possessing extraordinary power. Paul endeavors to assure his readers that the one true God is unexcelled in power.[26]

Arnold may have somewhat overstated the rarity or specificity of this particular term. While the participle form of ὑπερβάλλω does not occur in the LXX, verb forms occur six times, including with the meaning of *great* or *surpassing*.[27] The adjectival participle form (ὑπερβάλλον) is found ten times in Philo, at times denoting the greatness of God.[28] Therefore, it is a term not restricted to Ephesus or the Artemis cult. We will evaluate the plausibility of taking the specific religious context of Ephesus as the background to Ephesians in chapter 12, below.

Furthermore, the prayer report of v. 17, with its use of (ἐπίγνωσις) for knowledge of God, may well be adopting terminology from the religious milieu as a means of contextualizing the Christian message. Lincoln says:

> These are terms which would have been congenial to Hellenistic syncretistic religion with its concern for the communication of esoteric knowledge. It could well be that their use in these letters suggests a contrast with this emphasis in the syncretistic

---

25. Nissen, *New Testament and Mission*, 139; Wink, *Naming the Powers*, 39.
26. Arnold, *Ephesians*, 109.
27. E.g. Sir 25:11; 2 Macc 4:13; 3 Macc 2:23.
28. E.g. Philo, *Deus* §116; *Her.* §24. The form ὑπερβάλλον also occurs over nine hundred times in secular Greek, though rarely with reference to spiritual powers.

philosophy, indicating that this is a prayer for the genuine article, real knowledge of God.[29]

Knowledge vocabulary is not more frequent in Ephesians than in 1 Corinthians, for example, where words from the root γινωσκω occur forty-one times compared to fourteen occurrences in Ephesians. While it may be broadly appropriate to connect knowledge terminology in NT letters with the Hellenistic religious milieu of the first century, a more focused study of Ephesians would be needed before concluding that it was particularly adapted to a local cultural and religious context. This will be addressed in chapter 13, below.

3.7 Portrayal of the Character and Mission of God's People in the World

As noted above (§3.2), God's people are privileged because they constitute part of God's inheritance (v. 18). They are also empowered with the same death-conquering power at work in the resurrection of Christ (vv. 19–20). Their receipt of divine wisdom and revelation fosters relational closeness to God (v. 17). The most significant element of the character and mission of God's people is stated in vv. 22–23, the church is Christ's body, which has a role to play in manifesting to the world the fullness of life and salvation that it enjoys in Christ.

Meyer sees these verses as the key to understanding the church's mission according to Ephesians. The concept of all things being given to Christ for the church indicates to her that the church is called to participate in God's goal of proclaiming salvation to the whole cosmos.[30]

> Taking up again the idea of Eph 1:22b–23a, it should now be supplemented in the following way: God has enabled the church to serve the world by giving it Christ as Lord to the gentiles. The exalted Christ brings the fullness of God's power of grace (cf. 1:19–20) into the church as his body, so that he enables and guarantees its ministry. In other words, insofar as Christ makes use of charisms and services (cf. 4:7–16) in the church in his ministry towards the world, the church is his *pleroma*.
>
> The fact that the church is the *pleroma* of Christ thus means a specific belonging of the church to Christ, namely belonging in the form of ministry, in such a way that Christ Himself performs

---

29. Lincoln, *Ephesians*, 58; cf. Barth, *Ephesians 1–3*, 149.
30. Meyer, *Kirche und Mission*, 33; cf. Adai, *Heilige Geist*, 341.

the "ministry" (πληρουμένου) while the church is the means of his ministry. Considering that in 1:23b πλήρωμα is a condensed concept of the relationship between God-Christ-church-all, it is appropriate to understand it (in so far as there is an *ecclesiological* statement here) as the expression by the author of Ephesians to describe the charismatic-missionary enabling and the driving force of the body of Christ towards the world.[31]

Meyer's work was undertaken to test whether Rahner's conception of universal salvation was compatible with Ephesians. Her interpretation of Eph 1:22–23 seems to be shaped by an inclination to find scriptural warrants for universal salvation. For example, she conceives of the church as follows: "As the body of Christ, the church is the *pleroma* (fullness) of Christ who embraces all of humanity and wants to include it in his sphere of salvation."[32] So, although at the least Eph 1:23 indicates there is significance for the church in relation to the world by virtue of its identity as the body of Christ, Meyer may have incorporated extrabiblical ideas of universal salvation into her interpretation of the verse. A more measured interpretive conclusion is voiced by Thomas Winger, who says:

> The church and the world have been compared to concentric circles in which the church, the inner circle, is ever widening and laying claim to the rest of creation. Because Christ is the Head of all things, the church may view the world around it as a gift, not an enemy.[33]

This image of circles is a helpful way of not conflating the church and the world (as Meyer may be in danger of doing), while capturing the implication of the fullness vocabulary which is that the church as the body of Christ is progressively expanding its sphere of impact.[34] Gorman also uses the analogy of concentric circles, specifying the spheres in which the church's peacemaking takes place: "within the church itself, and extending to the home, the community, the nation, and the world."[35] As Barth argues, the *body of Christ* metaphor has a functional sense: "the church is the *manifestation of Christ to the world*."[36] The world remains separate from the church; the world is the beneficiary and field in which the church

---

31. Meyer, *Kirche und Mission*, 45, my translation.
32. Meyer, *Kirche und Mission*, 80, my translation.
33. Winger, *Ephesians*, 274.
34. Cf. Schnackenburg, *Ephesians*, 308.
35. Gorman, *Becoming the Gospel*, 208.
36. Barth, *Ephesians 1–3*, 198 italics in original.

acts in mission as a servant bringing "the life, growth and salvation" of God to all creation.[37] This understanding of mission avoids Hoekendijk's erroneous interpretation of *missio Dei*, popular in the 1960s and 1970s, that overemphasized mission as humanization and liberation and, in its eagerness to affirm God's work in the world apart from the church, often disparaged the church's role in mission.[38]

3.8 Conclusion

Ephesians 1:15–23 extends the lengthy opening *berakah*, transitioning into thanksgiving and prayer. The missional reading of this passage has highlighted the centrality of Christ's resurrection and heavenly session in God's salvation plan, since these are the means by which believers are empowered for mission. Further, in agreement with Meyer, we have seen that 1:22–23 is vital for understanding the role of the church in mission, but Barth's understanding of body and fullness are preferable to Meyer's approach. The fullness of Christ in the world is not universal salvation, but the church manifests Christ to the world, acting as a servant bringing revelation and a lived expression of the life and salvation that will ultimately fill the cosmos when all opposing powers are subjected to Christ.

---

37. Barth, *Ephesians 1–3*, 209.
38. Ott, *Mission of the Church*, xv.

4

Ephesians 2:1–10

4.1 Introduction

FLOWING FROM THE EXERTION of God's power to raise Christ from the dead in Eph 1:20, Eph 2:1–10 now focuses on how God acts to bring life to the recipients who were dead in trespasses (2:1, 5). God acts decisively to overcome the dire state of the recipients, giving them life and an exalted spiritual position (2:5–6). The passage also speaks of God gifting the recipients with salvation by grace (v. 8), which is the unmerited "gift of God and not a human achievement."[1] The passage concludes with a succinct summary of missional identity: believers are new creations walking in good works (2:10).

The missional hermeneutics focal issues we will explore include: the *missio Dei*, especially how God acts to overcome the dire state of humanity in its natural state; God's character focused on his mercy and love; the missional significance of echoes from Exod 34 and Deut 7, and allusions to Ezek 36–37; the portrayal of humanity's plight in 2:1–3; the missional context implied by the passage; and the character and mission of God's people revealed by the passage. The passage does not mention Paul's involvement in mission, and so that issue will not be covered.

---

1. Muddiman, *Ephesians*, 111.

4.2 Portrayal of God's Intentions, Actions, and Purposes (the *missio Dei*)

God's actions of making alive, raising and seating believers are prominent in 2:5–6. God acts to overcome the human plight that is outlined in 2:1–3. The purpose for which God acts is found in 2:10, as God creates believers anew in Christ for a missional lifestyle of good works. God's actions are public demonstrations (2:7) of his grace, that is, a witness to his redemptive mission.

Throughout this paragraph (esp. vv. 5, 6, 7, 10), participation "in Christ" is the means by which individuals come to receive God's blessings, and is foundational for the development of Christian identity and ethics in the remainder of the letter.[2] There is, therefore, a strong link with the theme of God blessing believers *in Christ* in Eph 1:3–14. God's mission is consistently Christocentric, not anthropocentric. It is focused on God's purposes to create a redeemed and renewed people of God *in Christ*, rather than a pietistic individualized salvation or a renewed or improved humanity for its own sake.[3]

Verses 5 and 8 use the perfect passive participle σεσῳσμένοι to describe the saving action of God wrought for believers in Christ. The passive voice makes it clear that salvation is God's initiative and action, not the believer's ongoing or incomplete work. The traditional grammatical view of the perfect was that it expressed an event completed at the time of writing, though with continuing relevance. Lincoln compares the perfect with aorists in the surrounding verses,[4] but this approach focused on time rather than aspect is now questionable. Porter's characterization of perfect tense verbs as stative, and Constantine Campbell's categorization of the perfect as "imperfective" with "heightened proximity," better respect the significance of verbal aspect in the Greek verb.[5] The meaning is therefore focused on the resulting state in which believers stand: "you are saved." The realized eschatological emphasis of Ephesians expressed in these perfect participles complements, rather than contradicts, the broader Pauline tendency to use future verb forms (e.g. Rom 5:9–10; 10:9, 13).[6]

---

2. Arnold, *Ephesians*, 125, 144–45.

3. Cf. Tennent, *Invitation*, 61–64, 487–88.

4. Lincoln, *Ephesians*, 105.

5. Porter, *Verbal Aspect*, 468; Campbell, *Verbal Aspect*, 107.

6. Barth, *Ephesians 1–3*, 221; Best, *Ephesians*, 217. Though note that Paul also uses aorist at times when describing God's work on behalf of believers, e.g. Rom 8:24; 1 Cor 1:21; and in disputed Pauline letters 2 Tim 1:9; Titus 3:5.

God's overarching intention in carrying out these actions is stated in v. 7. God acts for humanity "so that in the ages to come he might show the immeasurable riches of his grace in kindness toward us in Christ Jesus." The *missio Dei* is a dynamic project with a clear eschatological end point. Further, the *missio Dei* is a visible demonstration of God's character (his actions in salvation history show the riches of his grace). The verb used for *showing* (or demonstrating) the riches of his grace is ἐνδείκνυμι. In other NT instances where God is the subject of the verb, ἐνδείκνυμι relates to God's sovereign oversight of salvation history (esp. Rom 9:17, 22).

Barth claims that the verb ἐνδείκνυμι is frequently used in Pauline writings with a nuance of judicial proof.[7] He interprets the verse to indicate that "the church is given a decisive function in the lawsuit of God ... God uses her as his evidence ... [God] has given the church the right and the task to make God's cause public."[8] However, this assertion goes beyond the evidence, since there are seventeen occurrences of the word in Pauline letters, and of these, only three have an unambiguously legal connotation (Rom 2:15; 3:26; and 2 Thess 1:5). The immediate context of Eph 2, Lincoln points out, also lacks a clear legal tone, which further weakens Barth's case.[9] While witnessing may not carry the connotation of a lawsuit, it nevertheless implies that God intends the salvation of believers to be a publicly visible demonstration of his mission to graciously renew the world.

The use of *riches* (πλοῦτος) to describe the quality of God's mercy in 2:4 and the abundance of God's grace in 2:7 creates a linkage to the same adjective employed in 1:7 and 18. In each case God's broader missional purpose is to make his glory visible and widely known through believers who receive grace, not just now but throughout all ages.[10] *Riches* therefore highlights the extensive quality of God's dispositions in the mission of salvation.

The phrase in v. 7, ἐν τοῖς αἰῶσιν τοῖς ἐπερχομένοις, "in the ages to come," is challenging to interpret. A few commentators have suggested that the literal temporal meaning is unsatisfactory since in the age to come all doubt will be removed as to God's gracious character, so it will be unnecessary to demonstrate it then.[11] Some commentators have suggested that, in the light of 3:10 where God's wisdom is made known to the powers, *aeons* be understood as supernatural beings, i.e. the riches of God's grace

---

7. Barth, *Ephesians 1–3*, 222, e.g. Rom 2:15.

8. Barth, *Ephesians 1–3*, 241–42. Cf. 3:10 where the verb γνωρίζω is used of the church's role to make known the wisdom of God to rulers and authorities in the heavenly places.

9. Lincoln, *Ephesians*, 109.

10. Cf. Arnold, *Ephesians*, 138; Muddiman, *Ephesians*, 109–10.

11. E.g. Best, *Ephesians*, 223.

are made known "among the attacking [hostile] powers."[12] There are six occurrences of αἰών in Ephesians. Ephesians 2:2 and 3:9 can plausibly bear a personal meaning,[13] while 1:21; 3:11, 21 are clearly temporal. Lincoln rejects the interpretation of αἰών as personal, since such a meaning would normally employ a dative to indicate a personal indirect object, rather than the preposition ἐν which more naturally bears a temporal meaning. Whether the phrase has a temporal or personal meaning, the broader point is that God's saving actions will be powerfully clear and opponents to his mission will be silenced.

This text expresses clearly four features of soteriology: the primacy of God's love as the motive and ground for human rescue; the contrast between humanity's fallen state (death, dominated by desires of the flesh, and wrath) and the exalted new life in Christ (characterized by good works); the eschatological dimension of God's actions which will culminate in the end times; and the emphasis on salvation as grace, an unearned gift (δῶρον, v. 8).

This passage therefore is a powerful summary of the impact of God's mission in the world—those addressed have had their status changed from under wrath to under grace, and from death to life; and this change constitutes a witness or demonstration to the whole world and all spiritual powers that God's redemptive mission has succeeded.

4.3 Portrayal of God's Person and Character

God's characteristics, as portrayed in this passage, are that he is "rich in mercy" (v. 4), and that he is moved by "great love" and kindness towards humanity (vv. 4, 7). The use of mercy and love, as discussed further below in §4.4, alludes to God's covenant characteristics of *hesed* mercy, faithfulness, and love (Exod 34:6). The passage stresses grace as the dominant aspect of God's disposition towards humanity and the world (vv. 5, 7, 8).[14] The lavish quality of God's grace is emphasized by the use of the participle ὑπερβάλλω ("immeasurable," ESV, NRSV, or "surpassing," NASB) together with the noun πλοῦτος ("riches").[15]

---

12. Barth, *Ephesians 1–3*, 222; Schlier, *Brief*, 112–13. τοῖς ἐπερχομένοις is then translated as "to come upon someone with force," i.e. to attack.

13. BDAG, s.v. αἰών, ῶνος, ὁ.

14. Lincoln, *Ephesians*, 103–4.

15. Arnold, *Ephesians*, 138. As noted in regard to 1:19, ὑπερβάλλω is found in texts connected to Ephesus, but it is by no means unique to that area (it also occurs in 2 Cor 3:10; 9:14; and in Philo).

God is the instigator of the steps of salvation and the shaper of all that has occurred to enable human beings to experience salvation through Christ. Christ is presented as God's agent in the salvation process (v. 5) and as the means by which believers are enabled to do good works as their new way of life (v. 10). As believers are united with Christ (v. 5), they are then able to participate in Christ's new (risen) life and exalted heavenly status (vv. 5–6).

4.4 Intertextuality—Literary and Thematic Links to the Wider Biblical Narrative

According to UBS5, there are no allusions or quotes from the OT in Eph 2:1–10.[16] By contrast, Hans Hübner and a number of commentators detect a range of echoes or allusions in the passage. Barth identifies an allusion to Exod 34:6 and Deut 7:7–9 in the characterization of God as rich in mercy, love, and grace (Eph 2:4). The walking terminology which frames this section (and which comes to greater prominence in 4:1 and following) is probably an echo of Deut 28:9: "The LORD will establish you as his holy people, as he has sworn to you, if you keep the commandments of the LORD your God and walk in his ways" (cf. Deut 26:17). Starling has detected an allusion to Ezek 36–37 in the death and life contrast. Cozart argues for the influence of Isa 26:14, 19 in Eph 2:5. Lastly, Jennifer Maclean has proposed that Eph 2:1–10 is literarily dependent on Rom 3:21–31, and that there are broad thematic parallels with Rom 1–3. These proposals will be examined in turn.

4.4.1 Exodus 34:6 and Deuteronomy 7:7–9

Barth and Lincoln both note the significance of God's covenantal self-identification in Exod 34:6 and Deut 7:7–9 for the portrayal of God in Eph 2.[17] God is characterized in Eph 2:4 as "rich in mercy, [acting] out of the great love with which he loved us" (ὁ δὲ θεὸς πλούσιος ὢν ἐν ἐλέει, διὰ τὴν πολλὴν ἀγάπην αὐτοῦ ἣν ἠγάπησεν ἡμᾶς). The verbal similarity between Eph 2:4 and Exod 34:6–7 (LXX) consists of three variations on the root ἔλεος: the adjective *merciful*, a compound noun *full of mercy*, and the root noun *mercy* (Κύριος ὁ θεὸς οἰκτίρμων καὶ ἐλεήμων, μακρόθυμος καὶ πολυέλεος καὶ

---

16. UBS5, 864–83; NA28, 592 identifies an echo of Wis 5:6; 13:1 in Eph 2:3 but this link is not supported in standard commentaries.

17. Barth, *Ephesians 1–3*, 218; Lincoln, *Ephesians*, 100; cf. Arnold, *Ephesians*, 134–35; Hübner, *Vetus Testamentum*, 2:436–39.

ἀληθινὸς καὶ δικαιοσύνην διατηρῶν καὶ ποιῶν ἔλεος εἰς χιλιάδας). In Deut 7:8, 9 both *love* and *mercy* are key aspects of God's relationship with Israel: "the Lord loved you" (ἀλλὰ παρὰ τὸ ἀγαπᾶν κύριον ὑμᾶς, Deut 7:8), and "keeping covenant and mercy to those that love him" (φυλάσσων διαθήκην καὶ ἔλεος τοῖς ἀγαπῶσιν αὐτὸν, Deut 7:9). These similarities in vocabulary reach a modest threshold for Hays's test of *volume*. Regarding *recurrence*, Deut 7:9 is echoed at 1 Cor 1:9 and Exod 33:19 (part of the Sinai narrative) is cited at Rom 9:15.[18] Further, it was argued above (in §2.4.2) that Eph 1:3–14 alludes to Deut 7, so collectively there are strong indicators that Hays's tests of *availability*, *recurrence*, and *thematic coherence* are present.

The portrait of God as merciful and abounding in steadfast covenant love (*hesed* חֶסֶד) is certainly an apt theological background to Eph 2. God's steadfast covenant love is the driving motivator for his sovereign choice of believers (Eph 1:3–14), his redemptive action in Christ that rescues them from death and slavery to the powers (2:1–10), through the blood of the cross (2:13–14). This same love becomes the rationale for believers to live out a self-sacrificial ethic of love in 5:2, 25. The allusion to Exod 34 and Deut 7:7–9 reinforces covenant love as a prominent aspect of God's missional character.

4.4.2 Ezekiel 36–37

Starling argues that the recitals of salvation history in Eph 1–2 are "strikingly redolent of the salvation-history recitals of the OT scriptures."[19] The description in 2:3 of Paul and his fellow Jews being ensnared in the sin of the gentiles "among whom we all once lived" (ESV), evokes the exile. He identifies Ezek 36:19–23 as the most probable antecedent text, which six times describes Israel as living "among the nations" (εἰς τὰ ἔθνη/ἐν τοῖς ἔθνεσιν). There are further parallels between Eph 2:1–10 and Ezek 36–37: the imagery of death (Eph 2:1 and uncleanness, desolation, the corpses of Ezek 37:9); God making alive (Eph 2:5; Ezek 37:3, 6, 9–10, 14); the mention of wrath (ὀργή, Eph 2:3; θυμός, Ezek 36:5, 6, 18); God's salvation as "not your own doing . . . not the result of works" (Eph 2:8, 9), and God's salvation "not for your sake" (Ezek 36:22, 32).[20] To this we might add the coincidence of walking in God's ways (Eph 1:10, περιπατέω; Ezek 36:27 using πορεύω; 37:24). Starling concludes:

18. Hübner, *Vetus Testamentum*, 2:222.
19. Starling, "New Exodus," 141.
20. Starling, *Not My People*, 191–92.

The reminder of the readers' salvation in Eph. 2:1-10 is thus strongly reminiscent of the end-of-exile soteriology of the prophets. Specifically, the dominant image of salvation as resurrection from spiritual death echoes the imagery and ideas of Ezek. 36-37, which foretell the return of Israel from the spiritual death and uncleanness of exile as a miracle of national resurrection brought about by the grace and power of God.[21]

Starling's analysis aligns well with the broader thesis of Cozart that Ephesians is shaped by a new exodus theme.[22] The author of Ephesians understood God to have acted in Christ to bring about the promised redemption of his people from slavery among the nations.

Windsor endorses Starling's conclusion that Ezek 36-37 stands behind Eph 2:1-10.[23] The missional implication of the Ezekiel echo becomes more explicit in 2:11-22. God has acted not only to restore life and end exile, but to overcome the human estrangement between Jew and gentile as proof of the arrival of his reign.[24] Restricting our view for the moment to Eph 2:1-10, it is nevertheless clearly apparent that Ezek 36:23, 27 announce God's missional purpose to display his holiness to all nations, and to bring about both spiritual and ethical transformation of his redeemed people.

> I will sanctify my great name, which has been profaned among the nations, and which you have profaned among them; and the nations shall know that I am the LORD, says the Lord God, when through you I display my holiness before their eyes . . . I will put my spirit within you, and make you follow my statutes and be careful to observe my ordinances.

4.4.3 Isaiah 26:19

Cozart, drawing on a passing comment of Moritz,[25] argues that the death to life image of Eph 2:5 (καὶ ὄντας ἡμᾶς νεκροὺς τοῖς παραπτώμασιν συνεζωοποίησεν τῷ Χριστῷ, "even when we were dead through our trespasses, made us alive together with Christ") is an echo of the death to life promise in Isa 26:19. He notes the following verbal or conceptual correspondences: νεκρός (Eph 2:1; Isa 26:14, 19); συζωοποιέω (Eph 2:5; cf. ζωή, Isa

21. Starling, *Not My People*, 192.
22. Cozart, *Present Triumph*.
23. Windsor, *Reading Ephesians*, 116-17.
24. Cf. Starling, "New Exodus," 146-48.
25. Moritz, *Profound Mystery*, 109, n. 40.

26:14); συνεγείρω (Eph 2:6; cf. ἐγείρω and ἀνίστημι, Isa 26:19). Cozart also identifies a number of conceptual parallels between Eph 2 and Isaiah:

> spiritual reversal (Eph 2:1, 3–4), triumph over enemies (Eph 2:2), slavish conditions reversed (2:3), enthronement as a display to the enemy (Eph 2:5–7), divinely initiated salvation and righteousness (Eph 2:8–10).[26]

Cozart's analysis supports the broader pattern of OT appropriation in Eph 2:1–10. The author understood his recipients to be experiencing the new, redeemed life promised by the OT prophets based on the exodus motif and God's covenant faithfulness to his promises to create a people for himself who will receive his blessings. These correspondences are sufficient to establish literary echoes, but there is insufficient lexical and syntactic volume to claim them as allusions.

The allusions to Ezek 36–37, strengthened by the thematic echoes of Deut 7:7–9 and Isa 26:19, are unified by their focus on God acting to overcome the sin of his chosen people in order to display his holiness among the nations for the sake of his covenant love and mercy. Eph 2:7, which announces the purpose of God's actions as demonstrating his grace in Christ Jesus, is confirmed as the focal verse of the pericope. God's mission is, in the light of these OT echoes, that humanity be rescued from deadly enslavement to spiritual powers to live in holiness by God acting in mercy and love, so that his grace is made visible in all ages and to all creatures on heaven and earth.

4.4.4 Romans 3

One further potential intertextual link from Eph 2:1–10 is worth noting. Maclean believes that Ephesians represents a post-Pauline redaction of Pauline traditions. In the case of Eph 2:5–10, she argues that the passage is literarily dependent on Rom 3:21–31, and that the goal of the redaction was to argue against the boasting of gentile Christians that their faith was superior to Jewish Christian piety. She notes that there are verbal similarities centered on six terms:[27]

---

26. Cozart, *Present Triumph*, 144, cf. 127–133.
27. Maclean, "Ephesians and Colossians," 189.

χάρις	grace	Rom 3:24	Eph 2:5, 7, 8
ἔνδειξις/ἐνδείκνυμι	demonstrate	Rom 3:25, 26	Eph 2:7
διὰ πίστεως	through faith	Rom 3:25 (22)	Eph 2:8
δωρεάν/δῶρον	gift	Rom 3:24	Eph 2:8
ἔργα	works	Rom 3:27, 28	Eph 2:9
καύχησις/καυχάομαι	boast	Rom 3:27	Eph 2:9

Table 2: Parallel Terms in Romans 3 and Ephesians 2

While Lincoln had claimed that Eph 2:8–9 drew upon Rom 3:24–28,[28] Maclean argues for a more deliberate appropriation of the Rom 3 material in Ephesians, whose author had the rhetorical goal of challenging the recipients' false pride in their own faith, which they had elevated to a human work.[29] Maclean's proposal has not been accepted in subsequent scholarship. There is insufficient syntactic equivalence to pass Hays's threshold of *volume*. Pauline vocabulary of grace, faith, works, and boasting is prevalent in 2 Corinthians and Galatians in equal measure to Rom 3. An equally plausible explanation for the presence of so much Pauline vocabulary is that the author of Ephesians was Paul (working with a different amanuensis) or a disciple of Paul faithfully reflecting the Pauline theological heritage.

The common theological framework in Romans and Eph 2 affirms the preeminent importance of faith as the basis for both Jewish and gentile salvation in the light of universal sinfulness (cf. Eph 2:3, 8). God's mission is to see all humanity justified through Christ for the sake of God's righteousness (and so God will be glorified among the nations, Rom 9:23; 15:9; cf. Eph 2:7, 10). This emphasis on the universal scope of salvation clarifies that the readers of Eph 2:1–10 should not pridefully see themselves in a privileged and exclusive position, but rather as forerunners in God's mission that is unfolding throughout the ages and encompassing all humanity.[30]

Despite UBS5 not detailing any OT allusions for Eph 2:1–10, there is a strong case for accepting Ezek 36–37 as an intentional allusion (especially since there are continuing links to the passage in Eph 2:11–22). The proposals by Barth, Lincoln, and Cozart of influence from Exod 34:6; Deut 7:7–9; and Isa 26:19 can also be accepted, noting that these links are echoes, rather than intentional allusions. The narrative of God's mission in Eph 2 therefore

28. Lincoln, *Ephesians*, lvii.
29. Maclean, "Ephesians and Colossians," 201.
30. Cf. Maclean, "Ephesians and Colossians," 204.

affirms God's covenant faithfulness, love, and mercy as the ground for his salvation plan. The links to Ezekiel and Isaiah demonstrate that Eph 2 reflects the realization of the prophetic hope of a new exodus. This is seen in the movement from death to life, from slavery to redemption, and from judgment and wrath for disobedience to righteous living and good works. Maclean's claim of direct literary dependence of Eph 2:1–10 on Rom 3 is not convincing. Nevertheless, it is reasonable to see a number of important Pauline theological themes in both texts, particularly universal sinfulness and the fact that salvation comes to both Jews and gentiles by grace not works, as God acts out of love for the sake of his own righteousness.

4.5 Portrayal of Humanity and the World in Relation to God's Mission

This passage presents both humanity's plight (vv. 1–3) and humanity's status and task following God's gracious intervention (vv. 4–6, 10). The nature of humanity's plight is summed up by the phrase "dead in transgressions and sins" (νεκροὺς τοῖς παραπτώμασιν καὶ ταῖς ἁμαρτίαις) in v. 1 (and essentially repeated at v. 5). Death here figuratively expresses the recipients' moral or spiritual state before God, similarly to Luke 15:24, 32, Rev 3:1, and a range of classical Greek authors.[31] As the dead are powerless to revive themselves, so the spiritually dead are unable to animate their spiritual status before God.[32] The dative has both a locative and causal sense, "dead in the sphere of your sins" and "dead because of your sins."[33] Trespasses and sins are synonymous, and include deliberate law breaking as well as failure to live in accordance with God's purposes for humanity.[34]

The plight of those outside of Christ is specified in v. 3 as "by nature children of wrath." The use of φύσει, *by nature*, indicates that the human condition, as determined by birth rather than through actions, is inherently subject to God's wrath because of sin, i.e. the sinful nature.[35] Humanity is seen in v. 3 as enthralled to the desires (ἐπιθυμία) of the flesh (σάρξ). Both

31. BDAG, s.v. νεκρός, ά, όν.

32. L&N, §74.28.

33. Arnold, *Ephesians*, 130; Lincoln, *Ephesians*, 93; Barth, *Ephesians 1–3*, 213 prefers an even wider range of meanings: "the cause, the instrument, the manifestation, the realm, and the consequence of death." In the light of the clause that immediately follows in v. 2 which begins with the preposition ἐν, and the main verbs in vv. 4–5, namely, made alive, raised and seated in Christ, the locative sense should be given priority.

34. Hoehner, *Ephesians*, 308; Muddiman, *Ephesians*, 102.

35. Best, *Ephesians*, 211; BDAG, s.v. φύσις, εως, ἡ; Lincoln, *Ephesians*, 99 links Eph 2:1–3 to Rom 5:12–21 and the theological concept of original sin.

phrases are found elsewhere in the NT, predominantly with the negative moral connotation they carry here (e.g. Rom 13:14; Gal 5:14; 2 Pet 2:10; 1 John 2:16). This negative connotation is confirmed by the next clause, "following the desires of flesh and senses." The imagery is reminiscent of Rom 8:5–7 where those who set their mind on the flesh are said to be hostile to God and unable to submit to God's law.³⁶

A number of commentators (such as Barth, Muddiman, and Schlier) take the second person plural "you" of Eph 2:1 as referring primarily or exclusively to gentile Christians, while the first person plural "we"/"us" of 2:3, 5 is used in contrast to refer to Jewish Christians.³⁷ However, unlike Rom 1–3, where Paul deliberately treats the two groups separately before indicting them both as guilty before God, here there is no obvious polemic against Jewish presumptions of moral superiority as against gentiles. The author's concern is to establish that all humanity (whether Jew or gentile) were caught in sin ("all of us . . . like everyone else" ὡς καὶ οἱ λοιποί).³⁸ God's mission is not, therefore, a cooperative endeavor in partnership with seeking humanity (a semi-Pelagian idea); rather, God's mission to save is entirely gracious and unprompted by human works, as explicitly stated at vv. 8–9.³⁹

Verses 1–5 present a picture of humanity "dead" in relation to God (v. 1, 5) and "subject to God's wrath" (v. 3) due to sin and the controlling influence of "the ruler of the power of the air." While *ruler* (ἄρχων) generally refers to a political leader, it is used of the devil in Matt 9:34; 12:24–26 and John 12:31; 14:30; 16:11.⁴⁰ It is therefore the same spiritual being as the author later refers to as *the devil* διάβολος, in Eph 4:27 and 6:11.

Barth highlights the significance of the three compound verbs "together with Christ" in v. 5. It "connotes the combination of Jews and Gentiles in common resurrection, and their resurrection with Christ."⁴¹ Resurrection is "a social event" in which humanity is "united out of dispersion and division."⁴² Muddiman adds that believers are "'raised and seated *with each other* in Christ.' The vertical relation *with* Christ . . . is complemented with a

---

36. L&N, §26.14 διάνοια (Eph 2:3) and 26.15 φρόνημα (Rom 8:5–8) are closely related terms.

37. Barth, *Ephesians 1–3*, 212; see also Muddiman, *Ephesians*, 105–6. The inclusion of *all* in v. 3 ("we all were formerly living" ἡμεῖς πάντες) makes any purported limitation of the first-person plural to Jews highly unlikely. Hoehner, *Ephesians*, 317.

38. Best, *Ephesians*, 207–8; cf. Winger, *Ephesians*, 304–5.

39. Cf. Winger, *Ephesians*, 292–93.

40. Best, *Ephesians*, 204; Hoehner, *Ephesians*, 311.

41. Barth, *Ephesians 1–3*, 220.

42. Barth, *Ephesians 1–3*, 220.

horizontal relation with other Christians *in* Christ."[43] Reconciliation is thus a central aspect of God's mission amongst humanity.

Verse 9 is thoroughly Pauline in asserting that salvation by faith cannot derive from human works, so that boasting is excluded. However, Muddiman detects a development from Romans and Galatians, where *works* often refers to "'works of the law,' the marks of Jewish identity, chiefly circumcision, Sabbath observance and the food regulations."[44] In Ephesians, the issue is not Jewish ethnic privilege but human ethical and religious behavior generally. The meaning of *works* (ἔργον vv. 9, 10) in Ephesians is developed in 4:1—6:20 (cf. especially 4:12; 5:11). God's mission cannot be restricted to salvation in the sense of a restored relationship with God but must also encompass the ethical transformation of individuals and their communities.

Verse 10 adopts creation language to describe believers: "we are *what he has made us*, created in Christ Jesus." Κτίζω is used here for the first time in the letter but will recur in 2:15, 3:9, and 4:24. It constitutes one of the significant themes of the letter. The believing community is a new creation, united across previous ethnic and religious divides (cf. 2:15). The linking of our identity as God's workmanship (ποίημα, "what he has made us" NRSV, "workmanship" ESV, CSB; "God's handiwork" NIV) with creation language, indicates that salvation and creation are closely connected activities of God (cf. Isa 45:7-8).[45] In the following passage, God's creative (building) activities are further elaborated; believers are being built into an ever-growing temple of God's Spirit (2:19-22).

Humanity is intended to *walk* (i.e. live) not according to the sinful ways of the world (v. 2), but in the good works pre-prepared by God for each believer (v. 10). Walking, therefore, constitutes an *inclusio* defining the boundaries of this particular pericope, and enables us to see that the movement from sin to good works and from death (v. 1) to life (v. 5) and new creation (v. 10) is the primary theological emphasis of the pericope.[46] Walking (περιπατέω), as a metaphor for manner of life, recurs in Eph 4-6 where it encapsulates the ethical vision of the author, e.g. "walk in a manner worthy of the calling to which you have been called" (4:1 ESV; cf. 4:17; 5:2, 8, 15).

The word used to specify the nature of the works believers now walk in, προετοιμάζω *prepared beforehand* (v. 9), creates a verbal echo with the numerous προ- prefix words in 1:3-14. Believers are chosen before the world's creation (πρὸ καταβολῆς κόσμου, v. 4), predestined (προορίζω, vv. 5,

---

43. Muddiman, *Ephesians*, 109.
44. Muddiman, *Ephesians*, 111. E.g. Rom 3:20, 28; Gal 2:16; 3:2, 5, 10.
45. Barth, *Ephesians 1-3*, 243.
46. Lincoln, *Ephesians*, 85.

11), beneficiaries of God's plan (προτίθημι, v. 9), and the first to hope in Christ (προελπίζω, v. 12). So too believers' good works have been *prepared beforehand* (προετοιμάζω, v. 9). These works are the result of God's sovereign choice, and are an expression of their lives being lived to the praise of God's glory.[47] This verbal connection confirms that God's mission encompasses the ethical transformation of humanity; as believers walk in good works, their lives redound to God's glory (1:6, 12, 14).

In summary, Eph 2:1–10 portrays the past, present, and future of humanity in God's mission. All humanity (both Jew and gentile) is by nature under God's wrath, enslaved to cultural and spiritual forces opposed to God (vv. 1–3). From this state of spiritual death, vv. 5–6 announces God's actions to make humanity alive, and to raise and seat believers with Christ. Mission as reconciliation is paramount here. Salvation leads not to boasting, but to ethical living (vv. 8–9). Verse 10 concludes the section; using the language of new creation to affirm that God's ethical program for humanity will bring praise to his glory.

4.6 Evidence of a Missional Context in the Problems, Crises or Issues Addressed

The missional context of 2:1–10 is strong. The plight of humanity as a whole in vv. 2–3 is under the sway of the ruler of the power of the air, and the desires of the flesh. Verse 10 then sets forth a vision for the recipients to know and put into action their God-given life which is meant to be oriented towards good works. Thus, the problem in the background of vv. 1–3 is human bondage to spiritual powers. The issue in the background of vv. 5–8 is (to use mirror-reading) a failure to grasp one's new identity as beloved object of God's mercy and rescue. In v. 10 an implied problem is a failure to walk in God's ways (and thus be an effective new creation in the midst of the conflict with the spiritual powers).

Thielman discusses the likely background to this passage if an interpreter accepts Pauline authorship and therefore an earlier dating of the epistle.

> If Paul were addressing Christians who were tempted for various reasons to fear the rulers and authorities in heavenly places and to placate them with worship . . . When they heard and believed the gospel (1:13–14), Christ's victory over the evil powers

---

47. Lincoln, *Ephesians*, 86; Yoder Neufeld, *Ephesians*, 101.

became their victory also, for they were released from captivity to the Ruler of the realm of the air.[48]

The explicit mention in v. 2 of "the ruler of the power of the air, the spirit that is now at work among those who are disobedient," considered together with 6:11–12 indicates that God's mission involves spiritual conflict with "ontologically real beings."[49] The available literature and range of Christian approaches to spiritual warfare is diverse.[50] At the least, Eph 2:1–3 indicates that spiritual beings are at work in nonbelievers, particularly through human cultures ("following the course of this world," v. 2) and the flesh (v. 3).[51] Ephesians is therefore understandable as a missional document that highlights some strategies of powers opposed to God's work in the world. By cataloging the plight of humanity outside of Christ and the privileges of believers, the author puts forward a strong motivation for gospel outreach to non-Christians, while simultaneously reinforcing the faith of believers by reminding them that outside of Christ, "we were by nature children of wrath, like everyone else" (v. 3).

The reference to the church as proof of God's grace in the ages to come in 2:7 implies a contest between God's power and claims over the world on the one hand, and rival human institutions on the other hand. Barth notes that whether in political form such as the imperial Roman Empire, ideological/philosophical form such as the enlightenment or age of colonialism, human societies and their institutions constantly produce *powers* that claim "uniqueness, worthiness, respect, if not worship."[52] The mission of the church is to embody and witness to God's greater worth and glory in the face of social forces that deny God's ultimate claims over humanity for worship.

The mention of faith and works in this passage, while bearing a resemblance to Rom 3:20, 28 and Gal 2:16, does not indicate the author is engaging in polemic against Jewish works-righteousness. The phrase "works of the law" (ἔργα νόμου) does not occur in Ephesians (indeed, law is mentioned

---

48. Thielman, *Ephesians*, 136–37.

49. Lausanne Movement, "Deliver Us From Evil."

50. E.g. Schlier, *Principalities and Powers*; Carr, *Angels and Principalities*; Wink, *Naming the Powers*.

51. τὸν αἰῶνα τοῦ κόσμου τούτου, v. 2, "the course of this world" (NRSV, ESV, NASB), "the ways of this world" (NIV, CSB); αἰών indicates not a particular deity (contra most German commentators, e.g. Schlier, *Brief*, 101–2; Sellin, *Brief*, 167) but is used consistently with Eph 1:21; 2:7; 3:9, 11, 21 to indicate culture; Graham, *Exegetical Summary*, 108: "Αἰών 'age' is put by metonymy for what takes place within its time-span; i.e., the practices, customs, and follies of the world."

52. Barth, *Ephesians 1–3*, 223.

once only in 2:15). Best portrays this passage as "a transplanting of the Pauline doctrine of justification into Hellenistic soil."[53] The context in which the author is operating is no longer dominated by conflict with Jewish or Judaizing groups. Instead, the more universal concern of how salvation is achieved is now in focus. Thus, the author rejects reliance on morality, philosophical or Gnostic insights into truth, and ritualism as unable to save.[54] Grace through faith, not works, is the path of salvation the author presents.

In the light of Maclean's redactional analysis of Eph 2, discussed above, we might also add that the predominantly gentile recipients who are the focus of Eph 2 may have fallen into an erroneous understanding of faith. She states:

> In the present passage the author heightens his critique of his audience's status. Not only have they relied upon faith without adequate attention to love or hope, he now implies that in a twist of irony for followers of Paul, they have elevated faith to a human endeavor separated from grace and worthy of boasting before God. The author of Ephesians displays the inadequacy of this position by showing that such boasting in one's faith is tantamount to claiming it as a "work," not unlike the "works of the law," which Paul had shown to be an inappropriate basis for boasting.[55]

This reconstruction of the circumstances prompting the letter has merit. In 2:11–12 the author admonishes his audience to remember their former status excluded from the covenants, "having no hope and without God in the world" (2:12). In 3:17, 19, Paul's prayer is for them to grow in love. Similarly, in 4:2 the author begs his readers to pursue "humility and gentleness, with patience, bearing with one another in love." Therefore, 2:1–10 shows the author beginning a response to the pastoral issue of pride and exclusivity on the part of his recipients. Grace as the basis of salvation means that believers may not boast about God's saving work in their lives.

This passage also addresses the human plight of being "dead through the trespasses and sins . . . by nature children of wrath" (vv. 1, 3). Divine judgment of all those outside of Christ is one of the enduring Christian motivations for mission in the form of evangelistic outreach. By explicitly

---

53. Best, *Ephesians*, 228.

54. Best, *Ephesians*, 228. It is beyond the scope of this project to explore the relationship of Eph 2:8–10 to the terminology and theology of justification and works (of the law) in the undisputed Paulines. While Best contrasts the material of Eph 2:8–10 with Pauline polemic against Judaizing (e.g. Gal 2:16; 3:2–5; Rom 3:20, 29), this need not mean that Ephesians is deutero-Pauline, merely that it addresses a distinct situation from Galatians and Romans.

55. Maclean, "Ephesians and Colossians," 201.

addressing the condition of humanity without Christ, the author is not merely seeking to reassure his recipients that they are now secure from divine wrath and the influence of spiritual powers, but is praying and urging his recipients to understand their position in God's broader program of revelation and redemption (1:17–19). The missional context is that unbelieving humanity and the powers are yet to be fully confronted with the vastness of God's mercy, love, and grace at work in salvation (2:7). Therefore, anybody who is a recipient of God's saving grace is automatically and necessarily drawn into the role of being a witness to that salvation (noting the force of ἐνδείκνυμι in 2:7, discussed above).

Furthermore, the manner of life of believers, who now walk in good works (2:10) as distinct from their former pattern of walking in sin (2:1–2), indicates that God's mission is concerned with removing the blight of sin in the world, and replacing it with good works. The missional context is that human societies walking in sin are incapable of fulfilling their reason for existing—to live to the praise of God's glory by being made alive together with Christ and walking in good works (1:6, 12, 14; 2:5, 10). Therefore, wherever human societies exist without an active witness to God's mercy, love, and grace found in Christ, there is a missional need for the church, as the body of Christ, his fullness in the world, to establish a presence there.

This passage addresses a number of issues that highlight the nature of early Christian mission. Firstly, the plight of humanity, spiritually dead and in bondage to spiritual powers is the backdrop to appreciating God's gracious rescue of Christ believers. Eph 2:1–3 prepares the way for later discussions of spiritual warfare (especially 6:10–17), and here alerts the contemporary interpreter to the need to take seriously the religious context of the recipients of Ephesians, in which spirits and powers cast a destructive shadow over the world. Barth notes that human institutions too, such as imperial Roman rule or contemporary ideologies, can become idolatrous as they usurp the worship that is due to God alone. Any human tendency to pursue works-based righteousness is undercut by the nature of grace as elaborated in vv. 8–9. Finally, the passage provides a strong motivation for evangelistic outreach to those yet dead in sin and under the thrall of the powers in its celebration of salvation by grace through faith in Christ.

4.7 Character and Mission of God's People

The passage largely focuses on God's actions for believers, but even so, there are strong indicators of the character of God's people that is a result of God's work in them. Verse 7 gives the rationale for the raising of believers to be seated with Christ: "so that in the ages to come he might show the immeasurable riches of his grace in kindness toward us in Christ Jesus." God's people are a demonstration (ἐνδείκνυμι) of God's immeasurable grace (cf. Rom 3:25–26; 9:17, 22; 1 Cor 2:4). God's actions to publicly demonstrate his saving and reconciling agenda have as their intended audience all things in heaven and earth (1:10), and so certainly include human society as an arena in which the church is to display God's grace.

A significant purpose of God is also declared here. Believers have been "created in Christ Jesus for good works, which God prepared beforehand to be our way of life" (v. 10). God's mission is therefore to create a new humanity. *New creation* will be elaborated further in 2:15 where the focus is reconciliation between Jews and gentiles, while the entire paraenetic section of the letter in Eph 4–6 also aims to elucidate the nature of the new life created by God for believers (noting especially 4:24). Similarly, the good works (ἔργοις ἀγαθοῖς) that are to characterize the lives of believers are all those actions that promote the ethical transformation of individuals and their communities detailed in Eph 4–6. Specific examples there include honest (ἀγαθός) work to enable generous charity (4:28) and good speech that gives grace and edifies the hearers (4:29).

4.8 Conclusion

Ephesians 2:1–10 vividly portrays the *missio Dei* as God's actions to transform humanity's desperate situation based on his covenant faithfulness, love, and mercy (noting the echoes of Exod 34 and Deut 7). God's redemptive plan sees his people move from death to life, from slavery to redemption, and from judgment and wrath for disobedience to righteous living and good works, so fulfilling the prophetic hopes of a new exodus (Ezek 36–37; Isa 26). The missional context again sets spiritual forces in prominent focus and highlights the impotence of human efforts at salvation through works. God's redeemed and transformed people are a demonstration of the victory of God's redemptive plan over the forces of sin and evil.

5

Ephesians 2:11–22

5.1 Introduction

Having surveyed the contours, goals, and dynamic of the *missio Dei* in Eph 1 and introduced the dynamics of God's saving actions for individuals in 2:1–10, this next section of Ephesians (2:11–22) explores the corporate dimensions of God's mission: bringing unity, peace, and incorporation into a new organic dwelling place for God. Ephesians 2:11–22 is regarded by a number of commentators as the theological center of the letter.[1] The literature review at §1.5 also established that it is referred to more frequently in missiological works than any other part of the letter. Its explicit themes of reconciliation, incorporation of "the far off" into God's people and the growth of the believing community as a temple dwelling place for God, all have obvious missional weight. Our goal will be to add depth and rigor to the existing discussions within the fields of missiology and biblical studies. As with the previous section, we will address the missional hermeneutics questions in turn (the *missio Dei*, the character of God, intertextuality, humanity and the world, missional context, and the mission of God's people), excluding the portrayal of Paul in mission, since the passage is silent on that topic.

---

1. Schnackenburg, *Ephesians*, 102; Barth, *Ephesians 1–3*, 275; Gnilka, *Epheserbrief*, 132.

5.2 Portrayal of God's Intentions, Actions, and Purposes (the *missio Dei*)

Reconciliation, a powerful missional concept, lies at the heart of this passage. The author employs a range of metaphors including political, familial, cultic, and architectural in order to convey the reality of believers' changed status in Eph 2:11–22. The passage is structured around a contrast (ποτὲ . . . νῦν, *once . . . now*) which extends the contrasts that featured in the previous section (such as from death to life) and applies them more broadly to human-divine reconciliation and communal reconciliation. God's actions on behalf of humanity are portrayed using four broad concepts in this theologically dense passage. Firstly, humanity is reconciled and granted access to God (vv. 13, 16, 18, 19). Secondly, ethnically and religiously divided humanity is reconciled (vv. 14–15). Thirdly, Christ is established as the universal proclamation of peace (v. 17). Lastly, those reconciled are built into God's growing household and dwelling place (vv. 20–22).

5.2.1 Reconciliation with God

God has acted to overcome the alienation and exclusion of gentiles, who were previously hindered from experiencing God's salvation by five conditions, framed as an inverse of Rom 9:3–5 which cataloged the benefits of being a Jew.[2] Gentiles were, according to v. 12: (a) without Christ, (b) aliens from the commonwealth of Israel, (c) strangers to the covenants of promise, (d) having no hope, and (e) without God in the world. God's mission removes the spiritual and social-political obstacles otherwise preventing gentiles from experiencing life as part of his chosen people. This verse adopts political terminology (v. 12 alienated from the polity of Israel, ἀπηλλοτριωμένοι τῆς πολιτείας τοῦ Ἰσραὴλ; legal aliens/foreigners, ξένοι, to the covenants); as well as religious terminology to express the status of gentiles apart from Christ: "without hope and without God," ἐλπίδα μὴ ἔχοντες καὶ ἄθεοι.

In v. 16, God acts through the cross (διὰ τοῦ σταυροῦ), that is, through Christ's death, to reconcile humanity to himself. Reconciliation involves reestablishing "friendly interpersonal relations after these have been disrupted or broken."[3] The granting of access (προσαγωγή) to God through Christ (2:18, cf. 3:12), in the light of the temple imagery of 2:21 more likely draws on a cultic rather than a political context.[4] Both Lincoln and

---

2. Arnold, *Ephesians*, 154.
3. L&N, §40.1.
4. Best, *Ephesians*, 273. προσαγωγή is best understood intransitively (as "access")

Muddiman cite OT examples where gentiles are drawn to temple worship, due to the obvious blessings God has bestowed on Israel (e.g. 1 Kgs 8:41–43; Isa 56:6–8; Zech 8:20–23).[5]

5.2.2 Social Reconciliation

Reconciliation of Jew and gentile alike to God (the vertical dimension) is the context in which ethnic reconciliation between Jew and gentile (the horizontal dimension) becomes possible.[6] God acts to reconcile humanity, according to v. 16, ἐν ἑνὶ σώματι, "in one body," that is, in the church (the singular use of σῶμα elsewhere in Ephesians consistently indicates the church).[7] The language of membership in God's household (2:19) reinforces the point that reconciliation should have a concrete social manifestation: gentile believers "belong and are at home."[8]

The intent of God's mission is more than a cessation of mutual dislike or estrangement (noting the opening of the passage with pejorative name-calling from both sides, v. 11). Verse 14 portrays God creating one new entity out of two formerly distinct ethnic groups (ὁ ποιήσας τὰ ἀμφότερα ἕν). This act is accomplished in Christ, who is "our peace" (ἡ εἰρήνη ἡμῶν), who makes peace "in his flesh" (ἐν τῇ σαρκὶ αὐτοῦ). In the modern world, powerful examples of social reconciliation are encountered in the experiences of believing Dalits in India and previously warring tribes in Burundi.[9]

The peace promised in Eph 2:14–17 may speak to the Jewish idea of *shalom* as rest and wholeness, and provide an alternative to imperial Roman political peace (the elimination of hostility and resistance and the imposition of tyrannical rule).[10] The ethical implications of the reconciliation and peace enjoyed by believers are developed in 4:1—6:9, encompassing life in civic community, in the community of faith and in the household.[11] Since Ephesians paints the results of God's reconciling actions in the broadest possible terms, the narrow view of the dividing wall (which is the focal point of the

---

since the mention of the Spirit makes a transitive sense ("introduction," "being brought to God") awkward; cf. Graham, *Exegetical Summary*, 174.

5. Lincoln, *Ephesians*, 149; Muddiman, *Ephesians*, 138.
6. Cf. Lincoln, *Ephesians*, 148.
7. Best, *Ephesians*, 265.
8. Muddiman, *Ephesians*, 139.
9. Lausanne Committee for World Evangelization, "Reconciliation."
10. Muddiman, *Ephesians*, 125; cf. Faust, *Pax Christi*, 474–75; Maier, *Picturing Paul*, 137–42.
11. Muddiman, *Ephesians*, 126.

problem needing resolution in v. 14) as the Jewish law (referenced explicitly in v. 15),[12] or a physical barrier in the Jerusalem temple that excluded gentiles from the inner courts,[13] should be rejected in favor of a comprehensive understanding: the wall symbolized Israel's distinctive history, culture, cult, and relationship to God, which effectively excluded gentiles from the covenant people of God.[14] Two further reasons for rejecting narrow interpretations of the dividing wall are that the predominantly gentile audience of Ephesians was probably unaware of the physical barrier in the temple, and the law *per se* is nowhere else mentioned in Ephesians and is not identified as the problem to which Christ provides the solution.[15]

God's intentions and actions for humanity are not merely restorative but creative, "that he might create in himself one new humanity," v. 15. The verb for create (κτίζω) is repeated from 2:10, and thus links this section with God's purposes as elaborated in 2:1–10 that renewed humanity is created for good works (cf. 4:24 where καινός and κτίζω recur once more). Lincoln argues that the new creation:

> is not merely an amalgam of the old in which the best of Judaism and the best of Gentile aspirations have been combined. The two elements which were used in the creation have become totally transformed in the process.[16]

The nature and appropriate behaviors of the new humanity become the focus in Eph 4–6, where it is clear that the ethical framework for the new life is solidly grounded in the moral ideals set for Israel in the prophetic and wisdom traditions.

5.2.3 Universal Proclamation of Peace

Verse 17 continues the description of Christ's work in reconciliation, introducing for the first time in Ephesians the idea that Christ εὐηγγελίσατο εἰρήνην, "proclaimed the good news of peace" (CSB). This usage of εὐαγγελίζω is distinct from normal Pauline patterns where it denotes the apostolic proclamation of the gospel.[17] The usage here clearly reflects Isa 52:7, which

---

12. Schnackenburg, *Ephesians*, 114; Hoehner, *Ephesians*, 368–71.
13. Arnold, *Ephesians*, 159–60.
14. Barth, *Ephesians 1–3*, 282; Talbert, *Ephesians and Colossians*, 79–80; see also Muddiman, *Ephesians*, 128.
15. Cf. Yee, *Ethnic Reconciliation*, 144–51.
16. Lincoln, *Ephesians*, 144.
17. E.g. Rom 1:15; 1 Cor 1:17; 15:1; Gal 1:8, 9, 11.

emphasizes the object of the proclamation, peace, within the context of the redemption of God's people. The proclamation of peace is to both "the far off" and "the near," which in context encompasses gentiles in addition to Jews. God intends for the gospel of peace to be universally proclaimed.

5.2.4 Building the Household of God

Verses 19–22 extend the metaphorical language already employed for the people of God into a new field, that of architecture. Believers, as members of the household of God, are being *built* ἐποικοδομηθέντες (v. 20 an aorist passive participle, with God as the implicit agent of action). Using building terminology connects the ecclesial identity of God's people with God's purposes expressed progressively throughout the OT and NT. While ἐποικοδομέω does not occur in the LXX, the root verb οἰκοδομέω (בנה, MT) is regularly encountered. Where the word is used with God as the agent, particular themes emerge, many noted by Fouts and Hulst.[18] God is the builder of creation (Ps 78:69; Amos 9:6) and humanity (Gen 2:22). God promised to build David's house (his dynasty) in connection with the choosing and establishment of Israel as his own people (2 Sam 7:27; 1 Kgs 11:38; 1 Chr 17:10; Ps 89). God promised to restore and rebuild his people after the exile (Jer 24:6; 31:4; 33:7; 42:10; Amos 9:11). God is also the builder/rebuilder of Jerusalem/Zion as the place where former outcasts and exiles can find rest and security (Ps 51:20; 68:35–36 LXX; Isa 44:26). God is the builder/planner of the tabernacle and temple (Exod 25:8–9, though a different Gk./Heb word is used; 1 Chr 28:19).

Ephesians' use of the participle ἐποικοδομηθέντες *built* neatly encapsulated the completion of these varied divine building projects. The new household of God is a new humanity, a new people under a restored Davidic king, dwellers in a restored community, where God himself is present as he was in the temple and in Zion. Ἐποικοδομέω also occurs in 1 Cor 3:10–17, one of the other key NT passages which describes the church as a temple. Thus, Eph 2:20, by adopting architectural language, links the identity of the community of believers with God's building projects, especially the founding and restoration of his covenant people, and prepares us for the explicit discussion of the community as a temple, which follows in v. 21.

The climax to the section is the statement that members of the household of God are growing into a temple (v. 21), being "built together spiritually into a dwelling place for God" (v. 22). These two verses stress that the

---

18. Fouts, "בנה *bnh* 1215," 677–80; Hulst, "בנה *bnh* to build," 245–46; the following discussion includes additional references based on the author's own word study.

church as a temple is growing.[19] It is not therefore a static and localized concept of God's dwelling place, as might be expected based on the type of the Jerusalem temple. As will be demonstrated below in §5.4.7, a biblical theology of temple actually points to the temple as the ever-expanding presence of God on earth. God's mission through the church is to be present in the world, and to expand that presence over time.

5.3 Portrayal of God's Person and Character

God's actions are centered on Christ: it is through "the blood of Christ" (v. 13) that those far off are brought near; and "in his flesh" that unity is created (v. 14). Christ has abolished the law (v. 15) and reconciled both groups within humanity to God "in one body through the cross" (v. 16). Reconciliation is thus very much at the core of Christ's mission on earth; he is the agent of reconciliation and his body (the church as a community of reconciled and redeemed former aliens and enemies) becomes the goal of reconciliation.[20] Furthermore, it is Christ who proclaims the good news of peace (v. 17), who enables access to the Father (v. 18), and who is the keystone in the household of God (v. 20).[21] The divine peacemaking mission reaches a climax in 2:14–17, with the key declaration "for he [Christ] is our peace" (2:14). All the hostility and alienation of 2:12–19 is removed through Christ's death. As Gorman explains:

> For Paul, then, Jesus on the cross embodied and performed the divine act of peacemaking that constitutes the human dimension, so to speak, of the eternal, cosmic mystery and plan of God. The cross is the divine performative utterance of reconciliation. Or, more simply, Christ is our peace, our *shalom*. He is God's peace in person—*in the flesh*.[22]

Christ "gathers, forms, purifies, builds, instructs, seals, and proclaims" the church as the people of God saved through his sacrificial death.[23] The passage is thus a rich source of Christology, the themes of which lead to prayer and doxology in 3:18–21.

While Christ is the focus of the passage, v. 18 encapsulates the theme of access to God in language that supports a Trinitarian conception of God:

19. Cf. Arnold, *Ephesians*, 172.
20. Barth, *Ephesians 1–3*, 266; Stuhlmacher, "Er Ist Unser Friede," 348.
21. Lincoln, *Ephesians*, 161.
22. Gorman, *Becoming the Gospel*, 193, italics in original.
23. Barth, *Ephesians 1–3*, 313.

"through him [Christ] both of us have access in one Spirit to the Father."[24] Fee interprets ἐν ἑνὶ πνεύματι as a locative, in the light of the parallelism with 2:16 "in one body" and 4:4 "one body and one Spirit."[25] It also conveys an instrumental sense, because the Spirit enables access to God's presence. Fee concludes, "This is yet one more passage in Paul in which 'salvation in Christ' is conveyed in trinitarian terms."[26]

In v. 20, Christ's role in relation to the household of God is stated using an architectural metaphor, he is the ἀκρογωνιαῖος, traditionally understood as *foundation stone*. Joachim Jeremias, followed by Barth and Lincoln, argues for *keystone* or *capstone* on the basis of the term's usage in T. Sol. 2:27.[27] Against this newer interpretation, it should be noted that the term occurs only once in the LXX, at Isa 28:16, where ἀκρογωνιαῖος is clearly the stone laid at the commencement of building, since θεμέλιος (*foundation*) is used to clarify the meaning of ἀκρογωνιαῖος. Arnold further points out that the imagery used in Eph 2:20 is of a building which is not yet complete, one that is still under construction, and so a capstone logically would not yet be employed.[28] In Isa 28:16 the symbolism of the cornerstone:

> encompasses the reality of the new community, a faithful remnant, which is a foretaste of the coming righteous reign of God and which is ushered in by the promised messianic rule of Zion.[29]

The conception of the community and its leaders constituting the foundation of God's temple is echoed in the Dead Sea Scrolls, 1QS8.5–7 and 1QS11.7–9. In Ephesians, the significance of Christ as cornerstone is that all believers are now connected (συναρμολογέω "joined together") with every other member of the new people of God in a spiritual building which cannot be dismantled by human powers or the vagaries of the rise and fall of political powers across human history, as had happened to Israel.

A final reference to God's person is arguably also present in v. 22, where it states, "in whom [Christ] you also are built together spiritually [in the Spirit, ἐν πνεύματι] into a dwelling place for God." Fee argues that ἐν πνεύματι does not primarily indicate a non-earthly church universal, but rather, in the light of Eph 5:18–20, the church which is filled by the Spirit

---

24. Lincoln, *Ephesians*, 150.
25. Fee, *God's Empowering Presence*, 684.
26. Fee, *Empowering Presence*, 285; cf. Best, *Ephesians*, 274.
27. Jeremias, "ἀκρογωνιαῖος," 792; Barth, *Ephesians 1–3*, 271, 317–19; Lincoln, *Ephesians*, 154–56.
28. Arnold, *Ephesians*, 171.
29. Childs, *Isaiah*, 209–10, cf. 1 Pet 2:4–6.

as local congregations "are gathered to worship him and to instruct one another."³⁰ Lincoln notes that as with 2:18, "The readers' experience as part of the Church is described in this verse by means of a 'trinitarian' pattern of thought—'in Christ,' 'dwelling place of God,' and 'in the Spirit.'"³¹ This passage in Ephesians, then, is a strong basis for understanding the dynamic of mission as thoroughly Trinitarian.

5.4 Intertextuality—Literary and Thematic Links to the Wider Biblical Narrative

Ephesians 2:11–22 has literary or thematic linkages with a number of OT texts: Ezek 36–37; Isa 9:5–6; 52:7; 57:19; Zech 6:12–15; 2 Chr 6:32–33.³² The strength and significance of these links to OT referent texts will be explored in turn.

5.4.1 Ezekiel 36–37

Robert Suh and Starling have both argued for Ezek 37 to be understood as a literary influence on Eph 2. However, there are sufficient reasons to extend the boundaries of the precursor text to Ezek 36 as well. The following table of over twenty words common to Eph 2 and Ezek 36–37 includes vocabulary from Ezek 36 not mentioned by Suh or Starling. Although all of these words occur thirty or more times in the NT, the close proximity of so many is statistically unique.

Greek lemma		NT Frequency	Ezek 36–37	Eph 2
νεκρός	dead	128	37:9	2:1
ἁμαρτία	sin	173	36:19	2:1
σάρξ	flesh	147	36:26; 37:6	2:3, 11, 14
λοιπός	rest	55	36:5	2:3
ζαω	live	275+	37:3	2:5 συζωοποιέω

---

30. Fee, *Empowering Presence*, 689; a number of commentators take ἐν πνεύματι as a reference to God's Spirit, e.g. Schnackenburg, *Ephesians*, 125; Best, *Ephesians*, 290.

31. Lincoln, *Ephesians*, 158–59.

32. Kreitzer, *Hierapolis*, 126–27, noting particularly the rare word κατοικητήριον; Lincoln, *Ephesians*, 149.

Greek lemma		NT Frequency	Ezek 36–37	Eph 2
σῴζω	save	106	36:29	2:5, 8
αἰών	age	122	37:25	2:7
Ἰσραήλ	Israel	68	36:1; 37:11	2:12
διαθήκη	covenant	33	37:26	2:12
ἐλπίς	hope	53	37:11	2:12
εγγυς	near	31	36:8	2:13, 17
εἰρήνη	peace	92	37:26	2:14, 15
δύο	two	135	37:22	2:15
εἷς	one	345	37:17	2:15, 16, 18
καινός	new	42	36:26	2:15
θεός	God	1317	36:28; 37:23	2:16, 19
ἔρχομαι	come	632	36:8; 37:9	2:17
πνεῦμα	Spirit	379	36:26; 37:1	2:18, 22
οὐκέτι	no longer	47	36:14; 37:22	2:19
ἅγιος	holy	233	36:20; 37:26	2:19, 21
οικος (root)	house	420	36:10; 37:11	2:19, 20
περιπατέω	walk	95	37:24 (πορεύομαι)	2:2, 10

Table 3: Parallel Terms in Ezekiel 36–37 and Ephesians 2

The number of identical words or words from the same root creates a strong prima facie basis for seeing a literary relationship between Eph 2 and Ezek 36–37 (Hays's test of *volume*). We have already noted that the imagery of death to life in 2:1–10 is seen by scholars, including Starling, to derive from Ezek 36–37. Suh published an extended analysis of the links between 2:11–22 and Ezek 37, concluding that the author "used Ezekiel 37 as a framework for building his own argument in Ephesians 2."[33] The basis for Suh's conclusion consists in three areas of similarity: strong verbal parallelism, with fifteen significant words occurring in Eph 2 and Ezek 37; structural parallelism following the pattern life from death, explanation, then unification of two groups; and nine points of thematic parallelism. The parallel themes Suh identifies are:

33. Suh, "Use of Ezekiel 37," 733.

a. the new creation from death to life (Ezek 37:1-10/Eph 2:1-10);
b. walking in the way of the Lord (Ezek 37:24/Eph 2:10);
c. covenant (Ezek 37:26/Eph 2:12);
d. peace (Ezek 37:26/Eph 2:14-15, 17);
e. the promised Messiah of David/Jesus (Ezek 37:22, 24-25/Eph 2:13-17, 20);
f. the temple (sanctuary/dwelling place τὰ ἅγιά) of God (Ezek 37:26-28/Eph 2:19-22);
g. unity (Ezek 37:15-28/Eph 2:11-22);
h. the people of God (Ezek 37:23, 27/Eph 2:19); and
i. the Holy Spirit (Ezek 37:1-14/Eph 2:18, 22).[34]

Hays's test of *thematic coherence* is clearly also satisfied. The tests of *historical plausibility, availability*, and *recurrence* are also satisfied: Ezek 37:27 is quoted in 2 Cor 6:16; there are allusions to Ezek 36:26 at 2 Cor 3:3, and to Ezek 36:26; 37:14 in 1 Thess 4:8.[35] Accordingly, this part of Ezekiel was available to Paul, and an application of Ezekiel's renewal and temple imagery to the church is a move Paul had made previously, and so is *historically plausible*.[36]

There is a growing *history of interpretation* arguing for an influence by Ezekiel in Eph 2. The published works are by Ralph Martin, Charles Talbert, Ira Jolivet, Starling, and Suh,[37] while two theses by Joshua Greever and Andrew Stirling also argue for a relationship between Ezekiel and Eph 2.[38] The significance of this link for the portrayal of mission in Ephesians has, however, not yet been explored.

---

34. Suh, "Use of Ezekiel 37," 724-32.
35. UBS5, 859, 879; Hübner, *Vetus Testamentum*, 2:324, 366, 560.
36. Cf. Hayes, "Influence of Ezekiel 37," 123-36.
37. Martin, *Reconciliation*, 190; Talbert, *Ephesians and Colossians*, 81; Jolivet, "Ethical Instructions," 193-210; Starling, "New Exodus," 145; Suh, "Use of Ezekiel 37"; cf. Barth, *Ephesians 1-3*, 233, 293 who mentions Ezek 37, without exploring the extent of its literary influence.
38. E.g. Greever, "New Covenant," 200; Stirling, "Transformation and Growth," 101-3.

5.4.1.1 Old Testament Context

Turning now to the OT context of the allusions, we see that Ezek 36–37 occurs in the context of oracles on renewal and restoration: renewed shepherd leadership (Ezek 34), a restored land (Ezek 35:1—36:15), and a resurrected people (Ezek 36:16—37:28).[39] Ezekiel 37:21 announces a new exodus: God will take "the people of Israel from the nations among which they have gone, and will gather them from every quarter, and bring them to their own land" (cf. 36:24-33; 37:25).

In Ezek 36–37, the prophet's oracle looks to the time when God, for the sake of restoring the holiness of his name before the nations (36:23, 36; 37:28), acts to restore his chosen people to the holy land (36:24); cleanse them from their sins, which included idolatry (36:18, 25; 37:23); give them a new heart and spirit (36:26) thus enabling them to walk in his statutes (36:27; 37:24); and become his people (36:28). The renewed, sanctified people then become a fitting community in which the temple can be rebuilt, and God's dwelling among his people resumed (37:25-28; 40-48). The theme of unity is emphasized by repetition of the word *one* (37:16, 17, 19, 22, 24). The political reunification of Israel and Judah (pictured as two sticks rejoined) is God's act (37:21-22). There is also the promise of a new Davidic king (37:22, 24), and a new covenant of peace (37:26). Following the oracles concerning Gog in Ezek 38–39, the closing chapters of Ezekiel (40–48) concern the new temple, which ultimately becomes a source of life and healing for the whole world (47:1-12).

5.4.1.2 Ephesians' Theological Use of the Ezekiel Allusion

Ephesians 2 clearly portrays the fruits of God's acts of salvation and restoration on behalf of a renewed humanity (2:10, 15). The exile of Israel depicted in Ezek 36:19, 31 serves as a parallel to the exclusion of gentiles from God's people depicted in Eph 2:11-13. The prophesied return from exile (Ezek 36:24, 28) is therefore a parallel concept to those who are *far* being brought *near* in Eph 2:13, 17, accepting that the vocabulary is different. The reunification of the two kingdoms (Ezek 37:15-22) prefigures the creation of one new humanity from Jew and gentile (Eph 2:14-16). The promised Davidic shepherd servant-king (Ezek 37:24-25) is seen to be fulfilled in Christ, who has rescued those who were far off and brought them near, into God's household, through his own blood (Eph 2:13, 17, 19).

---

39. Blenkinsopp, *Ezekiel*, 155–78.

The promise of God's sanctuary dwelling place being in the midst of his restored people (Ezek 37:26–28) finds fulfillment in the church as the spiritual temple under construction in which God dwells (Eph 2:20–22). The final verse of Ezek 37:28 explicitly ties these acts of restoration and renewal to witness to the nations: "the nations shall know that I the Lord sanctify Israel, when my sanctuary is among them forevermore."[40] This missional witness to the nations is partially fulfilled by those gentiles who have already become believers in Eph 2, but it is also an ongoing imperative that shapes the Pauline mission (3:3–6, 9–10) and by implication shapes the mission of the churches already founded by his circle. The role of the church as the bearers of God's presence and blessing to the nations is also suggested by the vision of Ezekiel's new temple, out of which flows water that brings life and healing to the world (Ezek 47:1–12).[41]

5.4.2 Isaiah 9, 52, and 57

The presence of allusions to Isa 9, 52, and 57 in Eph 2:14–18 has long been observed, including by church fathers and in early commentaries such as by Brooke Westcott.[42] Peter Stuhlmacher proposed that in Eph 2:13–18, " the author offers a christological exegesis of Isa 9:5–6; 52:7; 57:19 . . . From the key word εἰρήνη it connects three scriptures with one another, namely Isa 57:19 (v. 13 and 17), Isa 9:5f (v. 14) and Isa 52:7 (v. 17)."[43] The overlapping vocabulary and phrasing is marked in the following table with italics.

---

40. Beale, *Temple and Mission*, 110–11.
41. Beale, *Temple and Mission*, 342.
42. Westcott, *Ephesians*, 101; John Chrysostom, *Hom. Eph.* 2:11,12; cf. Origen, *Cels.* 8.19, linking Eph 2:20 to Isa 54:11–14.
43. Stuhlmacher, "Er Ist Unser Friede," 347, my translation.

Isaiah (LXX)	Ephesians 2
9:6–7a (5–6a) NETS because a child was born for us, a son also given to us, whose sovereignty was upon his shoulder, and he is named Messenger of Great Counsel, for *I will bring peace* (ἐγὼ γὰρ ἄξω εἰρήνην) upon the rulers, *peace* (εἰρήνην) and health to him. His sovereignty is great, and his *peace* (εἰρήνης) has no boundary upon the throne of David and his kingdom 52:7 NETS I am here, like season upon the mountains, like the feet of *one bringing glad tidings* (εὐαγγελιζομένου) of a report of *peace* (εἰρήνης), like *one bringing glad tidings* (εὐαγγελιζόμενος) of good things, because I will make your salvation heard, saying to Sion, "Your God shall reign." 57:18–19 NETS I have seen his ways, and I healed him and comforted him, yes, gave him true comfort—*peace upon peace to those that are far and to those that are near* (εἰρήνην ἐπ' εἰρήνην τοῖς μακρὰν καὶ τοῖς ἐγγὺς οὖσιν). And the Lord said, I will heal them.	2:13–18 But now in Christ Jesus you who once were *far off* (μακρὰν) have been brought *near* (ἐγγὺς) by the blood of Christ. 14 For he is our peace (Αὐτὸς γάρ ἐστιν ἡ εἰρήνη ἡμῶν); in his flesh he has made both groups into one and has broken down the dividing wall, that is, the hostility between us. 15 He has abolished the law with its commandments and ordinances, that he might create in himself one new humanity in place of the two, thus making peace, 16 and might reconcile both groups to God in one body through the cross, thus putting to death that hostility through it. 17 So *he came and proclaimed peace* (εὐηγγελίσατο εἰρήνην) *to you who were far off* (τοῖς μακρὰν) and *peace to those who were near* (εἰρήνην τοῖς ἐγγύς); 18 for through him both of us have access in one Spirit to the Father.

Table 4: Parallels between Isaiah 9, 52, 57 and Ephesians 2

Similarly to Stuhlmacher, Muddiman sees the repeated use of εἰρήνη (occurring at 2:14, 15 and 17, twice) as an example of the Second Temple Jewish exegetical principle of *gězērā šāwā*, whereby a number of passages containing the same hook word are brought together to illuminate a concept.[44] The linguistic overlap is strongest between Eph 2:17 and Isa 57:19 where the terms *near*, *far*, and *peace* are all common; while in Eph 2:13 *the far* (μακρὰν) and *the near* (ἐγγύς) are mentioned. In Eph 2:17 the term εὐηγγελίσατο (*proclaim the good news*) strengthens the link with Isa 52:7 where two participle forms of εὐαγγελίζω are present (εὐαγγελιζομένου ἀκοὴν εἰρήνης, ὡς εὐαγγελιζόμενος ἀγαθά). This level of linguistic similarity, especially for Isa 57:19, satisfies Hays's first test of *volume*.

---

44. Muddiman, *Ephesians*, 137.

There is *thematic coherence* since the Isaiah texts (or their immediate contexts) speak of judgment on sin, idolatry, or unfaithfulness (Isa 9:8–21; 57:1–13; Eph 2:1–5, 12–13); restoration of an exiled or oppressed community (that is, a new exodus, Isa 9:2–7; 52:1–12; 57:15–19; Eph 2:13–19); and God present among his people (Isa 57:15; Eph 2:22).

Hays's test of *historical plausibility* concerns the likelihood that the texts would be employed in the proposed manner. A messianic interpretation for Isa 9 emerged early in Christian tradition,[45] and so it is entirely reasonable for Eph 2:14 to adopt a messianic interpretation of Isaiah texts (not only 9:5–6, but Isaiah associates peace with a messianic figure or new age in 52:7; 54:10, 13; 57:19; 60:17; 66:12). Hays's tests of *availability* and *recurrence* are also readily demonstrated. These Isaiah texts were certainly known to Paul and the early Christian movement. Isaiah 9:2 is likely used in 2 Cor 4:6. Isaiah 52:5 is cited at Rom 2:24. Isaiah 52:7 is cited at Rom 10:15.[46] Isaiah 57:19 is alluded to at Acts 2:39.[47] A link with Isa 52:7 in Eph 2 is strengthened by the allusion to Isa 52:7 at Eph 6:15.

In the light of the *verbal similarities*, the *availability* of the texts and *recurrent usage* in other Pauline letters, and the *thematic coherence*, it is fair to conclude that these three texts from Isaiah constituted precursor texts to Eph 2:13–17.

5.4.2.1 Old Testament Context

Isaiah 8–9 portrays the unfaithful people of God living under the threat of war and invasion by gentile nations. Against this threat of war, the messiah will usher in peace (9:2–7), but the majority will continue in rebellion and ungodliness (8:19–22; 9:8–10:4). Isaiah 52 announces the end of exile and a return of God's people to Jerusalem. God himself (ἐγώ εἰμι αὐτός, emphatic 52:6 LXX) is present and speaks as the feet of one who brings the good news of peace and of good things (52:7 LXX). Isaiah 57:19 announces healing and comfort to "those far off and to those who are near." The context of the passage includes the promise of gentile incorporation into the covenant (56:2–8); corrupt leadership (56:9–12); polemic against idolatry (57:1–13); and judgment on injustices (58–59).

---

45. E.g. Matt 4:15–16; Luke 1:32–33, 78–79; Justin, *1 Apol.* 35; Irenaeus, *Haer.* 4.33.
46. Hübner, *Vetus Testamentum*, 2:44, 172, 405; Seifrid, "Romans," 661; cf. Isa 52:11 quoted at 2 Cor 6:17; Isa 52:15 is cited at Rom 15:21.
47. Marshall, "Acts," 543.

5.4.2.2 Theological Use of the Old Testament

The messianic hope encountered in Isa 9 is surprising because it arises on the borders between Israel and gentile territory, and so foreshadows the "far off" motif as well as gentile incorporation into the people of God that is central in Eph 2:11–18.

In Isa 52 the redemption of God's people (52:2–3) by God as Divine Warrior (52:10, 12) leads to universal salvation (52:10) and divine self-revelation (52:6). Similarly, in Eph 2, redemption by the blood of Christ (2:13) is the means by which universal salvation is achieved for both Jew and gentile (2:13–17). A hint of warfare is present in 2:16 where the hostility between the two groups has been "put to death" (2:16). Divine revelation is implicit in people gaining access to God (2:18) and becoming his dwelling place (2:22). A number of Second Temple Judaism texts interpreted Isa 52:7 as promising eschatological salvation (e.g., *Lev. Rab.* 9:9 [119]; *Deut. Rab.* 5:15 [117]).[48] However, Second Temple Judaism did not give prominence to gentile inclusion in the awaited salvation.

The major theme of Eph 2:14–22 of gentile incorporation is also prominent in Isa 52. The previous failure of Israel to rightly present God to the nations (Isa 52:4–5) is the negative background against which the good news is set. That news is not just for Israel, but for the nations: "The Lord will reveal his holy arm before all the nations, and all the ends of the earth will see the salvation that is from our God" (Isa 52:10; itself echoing Isa 40:5, 9).

The themes of Isa 57 include an anti-idolatry polemic (57:4–13) which sets the scene before the announcement of an end to God's judgment (57:16–19), which brings healing and peace for God's people (15, 19). The theme of escape from idolatry is present in Eph 2:1–3, and healing is a prominent component of biblical peace (2:14–17). Isaiah 57:14 commands "remove every obstruction from my people's way," which parallels the breaking down of the wall in Eph 2:14–15. More broadly, Moritz notes that a concern for gentile incorporation into God's people is characteristic of Isaiah's theology in chapters 49, 56, and 60.[49]

---

48. Wilk, *Bedeutung des Jesajabuches*, 173–75; see also Strack and Billerbeck, *Kommentar*, 3:282–83.

49. Moritz, *Profound Mystery*, 47.

5.4.2.3 Missional Significance of Allusions to Isaiah 9, 52, and 57 in Ephesians 2

In the light of the link in Eph 2:14 to Isa 9, we can affirm that mission fosters peace between previously estranged groups as a direct outcome of the messiah's reign.[50] Ephesians 2:13–17 evokes the eschatological shalom of the OT.[51] Thielman particularly notes how Isaiah regularly portrays the gentile nations finding peace with God in the eschatological age (Isa 2:2–4; 11:10; 19:24–25; 45:14, 22; 51:4–5; 52:10; 55:5; 56:6–7; 60:11; 66:18–23).[52] This is a fulfillment of the Abrahamic covenant alluded to in Eph 2:12. The anticipated pilgrimage to Zion as the locus of God's presence and salvation leads to the gentiles experiencing God's blessings, acknowledging God, following God's laws/ways, praying, and bringing tribute to Jerusalem. Owens has argued for the passage to be understood as proclaiming the inauguration of a new covenant and new creation, as a fulfillment of Isaiah's new exodus prophecy.[53] Moritz also argues that the eschatological orientation of Isa 56–57 (in which sin has been overcome and gentiles are incorporated into the people of God) accords with the view of the author of Ephesians that Christ has inaugurated the eschaton.[54]

Interpreting Eph 2:11–22 in this way is preferable to the somewhat strained attempts of scholars to link it to Gnostic, Qumran, or rabbinic literature.[55] The history of religions approach adopted by Schlier, Karl Kuhn, and to a lesser extent Lincoln, involves deliberately setting aside the close verbal and thematic links with Isaiah, in pursuit of looser thematic correspondences to texts where there are not clear indicators of availability to the author or original recipients of Ephesians.[56]

Commentators on Ephesians have not fully drawn out the missional significance of Isaianic material in Ephesians. Drawing together the analysis above, a number of important insights emerge. By alluding to passages within Isaiah that evoke the hope of a new exodus and new creation, inaugurated by the messiah, Ephesians taps into the broader canvas of eschatological

---

50. Winger, *Ephesians*, 317, citing Isa 2:2–4; 56:6–8; 57:19; 66:12; Mic 4:1–4; Zech 8:20–23.

51. Schnackenburg, *Ephesians*, 113; Muddiman, *Ephesians*, 125–26; Yoder Neufeld, *Ephesians*, 111–12.

52. Thielman, *Ephesians*, 197.

53. Owens, *As It Was*, 169.

54. Moritz, *Profound Mystery*, 32–34.

55. E.g. Schlier, *Christus*, 20–23; Schlier, *Brief*, 133–34; Kuhn, "Light of Qumran"; Lincoln, "Use of the OT," 27–28, 46; cf. Moore, "Ephesians 2:14–16," 163–68.

56. Barth, *Ephesians 1–3*, 277–78.

renewal portrayed by Isaiah.[57] The most pertinent feature of this renewal for our study is the ingathering of the nations to Zion, and the consequent universal scope of God's salvation. The key verses that stand in close proximity to the precursor texts studied above are Isa 52:10

> The Lord has bared his holy arm
> before the eyes of all the nations;
> and all the ends of the earth shall see
> the salvation of our God.

and Isa 56:6–8.

> And the foreigners who join themselves to the Lord,
> to minister to him, to love the name of the Lord,
> and to be his servants,
> all who keep the sabbath, and do not profane it,
> and hold fast my covenant—
> these I will bring to my holy mountain,
> and make them joyful in my house of prayer;
> their burnt offerings and their sacrifices
> will be accepted on my altar;
> for my house shall be called a house of prayer
> for all peoples.
> Thus says the Lord God,
> who gathers the outcasts of Israel,
> I will gather others to them
> besides those already gathered.

In the light of these verses, the ethnic reconciliation described in Eph 2:14–17 does not stand in isolation from the course of salvation history, but is a prominent indicator that the age of the messiah foreseen by Isaiah has arrived (cf. Isa 2:2–4; 60:1–7). The influx of gentiles who come to be incorporated into the people of God are evidence that God's purposes for renewing the earth and human society are underway. Ethnic diversity within the church is therefore a positive characteristic for the mission of the church, serving as an invitation for those who otherwise experience alienation in their social interactions to experience reconciliation as an expression of God's peacemaking work in the world. More than that, Ephesians portrays

---

57. Owens, *As It Was*, 150, 158–59, 162, 169–70.

the body of Christ as the means by which God's eschatological program of bringing reconciliation and salvation to the nations is achieved. In the OT period, Israel had not lived up to its calling to be a light to the nations (Isa 49:6; 58; cf. Mark 11:17). But now, Christ as the great ingatherer (Eph 1:10), carries out Israel's original calling to be a source of blessing to the nations, bringing reconciliation and incorporation into God's covenantal people (Eph 2:11–20). Believing gentiles, alongside believing Jews, now constitute the eschatological people of God, they are a new humanity "in Christ," and exist as the "body of Christ" to continue Christ's worldwide mission revealing God's salvation to all nations.[58]

While Isaiah has rightly dominated scholarly investigation of the intertextual background to Eph 2:11–22, there are other plausible precursor texts and also a number of themes to consider.

5.4.3 Zechariah 6:12–15

Stirling has argued that Zech 6:12–15 "provides an OT precedent for the 'far off' coming near, it shares 'peace' language with the Isaiah texts and Ephesians, and it centers on the concept of a Davidic priest/king who builds the temple of God."[59] Zechariah 6:13b, 15a (LXX) states καὶ βουλὴ εἰρηνικὴ ἔσται ἀνὰ μέσον ἀμφοτέρων . . . καὶ οἱ μακρὰν ἀπ' αὐτῶν ἥξουσιν καὶ οἰκοδομήσουσιν ἐν τῷ οἴκῳ κυρίου, καὶ γνώσεσθε διότι κύριος παντοκράτωρ ἀπέσταλκέν με πρὸς ὑμᾶς, καὶ ἔσται, ἐὰν εἰσακούοντες εἰσακούσητε τῆς φωνῆς κυρίου τοῦ θεοῦ ὑμῶν "there will be a *peaceful* plan between *both* . . . And the ones *far away* from them will come and *build in the house of the Lord*" (LES).

Although there is verbal similarity in the words used for *peace, both, the far,* and *build,* the *thematic alignment* of the two passages is less clear than in the case of Isaiah. Further, the fact that Zech 6 is not clearly alluded to elsewhere in the Pauline corpus calls into question the *availability* of the text for appropriation in Ephesians. The *history of interpretation* of Zech 6 in relation to Eph 2 does not establish a strong case for its recognition as a precursor text.[60] Nevertheless, Zech 6 should not be entirely discarded, since if it is taken together with Zech 2:11 and 8:22, it confirms the prophetic vision of an ingathering of gentiles as a mark of the messianic age (there is a strong connection to Zech 8:16 at Eph 4:25, discussed in §9.4.2 below). The promise of Zech 2:11, "many nations shall

---

58. Goheen, *Light to the Nations*, 173.
59. Stirling, "Transformation and Growth," 83.
60. Cf. Unger, *Zechariah*, 114; Stirling, "Transformation and Growth," citing Thomson, *Chiasmus*, 107.

join themselves to the LORD on that day, and shall be my people; and I will dwell in your midst," also includes the idea present in Eph 2:22 of the multiethnic restored people of God as his dwelling place. In conclusion, while Zech 6:12–15 probably does not reach the threshold for a literary allusion, Zechariah includes a chain of prophetic texts which elaborate the characteristics of the messianic age in which gentiles will be joined to the people of God and a new temple will be built.[61]

5.4.4 2 Chronicles 6:32–33

Larry Kreitzer has suggested that there are sufficient similarities between Eph 2:17–19 and 2 Chr 6:32–33, Solomon's temple dedication speech, to warrant its discussion as an influence on the passage. He notes particularly the words ἀλλότριος (stranger), ἐκ γῆς μακρόθεν (from a far land), and the rare word κατοικητηρίου σου (your dwelling place, which occurs only in Eph 2:22 and Rev 18:2).[62] Hays's tests of *availability* and *history of interpretation* are not satisfied by this possible allusion, and the level of verbal agreement is slender, so Hays's test of *volume* is barely met. Kreitzer himself merely suggests that the verbal and thematic alignment supports his thesis that Eph 2:13–22 presents Jesus Christ, who is "our peace" (2:14), as a new Solomon, (whose name *šᵉlōmōh* bears similarity in Hebrew to peace, *šālôm*). Kreitzer's thesis is more conjecture than proof, but at a broad thematic level, we might affirm that, in the light of the more defensible allusion to 1 Chr 16 in Eph 1:3–14, an echo of the concern for gentile inclusion in Solomon's temple dedication speech in 2 Chr 6 is possible, but by no means certain. (See further discussion at §5.4.7 below on temple theology and mission.)

5.4.5 Peace/Shalom

Peace is a very significant concept in Eph 2:11–22. By allusion to Isa 9:5 (and some would add Mic 5:5),[63] Ephesians evokes the idea that the messianic age will be an age of *shalom* (שָׁלוֹם). While the removal of hostility is explicitly discussed in Eph 2:14–16, the broader concept of *peace* (εἰρήνη) as well-being, wholeness, and eschatological salvation, has also been won for believers by Christ. Barth states, "It is a gift of God affecting the totality of

---

61. Cf. Goheen, *Light to the Nations*, 177.

62. Kreitzer, *Hierapolis*, 126–27.

63. Witherington, *Philemon*, 259; NA28, 593; Hübner, *Vetus Testamentum*, 2:440–41.

psychic, physical, personal, familial, economic, and political dimensions of man's life."[64] As a missional concept it powerfully captures the broad scope of salvation that God wishes for the world: a comprehensive response to the impotence, death, immorality, alienation, and hopelessness of human existence apart from Christ (1:19; 2:1, 3, 12).[65]

5.4.6 New Creation

As noted above in §§5.2.2, 5.4.1, and 5.4.2 the use of new creation language (καινός and ποιέω/κτίζω) in Eph 2:10, 15 echoes prophetic texts that associate social and environmental renewal with the eschaton. Muddiman cites Isa 56–66 and 2 Bar 73–74 as relevant background, while Thielman also mentions the link to Ps 8:6 in Eph 1:22.[66] In the Pauline corpus, Gal 6:15 and particularly 2 Cor 5:17 confirm the eschatological interpretation: "So if anyone is in Christ, there is a new creation (καινὴ κτίσις): everything old has passed away; see, everything has become new!" Moyer Hubbard's published thesis examined new creation in Paul and found that the concept incorporates death to life symbolism, new birth, and pneumatology, concepts which are all present in Eph 2 (2:5, 18, 22).[67] Owens has also argued that in Eph 2:11–16,

> the author is implicitly appealing to Scripture's grand story of redemption by directly correlating the fulfillment of the Abrahamic covenant with the inauguration of the new covenant and new creation.[68]

Moreover, Owens argues that the temple imagery in Eph 2:19–22 suggests the inauguration of the vision of a "new heavens and new earth" in Isa 65–66. New creation is therefore not merely anthropological, but cosmological and ecclesiological.[69]

The missional people of God are those who have graciously been given new life, animated by the Spirit, as participants in and heralds of a new society and new creation, in which the death, alienation, and hostility of the old creation has been decisively broken.

---

64. Barth, *Ephesians 1–3*, 74; Von Rad, "εἰρήνη," 402–6.
65. Cf. Gorman, *Becoming the Gospel*, 189–93.
66. Muddiman, *Ephesians*, 133; Thielman, "Ephesians," 814.
67. Hubbard, *New Creation*, 233–36.
68. Owens, *As It Was*, 169.
69. Owens, *As It Was*, 170.

5.4.7 Temple

The temple metaphor of Eph 2:21–22 is a rich source of missional material. Through the background biblical theology, it conveys ideas of access, worship, community, growth, holiness, God's sovereignty, God's glory filling the earth, and God's dwelling place. Despite claims of similarity with the Dead Sea Scrolls, Ephesians' temple theology is quite distinct from that of the Qumran community. Beale's study of temple and mission provides the groundwork for the following discussion, which aims to extend and sharpen his insights.

Christ's sacrificial death (2:16) has provided both Jews and gentiles with "access (προσαγωγή) in one Spirit to the Father" (2:18). A minority of interpreters adopt the political meaning of being granted an audience with a king in the light of classical usage of the noun and the political language of aliens and citizenship is evident in 2:12, 19.[70] The more likely sphere of meaning is the temple cult. Through his shed blood (2:13–14), Christ secures access to God's presence for all believers (2:22).[71] Unhindered access to God's presence indicates that believers enjoy a restoration of the fellowship enjoyed in Eden before the fall, and an anticipation of the heavenly communion with God depicted in Rev 21:3.

Christ's work has not merely enabled access to God by those formerly excluded from participation in temple worship, but 2:18–19 indicates that a new inclusive and unified worshipping community is created. Fee argues that God's action to unify Jews and gentiles "in one Spirit" (v. 18) creates a new entity—a new community which enjoys access to God precisely because of their reconciliation and unity.[72] On this understanding, mission fosters the multiethnicity and inclusivity of the church. Without diversity and inclusion, the body of Christ is incomplete.

The temple metaphor utilizes two architectural terms to illustrate the nature of the worshipping community: συναρμολογέω (joined together, 2:21) and συνοικοδομέω (built together, 2:22). Συναρμολογέω uses the preposition συν as a prefix to emphasize the interconnected nature of relationships and interactions that characterize the Christian community when it is properly united and working together *in Christ* (cf. 4:16).[73] Συνοικοδομέω, *built together*, is unique in the NT and conveys a similar idea: construction from

---

70. BDAG, s.v. προσαγωγή, ῆς, ἡ; Caird, *Paul's Letters*, 60.

71. Arnold, *Ephesians*, 167; Best, *Ephesians*, 274; Barth, *Ephesians 1–3*, 312; Thielman, *Ephesians*, 174; cf. Gupta, "Metaphors in Paul," 169–81.

72. Fee, *Empowering Presence*, 683.

73. Hoehner, *Ephesians*, 409.

disparate parts.⁷⁴ God has acted to unite previously separated and heterogenous people into a new unified, functional entity.

Ephesians 2:21 also employs the term verb αὔξει, which connotes *organic growth* (frequently of plants, e.g. Mark 4:8; less commonly of people, 1 Pet 2:2). It thereby introduces the concept of growth as an ongoing feature of the community of believers. The church as temple (ναός) is continually expanding, as increasing numbers of believers are incorporated into the church.⁷⁵ As Bauckham puts it, biblical mission is a movement from a center to a periphery, and from one to many.⁷⁶ A growing temple reflects God's original pattern in the garden of Eden, which, according to Beale, was a temple dwelling place for humanity and God walking together, designed to progressively fill the earth (Gen 1:27–28; 3:8; Lev 26:12). Humanity's role in the garden temple was to be priest-regents maintaining the purity of the sacred space, but also expanding the garden's borders through cultivation into previously uninhabitable regions.⁷⁷ The end point of this expansion, as portrayed in Rev 21:1–3, 10, 22, is for the true temple, God's glorious presence, to encompass the whole new earth and heaven because of the work of Christ.⁷⁸

The temple in the OT was the physical manifestation of God's holiness and cosmic reign (Exod 15:17–18). In particular, the ark of the covenant, set in the holy of holies is understood to be the locus of God's reign on earth, his footstool (1 Chr 28:2; Ps 99:1–5; Isa 66:1).⁷⁹ The application of this principle in Ephesians shapes the letter. The risen and exalted Christ is sovereign over the whole cosmos (1:22–23), and as his body, believers manifest that sovereignty wherever they are. Believers must also embody holiness (Eph 1:4; 5:26–27; cf. 1 Cor 3:16–17; 1 Pet 2:5, 9). The church as "a holy (ἅγιος) temple in the Lord" (2:21) is therefore the ongoing manifestation of God's holiness and reign in the world. As Beale summarizes:

> They [Abraham's descendants] were to be God's instruments through whom God caused the light of his presence to shine in dark hearts of people in order that they too might become part of the increasing expansion of the temple's sacred space and

---

74. Philo, *Spec.* 1.274.

75. Goheen, *Light to the Nations*, 180, and see more generally his discussion of temple as a missional image for the church at 173–80.

76. Bauckham, *Bible and Mission*, 27, 76–78.

77. Beale, *Temple and Mission*, 81–85, and note "filling the earth/cosmos" as the goal of the church in Eph 1:23.

78. Beale, *Temple and Mission*, 369–70.

79. Beale, *Temple and Mission*, 35–36, 50, 63, 134.

of the kingdom. This is none other than performing the role of "witness" to God throughout the earth.[80]

In Eph 2:22, the author uses the rare word κατοικητήριον *dwelling place* (of God) as a further descriptor for the people as a living temple. It is used only eleven times in the LXX to refer to God's dwelling place, with a cluster of references in 3 Kgdms 8:39, 43, 49, par. 2 Chr 6:30, 33, 39, in which the ark is brought into Solomon's temple, and Solomon prays. Solomon foresees both Jews *and* gentiles praying towards the temple, God's dwelling place (κατοικητήριον), as the earthly focal point of God's name, and being heard with mercy by God from the temple. God answers the foreigner's prayer "so that all the peoples may know of your name and may fear you, just as your people Israel" (v. 43). While this passage lacks sufficient indicators to constitute an allusion, it nevertheless confirms the missional nature of the temple as a witness to God's presence, sovereignty and mercy for all peoples, not just Israel.[81] This function is now continued by the church. The more certain allusion discussed above at §5.4.1, Ezek 37:26–28 is equally explicit that God's sanctuary (ἅγιος) dwelling place (κατασκήνωσις) amongst his people constitutes a witness to God's saving covenant for all nations.

We note in passing claims by Bertil Gärtner and C. Marvin Pate that the Qumran community saw itself as a *replacement* for the Jerusalem temple, and in so doing, constituted a precursor to Christian texts like Eph 2:18–22 which envisaged a community as temple replacement.[82] The texts cited do not explicitly speak of the community as replacing the true temple. Rather they aim at reestablishing holiness and purity in the land in preparation for an eschatological physical temple. Any conception of the Qumran community as the "true temple" was a temporary identification in the period prior to the *eschaton* and emerged as a corollary from the corruption of the Jerusalem temple. God's glory or presence is not said to dwell with the Qumran community in the way that Eph 1–2 depicts God's presence filling believers. Rather, God's glory would return to a new physical temple (11Q19, col. 29.7–10). The concern of the Dead Sea Scrolls is consistently with the regulation of life for the *Yahad*, the Essene community, and there is no discernible vision to incorporate others, especially gentiles, into the chosen community.[83]

---

80. Beale, *Temple and Mission*, 117.

81. Cf. Bauckham, *Bible and Mission*, 38.

82. Gärtner, *Temple and Community*, 16–46, 60–64; Pate, *Communities*, 47, 206, citing 11Q19, col. 45–47; 4QFlor 1:1–10; 4QTestimonia 1:5–8; 1QS 8:5–25.

83. Cf. Regev, "Community as Temple," 624–31 for a recent reappraisal of this issue.

It is apparent from this survey that the temple metaphor in Eph 2:18–22 powerfully encapsulates many of the missional themes in Eph 2: access to God, the creation of a new heterogenous, yet unified worshipping community, and the growing church as a witness to and bearer of God's glory, holiness, and cosmic reign.

5.4.8 Summary

Ephesians 2:11–22 has a particularly dense cluster of OT allusions, echoes, and themes. The dominant precursor text is Ezek 36–37, which speaks of national renewal, cleansing from sin, death to life, reconciliation, and reunification, covenant renewal and the sanctuary (temple) as God's dwelling place among his people. Three texts from Isaiah (9, 52 and 57) are also skillfully woven together and incorporated into the passage through the hook words *near*, *far*, and *peace* to justify the incorporation of gentiles into God's covenant community. Hays readily affirms that "significant writing often mingles the echoes of multiple precursors."[84] We should not begrudge the author of Ephesians the capacity to combine two significant prophetic voices into his elaboration of Christ's saving work and its implications. As noted in the discussion, echoes from Zech 6 and 2 Chr 6 are plausible, but by no means certain. The themes of peace, new creation, and temple are also important motifs in this text, which effectively proclaims the presence of the anticipated messianic age with all its blessings for those in Christ.

5.5 Portrayal of Humanity and the World in Relation to God's Mission

The portrait of humanity in 2:11–22 is dominated by the categories of Jew and gentile, who stand in hostile opposition to each other (vv. 14, 16). Verse 12 commences the dichotomy by adopting the pejorative terminology of "the foreskin/the uncircumcision" and "the circumcision," thereby provoking feelings of division and otherness in both camps.[85] The gentiles were, according to v. 12: (a) without Christ, (b) aliens from the commonwealth of Israel, (c) strangers to the covenants of promise, (d) having no hope, and (e) without God in the world. The second and third labels, strangers and aliens, are repeated at v. 19. Verse 14 speaks of a dividing wall

---

84. Hays, *Conversion of the Imagination*, 15.
85. Best, *Ephesians*, 256; Yee, *Ethnic Reconciliation*, 87; Windsor, *Reading Ephesians*, 122.

(μεσότοιχον) that is demolished by Christ. Verse 15 elaborates the factor that separates Jews from gentiles as τὸν νόμον τῶν ἐντολῶν ἐν δόγμασιν "the law with its commandments and ordinances." Tet-Lim Yee has explored the characterization of gentiles in Eph 2 and concluded that it represents the viewpoint from a Jewish "covenantal ethnocentrism."[86] This viewpoint sought to preserve Jewish ethnic and religious identity as distinct from every other human society through ethnic and religious boundaries. The law was "the embodiment of Jewish particularism, introversion, and group identity, and the occasion for pride in being a select people."[87] Windsor draws on texts like Pss. Sol. 17 to argue that Eph 2:12 represents "a description of the plight of gentiles from the point of view of Jews who viewed gentiles primarily as enemies."[88]

This dismal catalog of disadvantages is the background against which Christ's reconciling death is painted (vv. 14, 16). The key descriptors of what is achieved by Christ's action on the cross are demolition of the dividing wall (v. 14), abolishing the law with its commandments and ordinances (v. 15), creating one new humanity (v. 15), making peace (v. 15), reconciling both groups to God (v. 16), and opening up access to God (v. 18). These actions, using a variety of images, center on reconciliation. Thus, the state of humanity prior to God's intervention was alienation from each other and from God. The effect of God's mission is to create the basis for peace and reconciliation in the social, racial, and spiritual spheres of human existence for all of humanity, not just Israel.[89] However, it goes too far to suggest as F. C. Baur did, that Ephesians presents Christianity as "a unity standing above the antitheses of Jew and Gentile."[90] Yee argues that God's mission is to deconstruct Jewish exclusivism and ethnocentric attitudes, not deconstruct ethnicity or the entity Israel.[91] More recently, Windsor has argued that the abolition of the law in 2:15 should not be taken to extremes. The OT law was still valid as the source of the gospel and eschatological promises, but invalid when *decrees* (δόγμα) drawn from the law fostered enmity or hostility between Jews and gentiles.[92]

Each verse and phrase in Eph 2:12–18 has been debated, with a variety of possible interpretations offered for the meaning of the *dividing wall*,

---

86. Yee, *Ethnic Reconciliation*, 71–72.
87. Bosch, *Transforming Mission*, 157.
88. Windsor, *Reading Ephesians*, 126.
89. Cf. Bosch, *Transforming Mission*, 172.
90. Rader, *Church and Racial Hostility*, 171–72.
91. Yee, *Ethnic Reconciliation*, 216–18.
92. Windsor, *Reading Ephesians*, 134–40.

abolish, the law, its *commandments and ordinances,* and *hostility.* Within the scope of this study, it is not possible to review all the positions. What is widely agreed is that Christ's death overcomes the hostility between Jew and gentile and creates the basis for a new unity and a new expression of humanity in which there is no barrier to gentile enjoyment of all God's covenant blessings previously focused on national/ethnic Israel.[93] God's mission for humanity is conceived in Eph 2 not simply as a reform movement within Judaism, or as an opening up of Judaism to gentiles by removing ethnic or religious boundary markers; rather, God's mission is to create a new humanity (v. 15).[94] The new humanity is characterized by being at peace (v. 15), having access to God (v. 18), sharing a common citizenship and membership in the household of God (v. 19), realizing a unity and interconnectedness in Christ (v. 21), so that it constitutes a dwelling place for God (v. 22).

5.6 Evidence of a Missional Context in the Problems, Crises or Issues Addressed

An immediately apparent concern of this passage is Jewish-gentile relations. This has led a number of commentators to propose that Ephesians was confronting conflict between these two groups within the church communities addressed.[95] However, this probably overstresses the issue. Elsewhere in the letter there is no indication of Judaizers troubling the church (as prompted Galatians, e.g. Gal 3:1–5, 5:4), nor is a problem of gentile arrogance towards Jewish believers discernible (as is reflected in Romans, e.g. Rom 11:17–24).[96] Schnackenburg provides a measured assessment, when he says, "the most we can say is that there were tensions between Christians from different backgrounds in the then predominantly Gentile-Christian congregations."[97] Lincoln proposes the following setting:

> predominantly Gentile churches in Asia Minor toward the end of the first century, when Jewish Christian/Gentile Christian struggles were past and when there was a diminishing awareness of the Church's roots and therefore a deficient sense of their identity on the part of Gentile Christians . . . [The author wanted his audience] to remember their own history in terms of the

93. Barth, *Ephesians 1–3*, 310; Yee, *Ethnic Reconciliation*, 216–17; Campbell, "Unity and Diversity," 18.
94. Cf. Lincoln, *Ephesians*, 163.
95. Fischer, *Tendenz und Absicht*, 86–88; Arnold, *Ephesians*, 174–76.
96. Contra Martin, *Reconciliation*, 167.
97. Schnackenburg, *Ephesians*, 119.

history of salvation, not in order to dwell on their old identity in distinction from Israel or on any continuing distinction from Jewish Christians, but in order to appreciate their new identity as part of the one new humanity.[98]

According to Lincoln's reconstruction, the missional context is therefore not an acute conflict or crisis, but an inadequately developed understanding of Christian identity. This position cannot be faulted for what it says, but perhaps fails to connect theological growth with concrete social issues. Ben Witherington goes a step further by noting that the letter's recipients, by being reminded of their former dire plight and the benefits of their new situation, are being primed for the ethical injunctions that will follow in subsequent chapters.[99] In sociological terms, one function of this passage is to legitimate the new identity of gentile believers in the face of hostility from their communities.[100]

This passage stresses through a variety of metaphors (political, architectural, family) that Christ's work has created a new community, and that newly reconciled community is very much an expression of God's intent for humanity. Therefore, all forms of social hostility and disunity are inimical to God's purposes for the world. The broader concern of the letter for unity is reflected in several statements in this passage: "both groups into one" (v. 14), "one new humanity" (v. 15), and "one body through the cross" (v. 16, cf. 4:2–6, 13). So, although the passage frames its theological stance against a portrait of Jewish-gentile hostility, broader manifestations of community dysfunction may well be an issue that prompted the letter.

The social world of Western Asia Minor, as portrayed in Acts, was cosmopolitan, but prone to ethnic and religious hostility (e.g. Acts 19:21–41). Converts to Christian faith from such a background may have carried into their church communities social prejudices that were damaging the internal cohesion and witness of the church (cf. 1 Cor). With this setting in mind, the emphasis on unity in vv. 14–16 is not theoretical or intellectual, but intensely practical. The church would only be the new community, the place in which new humanity flourishes, if it practiced reconciliation between all previously estranged social parties. As Stuhlmacher says:

> The church as temple, building and dwelling place of God is held together by Christ as the keystone, but is itself only in the process of becoming, i.e. a missionary community created by Christ, aimed at enlargement and probation [a period of growth

---

98. Lincoln, *Ephesians*, 164–65; see also Martin, *Reconciliation*, 165–66.
99. Witherington, *Philemon*, 263.
100. Tidball, "Social Setting," 890.

and testing], the basis and everyday reality of which is called reconciliation and peace (cf. 4:1ff; 6:15).[101]

One further element in the missional context of Eph 2:11–22 should be noted. Although the intertextual analysis above clearly shows that the temple imagery of the passage alludes to OT prophetic hopes of the eschatological temple, that does not rule out the recipients hearing temple language in the light of notable temples in their contemporary context. Ephesus was the location for the temple of Artemis, one of the wonders of the ancient world. By stressing that believers are the dwelling place of God, the author is disputing the cult of Artemis's claims that the temple was the foundation for the city and region's fame and security (as vividly reflected in the words of Demetrius the silversmith, Acts 19:26–27).

In the light of the emphasis in Eph 2 on new community identity as a living temple, it seems entirely reasonable to posit the city and surrounds of Ephesus as the location for some of the letter's original recipients. The passage then helps to reorient its first readers away from their former identities, as shaped by the Artemis cult and the presence of the temple, and to consolidate their commitment to Christ.

5.7 The Character and Mission of God's People

Words deriving from the stem οἶκος abound in this section,[102] but particularly significant is οἰκεῖοι, *members of the household* (v. 19). Roman households provided members with security and identity, a sense of belonging that went beyond political status to encompass financial support, influence, and advice.[103] Gehring argues that the household language in Ephesians is not merely metaphorical, but reflects the self-conception of the early believers that their communal arrangements were those of an οἶκος (cf. Eph 5:21— 6:9).[104] Membership in the "household of God" entailed a particular social existence, where the believers' relationship to God in Christ gave them the privileges of covenant membership, namely access to God, cleansing from sin, shalom (wholeness and peace), a new birth, and ongoing life of holiness

---

101. Stuhlmacher, "Er Ist Unser Friede," 353, my translation.

102. See v. 19, πάροικοι (*aliens, outsiders*), οἰκεῖοι (*members of the household*), v. 20, ἐποικοδομηθέντες (*built on*), v. 21, οἰκοδομή (*building*), v. 22, συνοικοδομεῖσθε (*built together*), and κατοικητήριον (*dwelling place*).

103. Towner, "Households," 417–19. Cf. Seneca *Ben.* 1, 2.4 cited in Gardner, *Roman Household*, 171.

104. Gehring, *House Church*, 261.

empowered by God's Spirit. Complementing these privileges are the communal responsibilities so prominent in Eph 4–6.

Eph 2:18 has become a key text for a number of missiologists. Andrew Walls particularly refers to "the Ephesians Moment" as "the social coming together of people of two cultures to experience Christ."[105] Historically, this occurred during the first century as Jewish and gentile believers experienced unity in Christ; but then a monocultural predominantly gentile Christianity became the norm. For Walls, another significant moment in contemporary church history has arisen as Western Christendom has declined and African, Asian, and Latin American Christianity has grown. Walls challenges the global church to recognize that in this new context the church has an opportunity to become the "fullness of God" (Eph 1:23). In order to seize this moment, Western Christianity has to surrender a desire to protect its presumed status as defenders of *standard* Christian culture and theology, while also not allowing a postmodern pluralism of separateness to become the new norm. Fullness will be achieved when the global diversity of the contemporary church drives the theologizing and contextualizing of Christianity in the twenty-first century.[106]

Tennent also sees particular potential in Eph 2:18 as it highlights the missiological importance of creating opportunities for access to God in Christ by people groups who are "far off" from Christian witness in the contemporary world. For Tennent there is a Trinitarian theological imperative in the incarnation, which created access for gentiles "to the good news of God's redemption in Jesus Christ."[107] Similarly, C. J. H. Wright sees the "near" and "far" language of Eph 2 as supportive of the dual directions of mission: "the gospel goes out to the nations (centrifugal) [and] the nations are gathered in to Christ (centripetal)."[108] This image is a better reflection of the church acting in mission than the classic concept of simply being *sent*, which sometimes fostered a colonialist mentality of superiority in the senders, and a slowness to recognize the Spirit's work in gatherings of Christ-followers that looked culturally different to the senders.

N. T. Wright sees the temple metaphor as an important element in the symbolic reality that defined the church as missional. Believing communities were "the advance signs of that time when the whole world would

---

105. Walls, *Cross-Cultural Process*, 78.

106. Walls, *Cross-Cultural Process*, 79–81; cf. Katongole, "Ephesian Moment," 183–200, who sees believers from diverse backgrounds and settings coming together in pilgrimage and table fellowship as examples of the kind of contemporary mission practice envisaged by Walls.

107. Tennent, *Invitation*, 355.

108. Wright, *Mission of God*, 524.

be filled with the divine glory."[109] As the church experiences and promotes justice, peace, and joy, it demonstrates that the prophetic hopes associated with God's future return in glory to his temple are now coming to pass and history is edging closer to the day in which the whole earth will be filled with the knowledge and glory of God.[110]

5.8 Conclusion

Ephesians 2:11–22 contains a dense concentration of missional material. It proclaims a number of potent missional ideas: (a) the Christian community is *inclusive*, it incorporates persons previously excluded from membership in God's people (v. 19); (b) the Christian community is intended to *grow* (v. 21), that is, to increase in number and in geographic distribution; (c) the community and its members are to be *holy* (v. 21), that is, ethically set apart for God's use, in distinction to their pagan lives prior to incorporation into the people of God; (d) the community is to be *unified*, former enemies are reconciled, "joined together" (v. 21) and "build together" (v. 22) into a new corporate entity; and (e) the community is to be a *dwelling place* for God (v. 22), that is, to be the locus of God's presence in the world and the witness to God's saving purposes for all humanity. This mission is thoroughly Christocentric: Christ's death brings reconciliation, Christ is peace personified, and Christ is the orienting foundation for the temple community being built *in him*. The dense concentration of intertextual links in Eph 2:11–22 emphasizes the point that God's purposes are consistent with the prophetic hopes of a new exodus, new creation, universal witness, and renewed temple seen particularly in Ezekiel and Isaiah. The image of God's temple is a particularly powerful missional theme, as it indicates that the new Christian community is intended to grow, to be holy, to be unified, and a means by which God's presence can progressively expand to fill the whole earth. Our missional reading of Eph 2:11–22 has confirmed the significance of the passage for mission, and has integrated hitherto disparate treatments of its thematic concerns with reconciliation, peace, and growth with its rich scriptural background to produce a more detailed account of mission that breaks down ethnic barriers, both goes out and gathers in, and is visible through the holiness of life of the believing community living in intimate communion with God.

---

109. Wright, *Faithfulness of God*, 437.
110. Wright, *Faithfulness of God*, 437.

6

Ephesians 3:1–13

6.1 Introduction

HAVING OPENED WITH A *berakah* praising God for his manifold blessings to believers in Eph 1:3–14, Eph 2 contrasted the human plight of death and alienation with their new status as a reconciled new humanity in Christ. Now in Eph 3:1–13, the focus moves to Paul's particular role in the *missio Dei* bringing the gospel to the gentiles. The following discussion will explore how the incorporation of gentiles into God's people is a central aspect of the *missio Dei*, how grace and power are key missional characteristics of God, how intertextual links enrich our appreciation of Paul as an agent of God's mission, the missional context of this passage, the church's role in making known God's wisdom, and the characterization of Paul.

6.2 Portrayal of God's Intentions, Actions, and Purposes (the *missio Dei*)

This passage is a theologically rich elaboration of God's purposes to incorporate gentiles into his redeemed people as a witness to the powers that his salvation plan is prevailing. The key elements of the *missio Dei* we will focus on here are: God's salvation historical plan and mission (οἰκονομία), the concept of mystery, God's revelation, and God's creative purposes.

6.2.1 God's Salvation Historical Plan (οἰκονομία)

The incorporation of the gentiles into an inclusive body of God's people was a paramount goal of salvation history. Schnackenburg describes it as "the fulfilment of his plan for salvation."[1] Three συν- compound words in v. 6 (συγκληρονόμα, σύσσωμα, and συμμέτοχα "co-heirs, con-corporate, co-partakers in the promise"[2]) make it emphatically clear that gentiles and Jews together have been reconciled to God, and are now joint members of the household of God, reiterating the central theme of 2:14–22. Gentile and Jewish incorporation into the people of God necessarily involves their incorporation into God's purposes for the world, that is, the *missio Dei*.[3]

The key term indicating God's plan is οἰκονομία. Verse 2 begins "surely you have heard of the commission (οἰκονομία) of God's grace that was given me for you." This thought is continued in v. 9 where Paul's role is to "make everyone see what is the plan (οἰκονομία) of the mystery hidden for ages." For Best, οἰκονομία emphasizes "the (divine) charisma"[4] given to Paul for the sake of the gentiles. The majority of translators and commentators render οἰκονομία as commission (NRSV), administration (NIV), stewardship (ESV), or plan (NRSV, ESV in v. 9), based on the word's root οἶκος denoting household matters.[5] It is likely, however, that here in Eph 3 the word carries a stronger nuance of God's plan of salvation for humanity, *Heilsgeschichte*. BDAG lists Eph 3:9 and Eph 1:10 as examples where οἰκονομία denotes "the *plan of salvation* which God is bringing to reality through Christ, in the fullness of the times."[6] Reumann has surveyed patristic usage and notes that Ignatius, Tertullian, and Origin all can use οἰκονομία to mean God's covenantal arrangements for the salvation of humanity, and that it can be used in preference to διαθήκη.[7] While Reumann makes a valid observation about the connotations of οἰκονομία in the patristic era, his data cannot support reading a covenantal nuance into the NT occurrences of the word.

1. Schnackenburg, *Ephesians*, 134; cf. Yee, *Ethnic Reconciliation*, 126; Eph 4:3–6.

2. Barth, *Ephesians 1–3*, 337.

3. Cf. Gorman, *Becoming the Gospel*, 33–34 where *syn-* vocabulary in Rom 8 similarly conveys the idea that believers' participation with Christ in suffering and glory incorporates them into his mission.

4. Best, *Ephesians*, 299.

5. Hoehner, *Ephesians*, 422; Lincoln, *Ephesians*, 173–74; Thielman, *Ephesians*, 192–93. In v. 2: NRSV *commission*, NASB *stewardship*, NIV and CSB *administration*; in v. 9 NRSV *plan*, NASB, NIV, CSB *administration*.

6. BDAG, s.v. οἰκονομία, ας, ἡ 2.b., 697–98, italics in original; cf. Goetzmann, "House," 255.

7. Reumann, "OIKONOMIA," 282–92 esp. at 283, citing, inter alia, *IEph* 18:2; 20:1; Tertullian, *Marc.* 4.1; 5.4; Origin, *Cels.* 4.8, 9; 5.50.

Van Aarde argues that οἰκονομία should be understood to specifically mean *mission*. He states, "the sense of οἰκονομία in Ephesians 3:2 is the entrusting to Paul of the missionary assignment to the Gentiles."[8] In v. 9 Van Aarde then claims the emphasis shifts to the role of the church in God's mission, bearing witness to "the plan [οἰκονομία] of the mystery hidden for ages in God." It is consistent with the context of Ephesians to understand the plan and commission in vv. 2, 9 as connoting the broader mission of God which Paul is serving. However, the emphasis in v. 9 remains with Paul as the pioneering agent of mission, and as we will explore in §6.6, below, the church participates *derivatively* in that mission. Van Aarde's claims for v. 9 go too far.

6.2.2 The Mystery

The μυστήριον *mystery* entrusted to Paul is mentioned three times in this passage (3:3, 4, 9). A variety of interpretations of mystery exist in the scholarly literature. We will examine the views of G. K. Beale and Benjamin Gladd, Caragounis, and Steve Baugh.

Beale and Gladd argue that the key idea here is that the Christ is true, end-time Israel, and that the mystery is that gentiles could become part of true Israel:

> The revealed mystery is that Gentiles can become true Israel only by identifying by faith with Christ, the true Israel, and not having to identify with the nationalistic marks of an Israelite of the old epoch (whether that be circumcision, Sabbath laws, dietary laws, etc.). Christ's identity as true Israel is the key to the mystery: Gentiles identify with him, not Israel's law, to become true Israelites.[9]

While this interpretation is plausible, there is nothing in Eph 3 that indicates the abrogation of the nationalistic identity markers is the key aspect of the mystery. In Eph 2:14–15 one of the interpretive possibilities for the breaking down of the wall between Jews and gentiles is the abrogation of Israel's nationalistic boundary markers, but only circumcision is explicitly mentioned (2:11). Sabbath and dietary laws are not mentioned explicitly, and a comprehensive view that sees the barrier as comprising cultic, historical, social, ethnic, and geographic elements is more likely.[10] Therefore, Beale and

---

8. Van Aarde, "Οἰκονομία for Missions," 6.
9. Beale and Gladd, *Now Revealed*, 166.
10. Barth, *Ephesians 1–3*, 282; Muddiman, *Ephesians*, 128.

Gladd's explanation of the mystery appears to be an overreading of the text. The mystery involves at least the incorporation of gentiles into the people of God, but not necessarily as Beale and Gladd construe it.

A second contested issue relating to mystery is the degree to which God's salvation plans were unknown prior to the NT era. The mystery of Christ (v. 4) which has been revealed to Paul was "not made known to former generations" (v. 5). This idea is also reflected in Rom 16:25 and Col 1:26. Some commentators including Caragounis suggest that the contrast between what was not previously known and the now-revealed mystery is one of degree.[11] The OT prophets had incomplete knowledge about God's salvation historical plan. The majority of modern scholars reject this interpretation on the grounds that the conjunction ὡς indicates an absolute, not relative, contrast.[12] While grammatically more defensible, this stance seemingly implies that nothing was discernible about gentile salvation from the OT—a position that seems overly negative in the light of numerous passages in the OT that envisage gentiles coming to receive God's blessings in an eschatological age (e.g. Gen 12:3; Isa 2:2–4; 59:20–21; 66:20; Zech 9:9–10).[13]

The Pauline tradition routinely appeals to texts in Isaiah and Psalms that foresee gentiles included in the scope of God's saving acts.[14] Baugh argues that while one strand of the OT anticipated an eschatological pilgrimage of gentiles, this would be problematic for the author of Ephesians because:

> the Gentiles appear in those places as captives or subject peoples bearing tribute to God, who comes in judgment and for the glory of a revived, conquering Israel (e.g., Gen 49:10; Psa 96; 98; Isa 18:3–7). Yet Paul [in Ephesians] says the Gentiles do not come in as enslaved captives or subjects but as "coheirs" and sharers in the OT covenant promises.[15]

---

11. Caragounis, *Ephesian Mysterion*, 102–3; Edwards, *Galatians*, 139.

12. See Arnold, *Ephesians*, 189, nn. 13, 14 for a list of key commentators supporting each alternative.

13. Fowl, *Ephesians*, 108–9; Grindheim, "OT Prophets," 533.

14. E.g. Rom 1:16–17 alluding to Ps 98:2–3, discussed in Hays, *Echoes of Scripture*, 36–37; Rom 10:15; 15:21, citing Isa 52:7, discussed in Seifrid, "Romans," 661; see also Barth, *Ephesians 1–3*, 333–34; a contrary view is put by Donaldson, *Paul and the Gentiles*, 194–95 who claims that the undisputed Pauline letters do not clearly adopt eschatological pilgrimage texts, but his view is only sustainable by a narrow reading of Rom 15, and not a full survey of the Pauline corpus.

15. Baugh, *Ephesians*, 235, citing Gen 9:27; Ps 86:9; Isa 2:2; 60:3; 66:18–23; Mic 4:1–3 as gentile pilgrimage texts.

In making this claim, Baugh only refers to a selection of gentile pilgrimage passages, neglecting those that are alluded to within Ephesians itself (for example, Eph 2:11–22 alluding to Isa 52, 57, discussed at §5.4.2, above). Eph 3:3 states καθὼς προέγραψα ἐν ὀλίγῳ, "as I wrote above in a few words," making the link between Eph 3 and Eph 2 explicit. Keeping the focus on the immediate context (rather than broader Pauline theology) helps to confirm that the contrast in v. 5 is not about degree of knowledge of God's plan, but simply that in the past it was not known that God would welcome gentiles as *equal members* of his saved people in the eschatological age, by faith in Christ.

Talbert summarizes the meaning of mystery as used in Eph 3 as comprising four elements: "(1) God's will [v. 2], (2) hidden for ages [v. 5], (3) revealed to someone now [vv. 3–5], and (4) associated with Christ and the gospel [vv. 4, 6]."[16] The mystery terminology of Ephesians does not indicate hidden, esoteric truths, as was often the case in mystery religions and as came to be valued in Gnosticism; rather, the mystery designates divine truth now publicly revealed and proclaimed (3:9–10).[17] This usage of mystery is entirely consistent with Pauline usage elsewhere (esp. Rom 16:25–26, where the same three terms are found; and 1 Cor 2:1–10).[18]

6.2.3 Revelation

In v. 3 three words are particularly associated with revelation, ἀποκάλυψις, γνωρίζω, and μυστήριον, "the *mystery made known* to me by *revelation*" (cf. Rom 16:25–27). This indicates that God's purposes in history are to make himself and his plans known. The revelation takes place by the agency of the Holy Spirit (v. 5), which legitimizes Paul as the channel of revelation, and emphasizes once more that God was actively and deliberately communicating his intention to incorporate gentiles into the community of beneficiaries of his promise, the focus of Eph 2.[19]

God's intention is that this gospel of the inclusion of gentiles (v. 6) is widely announced to "everyone" (v. 9), initially through Paul's ministry, then subsequently through the existence and ongoing witness of the multi-ethnic church. The wide dissemination of the gospel among all people then also furthers God's plan that his wisdom be "made known to the rulers and

---

16. Talbert, *Ephesians and Colossians*, 98.

17. Baugh, *Ephesians*, 585–86; cf. Schnabel, *Paul the Missionary*, 147; Caragounis, *Ephesian Mysterion*, 32–34, 118–21.

18. Beale and Gladd, *Now Revealed*, 161; Talbert, *Ephesians and Colossians*, 97–98.

19. Fee, *Empowering Presence*, 691–93; Barth, *Ephesians 1–3*, 354.

authorities in the heavenly places" (v. 10). God's missionary purpose is therefore revelatory: to reveal a benefit (the gospel) to all humanity, and in this process to reveal his wisdom to spiritual powers. Verse 11 emphasizes that God's purpose is an eternal one (that is, it is not merely an incidental, recent, or passing purpose), and that Jesus, as Christ and Lord, is central to God's purposes for the world.

6.2.4 God's Creative Purposes

Timothy Gombis sees the use of creation language in v. 9 (ἐν τῷ θεῷ τῷ τὰ πάντα κτίσαντι "in God who created all things"; cf. 2:10, 15; 4:24) as a polemical contrast with "the powers and authorities who are powerless to create, and whose rule over this present evil age is characterized by destruction, division, and leading humanity astray into idolatry."[20] God's mission (his manifold wisdom, ἡ πολυποίκιλος σοφία τοῦ θεοῦ, v. 10), brings life, reconciliation, peace, and God's presence to earth (2:5, 14–22) in the church, thereby defeating the agenda of the powers that stand opposed to God.[21]

In summary, the *missio Dei*, as announced largely through Paul's gospel proclamation and reflected in Eph 3:1–13, is to incorporate gentiles by faith as equal beneficiaries of his salvation plan, creating a unified and reconciled church, whose existence and growth continues the process of Christ filling the cosmos with his lordship, thereby defeating the darkness, death and destruction that the powers represent.

6.3 Portrayal of God's Person and Character

This passage conveys a number of facets of God's character, pre-eminently his grace, self-disclosure, and power at work in the apostolic mission and gospel proclamation.

Verses 2 and 7 particularly note "the grace of God" (τῆς χάριτος τοῦ θεοῦ) as foundational for Paul's ministry. This genitive is best understood as an objective genitive, "the grace of God," indicating specifically here the grace Paul experiences by being appointed to a ministry of proclaiming salvation (cf. Eph 2:8; Col 1:5–6; 2 Cor 6:1).[22] In combination with δίδωμι, grace often signifies Paul's specific role in communicating the gospel and its implications to the gentiles (e.g. Rom 15:15; 1 Cor 3:10; Gal 2:9) as it clearly

---

20. Gombis, "Ephesians 3:2–13," 321.
21. Gombis, "Ephesians 3:2–13," 322; cf. Gnilka, "Paulusbild," 189.
22. Caragounis, *Ephesian Mysterion*, 98.

does in 3:8, "this grace was given to me (ἐδόθη ἡ χάρις αὕτη) to bring to the gentiles the news of the boundless riches of Christ."[23]

As noted above, the passage is replete with vocabulary of revelation and God's self-disclosure. The terms include γνωρίζω "make known" (vv. 3, 5, 10); ἀποκάλυψις/ἀποκαλύπτω revelation/reveal (vv. 3, 5); εὐαγγελίζω "to proclaim the good news" (v. 8); φωτίζω "to bring to light" (v. 9). These variations on the idea of communication and revelation indicate that God's purposes in history are to make himself and his plans known. The revelation takes place by the agency of the Holy Spirit (v. 5), which legitimizes Paul as the channel of revelation.

God's power is particularly exercised in commissioning and enabling Paul to carry out his apostolic mission (v. 7 κατὰ τὴν ἐνέργειαν τῆς δυνάμεως αὐτοῦ) of preaching the riches of Christ among the gentiles (v. 8).

The Spirit is active in revealing God's mystery to apostles and prophets (v. 5). Adai comments that therefore, "This revelation, given 'in the Spirit,' was the starting point of the missionary activities of the apostles and prophets."[24] Adai further adds that the apostles and prophets, by proclaiming the gospel, become emissaries (Abgesandte) or mediators (Vermittler) of the Spirit of God to new believers. Thus, the Spirit of God both initiates the missionary activity of the church and, as God's presence with believers, is a fruit of the missionary proclamation of the gospel.

The insight or understanding Paul refers to in 3:4 is τῷ μυστηρίῳ τοῦ Χριστοῦ "the mystery of Christ." This genitive is interpreted as either an objective genitive, the mystery "about Christ," or a genitive of apposition, the mystery "that is Christ."[25] On either approach, the emphasis is that Christ's person and work are the means by which God's will to save is realized. Verse 11 contains a relative clause ἣν ἐποίησεν ἐν τῷ Χριστῷ Ἰησοῦ τῷ κυρίῳ ἡμῶν, elaborating God's eternal purpose "which [God] achieved in Christ Jesus our Lord." Christ is thus specified as the focal point and means by which God's eternal salvation purpose was realized. Most modern commentators prefer the meaning of *achieve* rather than *conceive* for ἐποίησεν, based on the following idea that access has been granted and the reference to the church in v. 10, both of which are the outcomes of Christ's ministry.[26] The explanation of Christ's vital role in salvation history is carried into the next verse, where it is stated that in Christ (ἐν ᾧ) believers "have boldness and confident access to God" (v. 12 CSB). Hoehner sees the verb ἐποίησεν in v. 11 as incorporating

---

23. Hoehner, *Ephesians*, 423.
24. Adai, *Heilige Geist*, 277, my translation.
25. Hoehner, *Ephesians*, 436–37.
26. Lincoln, *Ephesians*, 189.

a reference to Christ's *death* as the particular means by which God's plan was accomplished, based on verb form and the context of Eph 2:14–15.[27] While theologically true, the cross is only explicitly mentioned in 2:13–16, and the idea of access to God in v. 12 is related to believers' faith rather than to the death of Christ, so Hoehner's preference lacks support.

While not explicitly Trinitarian, this passage nevertheless communicates the economic Trinity. The role of God in purposing salvation and appointing apostles to proclaim his salvation plan, the role of Christ in achieving salvation for Jews and gentiles and therefore creating the church, together with the role of the Spirit in revealing God's purposes to prophets and apostles encompasses a broad sweep of divine saving action.

6.4 Intertextuality—Literary and Thematic Links to the Wider Biblical Narrative

There are connections in this passage both with NT texts that speak of Paul's imprisonment and commissioning as apostle to the gentiles, as well as with OT themes of revelation, the Isaianic suffering servant, and witness or revelation to the nations (Ps 97:2 [LXX]; Isa 52:10; Dan 2).

Firstly, there are clear biographical linkages in this passage with Paul's imprisonment and calling narratives found in Acts and the Pauline letters. Ephesians 3:1 refers explicitly to Paul as "a prisoner for Christ Jesus (ὁ δέσμιος τοῦ Χριστοῦ ['Ιησοῦ]) for the sake of you Gentiles." The imprisonments of Paul are also referred to in the undisputed letters 2 Cor 6:5; 11:23; Phil 1:7, 13–16; Phlm 1, 9 (where the same combination δέσμιος Χριστοῦ 'Ιησοῦ is found); as well as the disputed letters, Col 1:24; 4:3, 18; 2 Tim 1:8, 16; 2:9. Ephesians does not indicate the location of Paul's imprisonment referenced in Eph 3:1. In his final years, he was imprisoned in Jerusalem, Caesarea, and then Rome (Acts 21–26; 28; cf. 2 Tim 1:16–18).

The significance of his imprisonment for his ministry was that rather than proving the illegitimacy of his mission or message, it only served to increase its audience (Phil 1:13–14; Eph 6:20), and demonstrated the essential continuity of his ministry with that of Christ, who also suffered (Phil 1:29; 2 Cor 13:4). As Hafemann says, "Paul's suffering was the instrument by which he 'publicly portrayed' the crucified Christ 'before [the Galatians'] eyes' (Gal. 3:1)."[28] His sufferings are thus not something to be ashamed of, rather they are a paradoxically glorious manifestation

---

27. Hoehner, *Ephesians*, 463–64.
28. Hafemann, "Because of Weakness," 136.

of God's pattern of salvation and power through weakness (Eph 3:13; cf. 1 Cor 1:19–27; 4:9; 2 Cor 14:1–6).²⁹

The portrayal of Paul as a suffering servant of God both in Eph 3:1–9 and in the wider Pauline corpus creates a thematic linkage firstly with Christ and secondly (in broader biblical perspective) the Isaianic suffering servant (Isa 52:13–53:12).³⁰ Ciampa and Brian Rosner note that especially in Acts' portrayal (esp. Acts 9:15), Paul is:

> the Lord's Isaianic Servant, who, through suffering, trials, and rejection by his own people, testifies to the name of the Lord and his Christ before "kings" (Isa. 49:7). Paul in his own person takes on the prophetic role of Israel—he is the light to the nations, the bringer of salvation.³¹

Thus, the comment in Eph 3:1 that Paul is a prisoner "for the sake of you Gentiles" (ὑπὲρ ὑμῶν τῶν ἐθνῶν) indicates the theological importance of Paul's suffering as a vital part of God's salvation purposes in reaching the nations.

In both Eph 3:2 and 3:7–9 the author alludes to Paul's Damascus Road experience in which he was commissioned to take the gospel to the gentiles (cf. Acts 9:3–16, esp. 15; 22:6–16; 26:12–18; Gal 1:15–17). The commission which Paul bears is therefore inherently concerned with gentile witness.

Hübner sees a link in the combination of *making known* vocabulary in Eph 3:5 (οὐκ ἐγνωρίσθη . . . νῦν ἀπεκαλύφθη "not made known . . . now revealed"), v. 9 (φωτίσαι *to bring to light*), and v. 10 (γνωρισθῇ *be made known*) and *gentiles* in v. 6 (τὰ ἔθνη) and v. 8 (τοῖς ἔθνεσιν) to the wording of Ps 97:2 (LXX), ἐγνώρισεν κύριος τὸ σωτήριον αὐτοῦ, ἐναντίον τῶν ἐθνῶν ἀπεκάλυψεν τὴν δικαιοσύνην αὐτοῦ (the Lord *made known* his salvation, before *the nations he disclosed* his righteousness).³² While Hays's test of *volume* is thereby satisfied, Hays's other tests (especially *availability, recurrence*, and *history of interpretation*) are not met. This suggested intertextual link is not noted in commentaries, though it is compelling since only in Ps 97:2 and Isa 52:10 are nation and revelation language found together. Given Isa 52:10 has already been noted in the discussion above as relevant

---

29. Cf. Ciampa and Rosner, *1 Corinthians*, 11–12; Gombis, "Ephesians 3:2–13," 322.

30. Kruse, "Servant, Service," 870: "there are hints in his writings (Rom 15:21/Is 52:15; Gal 1:15/Is 49:1; Phil 2:16/Is 49:4) that he understood the Isaianic servant's sufferings to have prefigured his own sufferings as well as Christ's." Cf. O'Brien, *Gospel and Mission*, 12.

31. Ciampa and Rosner, *1 Corinthians*, 12.

32. Hübner, *Vetus Testamentum*, 2:444–45.

to Eph 2:17, this strengthens the argument that the author of Ephesians was alluding to Isa 52. The link with Ps 97:2 conveys the idea that has consistently emerged from allusions in Eph 1–2, namely that the reconciliation and new life now enjoyed by the letter's recipients was meant to be a witness to the nations of God's universal plan of salvation. At best this is an echo that reinforces a recurrent theme.

Thielman and Caragounis both see an allusion to the Dan 2 narrative of Nebuchadnezzar's dream in Eph 3:3–13.[33] (Caragounis also notes parallels with Dan 7, discussed further below.) A number of verbal similarities are present in the two texts.

Daniel	Ephesians
2:18 concerning this *mystery* (μυστηρίου)	3:3 the *mystery* (μυστήριον)
2:19 the *mystery* (μυστήριον) of the king was revealed	3:4 my understanding (σύνεσίν) of the *mystery* (μυστηρίῳ)
2:21 giving to the wise wisdom and *understanding* (σύνεσιν) to those with skill	3:4 my *understanding* (σύνεσίν) of the mystery
2:28 but there is a God in heaven who *reveals* (ἀνακαλύπτων) mysteries	3:3 the mystery was made known to me by *revelation* (ἀποκάλυψιν)
	3:5 now revealed (ἀπεκαλύφθη)
2:14 then Daniel responded with counsel and *advice* (γνώμην)	3:4 concerning this, you are able to understand (ἀναγινώσκοντες)
	3:5 not made known (ἐγνωρίσθη)
2:44 this kingdom will not be given to another *people* (ἔθνος)	3:6 to be a *people* (ἔθνη)
	3:8 to proclaim the good news to the *Gentiles* (ἔθνεσιν)
2:37 to you the Lord of heaven has given the authority (ἀρχὴν) and the kingdom and the might and the honor and the glory	3:10 now be made known to the rulers (ἀρχαῖς) and authorities in the heavenly places

---

33. Thielman, "Ephesians," 819; Caragounis, *Ephesian Mysterion*, 123–26.

Daniel	Ephesians
7:12 And he took away their *authority* (ἐξουσίας) from all those around it, and a duration of existence was granted to them, for a time and a season (LES)	3:10 now be made known to the rulers and *authorities* (ἐξουσίαις) in the heavenly places (ἐν τοῖς ἐπουρανίοις)
7:14 *Authority* (ἐξουσία) was granted to him, and all the peoples of the earth according to races, and all honor will be directed to him, and his *authority* (ἐξουσία) is an everlasting *authority* (LES)	
7:27 Then the kingdom and the *authority* (ἐξουσίαν) and the majesty of them, and the *dominion* (ἀρχὴν) of all under the kingdoms of *heaven* (οὐρανὸν), he gave to the holy people of the most high to rule an everlasting kingdom. And all *authority* (ἐξουσίαι) will be placed under him, and they will obey him until the overthrow of the word (LES)	3:10 now be made known to the rulers and authorities in the *heavenly* places (ἐν τοῖς ἐπουρανίοις)

Table 5: Parallels between Daniel 2, 7 and Ephesians 3:3–10

The verbal repetition meets Hays's test of *volume*. Further, Daniel was *available* to Paul (e.g. 2 Thess 2:4; Dan 11:36) and Dan 2:44, 47 is alluded to in 1 Cor 14:25; 15:24, indicating *recurrence* of use.[34] The *thematic coherence* and *plausibility* of an allusion to Dan 2 also seems reasonable. The missional significance of an allusion to Dan 2 is that in Dan 2:29, 44 "God's sovereignty over the course of history"[35] is affirmed by Daniel and then by Nebuchadnezzar, who proclaims, "Truly, your God is God of gods and Lord of kings and a revealer of mysteries, for you have been able to reveal this mystery!" (2:47). This allusion suggests that Paul, like Daniel, is acting as God's chosen means of revealing God's purposes to gentiles.

The linkages to Dan 7 are more complex. Caragounis sees the ἀνακεφαλαιώσασθαι τὰ πάντα ἐν τῷ Χριστῷ "summing up of all things in Christ" (Eph 1:10), as a key concept for the letter. The spiritual potentates (ταῖς ἀρχαῖς καὶ ταῖς ἐξουσίαις "rulers and powers") mentioned in Eph 1:21 and 3:10, are defeated by Christ, just as the power of the beasts is given to the "Son of Man" in Dan 7:12–14. The role of the church is analogous to the "people of the holy ones of the Most High" (Dan 7:27), who exercise

---

34. UBS5, 880; Hübner, *Vetus Testamentum*, 2:290.
35. Thielman, "Ephesians," 819.

a derivative dominion, won by the Son of Man (Christ) over the rulers and powers.[36] In the light of this background, the role of the church in Eph 3:10–12 is to realize that the powers already stand defeated, and that the church's ongoing existence and progressive expansion through mission is in accordance with God's purposes to see the powers fully subjugated under Christ's reign.

Caragounis's proposal, while based on verbal parallels between Dan 2, 7 and Eph 1, 3, is not particularly satisfactory as a christological reading, since so few of the Son of Man attributes in Dan 2 and 7 are explicitly connected with verses mentioning Christ in Ephesians other than Eph 1:10. The imagery of Christ as sovereign in Eph 1:20–23 connects much more closely with Pss 8 and 110. Therefore, we must reject Caragounis's intertextual reading of Ephesians' Christology. Nevertheless, the verbal parallels around ταῖς ἀρχαῖς καὶ ταῖς ἐξουσίαις "rulers and powers" do support reading the divine warfare subtheme within Ephesians in the light of Dan 2 and 7. The most pertinent text to evoke this intertextual link is therefore Eph 6:10–20, rather than Eph 3.

This passage, through intertextual links to Pauline imprisonment and suffering texts, demonstrates the continuity of Paul's ministry with the suffering Christ, and God's pattern of demonstrating his power through weakness. Through allusions to the suffering servant of Isa 52–53 and Ps 97:2 (LXX), Paul is understood to be God's appointed agent to bring light and revelation to the nations, a theme also evident in Damascus Road texts (esp. Acts 9:15) and Dan 2.

6.5 Evidence of a Missional Context in the Problems, Crises or Issues Addressed

This passage seeks to ground the gentile mission in Paul's authority and divine commissioning. Flowing from that foundation, the Pauline churches may continue secure in their assurance that their existence is part of God's plans, even under a new generation of leaders, in a situation where they are a social minority. The passage also addresses their role with regards to the cosmic powers (Eph 3:10).

The passage reflects the Pauline mission to the gentiles, and is framed as a discussion of the validity and power of that mission, despite the imprisonment of Paul noted in 3:1, 13. As noted above, Paul's imprisonment might wrongly be interpreted as "a source of shame that undermines God's

---

36. Caragounis, *Ephesian Mysterion*, 124, 157–61.

purposes."[37] Instead, the author focuses on Paul as an authoritative recipient and promoter of God's salvation historical plan. For scholars who place Ephesians in the post-Pauline period, Martinus de Boer argues "the image of Paul as the suffering apostle who brought the gospel to the world is not only the basis for their own missionary vision and endeavor";[38] it helps them understand their minority status in a largely unbelieving world, and as a distinct group with Jewish heritage but separate from the synagogue and Jewish Christianity.[39] MacDonald, as a representative commentator adopting a post-Pauline provenance for Ephesians, sees this passage "tying the authority of current church leaders to the authority of foundational leaders [as a way of] guaranteeing the survival of the Pauline churches after Paul's disappearance."[40] The passage lays the groundwork for the more explicit discussion of leadership presented in 4:11–16, which is concerned to shape the church for long-term survival through adoption of Pauline teaching.

The context of the letter is a primary audience made up of gentiles who have benefited from the apostolic proclamation of the gospel (v. 1 "you Gentiles"; v. 8 "to proclaim to the Gentiles the incalculable riches of Christ"). These relatively recent newcomers to a faith based in Judaism needed education and ongoing encouragement that the gospel they had believed was of divine origin (vv. 2, 3, 5, 8), was well-founded in God's eternal purposes (v. 11), and provided significant benefits (vv. 6, 8, 12).[41]

The phrase "his holy apostles and prophets" (3:5) has aroused considerable debate. While some scholars have seen it as phraseology that they judge Paul could never have used, the pertinent element for us is that it is used to say something about the revelation of God's saving purposes in the world. In brief, the apostles and prophets have a significant salvation historical role to play in announcing the reconciliation of Jews and gentiles, and their joint inclusion under the new covenant blessings made possible by Christ's death (2:11–18). The adjective ἁγίοις indicates not some process of ecclesiastical honoring of the group, but is a designation indicating that apostles and prophets (of the

---

37. Sherwood, "Paul's Imprisonment," 97.
38. De Boer, "Images of Paul," 369.
39. Perkins, *Ephesians*, 87.
40. MacDonald, *Colossians and Ephesians*, 272.
41. The emphasis on the need for maturity, and growth in understanding of the faith seen especially in the prayers of Eph 1:17–19; 3:18 suggests that there were a substantial number of relatively recent converts to Christ in the original audience; cf. Best, *Ephesians*, 3; Arnold, *Ephesians, Power and Magic*, 123, 167; Dahl, "Gentile, Christians, and Israelites," 38.

new covenant era) are "both special agents of divine disclosure . . . [they] are commissioned by and belong to God."[42]

Verse 10 gives the church a particular role in the cosmic mission of God. The church is designated as a witness to God's wisdom, particularly for the heavenly powers and authorities. As noted above, this does not entail preaching to powers (whether conceived literally as spiritual beings, or in demythologized form as politicians, corporations, and governments).[43] Instead, the church witnesses to the powers as an increasing number of gentiles (formerly living in darkness, under the dominion of evil spiritual powers) receive the benefits of the gospel, and so diminish the segment of humanity under Satan's thrall. Johannes Nissen emphasizes "the church's worshipping and serving presence in the world which unmasks the evil powers and brings light into darkness."[44]

Barth says:

> In Eph 3:10 the church is instructed to participate in that authentic "proclamation of peace" which was commenced and is still continued by Jesus Christ himself (2:17). The church of which Paul speaks is therefore by definition "evangelic and apostolic." Otherwise she would not be the church built and growing "in the Lord . . . into God's temple . . . on the foundation of the apostles and prophets" (2:20–21). In other words, the church is not an end in itself but a functional outpost of God's kingdom.[45]

While Barth's phrase "the church is instructed" is overstatement, the "essence and function"[46] of the church is necessarily "evangelic and apostolic," since the church publicly displays the power of Christ's proclamation of peace to create new life, forgiveness, reconciliation, and unity, and thereby extends God's kingdom on earth.

6.6 Character of the People of God in God's Mission

The church's role in mission comes to prominence in Eph 3:10. This verse represents the third purpose clause that follows Paul's statement that he

---

42. Baugh, *Ephesians*, 232, 233.
43. Cf. Barth, *Ephesians 1–3*, 365.
44. Nissen, *New Testament and Mission*, 136.
45. Barth, *Ephesians 1–3*, 364.
46. Barth, *Ephesians 1–3*, 364.

was made a servant by God's grace (vv. 7–8), and represents the climax of those preceding steps.⁴⁷ By bringing "to the Gentiles the news of the boundless riches of Christ" (v. 8), and by enlightening (φωτίζω *making known*) "the plan of the mystery hidden for ages in God" (v. 9), "the wisdom of God in its rich variety might now be made known to the rulers and authorities in the heavenly places" *through the church* (v. 10). This verse is clearly central to the author's understanding of God's missional intentions for the church and the world.

"Rulers and authorities in the heavenly places" are the audience of God's now-revealed wisdom. This surprises some interpreters since the focus of Paul's gospel proclamation is naturally Jews and gentiles in the regions he traversed around the Mediterranean. The rulers and authorities are not exclusively evil (those opposed to believers in 6:12), but as seems likely in 1:21, the heavenlies comprise both good and evil spiritual entities.⁴⁸

Walter Wink suggests that the church preaches to the powers, but this cannot be supported from the text.⁴⁹ It is the existence and relationships of believers in the church, composed of reconciled and redeemed Jews and gentiles sharing equal status in God's household (2:11–22; 3:6), and unhindered access to God (3:12), that provide a witness to the powers.⁵⁰ Baugh says, "it is in the church's existence as a multicultural and multiethnic body dwelling in unity that the church witnesses to the power of the new creation."⁵¹ The powers which previously held humanity in their thrall through sin and death (2:1–3), have had their captive subjects released from their power (2:6–7), and Christ affirmed as the true Lord of the cosmos and especially the church (1:10, 20–23; cf. 1 Cor 15:24–28; Col 1:13; 2:10–15). Neither Paul nor the church is charged with preaching directly to the powers, since the proclamation of the gospel to Jews and gentiles, and the resultant transfer of individuals from the domain of sin and death to the domain of reconciliation and life, inflicts a continual defeat on those powers opposed to God.

Windsor notes that the preposition used with τῆς ἐκκλησίας *the church* in v. 10 is διά *through*, which can indicate agency. Accordingly, he sees a grammatical basis for the church to have an active role as an agent of

---

47. Hoehner, *Ephesians*, 459.
48. Hoehner, *Ephesians*, 460.
49. Wink, *Naming the Powers*, 89, 95–96.
50. Lincoln, *Ephesians*, 186–87; Minear, "Invisible Powers," 97–98; Arnold, *Ephesians*, 196–97.
51. Baugh, *Ephesians*, 243.

revelation to the cosmos (cf. Eph 4:11–16).[52] Van Aarde goes too far, however, in arguing that "It is through the active proclamation of the gospel and not simply the existence of the church that the manifold wisdom of God is made known."[53] He bases this conclusion on his reading of Eph 3:2, whereby he sees a continuity between God's mission, Paul's mission, and the church's mission. "Paul commits to the church the apostolic mission, the mission he has received from the Lord (Eph 3:2)."[54] He interprets εἰς ὑμᾶς (*for you*, 3:2) in conjunction with διὰ τῆς ἐκκλησίας (*through the church*, 3:10). Van Aarde also links Eph 3:8–10 with Acts 20:24, 30–35 where he claims Paul commits the task of evangelism to the elders of the church in Ephesus; and 1 Cor 9:17–18 where οἰκονομία and εὐαγγελίζω are both connected.[55] Van Aarde's reading of Acts 20 goes beyond the text, since there is not an explicit charge to evangelize, and similarly in 1 Cor 9, Paul is speaking of his own practices, rather than exhorting the Corinthians to evangelize.

A more moderate position than Van Aarde that is better grounded in the text of Ephesians is found in Barth, who sees the church as having "a mediating role" in making known God's wisdom to the powers.[56] He states:

> By the revelation which [Jews and gentiles] receive through the preaching of the gospel they are not only enlightened, saved, and created to be a growing body, rather they are also made into carriers of revelation. As a lighthouse of God (cf. 5:8) they shine brightly among the powers of the world and prove God's goodness to them (2:7; 3:10). In fulfilling this mission they are not left empty. The missionary church is a worshiping church; all its members have free access to God.[57]

The church is missional by virtue of its worship and community life, rather than solely through verbal proclamation. Interpreters like Van Aarde and Windsor who strive to find support in the text for verbal proclamation perhaps fail to recognize the strength and validity of nonverbal forms of witness as expressions of NT mission.

---

52. Windsor, *Reading Ephesians*, 171.
53. Van Aarde, "Οἰκονομία for Missions," 8, n. 40.
54. Van Aarde, "God's Mission," 287.
55. Van Aarde, "God's Mission," 288–89.
56. Barth, *Ephesians 1–3*, 363.
57. Barth, *Ephesians 1–3*, 355.

6.7 Portrayal of Paul and His Involvement in God's Mission

Paul and his ministry to the gentiles also comes to the fore in this passage. The author claims for Paul a central role in God's mission for the world. As a God-appointed servant of the gospel (διάκονος, v. 7), Paul has served a unique function making known God's eternal purposes of granting access to his presence to all people by faith (vv. 8, 11–12).[58] Through the biographical elements of this passage, we gain an insight into the way Paul was motivated by the grace he had received to proclaim the gospel to gentiles, and so be a channel of saving grace to the nations.

God has given a particular role to "holy apostles and prophets" to receive and then announce widely God's mystery (v. 5); God's character is therefore not hidden, but outward-focused and open towards the world. Indeed, the purpose of the mystery now revealed is the cosmic demonstration of God's wisdom, that is, his plan to incorporate Jews and gentiles into one new humanity (2:15–16; 3:6). We will consider the role of apostles and prophets in mission in greater detail in §8.7, below.

Paul's driving motivation for involvement in God's mission as depicted in this passage is his consciousness of God's grace in commissioning him despite his unworthiness (3:2, 7, 8).[59] That this commissioning was God's doing, and not at all Paul's initiative, is emphasized through the use of passive verbs in connection with God's grace to Paul (δοθείσης μοι *given to me*, v. 2; τῆς δοθείσης μοι *given to me*, v. 7; ἐδόθη *given*, v. 8), the use of the word δωρεά (*gift*, v. 7), and by linking Paul's ministry to the gentiles with the working of God's power (κατὰ τὴν ἐνέργειαν τῆς δυνάμεως αὐτοῦ, v. 7).[60]

This passage also situates the apostle Paul as a significant (though not the only) herald commissioned by God to announce this good news. Verse 5 states that the mystery was revealed to holy apostles and prophets (plural), rather than to Paul alone. Verse 8 speaks of the grace given Paul to bring the gospel to the gentiles, but not in such a way as to preclude other believers from also being active in the propagation of the good news. Encouraging an active role for others in gospel proclamation becomes explicit in 4:11–16.

Paul's attitude of unworthiness to participate in God's mission is underscored by the phrase ἐμοὶ τῷ ἐλαχιστοτέρῳ πάντων ἁγίων "to me—the very least of all the saints" (v. 8). But rather than rendering Paul impotent,

---

58. Best, *Ephesians*, 292.

59. O'Brien, *Gospel and Mission*, 14.

60. O'Brien, *Gospel and Mission*, 14–15; Lincoln, *Ephesians*, 182; Gombis, "Ephesians 3:2–13," 317.

his consciousness of his sin (likely stemming from his former persecution of the church, cf. Gal 1:23; Phil 3:6) only enhanced his dedication to the mission he was entrusted with (cf. 6:20), and clarified that God's grace was the "foundation and the center of Paul's personal life, of his missionary work and of the life of the new believers who have been converted and of the churches that have been established."[61]

The primary action of Paul, as apostle to the gentiles, is clearly proclamation of the gospel, which is the means by which the church is created (3:8–10). Two verbs are used, εὐαγγελίσασθαι *to preach the good news* (v. 8) and φωτίσαι *to enlighten/make known* (v. 9), with the second indicating that the church, which is God's new creation called into existence through gospel proclamation, demonstrates the progress and success of God's salvation plan.[62] Senior and Stuhlmueller note that Paul's personal mission of making known God's salvation (Eph 3:8–9) *creates* the church. The church, in turn, continues and extends that mission because their "reconciled life concretizes the nature of God's redemptive work and helps to reveal it to the world."[63]

For Best, if Ephesians is pseudonymous, then 3:2–13 is a reminder to the readers "that Paul sealed his mission with a martyr's death in prison; in this way he will deepen the appeal of what he writes in setting out Paul as the architect of the church of Jews and gentiles."[64] The passage thus underscores the ultimate personal price that Paul paid to establish the church in which gentiles stood equally with Jewish believers. Wright, in developing a missional reading of Jeremiah, also notes that there is a "missional cost to the messenger," comprising physical, emotional, and relational suffering.[65] Paul embodies this model of the suffering prophet (3:13), and exhorts the original recipients to live in self-sacrificial love after Christ's pattern (Eph 5:1–2) as part of their calling. Any discouragement from Paul's imprisonment (which his recipients might have interpreted as a sign that the gospel of which Paul was an ambassador was less powerful than the civil authorities who have forestalled Paul) was unwarranted.[66] The author's rejoinder is that while Paul is a prisoner (3:1), and is suffering (3:13), this is consistent with God's pattern

---

61. Schnabel, *Paul the Missionary*, 146; cf. Best, *Ephesians*, 317, concerning Paul's self-assessment that he was the "very least of all the saints."
62. Gombis, "Ephesians 3:2–13," 320.
63. Senior and Stuhlmueller, *Biblical Foundations*, 205.
64. Best, *Ephesians*, 295.
65. Wright, "Prophet to the Nations," 128–29.
66. Gombis, "Ephesians 3:2–13," 316.

of working through weakness and surprising means to bring about his glory (3:6–8; cf. 1 Cor 1:17–25; 2 Cor 12:5–10).[67]

Best also discusses the scenario where Paul is the author, in which case the mention of his imprisonment indicates that *prisoner* is being used christologically, similarly to Phil 1:12–14 and Phlm 9, where it is for the good of the gospel.[68] "Paul" is motivated by his imprisonment to reassure his recipients that their status in God's plans for the cosmos are secure, despite his apparently defeated circumstances. Imprisonment is not a brake on the spread of the gospel through the apostle (cf. 6:19–20). Similarly, his apparent shame is in fact a source of pride, as he is suffering for the gospel, and therefore is suffering with Christ (cf. Col 1:24).[69]

Barth notes that the description of Paul's ministry as a grace entrusted to him by God is consistent with the "altruistic and missionary essence"[70] that is evident in Eph 3:2, 7, 8 and similar Pauline texts including 1 Tim 1:16 and Eph 2:7. Paul is an exemplar of the theological principle that grace is given in order that it be further dispersed, rather than held for oneself.[71] Grace "calls the former enemy of Christ and the church to fulfil a function among all who were hostile to God and to one another (2:15–16)."[72] This paradigm of grace given in order to serve others becomes more explicit in the discussion of ministry gifts in Eph 4:7–16.

6.8 Conclusion

Ephesians 3:1–13 is rich in missional themes and insights. The mystery of the gospel, as revealed to Paul (with other apostles and prophets) and proclaimed openly by him is that gentiles have been incorporated by faith as equal members of God's covenant people. As a unified and reconciled body, the existence and growth of the church continues the process of Christ filling the cosmos with his lordship, thereby defeating the darkness, death, and destruction that the powers represent. The economic Trinity is reflected in the roles played by God, the Spirit, and Christ. God is revealed to be gracious, ready to reveal his salvation plan for the cosmos; God's Spirit is particularly active in revelation and the proclamation of

---

67. Baugh, *Ephesians*, 212.
68. Best, *Ephesians*, 296.
69. Best, *Ephesians*, 293.
70. Barth, *Ephesians 1–3*, 359.
71. Cf. O'Brien, *Gospel and Mission*, 14.
72. Barth, *Ephesians 1–3*, 359.

the apostles; while Christ is the focal point of the mystery as the means by which salvation is won.

The numerous intertextual links in the passage to Pauline imprisonment and suffering texts, demonstrates the continuity of Paul's ministry with the suffering Christ, and God's pattern of showing his power through weakness. Through allusions to the suffering servant of Isa 52–53 and Psalm 97:2 (LXX), Paul is understood to be God's appointed agent to bring light and revelation to the nations, a theme also evident in Damascus Road texts (esp. Acts 9:15) and Dan 2. The portrait of humanity outside Christ is consistent with Eph 2, in that only through the enlightenment of the gospel will they gain access to the benefits of salvation achieved by Christ.

The missional context reflected in this passage is one in which Christians need reassurance of the divine origin and purposes of their believing community as a fruit of Paul's gentile mission, since they exist as a minority in a religiously hostile environment, and (for some interpreters) are facing the challenge of maintaining stability in the post-Pauline period when charismatic leadership gave way to institutional systems. The portrayal of Paul underlines his motivation to proclaim the gospel, and so create and empower the church, by being a conduit of grace.

7

Ephesians 3:14–21

7.1 Introduction

THE PRAYER OF 3:14–21 resumes the thought begun in 3:1 but interrupted by the autobiographical digression of 3:2–13. It is a prayer arising from the insights of Eph 2 that reconciled Jewish and gentile believers constitute a growing living temple in which God dwells.[1] We will explore how the present passage reveals the *missio Dei*, portrays God, relates to the wider biblical narrative of God's mission in the world, reflects a missional context, and gives insights into the character and mission of God's people in the world. The passage does not address the portrayal of humanity and the world in relation to God's mission, nor does it add to the portrait of Paul's role in mission, except insofar as it demonstrates that apostolic prayer for the formation of believers was part of the manner by which Paul carried out his missionary call.

7.2 Portrayal of God's Intentions, Actions, and Purposes (the *missio Dei*)

This passage refers to God's intention that believers be filled with the fullness of God (v. 19) and an overarching purpose of being glorified in the church and in Christ Jesus (v. 21).

---

1. Foster, "Temple in the Lord," 85–96; discussed in detail in §7.4, below.

The "fullness of God" (τὸ πλήρωμα τοῦ θεοῦ, v. 19), with which believers are to be filled, has been interpreted broadly in four ways.[2] It is interpreted by Best as referring to God's love (vv. 17, 19). Since God's nature is love and "his greatest spiritual gift is love . . . believers are summoned [in Eph 5:1] to imitate God, again in a context of love."[3] To be filled with the fullness of God is, therefore, to be filled with God's love, which will necessarily manifest itself in actions (Eph 4–6). Hoehner, as representative of the second view, refines Best's idea to say that God's fullness is his moral excellence, perfection, and power especially evident in the love between formerly estranged groups: Jews and gentiles. The fullness of God therefore equips the church for its witness to the broader unbelieving community.[4]

Thirdly, Lincoln takes a broader view that God's fullness is "his presence and power, his life and rule."[5] The broader view is preferable to Best's approach, since in 4:11–16 the work of ministry is characterized by love, but encompasses the goal of Christ-like maturity (reaching "the measure of the full stature (πληρώματος) of Christ," 4:13). Similarly, at 5:18 believers are to be filled (πληροῦσθε) with the Spirit, an imperative that functions as the conclusion to a comprehensive ethical renovation and life reorientation (5:1–20). The four instances of πλήρωμα in Ephesians (1:10, 23; 3:19; 4:13) consistently relate fullness to Christ, not to love or moral excellence, which undermines Best's interpretation. A supplementary idea regarding fullness is also evident in Arnold and Barth. They link fullness to the way in which God's glory and presence fill the temple.[6] We will argue below that temple echoes are present in this passage; nevertheless, Lincoln's broad view which is properly Christocentric together with Hoehner's insight that the loving relationships in the community (modeled on Christ and empowered by him, 3:17; 4:20) present a witness to the unbelieving world, are the most convincing approaches.

The second divine intention evident in this passage is that God's glory be manifest in the church and in Christ eternally (v. 21). For Best, God already possesses glory (cf. v. 16), so the verse cannot express a wish or prayer for God's glory to increase, but indicates that believers (as a body) should affirm and praise God for his glory (cf. 1:6, 12, 14).[7] Lincoln states

2. Merkle, *Ephesians*, 108.
3. Best, *Ephesians*, 348.
4. Hoehner, *Ephesians*, 491.
5. Lincoln, *Ephesians*, 214; Arnold, *Ephesians*, 218, also speaks of fullness as the "divine presence and the power of the Spirit" which believers enjoy by virtue of their union with Christ.
6. Arnold, *Ephesians*, 218; Barth, *Ephesians 1–3*, 374.
7. Best, *Ephesians*, 350.

that the church is "the sphere in which God's glory is acknowledged [especially through] the worship and praise of the redeemed community."[8] This recalls 3:10, where the church bears witness to the wisdom of God before the heavenly rulers and authorities. As the church progressively comes to embody the fullness of God, and so reflect his glory, God's mission to the whole cosmos is advanced.

The glory that is envisioned for the church in this passage is, according to Best, Christ's glory, since church and Christ are related as body to head (1:23; 4:15–16), building and cornerstone (2:20), and bride to groom (5:22–32).[9] Lincoln expresses the connection in a more nuanced way, saying:

> the Church's ascription of glory to God is dependent on Christ, both as the mediator of God's activity to humanity in the first place and as the mediator of humanity's response of praise to God.[10]

So God's purposes are to enable his glory to be increasingly manifest in the world through the church and then as the church is strengthened and grows, to receive the praise offered by the church.

7.3 Portrayal of God's Person and Character

This passage portrays God as Father (vv. 14–15), Christ as characterized by love that surpasses knowledge (v. 19), and the Spirit as the means by which God's power is made available to believers (v. 16).

Ephesians has already spoken of God as Father on several occasions (1:2, 3, 17; 2:18; 3:16). Each of these instances expresses an idea about God as Father working in concert with Christ and/or the Spirit, so a Trinitarian element to the usage is by now well established (3:16 mentions the Spirit and 3:17–19 focuses on Christ).[11] Schnackenburg summarizes the importance of this passage for its contribution to our understanding of God:

> Here we observe a certain trinitarian structure . . . a consideration of the Economy of Salvation in which the reality of God is opened up in its effect *on us*. The prayer to the Father in this perspective finds its appropriate culmination in the wish that the Christians may achieve the total fullness of God. The process of inclusion in the communion and life of God which the author

---

8. Lincoln, *Ephesians*, 217.
9. Best, *Ephesians*, 351.
10. Lincoln, *Ephesians*, 217.
11. Cf. Hoehner, *Ephesians*, 482.

expresses in an unusual way as "being filled" takes place when they gain strength in the inner person through the Spirit, allow Christ through faith to live in them, and increasingly come to understand and be penetrated by the love of Christ.[12]

The portrayal of God in this passage is also significant since God's fatherhood is related to the naming of "every family in heaven and on earth" (v. 15). While this prompted Muddiman to speculate that families "in heaven" refer to departed Christians, "the communion of saints,"[13] Thielman sees the idea of naming as offering the interpretive key. God, in naming all created beings (both earthly and heavenly), demonstrates his authority over them by virtue of his role as creator.[14] Thielman's approach is better supported by the intertextual echoes Hübner identifies for this verse, Ps 146:4 (LXX) and Isa 40:26, where God's naming is associated with his role as sovereign creator.[15] Schrenk suggests that "every πατριά on earth" refers to "Israel and the ἔθνη," mentioned explicitly at 3:1, 6, 8.[16] Accordingly, the affirmation of God's sovereignty over the nations and all heavenly beings leads naturally to the prayer for believers to be empowered by the Spirit (v. 16) for their role as bearers of God's fullness in the world (v. 19; cf. 1:20–23; 3:10).

The fatherhood of God, in the context of Trinitarian theology, is a potent concept for mission. Tennent, for example, argues that God as Father can particularly be identified as the source of mission, the initiator of mission, the sender of the Son and through him the church, and most pertinently for Eph 3:15, mission is an expression of God's relational, holy love.[17] The fatherhood of God is evident in the OT, particularly in association with the exodus (e.g. Exod 4:22–23) and the longed-for redemption of a new exodus (e.g. Hos 11:1–11).[18] Mission is an invitation for people from all nations to be reconciled to God through the work of the Son, by the power of the Spirit, and so to be drawn into the relational presence of the triune God. The following verses of Eph 3, which adopt evocative vocabulary to describe the fellowship that the author prays his recipients will enjoy, reinforce the idea that the *missio Dei* is concerned to fill the earth with the blessings of divine love. Verse 17 speaks of Christ dwelling

12. Schnackenburg, *Ephesians*, 152.
13. Muddiman, *Ephesians*, 157.
14. Thielman, *Ephesians*, 228, citing Ps 147:4.
15. Hübner, *Vetus Testamentum*, 2:446.
16. Schrenk, "πατριά," 1018.
17. Tennent, *Invitation*, 75–79; cf. Braaten, "Triune God," 415–27.
18. Ciampa and Rosner, *1 Corinthians*, 59–60, cf. Jub. 1:24–25.

in believers' hearts as they are "rooted and grounded in love," while in vv. 18–19 this love is so immense that it surpasses knowledge.

7.4 Intertextuality—Literary and Thematic Links to the Wider Biblical Narrative

This passage contains thematic and literary echoes of other biblical texts, particularly the ideas of all the families on earth (v. 15), dwelling (v. 17), measurement (v. 18), and fullness (v. 19). There are insufficient factors to warrant regarding the intertextual links as allusions. Rather, they are echoes which would likely only have been detected by a minority amongst the letter's original audience.

Lincoln observes that πατριά is rare in the NT, occurring only in Luke 2:4 and Acts 3:25, where it is found in a quotation of Gen 12:3, Καὶ ἐν τῷ σπέρματί σου [ἐν]ευλογηθήσονται πᾶσαι αἱ πατριαὶ τῆς γῆς, "And in your descendants all the families of the earth shall be blessed."[19] Schrenk notes that the use of πατριά in Acts 3:25 does not reflect the precise form of LXX of Gen 12:3 (which uses φυλαί, tribes), or Gen 18:18; 22:18 (which use ἔθνη, nations). He concludes that Acts and Ephesians are more dependent on liturgical texts such as the Psalter.[20] Notably, πατριά occurs in Ps 95:7 (LXX), which is one of the Psalms incorporated into 1 Chr 16, alluded to in Eph 1:3–14 (1 Chr 6:28 reads δότε τῷ κυρίῳ, πατριαὶ τῶν ἐθνῶν "give to the Lord, families of the nations"). A connection with the Abrahamic promise is appealing for a missional reading of Ephesians. As noted above in §7.3, the prayer asks for believers to be granted the blessings of relationship with God as Father, through the work of Christ and the Spirit, which amounts to a fulfillment of the Abrahamic promise.

In v. 17 the concept of Christ dwelling with believers relates to a number of NT and OT texts. Colossians 1:19 and 2:9 use κατοικέω of the fullness of God dwelling in Christ. A different verb μένω (remain, abide) is used in John 14:17 and 15:4–6 with a similar idea of God/Christ dwelling in believers. In the OT, κατοικέω regularly occurs with God as the subject in the Psalms and Isaiah to speak of God who dwells in heaven, or in Zion (Pss 2:4; 9:12; 21:4; 112:5; 122:1; 134:21; Isa 8:18; 33:5). An echo that scholars have not previously explored is also evident. The verb κατοικέω is found with God as the subject in 3 Kgdms 8:27 (LXX) and 2 Chr 6:18, the parallel accounts of Solomon's temple dedication prayer: εἰ ἀληθῶς κατοικήσει ὁ θεὸς μετὰ ἀνθρώπων ἐπὶ τῆς γῆς, "if God will truly *live* with

---

19. Lincoln, *Ephesians*, 202.
20. Schrenk, "πατριά," 1017.

people on the earth." Taken together with the idea present in the Psalms of Zion as the earthly locus of God's presence (Pss 9:12; 134:21), it is likely that *dwelling* may echo the temple scene of 3 Kgdms 8/2 Chr 6 (discussed above at §5.3.7). This intertextual background reinforces the conclusions drawn in relation to Eph 2:11-22, in §5.4 above, that God's people now corporately receive and reveal to the world God's presence, which in OT times was confined to the physical temple.

Turning to *fullness* (πλήρωμα, 3:19), it was noted above (§7.2) that the term implies more than God's love. It connotes God's "presence and power, his life and rule."[21] Robert Foster sees Eph 2:19-22 as the relevant context for the prayer in 3:14-21, and therefore explores the temple themes evident in 3:15-19. He claims that πλήρωμα (3:19) refers to God's glory that filled the temple at key points in salvation history (Exod 40:34-35; cf. 2 Chr 5:13-14; 7:1-3).[22] Verse 18, then, which mentions "the breadth and length and height and depth" of an unspecified object, might well be interpreted in the light of the temple echoes surrounding it (glory, dwelling, fullness). Commentators have proposed that it refers to the four arms of the cross, a magical formula, a Gnostic idea about a heavenly man, or God's wisdom.[23] All of these suggestions lack support in the text of Ephesians itself, and derive from presuppositions about the milieu of the letter. A sounder approach is to consider intertextual echoes. Muddiman, for example, relates the phrase to the heavenly Jerusalem (Rev 21:16, where πλάτος [width], μῆκος [length], and ὕψος [height] are used).[24] Measurement vocabulary is also concentrated in Ezekiel's vision of the temple, which we have suggested above (§5.4.1) is alluded to in Eph 2, (e.g. Ezek 40:18-21; 41:2-4; 42:15-20). If there is an echo of Ezekiel, then the climactic vision of 43:2-5 when the glory of the Lord returns and fills the temple is very likely behind the prayer of Eph 3:14-19. Foster has argued just this case, concluding that the church of reconciled Jews and gentiles in Christ is the dwelling place of God, filled with God's glory in fulfillment of the prophecy in Ezek 43.[25] The missional significance of the church being filled with God's glory is that it is a foretaste and sign to the whole earth of God's redemptive presence and purposes now at work in the world.

21. Lincoln, *Ephesians*, 214-15; see also Barth, *Ephesians 1-3*, 205; Arnold, *Ephesians*, 118, discussing its use in Eph 1:23.

22. Foster, "Temple in the Lord," 85-96; cf. Best, *Ephesians*, 350-51.

23. Referring to the cross, Schlier, *Brief*, 174; magical formula, Arnold, *Ephesians, Power and Magic*, 90-95; Gnosticism, Gnilka, *Epheserbrief*, 188; Dahl, "Cosmic Dimensions," 365-88.

24. Muddiman, *Ephesians*, 171.

25. Foster, "Temple in the Lord," 89-93.

Pauline doxologies are found at Gal 1:5; Rom 11:36; 16:25-27; 1 Tim 1:17; and 2 Tim 4:18. The doxology here at Eph 3:20-21 differs from other Pauline doxologies in its mention of God's power at work in believers (reiterating the prayer of 3:16). It has some affinity to the doxology at 1 Chr 29:10-11, where three identical ideas are present: *power, glory,* and *forever and ever.* The doxology of 1 Chr 29 is set at the time when freewill offerings for Solomon's planned temple were dedicated by David. This context adds weight to the probable echo of temple imagery in vv. 15-19.

7.5 Evidence of a Missional Context in the Problems, Crises or Issues Addressed

This prayer, which forms the conclusion of the first half of the letter, is a launching pad into the more explicitly ethical paraenesis to follow in chapters 4-6. As such, the themes of being strengthened (power), the indwelling of Christ, the foundation of love and having knowledge, represent the summary needs of the recipients as perceived by the author. These are generic enough that Ephesians (as viewed through this passage) could function as a circular letter, encouraging perseverance against opposition and continued faithfulness to Christ as the core of the recipients' spiritual life. There is insufficient evidence in this passage alone to be more specific about the nature of the opposition, or whether there were specific areas of underdevelopment in their faith life that warranted the prayers for progress.

A few commentators offer suggestions regarding the issues addressed by this passage. Best understands the passage primarily as preparatory for the paraenesis to follow since without the love that is the central request of the prayer, the author's elaboration of morality would be insufficient.[26] Lincoln concludes in the light of 4:14 and 6:10 that the prayer for strengthening indicates "some weakness or vacillation on their part."[27] Lincoln also sees the prayer for love and knowledge as indicative of "an insufficient sense of their identity and security."[28] He further speculates that the prayer for them to be filled up to the fullness of God may be offered in the face of syncretistic notions of reaching the πλήρωμα. There is insufficient evidence of active Gnosticism in Western Asia minor in the first century to support this suggestion.

For N. T. Wright, the prayer for strengthening and for God to dwell in believers' hearts by faith is not "self-indulgent pietism, but for Paul it is

26. Best, *Ephesians*, 335.
27. Lincoln, *Ephesians*, 219.
28. Lincoln, *Ephesians*, 219.

a human transformation which is designed to generate and sustain people who are part of this extraordinary community and who are facing outwards as they are called to those particular good works [which reflect the fullness and love of God at work in them]."[29]

7.6 Portrayal of the Character and Mission of God's People in the World

As noted above (in §§7.2 and 7.4), God's fullness equips the church to give a positive witness to the reconciling power of God's love as Jews and gentiles live and grow towards Christ-like maturity in faith together. Furthermore, the prayer for God's strengthening indicates that God's people will face struggles (unspecified in the immediate context). The mission of God's people, though, is to draw on the strong roots and foundations provided by the indwelling Christ and the empowerment of the Spirit, and to live lives that glorify God. The introduction of the prayer also reminds the recipients that God is a fatherly source and authority over the church (as a family), v. 15. Accordingly, the church's mission in the world is to be agents of God in his paternal desire to see the world redeemed and reconciled to him.

The character of God's people, as equipped by God for this mission, is to be grounded in Christ (especially Christ's love), empowered by the Spirit, knowledgeable of God's glorious power and purposes for the world, and intentional about manifesting God's glory in their reconciled inter-ethnic relationships.

7.7 Conclusion

This passage reveals God's intention that believers be filled with his presence, power, life and rule, and in so doing, God's fullness equips the church for witness. God also intends that his glory be manifest in the world through the church. The Trinitarian tone to the passage is unmistakable: mission is an invitation for people from all nations to be reconciled to God through the work of the Son, by the power of the Spirit, and so to be drawn into God's relational presence. This missional narrative is underpinned by echoes of the Abrahamic promise, the temple dedication narrative of 3 Kgdms 8, narratives and prophecies of the glory of God filling the temple (Exod 40; Ezek 40–43), and Pauline doxologies. No clear missional context is discernible in the passage, other than the need for

---

29. Wright, "Letter to the Ephesians," 17.

stronger identity formation that permeates the whole letter. Finally, the prayer highlights the missional character of God's people when they are grounded in Christ's reconciling love and empowered by the Spirit for their God-glorifying worship and life in the world.

8

Ephesians 4:1–16

8.1 Introduction

CHAPTER 4 BEGINS THE paraenetic section of Ephesians which develops the practical ethical implications of the theological argument propounded in Eph 1–3. In particular the good works prepared by God for believers to walk in (2:10), are here elaborated at length. We will explore how the present passage reveals the *missio Dei* which includes communal transformation and growth, how God is portrayed in strongly Trinitarian terms, how Ps 68 and other texts undergird the teaching of the passage, how humanity is portrayed, the missional context reflected in the passage, and how the character and mission of God's people is portrayed. The passage does not address Paul's role in mission.

8.2 Portrayal of God's Intentions, Actions, and Purposes (the *missio Dei*)

The overarching exhortation in Eph 4:1 "to lead a life [περιπατῆσαι, *to walk*] worthy of the calling to which you have been called" indicates that God's intention in calling people is to bring about a transformation in individual lives and communities, such that they are increasingly aligned to God's will (his "calling"). The construction combining a cognate noun and verb, "calling to which you have been called" (4:1) echoes similar constructions in 1:3, 6, 19, 20, 23; 2:4; 3:19, 20.[1] These phrases intensify the divine action, emphasizing

---

1. Lincoln, *Ephesians*, 234.

God's deliberate plan, motivated by love (cf. 1:4–6), to benefit the recipients of the letter.[2] Lincoln states, "God's sovereign initiative and human responsibility for living appropriately go hand in hand."[3]

The characteristics of this distinctive life to which believers are called are initially elaborated in vv. 2–3, but they are elaborated more fully in the paraenesis extending to Eph 6. Verses 2–3 stress individual attitudes that will foster communal harmony: humility, gentleness, patience, tolerance (attitudes that occur frequently in Pauline moral exhortations, e.g. Gal 5:22–23; Phil 2:3; Col 3:12). The goal is unity (ἑνότης, v. 3); though human effort is directed towards maintaining unity, rather than creating it, since the unity is a result of God's reconciling work (2:14–18). It is a unity "of the Spirit," a genitive of source or origin.[4] That God intends there to be a unified church is consistent with the vision of Eph 1:10 that all things will be gathered up and unified in Christ, since believers collectively constitute Christ's body, which will ultimately fill all things (1:23).

Verses 4–6 then further emphasize God's purpose of creating unity by the sevenfold repetition of the word εἷς, *one*. As believers realize and act consistently with the divine foundation of their one faith (expressed in confession of the oneness of God "one Lord," "one Spirit," "one God and Father," and of baptism as the sole sacrament of entry to God's people), God's goal of fostering unity is realized. Verse 13 returns to the idea of unity (ἑνότης) as the goal of God's work in the church. Maturity is equated with knowledge of Christ as Son of God and incorporation into his fullness.

In both v. 10 and v. 13 Christ's actions (be they descent-ascent or gift-giving) result in fullness: v. 10, ἵνα πληρώσῃ τὰ πάντα, "so that he might fill all things," and v. 13, τοῦ πληρώματος τοῦ Χριστοῦ, "until all of us come . . . to the measure of the full stature of Christ." When considered in the light of 1:22–23, which describes Christ as "the head over all things for the church, which is his body, the fullness of him who fills all in all (τὸ πλήρωμα τοῦ τὰ πάντα ἐν πᾶσιν πληρουμένου)," it is arguable that the church, through its ministers, contributes to the ultimate salvation historical goal of the cosmos being pervasively filled with Christ's presence and rule.[5] Thus, quantitative church *growth* is reasonably implied in vv. 15–16 as the purpose of all that Christ has done in his descent, ascent, and gift-giving. Giving due weight to the filling and fullness vocabulary of vv. 10, 13 means that restricting the goal of Christ's

---

2. Heil, *Ephesians*, 167.
3. Lincoln, *Ephesians*, 235.
4. Hoehner, *Ephesians*, 511–12.
5. Lincoln, *Ephesians*, 248.

actions to *maturity* (the formation of believers into Christlikeness), as Arnold, Best, and Hoehner do, is unsatisfactory.[6]

8.3 Portrayal of God's Person and Character

Ephesians 4:4–6 is a passage widely acknowledged by scholars as significant for its Trinitarian thought. Even those commentators who deny intentional incorporation of Trinitarian thought in Ephesians acknowledge that the mention of one Spirit, one Lord, and one God and Father, lends itself to Trinitarian interpretation. For example, Muddiman notes, "God is transcendent Father ('over all'), the same God in Christ is mediator of salvation ('through all') and in the Spirit indwells believers ('in all')."[7] Hoehner, who sees the author as consciously expressing Trinitarian ideas, states "the Triune God is the center and model for unity."[8] The portrayal of God in this Trinitarian manner is consistent with 1:3–14 and 2:11–22, where God's actions in salvation history and the achievement of reconciliation through Christ's death result in the present Spirit-empowered life of believers. The implications for mission are that ecclesial unity presents a witness to the unbelieving world and the yet-to-be-unified cosmos that God's triune character is the ultimate truth that will be realized in the eschaton.

Verses 7–16 are centered on the person of Christ who equips his gifted saints for the work of ministry, for building up the body of Christ, and for thorough-going maturity.[9] The path of Christ in salvation history is invoked through vocabulary of ascension, capturing captivity, descent, and headship (Eph 4:8–15).

Ascension (ἀναβαίνω) is prominent in vv. 8, 9, 10. The first participle form (ἀναβὰς, v. 8) indicates that Jesus ascends to the heights (ὕψος), a position of authority. It is this position of victorious authority that authorizes Christ to become divine gift-giver. The second occurrence in v. 9 is incidental, simply introducing the midrashic discussion of descent. The third occurrence in v. 10 uses a participle form which clarifies the initial reference in v. 8. Christ has ascended "(far) above all the heavens." In the light of similar terminology in 1:20–21, "far above every rule and authority and power and dominion," what is being emphasized is that Christ occupies the position of ultimate

---

6. Arnold, *Ephesians*, 265–66; Best, *Ephesians*, 399–401; Hoehner, *Ephesians*, 556–59.
7. Muddiman, *Ephesians*, 186; cf. Lincoln, *Ephesians*, 266.
8. Hoehner, *Ephesians*, 520–21; Barth, *Ephesians 4–6*, 466–67.
9. Hoehner, *Ephesians*, 547–49.

authority.[10] The purpose of Christ's ascension is filling, "that he might fill all things" (v. 10), which many commentators agree is a reference to Eph 1:23.[11] In the light of that link, Christ's ascension is the proof that he has God's full authority over the entire cosmos, not just the church, and that as Christ gifts particular persons to the church, they function as agents of the *missio Dei* to extend his ruling presence throughout the world.

A second idea in v. 8 is ἠχμαλώτευσεν αἰχμαλωσίαν, "he led captive a host of captives" (NASB). In the intertext, Ps 68, the captives are the Canaanites defeated as God leads his people into the promised land. While the church fathers tended to identify the captives with the freed souls of people caught by Satan, the close relationship of this passage with Eph 1:20–23 (established on the basis of ascension imagery) would suggest the captives are the spiritual powers and principalities defeated by Christ (cf. Col 1:24–25).[12] This second view makes better sense of the Divine Warrior theme that pervades this passage.[13]

The descent of Christ mentioned in v. 9 does not refer to a descent into hell (cf. 1 Pet 3:19) since in Ephesians the powers are active in the heavens (2:2; 6:12), not in a lower region.[14] Equally unlikely is a reference to Pentecost and the descent of the Spirit giving spiritual gifts to the church, since the author of Ephesians readily distinguishes the roles of Christ and the Spirit (4:3–6), and here Christ's ascent and descent is particularly emphasized, not the Spirit's action.[15] The most likely meaning of the descent is simply the incarnation (cf. Phil 2:7–8), since the earth (τῆς γῆς) may be taken as a genitive of apposition, and thus Christ is said to descend "to the lower regions, that is, to the earth."[16] The lower regions may be an allusion to Christ's tomb, which has the impact of upholding the death of Christ as the key soteriological moment when Christ brings about reconciliation (cf. 1:7; 2:13; 5:2, 25).[17] The ascent, descent,

---

10. Hoehner, *Ephesians*, 537.

11. E.g. Best, *Ephesians*, 387–88; Barth, *Ephesians 4–6*, 434.

12. Best, *Ephesians*, 382; e.g. Jerome, *Comm. Eph.* 2.4.8, cited in Edwards, *Galatians*, 154–55.

13. Arnold, *Ephesians, Power and Magic*, 56–57; Gombis, "Cosmic Lordship," 375; Schnackenburg, *Ephesians*, 179; Barth, *Ephesians 4–6*, 432.

14. Barth, *Ephesians 4–6*, 433–34; contra Arnold, *Ephesians*, 254; Irenaeus, Origen and Tertullian as cited in Best, *Ephesians*, 383.

15. Hoehner, *Ephesians*, 531–35; contra Caird, *Paul's Letters*, 74–75; Harris, *Descent of Christ*, 143–97.

16. E.g. Barth, *Ephesians 4–6*, 433–34.

17. Hoehner, *Ephesians*, 535–36; Gombis, "Cosmic Lordship," 376–78.

gift-giving movement thus climaxes in the achievement of unity for the sake of church growth and maturity (4:12–13).

A final aspect of the portrayal of Christ in Eph 4 is the notion of headship over the body at 4:15–16. The church as the body of Christ is introduced at 1:22–23, and recurs in 3:6 and 4:4. In Eph 4, the role of the gifted persons given by Christ is to build up the body of Christ (v. 12), which ultimately contributes to the growth of the body in love (v. 16). Best associates the thought of the passage with 2:20–22 where the building of the church, like a temple, expands to fill the world with Christ's presence.[18] Christ's headship therefore signifies that Christ is directing the growth of the church in mission (Eph 4:15–16).[19] The impediments to mission spelled out in v. 14 are immaturity, erroneous doctrine and human trickery. Christ gifts his body for mission through ministries focused on proclaiming, explaining, and applying the word of God (vv. 11–12), with every member of the church equipped and expected to play a role in this growth-producing task.

8.4 Intertextuality—Literary and Thematic Links to the Wider Biblical Narrative

The dominant intertextual link in this passage is the citation of Ps 68:18, however there are a few less frequently noted echoes in the passage which warrant mention as well.[20]

The vocabulary of calling in Eph 4:1 would firstly recall the opening *berakah* of 1:3–14, where God's choosing of the recipients in Christ is directed towards a goal of holiness (1:4). To be called by God, as understood in the OT, was to be called to holiness of life as defined by covenantal laws. Israel's vocation was to manifest God's holiness and name in its own social life and more broadly, to the nations (e.g. Lev 19:2; Deut 4:5–8; 1 Kgs 8:56–61; 1 Chr 16:23, 34, 35).

The oneness of God, as emphasized through the repeated use of "one" in Eph 4:4–6 recalls the *shema*, Deut 6:4–6, which evokes a multiplicity of theological ideas from God's sovereignty, to his rightful claim upon human private and social life.[21] While Israel did not routinely proselytize, within

---

18. Best, *Ephesians*, 408.

19. Arnold, *Ephesians, Power and Magic*, 144.

20. These echoes do not pass Hays's threshold tests, and so are discussed as illustrative background only for the missional reading being developed.

21. Barth, *Ephesians 4–6*, 464–66; Stuhlmacher, *Biblical Theology*, 464 notes that the allusion to Deut 6:4–6 in Eph 4:4–6 mirrors the contemporaneous Jewish text 2 Bar. 48:23–24.

the OT Scriptures are numerous texts that can support the monotheistic drive towards mission based on the fact that the one true God (God in his "transcendent uniqueness") should be known and rightly worshipped by all nations in God's world (e.g. Ps 86:8–9; 1 Kgs 8:60; Isa 45).[22]

Baugh comments that the confession of Jesus as the "one Lord" anticipates God's intention that all nations be refreshed and enfolded under his universal dominion, citing Zech 14:8–9, which reads:[23]

> On that day living waters shall flow out from Jerusalem, half of them to the eastern sea and half of them to the western sea; it shall continue in summer as in winter. And the LORD will become king over all the earth; on that day the LORD will be one and his name one.

The gift list of 4:11 overlaps with the gifts noted in Rom 12:6–8 (prophecy, teaching, and possibly leading as a parallel to the pastor/shepherd role of Eph 4:11) and 1 Cor 12:28 (apostles, prophets, and teachers). Like Eph 4, Rom 12 sets the context for the exercise of gifts within an explicit reminder that believers are part of one body (Rom 12:4–5). A similar reminder is present in 1 Cor 12, coupled with language similar to Eph 4, one Spirit, and a mention of baptism (vv. 4–5, 12–13). The gifts serve the common good (1 Cor 12:7); they are part of God's program for the building up of his people (Rom 14:19; 1 Cor 14:3–4, 26). Spiritual gifts must always be exercised in love (Eph 4:16; 1 Cor 8:1; 13:1–13). The specific gift of shepherd (ποιμήν), reminds us of Jesus's description of himself as the good shepherd (John 10:1–16), which draws on the OT prophetic hope of godly leaders like David (e.g. Jer 3:15; 23:4; Ezek 34:23).

The hapax legomenon κλυδωνίζομαι (tossed by waves) in Eph 4:14, occurs just once in the LXX, in Isa 57:20, where it is set as the fate of the wicked in contrast to the peace which God offers to the far and near.

> Peace, peace, to the far and the near, says the Lord;
>
> and I will heal them.
>
> But the wicked are like the tossing sea
>
> that cannot keep still;
>
> its waters toss up mire and mud.
>
> There is no peace, says my God, for the wicked.

---

22. Bauckham, *Bible and Mission*, 37; Bauckham, "Biblical Theology," 211; Wright, *Mission of God*, 126–35, 171–72.

23. Baugh, *Ephesians*, 303.

The incidence of this hapax in Eph 4:14 connects with and reinforces the allusion to Isa 57:19 in Eph 2:14, 17. The impact of this allusion across two passages is that the specific focus of the gifted apostles, prophets, evangelists, shepherds, and teachers is to foster the peace with God and resultant communal growth as God's expanding spiritual temple presence in the world that was the goal in Eph 2:11–22.

Another intertextual connection that continues this theme of God's intention to fill the earth with his presence is in Eph 4:10, where Christ's descent to the *earth* (τῆς γῆς), followed by his ascent far above all the *heavens* (ὑπεράνω πάντων τῶν οὐρανῶν) enables him to *fill all things* (ἵνα πληρώσῃ τὰ πάντα). Hübner notes Jer 23:24 as an antecedent text for this theme, where it states μὴ οὐχὶ τὸν οὐρανὸν καὶ τὴν γῆν ἐγὼ πληρῶ, "Do I not fill heaven and earth? says the LORD."[24] This text emphasizes God's omniscience as the reason that false prophets will be judged, while the faithful speakers of God's word are affirmed (Jer 23:28–32). We may conclude that the true proclamation of God's words is a core function of the five ministry roles of Eph 4:11, as this counteracts false prophecy which results in immaturity and apostasy.

Finally, we turn to the major intertextual link in this passage, Eph 4:8, with its quotation of Ps 68:18 (67:19 LXX). The text in 4:8 varies from the LXX and MT in two major ways: a change from second to third person, and the verb changed from *receive* to *give*. A number of commentators conclude these changes are the result of the author quoting from a different OT tradition (evident in *Targum Psalms*).[25] A satisfying explanation that does not rely on speculative reconstructions of first-century Jewish and Christian traditions is that the author drew on the broader literary context of the Psalm and aligned the verb with the theme of divine provision for his people that recurs throughout the Psalm (e.g. vv. 5–6, 9, 19, 35). Psalm 68 incorporates a number of motifs that feature in Ephesians, especially the idea of God as triumphant Divine Warrior (Ps 68:1, 4, 7, 17–21, 28 and Eph 1:19–22; 6:10–17), gentile pilgrimage to Zion to worship God (Ps 68:29–32; Eph 2:11–22; 3:6) and God's gracious provision for his people (Ps 68:5–6, 9–10, 19–20, 35; Eph 1:3–14; 3:16–19).[26]

Once again, we note that the author of Ephesians is drawing on an OT text that elaborates on the idea of God's presence coming to Jerusalem, as a symbol of his power and victory over the false gods of the nations, and his power made available to strengthen his chosen people, especially as they

---

24. Hübner, *Vetus Testamentum*, 2:452.

25. Ehorn, "Use of Psalm 68," 96–120; Best, *Ephesians*, 379–81; Lincoln, *Ephesians*, 243.

26. Baugh, *Ephesians*, 326; cf. Aletti, *Épître aux Éphésiens*, 206, 219.

praise him (Ps 68:17–18, 24–35).²⁷ As with earlier allusions to 1 Chr 16 at Eph 1:3–14 and 3 Kgdms 8:37–45 at Eph 2:18–22, prayers spoken at the time of the ark (God's presence) coming to the temple sum up a key pastoral message of Ephesians—that God's presence empowers the letter's recipients in their spiritual struggle against hostile spiritual forces. Furthermore, God's missional plan is moving towards an eschatological ingathering of the nations to worship God in Christ.

8.5 Portrayal of Humanity and the World in Relation to God's Mission

Humanity apart from Christ is presented, by implication, in Eph 4:2 as prone to divisive arrogance and conflict, and in v. 14 as prone to deception by a human sinful tendency to deceit and manipulation. This passage sets the body of Christ as the countermovement that overcomes such sinful human inclinations, especially as it is led and united by the Spirit (vv. 3–4) and engaged in gifted ministry for the benefit of the body's growth (vv. 11–16). The world is the sphere of God's action. Though he is already pervasively present in the cosmos (v. 6), Christ's descent (incarnation and death), followed by his ascension means that his reign and the church as his body now has a worldwide reach. God's intention is that the church grow in love (v. 16) to "the full stature of Christ" (v. 13), filling all things (v. 10).

8.6 Evidence of a Missional Context in the Problems, Crises or Issues Addressed

Although Eph 4:1–16 does not directly identify a crisis or theological problem facing its recipients, it nevertheless reveals several deficient approaches to communal organization and functioning. There is an implicit rejection of agonistic social models in which competitive striving is utilized to select leaders and to shape social compliance with accepted norms.²⁸ Instead, the Christian community is to cultivate attitudes of mutuality, humility, and love (vv. 2, 16), all aimed at guarding unity and fostering collective growth, rather than individual advancement.

---

27. Cf. Moritz, "Psalms," 181–95 who notes that "both texts [Eph 1:21–22, Eph 4:9–10] use motifs from the Psalms to express the subjugation of the evil powers under Christ."

28. Cf. Witherington, *Philemon*, 285; MacDonald, *Colossians and Ephesians*, 297.

The emphasis on unity in the body of Christ is a particular goal. While Greco-Roman society may have fostered unity through acceptance of social norms and communal worship of the dominant deities and the emperor as bringer of peace, the recipients of the letter were to reject such paths to conformity, instead acknowledging only one hope, one Lord, one faith.[29] MacDonald argues that the author of Ephesians aims to foster unity as a defense against the external threat of "menacing spiritual powers and increasingly hostile reactions from the outside world."[30]

In the light of the emphasis on maturity, stability, unity, and progress in faith in 4:13–15, Hoehner surmises that the recipients were in their spiritual infancy.[31] There may have been disunity, and an unwillingness to engage in mutual service, drawing on the gifts mentioned in v. 11. While the language is about body growth, the gifts (especially apostles and evangelists) are outward-looking roles, which may suggest that the recipients were too absorbed in internal concerns, and insufficiently engaged in attracting and seeking converts. Disunity was a problem with a number of Pauline communities, most notably Corinth, which the text of 1 Corinthians addresses (e.g. 1 Cor 1:10–13). The general tone of Ephesians does not allow speculation as to whether there was a particular form of disunity affecting the recipients' community, though Muddiman speculates that in the light of 1 John (a letter also traditionally addressed to a community in Western Asia Minor), there may have been a localized predilection to schism.[32]

The clearest negative statement is found in v. 14, where the author addresses the problem of false teaching and broader human deceitfulness. MacDonald sees the ocean imagery of being tossed by waves as being too generalized to involve a specific heretical idea, but "a general fear of instability."[33] Arnold argues that there is a danger of the letter recipients reverting to their former way of life in which magical practices had featured (cf. 2:2; 4:22).[34] Peter Gosnell notes that whether there was actual false teaching or merely the potential for it to threaten the recipients of the letter, this passage promotes group cohesion by elevating the value of teaching coming from Christ's designated envoys as listed in 4:11.[35]

---

29. Best, *Ephesians*, 376; for the emperor as bringer of peace, see Smith, *Christ the Ideal King*, 66–67.
30. MacDonald, *Colossians and Ephesians*, 298.
31. Hoehner, *Ephesians*, 560–62; cf. Lincoln, *Ephesians*, 226, speaks of "immaturity."
32. Muddiman, *Ephesians*, 183.
33. MacDonald, *Colossians and Ephesians*.
34. E.g. Arnold, *Ephesians, Power and Magic*, 123.
35. Gosnell, "Networks and Exchanges," 141.

8.7 Portrayal of the Character and Mission of God's People in the World

As the first passage of the predominantly paraenetic half of the letter (Eph 4–6), this passage transitions from the doctrinally rich first half by making a number of summary exhortations in vv. 1, 3, 14, 15. These imperatives urge the recipients to *walk* in a particular way in light of their calling, to make efforts to maintain unity, to leave behind immature susceptibility to false teaching, and to speak truth in love in a way that fosters church growth. The overarching concern is that their actions align with the redeeming and reconciling work of God already appropriated through faith into their lives (as foreshadowed in Eph 2:10).

In v. 1 the recipients of the letter are begged "to lead a life worthy of their calling." Their choice by God for incorporation into God's family is intended to have a noticeable impact on their public actions and relationships (cf. Phil 1:27; Col 1:10; 1 Thess 2:12; 2 Thess 1:11). The idea of *worthy* (ἀξίως) conduct presupposes a watching audience, who will either be attracted or repelled by the observed behavior. Ephesians' ethical discourse reflects a missional concern that the corporate life of the letter's recipients reflects God's holy and glorious character (cf. Eph 1:4, 6, 12, 14). Biblical ethics are therefore inherently missional, since the social interactions of believers can never be fully hidden from wider society.

This missional concern is further evident in v. 6, where God's universal presence ("above all, through all, in all") is realized as God's people live out godly virtues (v. 2). Just as the temple imagery of Eph 2 suggested, as God's people increase in number and distribution throughout the world, living out the values of God's kingdom, then God's mission to fill the earth is progressively realized through his redeemed and Spirit-filled image-bearers.

Gift-giving as the action of a victorious conqueror or ruler in the ancient world (vv. 7–8) is a striking image to adopt as a facet of God's mission. Tributes and largess were used in the ancient world to create financial dependency and loyalty on the part of vassals to their sovereign. Christ's pattern of gift-giving is not manipulative in this traditional human way (v. 14) but is designed to strengthen and equip the recipients of Christ's favor for healthy corporate growth. Nevertheless, growth separate from Christ the head is not countenanced, and the loyalty ties created by divine gift-giving do not deviate from the social expectations of benefaction in the ancient world.[36]

---

36. Talbert, *Ephesians and Colossians*, 23–25, 108.

The nature of mission for God's people is firmly in view in 4:11–13. While it is undeniable that there is an internal focus on maturity and unity in 4:13–16, this need not exclude a goal of ongoing growth through evangelistic proclamation to nonbelievers. The key issue is the identity and role of the apostles and evangelists mentioned in 4:11.[37]

Apostles (ἀπόστολοι) certainly designates the twelve, with the self-conscious addition of Paul (1 Cor 9:1–10; 15:9); this is its meaning in Eph 2:20; 3:5. Beyond that authoritative circle of witnesses to the risen Christ, *apostle* is also used of Barnabas and unnamed others (1 Cor 9:1–6; cf. Acts 14:14), Andronicus and Junia (Rom 16:7), Epaphroditus (Phil 2:25), perhaps Silvanus (1 Thess 1:1; 2:6–7), and Titus (2 Cor 8:23). Therefore, in addition to the twelve, there were arguably *apostles* whose role was to be envoys and church-planting missionaries (noting particularly 2 Cor 8:23; Phil 2:25).[38] Later Christian writings occasionally support the ongoing existence of apostles, understood as missionaries/itinerant evangelists (e.g. *Didache* 11.3–12; Eusebius, *Hist. Eccl.* 3.37).[39] This stance is, however, the minority view. A dogmatic concern to uphold the authoritative and unique role of the twelve and Paul in the founding of the church and the formation of the NT canon means that most church fathers and a majority of modern scholars do not readily allow for the continuing existence of apostles in the second century CE or beyond.[40]

Evangelist (εὐαγγελιστής) as a noun is found only three times in the NT (Acts 21:8; Eph 4:11; 2 Tim 4:5). Best interprets the role of evangelist as restricted to ministry within the existing church, on the basis of a restrictive reading of Acts 21:8 and 2 Tim 4:2, and the observation that the context of Eph 4:11–16 is concerned with maturity and unity within the existing church.[41] However, John Dickson has mounted a convincing argument for understanding evangelists as apostolic analogues, a group "who [proclaim] the gospel to those who do not yet believe or have not yet heard the news

---

37. Johnson, *Apostolic Function*, 51–75 gives a helpful overview of background literature regarding apostles while focusing on contemporary missiological application.

38. Hoehner, *Ephesians*, 541–42; Morris, *Expository Reflections*, 116–17; Witherington, *Philemon*, 290.

39. Cf. Clark, "Apostleship," 72–74.

40. Kruse, "Apostle, Apostleship," 76–82; McNair Scott, *Apostles Today*, 101–2; Winger, *Ephesians*, 450, exhibits a reluctance to admit the existence of apostles other than the twelve. Calvin, *Institutes* 4.3.4 and *Commentary Ephesians* 4:11, was essentially cessationist but conceded that a modern-day apostle may arise in extraordinary times of need.

41. Best, *Ephesians*, 390; Best, "Ministry in Ephesians," 163–66.

... they 'build' the church through mission."[42] Key elements of Dickson's argument are that Philip elsewhere carries out gospel proclamation to nonbelievers (Acts 8:4, 12, 35, 40); the εὐαγγελ root connotes the activity of conveying news to those who have not previously heard it; and 2 Tim 4 is not restricted to the existing congregation (2 Tim 3:5-7, 10-17). Therefore, it is incorrect to claim that evangelists were solely congregational teachers with no involvement in gospel proclamation to outsiders.[43]

In the contemporary Christian world, a number of movements identify Eph 4 ministries or functions, especially that of apostles, as essential to mission. The argument of these movements (often called Restorationist or New Apostolic) is that all the ministry gifts or functions of Eph 4:11 continue to the present day, and are necessary for the expansion of the church.[44] More modestly, Barth argues that there was no evidence in the text of Eph 4 that the ministries were "restricted to a certain period of church history and [were] later to die out."[45] While the exegetical foundation for new apostolic movements is rarely well developed, the simple observation that the gifts of Eph 4:11 are not, according to the text, restricted to the first generation of the church, means that an ongoing apostolic ministry of church planting and an ongoing evangelistic ministry of gospel proclamation are inherent to Christian ministry as conceived by Ephesians.[46]

8.8 Conclusion

The *missio Dei*, as depicted in Eph 4:1–16, is to foster unity, maturity, and church growth in order for the church to fill the world with a compelling witness to the reconciling power of the gospel. God (as Spirit, Lord and Father, 4:4–6) is the center and model for unity while Christ's ascent, descent, and gift-giving are aimed at overcoming the immaturity, error, and deception which would otherwise hinder the mission of his body in which all members contribute to growth, maturity, and witness (an idea reinforced

---

42. Dickson, *Mission-Commitment*, 318–36, quote at 328.

43. Silva, "εὐαγγέλιον," 2:312. "The term [εὐαγγελιστής] is thus clearly intended to refer to people who carry on the work of the apostles, who have been directly called by the risen Christ. But it is difficult to decide whether the ref. is to an office or more generally to an activity. These evangelists may have been engaged in missionary work (Acts 21:8) or church leadership (2 Tim 4:5)."

44. Hirsch, *Forgotten Ways*; McNair Scott, *Apostles Today*; Robertson, "Distinctive Missiology," 144–61.

45. Barth, *Ephesians 4–6*, 437.

46. As noted above (in §1.5.2), Hedlund, *Mission of the Church*, 209–16, 241, gives sustained attention to the importance of the "apostolate" in mission.

by the echo of Jer 23:24–32). The echo of the *shema* in Eph 4:4–6 alerts us to the importance of God's transcendent uniqueness as a key impetus for global mission. The citation of Ps 68:18 underscores Christ's gracious provision for ministry while also containing divine warfare and gentile pilgrimage motifs. The missional context reflected in Eph 4:1–16 is spiritual immaturity possibly manifest in disunity and susceptibility to erroneous teaching. The mission of God's people, especially as led and facilitated by the five ministries of 4:11, includes pioneering church planting, gospel proclamation, and ongoing discipleship to foster maturity.

9

Ephesians 4:17—5:20

9.1 Introduction

THIS PASSAGE, REPLETE WITH catalogs of virtues and vices, broadly aligns with the Jewish parenetic tradition of *two ways* texts such as Ps 1; Deut 30:15-20; and 1QS 3,4.[1] But it is more than a recitation of generic moral instruction. There are several links to the theological bases for transformed living outlined in the first half of the letter (e.g. 4:17-19 and 2:1-5; 4:30 and 1:13; 5:18 and 1:23; 3:19; 4:10). In its portrayal of the *missio Dei*, the character of God, its use of OT allusions, the portrayal of humanity, background issues and the missional role of God's people, this text seeks to foster communal life that is harmonious, unified, true to Christ as the prototypical new human, and reflective of God's goal to renew the whole cosmos in holiness and truth.

9.2 Portrayal of God's Intentions, Actions, and Purposes (the *missio Dei*)

The focus in this section is on the ethical implications of the recipients' conversion to Christ. Its content is focused on the human response to grace, with insights into the *missio Dei* arising as inferences from the goals set forth such as new creation holiness in Eph 4:24, forgiveness in 4:32, and Spirit-filling in 5:18-19.

---

1. Lincoln, *Ephesians*, 272.

Ephesians 4:24 reprises the new humanity (τὸν καινὸν ἄνθρωπον) and creation language (κτίζω) of 2:10, 15, thereby recalling Christ's saving action at the cross, and indeed implying that believers are to put on Christ himself, cf. Gal 3:27.[2] The significance of the ethical transformation that God intends to occur is that all ethical exhortation is grounded in the prior redemptive and creative work of God, who is acting to restore humanity to its intended role as his vice-regents in creation. Only as humanity acts in righteousness and holiness (4:24) is the influence of sin progressively diminished and Christ as the new humanity, through his body, comes to fill the earth (1:23).

The exhortation to mutual kindness and forgiveness is grounded in the reminder that "in Christ God has forgiven you" (4:32). Similarly, God's prior act of love is the rationale for believers to be loving in their relationships (5:2, 23, 25, 29 all using the καθώς, *just as* construction). The missional pattern envisaged is similar to 2 Cor 5:14–21, where Christ's love is the motivating force behind Paul's mission to see gentiles reconciled to God. God's saving and reconciling actions as elaborated in Eph 1–3 "now provides both the norm and the grounds for believers' own behavior."[3] Throughout the paraenetic section of Ephesians we encounter what Gorman describes as *theosis*: believers are called to "Spirit-enabled transformative participation in the life and character of God revealed in the crucified and resurrected Messiah Jesus."[4] Believers' ethical behavior, when grounded in the gospel, is a potent form of mission, since it publicly demonstrates the beauty and justice of human life lived in alignment with God's intentions (cf. Tit 2; *Ign. Eph.* 10:1–3).[5]

The exhortation in 5:18 to be filled with the Spirit utilizes πληρόω. In the light of earlier occurrences of πληρόω (at 1:23; 2:19–22; 3:19), Eph 5:18 is further confirmation that God's mission involves the progressive filling of the world with his presence through believers.[6]

Ephesians 4:17—5:20 provides a detailed vision of the ethical outworking of God's mission to recreate humanity and fill the earth with his presence through Christ's body. Believers are to be righteous and holy (4:24), not grieving the Holy Spirit through ungodly conduct (4:30), practicing mutual care and forgiveness motivated by the forgiveness they have received from

---

2. Winger, *Ephesians*, 549.

3. Lincoln, *Ephesians*, 310.

4. Gorman, *Becoming the Gospel*, 4, and cf. 195–99.

5. Dickson, *Mission-Commitment*, 290–92; Wright, *Mission of God*, 388; Wright, *God's People*, 108; Wright, *Bringing the Church*, 59.

6. Gombis, "Fullness of God," 260–62; cf. Ezek 44:4; Jer 23:24.

God (4:32). Their lives of self-giving love (5:1–2) will, in combination with the virtues previously cataloged, provide an ethical witness to the life God intends for humanity and enables through his indwelling Spirit. God's Spirit corporately fills the church (5:18) as its grateful and reverent attitudes and mutually edifying actions extend God's presence into all the earth. In short, Eph 4:17—5:20 reflects God's purpose to recreate humanity and draw his people into participation in the divine life of love.

9.3 Portrayal of God's Person and Character

Although this passage is not strongly theological, it nevertheless contains a few verses that portray Christ and the Spirit as active in shaping the lives of believers. Firstly, believers are said to have "learned Christ" (4:20), and thereby escape the futility, darkness, and alienation from God that characterizes life apart from Christ (4:17–19).[7] This concept is reinforced then with the claim that "truth is in Jesus" (4:21). The truth likely comprises both the historical example of Jesus for the ethical life of believers and the gospel of salvation, which is "the word of truth" (1:13).[8] Truth-speaking in love is the means specified for growth in maturity in the preceding section (4:15), and then is connected with goodness and righteousness as a fruit of the light in 5:9. This verse is therefore emphasizing that the source and norm for spiritual growth is Jesus himself (which is an idea also found in John 14:6 and 1 Cor 1:24).[9]

As noted in the discussion of 4:24 in §9.2, above, God's mission involves humanity being renewed in God's likeness (κατὰ θεὸν "according to God," 4:24, i.e. in the image or likeness of God, cf. Col 3:10).[10] God's divine characteristics of "righteousness and holiness" (e.g. Deut 32:4; Ps 144:17 LXX) are presented here as communicable attributes.

Ephesians 4:30 contains a negative imperative not to "grieve the Holy Spirit." This verse provides one of the clearest biblical supports for the personhood of the Holy Spirit, establishing that the Spirit is not an impersonal force.[11] Rather, the Spirit is the source and guardian of church unity (4:3–4), the one through whom a believer has access to the Father (2:18), the giver of power to know and live in divine love (3:16), and the seal guaranteeing God's redemptive work in the lives of the recipients (1:13–14; 4:30). The

---

7. Lincoln, *Ephesians*, 279–80.
8. Best, *Ephesians*, 429.
9. Baugh, *Ephesians*, 368.
10. Hoehner, *Ephesians*, 611.
11. Bloesch, *Holy Spirit*, 67; Muddiman, *Ephesians*, 229.

manner in which the Holy Spirit could be grieved is not directly stated, but the context of 4:25–32 strongly indicates that sins involving speaking abusively or falsely would grieve the Spirit since they destroy communal life, which the Spirit enlivens (4:3–4).[12]

Ephesians 4:30—5:2 mentions "the Holy Spirit of God" (v. 30), "God in Christ" (v. 32), "God" (vv. 1, 2), and "Christ" (v. 2). This concentration of terms denoting God's persons is set in the context of the command to imitate God in love, self-offering, and avoidance of divisive and hurtful behavior. This short passage therefore links God's Trinitarian relationality as paradigmatic for renewed human society and relationships.

In the poetic unit, "Sleeper awake! Rise from the dead, and Christ will shine on you," (5:14) Christ is presented as the one who illuminates his followers to know and do what is "good and right and true . . . what is pleasing to the Lord" (5:9–10). Light here is being used as an image connoting ethical behavior and is a summary for the positive virtues presented throughout the paraenesis of 4:17—5:20 (noting that it commenced with an injunction against persisting in the darkened futility and alienation from God typical of gentiles apart from Christ). Christ not only is a standard of ethical purity in himself, but is able to transmit that ethical purity to his faithful followers (5:8–14).[13] The impact of Christ's light shining on and through his followers is therefore missional, since it causes "works of darkness" to be exposed (5:11), and invites those in darkness who become aware of their spiritual state to come to Christ for the light of salvation (5:13–14).[14]

Lincoln detects a Trinitarian dimension to the theology of 5:17–20. It is the will of Christ as Lord that the community must seek to understand (5:17). Christ mediates believers' worship and thanksgiving to the Father (v. 20), while the Spirit mediates God's power and presence to believers (5:18), especially in their worship and speech.[15]

9.4 Intertextuality—Literary and Thematic Links to the Wider Biblical Narrative

Paul's use of the OT in Eph 4:17—5:20 is often characterized as based on Jewish traditions of ethical instruction.[16] There are a number of Second

---

12. Lincoln, *Ephesians*, 307.
13. Lincoln, *Ephesians*, 331.
14. Lincoln, *Ephesians*, 331–35.
15. Lincoln, *Ephesians*, 348.
16. Thielman, "Ephesians," 825, citing Lincoln, *Ephesians*, 300; cf. Gnilka, *Epheserbrief*, 234; Rosner, *Greed as Idolatry*, 56–58.

Temple Jewish texts that address, for example, anger, deceit, drunkenness, theft, and grieving the Holy Spirit (e.g. T. Iss. 7:3–4; T. Dan 2:1, 4; 3:5–6; 4:6–7; 5:1–2, 7; 6:8; Herm. Mand. 41:2–6; 42:2). While noting the presence of these ethical themes in extrabiblical Jewish texts, the following discussion will focus on the allusions to OT texts at 4:24, 25, 26, 30; 5:2, 14. Although echoes of OT texts are also listed by UBS5 for Eph 5:13, 18, 19, these texts fail to satisfy even two of Hays's criteria for OT echoes, and so they will not be discussed.[17]

9.4.1 Ephesians 4:24 and Genesis 1:27, Deuteronomy 32:4, Psalm 144:17

Ephesians 4:24 states: "Clothe yourselves with the new self, created according to the likeness of God in true righteousness and holiness." Hübner identifies six OT LXX texts with at least one word in common with Eph 4:24, namely:[18] Gen 1:27 (ἄνθρωπος humanity and θεὸς God); Deut 32:4 (ἀληθινός true, δίκαιος just and ὅσιος holy); 2 Chr 6:41 (ἐνδύω clothe); Job 29:14 (δικαιοσύνη just and ἐνδύω clothe); Ps 144:17 (δίκαιος just and ὅσιος holy); and Wis 9:1–3 (ποιέω and κατασκευάζω make/create as equivalent to κτίζω create; ἄνθρωπος humanity, ὁσιότης holiness, δικαιοσύνη righteousness). Another text not listed by Hübner where three words are common is Ps 131:9 LXX (ἐνδύω, δικαιοσύνη, and ὅσιος). The inclusion of 2 Chr 6:41 as a text echo is unwarranted since the single word ἐνδύω is the only point of connection.

An allusion to the Genesis creation account is obvious and uncontentious, despite the absence of εἰκών which is present in the parallel text Col 3:10.[19] Almost all commentators recognize it.[20] In the light of earlier references at 2:10, 15, this verse confirms that the author is presenting believers as God's new creation, aligned with his character and will, empowered to fulfill his mission of filling the earth with his blessings and presence. The verbal correspondence of the nouns righteousness and holiness (δικαιοσύνη and ὅσιος) to the descriptors of God's character in Deut 32:4 and Ps 144:17 LXX supports the idea that believers are restored divine image-bearers. Similarly, we can see the wisdom literature texts (Job 29:14 and Wis 9:1–3) as foreshadowing the importance of ethical living as a missional witness. Muddiman also links this verse with 1 Cor 1:30 and the

---

17. UBS5, 872, 874, 881, Ps 33:2,3 and Eph 5:19; Prov 23:31 LXX and Eph 5:18; Amos 5:13 and Eph 5:16.

18. Hübner, *Vetus Testamentum*, 2:454–57.

19. Owens, *As It Was*, 152.

20. E.g. Best, *Ephesians*, 436–37; Lincoln, *Ephesians*, 287.

earlier reference at Eph 4:13 to Christ as the perfect man, and with the support of 1 Cor 15:45, claims "The risen Christ is not just the agent of the new creation, he is also the first example of it."[21]

9.4.2 Ephesians 4:25 and Zechariah 8:16

Ephesians 4:25, "putting away falsehood, let all of us *speak the truth to our neighbors*," (λαλεῖτε ἀλήθειαν ἕκαστος μετὰ τοῦ πλησίον αὐτοῦ) is a quotation of Zech 8:16: "These are the things that you shall do: *Speak the truth to one another*, render in your gates judgments that are true and make for peace" (λαλεῖτε ἀλήθειαν ἕκαστος πρὸς τὸν πλησίον αὐτοῦ . . . only the preposition is altered). There are significant elements of overlap in the context of both Zech 8 and Eph 4, as noted by Yoder Neufeld, Hoehner, and Thielman.[22] Both texts are concerned with the appropriate conduct of the restored eschatological people of God (Zech 8:4–13; Eph 4:1, 20–25), both texts envisage Jews and gentiles jointly worshipping God in a renewed temple as a characteristic of the eschaton (Zech 8:18–23; Eph 2:13–22), and there is a concentration of truth vocabulary in both texts (ἀλήθεια Zech 8:3, 8, 16, 19; Eph 4:15, 21, 24, 25). Truth-speaking to one's neighbor is therefore a concept loaded with missional meaning. Muddiman thinks *neighbors* here means only fellow Christians, but this narrow view does not do justice to the intertext.[23] Neighbors likely does not just signify people in proximity to one another, but those from *afar* (cf. Eph 2:13, 17) who are being drawn (or "gathered up," cf. Eph 1:10) from all nations by God into the community of faith. Zechariah 8 pictures representatives from "nations of every language" grasping the clothing of a Jew, saying, "Let us go with you, for we have heard that God is with you" (Zech 8:23). Accordingly, truth-speaking may well have a nuance of gospel proclamation (as it does in 1:13; 4:21), by which diverse peoples come to experience the blessing of salvation and be counted among the people of God.

9.4.3 Ephesians 4:26 and Psalm 4:5

The wording of Eph 4:26, "Be angry but do not sin," reflects the exact wording of Ps 4:5 LXX ὀργίζεσθε καὶ μὴ ἁμαρτάνετε. The following phrase in

---

21. Muddiman, *Ephesians*, 221.

22. Yoder Neufeld, *Put on the Armour*, 133–34; Hoehner, *Ephesians*, 616–17; Thielman, "Ephesians," 825.

23. Muddiman, *Ephesians*, 224–25.

Eph 4:26b ("do not let the sun go down on your anger") also may represent a parallel idea to the Psalm, "ponder it on your beds." The context in both texts is an attack on falsehood (ψεῦδος, lies, Ps 4:3 LXX; Eph 4:25).[24] Arnold interprets the Psalm as containing a polemic against idolatry, seemingly on the basis of the NIV translation of Ps 4:2, "How long will you love delusions and seek false gods?"[25] Although the word כָזָב (Ps 4:2 MT) may imply idols (Amos 4:2), the NIV translation of "false gods" at Ps 4:2 is an overreading, unsupported by the immediate context, and not adopted in the majority of commentaries and other translations.[26] Therefore, Arnold's claim that Eph 4:25 may encompass permissible anger provoked "when a member of the community makes compromises with the pagan idolatry in their environment," attractive as it may be for a missional reading of the text, is unsupportable from the context of Eph 4 or Ps 4.[27] A more balanced reading of this text is found in Lincoln who notes that anger causes estrangement, which undercuts the reconciled relationships of members in the body of Christ, which is the explicit concern in Eph 4:25.[28] We may further note that the Psalm ends with an appeal for the light of God's face to bring peace and resolve the righteous person's angry frustration with sin. A similar climax to the paraenesis of Eph 4–5 is found at Eph 5:14 where the promise of Christ's light shining on the believer brings wisdom and fruitful conduct (5:9, 15).

9.4.4 Ephesians 4:30 and Isaiah 63:10

The majority of commentators see an allusion to Isa 63:10 in Eph 4:30 "do not grieve the Holy Spirit of God, with which you were marked with a seal for the day of redemption," although the verb is different in the LXX (καὶ παρώξυναν τὸ πνεῦμα τὸ ἅγιον αὐτοῦ (παροξύνω *provoke* or *irritate*), compared with καὶ μὴ λυπεῖτε τὸ πνεῦμα τὸ ἅγιον τοῦ θεοῦ (λυπέω, *vex, irritate, offend, insult* in Ephesians).[29] Isaiah 63 depicts Israel's exodus, exile and periodic unfaithfulness (63:10–19), which are set against the backdrop of God's consistent

---

24. Thielman, "Ephesians," 825.

25. Arnold, *Ephesians*, 301.

26. Klopfenstein, "כזב *kzb* to lie," *TLOT*, 2:608; deClaisse-Walford, et al., *Book of Psalms*, 79; NASB, ESV, NRSV, CSB all translate as "lies."

27. Arnold, *Ephesians*, 301.

28. Lincoln, *Ephesians*, 301–2.

29. Lincoln, *Ephesians*, 306; Muddiman, *Ephesians*, 229; cf. Best, *Ephesians*, 457 (rejects the Isa 63:10 background as the LXX uses a different word, and claims the author of Ephesians does not know the MT of Isaiah); BDAG, s.v. λυπέω.

covenantal love (63:7). To grieve the Holy Spirit is to walk inconsistently with the merciful salvation brought by a righteous, judging God in the long-awaited eschatological age (63:4, 7–10).

For Barth, the sealing of the Spirit in Eph 4:30 and 1:13 is more than an individual assurance of salvation, but is to be understood as the cumulative gifts of the Spirit among the people of God already mentioned in Eph 1–4, including rebirth, a life of praising God's glory, access to God, unity, corporate growth, verbal confession and witness. Therefore, the sealing of the Holy Spirit has a "ministerial, missionary, evangelistic character . . . [it] is a light kindled to the glory of God and the benefit of the whole world."[30] The immediate context in Eph 4:25–29 is concerned with conduct (including deceit, anger, theft) that will harm internal communal life, but the verses following 4:30 adopt the imagery of the people of God living "as children of light" (5:8), and their ethical conduct making visible Christ's glory (5:9–15). This context confirms Barth's interpretation, which is also consistent with the broader context of Isaiah, where God is exhorted to come down in a glorious theophany (Isa 64:1–5) that is seen by both his own people and his adversaries and the nations.

9.4.5 Ephesians 5:2 and Ezekiel 20:41

Ephesians 5:2, "and live in love, as Christ loved us and gave himself up for us, a fragrant offering and sacrifice to God," has echoes of Exod 29:18; Ps 40:6; and Ezek 20:41.[31] While the sacrificial vocabulary is common throughout the Pentateuch, the spiritualization of the imagery and application to God's people occur in only a handful of texts, of which the closest to Eph 5:2 is Ezek 20:41.

> As a pleasing odor I will accept you, when I bring you out from the peoples, and gather you out of the countries where you have been scattered; and I will manifest my holiness among you in the sight of the nations.[32]

This verse in Ezekiel is unmistakably clear in stating that the restored people of God, whose reformed way of life and renewed temple worship, will be a means by which God is made known to the nations.[33] In Eph 5:2, the sacrificial action has been offered by Christ, and his people merely imitate his

---

30. Barth, *Ephesians 1–3*, 143; Barth, *Ephesians 4–6*, 547.
31. Best, *Ephesians*, 78, 470–71; Lincoln, *Ephesians*, 298; UBS5, 866, 872, 878.
32. Lincoln, *Ephesians*, 471 also notes Dan 4:37a LXX; T. Levi 3:6; and Phil 4:18.
33. Cooper, *Ezekiel*, 208.

sacrificial love. Their words and loving deeds witness to Christ, similarly to the way in which the church disperses the "aroma of Christ" to believers and nonbelievers in 2 Cor 2:14-16.[34] While the missional connotations of Ezek 20:41 are rich, there is insufficient basis for claiming it as an intertextual allusion from Eph 5:2, since the subject in Ephesians is Christ and his sacrifice, rather than the witness of the people of God to the nations as in Ezekiel. The vocabulary in common (ὀσμή εὐωδία) is too common in the LXX to be able to narrow the referent text to Ezek 20. Accordingly, it is best treated as illustrative background rather than a deliberate intertextual link.

9.4.6 Ephesians 5:14 and Isaiah 26:19, 60:1

The saying in Eph 5:14, "Sleeper, awake! Rise from the dead, and Christ will shine on you," serves as the climax and rationale for the exhortations to live as children of the light in 5:8-14. It is not a quote from any single OT text and is regarded by many commentators as deriving from Christian tradition. Most of these commentators acknowledge the likelihood that the tradition drew on Isa 26:19 and 60:1.[35] Isaiah 26:19 has three words in common with Eph 5:14 (though in different form and order): ἐγείρω (awake), ἀνίστημι (rise), and οἱ νεκροί (the dead). Isa 26:19 reads: "The dead (οἱ νεκροί) will rise (ἀναστήσονται), and those in the tombs will be raised (ἐγερθήσονται)." Isaiah 26 is a song of Judah in which the prophet speaks of God's wrath which will fall upon impious people, while those people of righteousness, truth, and peace yet hope in God for his light and salvation. It is therefore quite compatible with the *two ways* material of Eph 4-5 in which ungodliness is contrasted with life *in Christ* (or *in the light*). There are shared concepts including *light* (Isa 26:9; Eph 5:8, 9, 13, 14), *truth* (Isa 26:2, 3, 10; Eph 5:9), *righteousness* (Isa 26:2, 9, 10; Eph 5:9), *wrath* (Isa 26:20, 21; Eph 5:6), *the dead* (Isa 26:19; Eph 5:14), *rising up* (Isa 26:14, 19; Eph 5:14), and *peace* (Isa 26:3, 12; cf. Eph 4:3).

Despite the scholarly preference for seeing the saying as an existing Christian tradition, adopted by the author of Ephesians, Jonathan Lunde and John Dunne have disputed this reconstruction, instead arguing that the author of Ephesians was capable of personally crafting the saying to echo the two Isaianic intertexts.[36] They note the context of Isa 60:1 and discuss its thematic coherence with Ephesians as well as some verbal

---

34. Barth, *Ephesians 4-6*, 560.

35. Barth, *Ephesians 4-6*, 574-75; Best, *Ephesians*, 497; Bruce, *Epistles*, 376; Lincoln, *Ephesians*, 318-19.

36. Lunde and Dunne, "Isaiah in Ephesians 5," 90.

parallels. However, their case can be strengthened even further. As noted above, Isa 26 also shares a number of themes with Eph 5. The following table demonstrates the multiple units of vocabulary in common between Eph 5:6–14 and Isa 59–60.

Vocabulary	Greek lemma/root	Isaiah (LES)	Ephesians
Empty words	κενός λόγος/ λαλέω	59:4 they *speak empty things* (λαλοῦσιν κενά)	5:6 Let no one deceive you with *empty words* (κενοῖς λόγοις)
Wrath of God	ὀργή θεός/ κύριος	59:19 *wrath* (ὀργή) will come from *the Lord*	5:6 because of these things the *wrath* (ὀργή) *of God* comes
Light	φῶς	59:9 While they were waiting for *light* (φῶς), darkness came upon them; while waiting for brightness, they walked in darkness 60:1 *Shine! Shine* (φωτίζω), Jerusalem, for your *light* (φῶς) is come 60:3 Kings will walk in your *light* (φῶς) 60:19 the sun will not be your *light* (φῶς) by day . . . the Lord will be eternal *light* (φῶς) for you 60:20 the Lord will be everlasting *light* (φῶς) for you	5:8–14 For once you were darkness, but now in the Lord you are *light*. Live as children of *light*— 9for the fruit of the *light* is found in all that is good and right and true . . . 13 but everything exposed by the *light* becomes visible, 14for everything that becomes visible is *light*. Therefore it says, "Sleeper, awake! Rise from the dead, and Christ will shine on you."
Visible/ appear/shine	φανερόω/ φαίνω/ ἐπιφαύσκω	60:2 but the Lord will *appear* (φαίνω) over you, and his glory will be seen upon you	5:13, 14 but everything exposed by the light becomes *visible* (φανερόω), for everything that becomes *visible* (φανερόω) is light . . . Christ will *shine* (ἐπιφαύσκω) on you

Vocabulary	Greek lemma/root	Isaiah (LES)	Ephesians
Darkness	σκότος	59:9 While they were waiting for light, *darkness* (σκότος) came upon them; 60:2 *Gloom* (σκότος) will cover the earth, and darkness will be upon the nations	5:8 For once you were *darkness* 5:11 Take no part in the unfruitful works of *darkness*
Children	τέκνον	60:4 see your *children* gathered together	5:8 Live as *children* of light
Right/righteous	δικαιοσύνη/δίκαιος	59:4 No one speaks *justice* (δίκαιος) 59:17 He put on *righteousness* (δικαιοσύνη) like a breastplate; 60:17 I will establish your rulers in peace and your overseers in *righteousness* (δικαιοσύνη)	5:9 the fruit of the light is found in all that is good and *right* (δικαιοσύνη) and true
True	ἀλήθεια ἀληθινός	59:4 there is not *true* (ἀληθινός) judgment 59:14 because *truth* (ἀλήθεια) has been used up in their ways 59:15 the *truth* (ἀλήθεια) has been taken away	5:9 the fruit of the light is found in all that is good and right and *true* (ἀλήθεια)
Pleasing	ἀρέσκω	59:15 the Lord saw it, and *it displeased him* (οὐκ ἤρεσεν αὐτῷ)	5:10 find out what is *pleasing* (ἀρέσκω) to the Lord

Table 6: Parallel Terms in Isaiah 59–60 and Ephesians 5:6–14

In the light of these substantial verbal correspondences, Hays's first criterion for an OT precursor text, *volume*, is readily satisfied. Hays's criterion of *availability* is also readily satisfied since Isaiah is so extensively used in Ephesians and other Pauline writings. *Recurrence* of the specific verses Isa 26:19 and 60:1–2 is not evident in Pauline writings (though Isa 60:1–2 is echoed in Luke 1:78–79), but allusions to the chapters do exist (Isa 26:3 in Phil 4:7; Isa 59:17 in Eph 6:14, 17; 1 Thess 5:8). Moritz cites Hippolytus as one patristic writer who saw a link to Isaiah in Eph 5:14, but the vast majority believed the saying derived from a tradition other than the OT.[37] Therefore the *history of interpretation* provides weak support until the modern period for seeing a connection to Isa 26 and 60.

The link is *historically plausible*, as Pauline usage of metaphors of light, darkness, and rising, and an ethical renewal for the eschatological people of God is present in other texts (Rom 2:19; 13:12; 2 Cor 1:9; 1 Thess 5:4–10). Hays's penultimate criterion of *thematic coherence* has been noted briefly by Moritz but argued more extensively by Lunde and Dunne.[38] They note that Isaiah's portrait of Israel's rebellious sinfulness is a type for the sinfulness of pre-Christian gentiles as portrayed in Eph 2–5. Furthermore, the redemption anticipated by Isaiah also typologically coheres with the redemption imagery of Eph 2–5.[39] Taking the cumulative weight of these criteria into account, we can conclude that there is a strong probability that metalepsis is at play. The following discussion will indicate whether such a link is also *satisfying* (Hays's final test).

Provisionally accepting a metaleptic impact of the intertext, a number of missional implications become evident. The faithful community of Isa 26 lives during a time when an outpouring of God's wrath on the ungodly is imminent, and God's final salvation is not yet fully manifest. Therefore the godly must persist with hope and absolute allegiance to the God who has promised to bring life to the dead, despite ongoing oppression by other lords (esp. Isa 26:13).[40] The role of God's people is to live righteously by God's laws so that God's light is made visible in the land (Isa 26:9–11). This ethical witness is prominent in Eph 5:8–11, while the need for faithfulness to God's ways in the midst of a hostile culture is the unifying theme of Eph 4:17—5:20.[41]

The other precursor text, Isa 59–60, also has missional themes. Following the catalog of transgressions in Isa 59:2–15, God himself comes as Divine Warrior to deliver and establish justice (59:16–18). Consequently "those in the west shall fear the name of the LORD, and those in the east, his glory" (59:19). God's intent is that he be known and glorified in the whole earth (cf. Eph 1:10, 23). Following his coming to Zion as redeemer, God covenants to bestow his Spirit, along with his words in the mouths of his faithful people and their future generations (Isa 59:20–21). This concept aligns well with the

37. Moritz, *Profound Mystery*, 100, citing Hippolitus, *Dan*, 4.56 and *Antichristo*, 65; Edwards, *Galatians*, 179, cites Jerome (*Ep. Eph.* 3.5.14) and Theodoret (*Eph.* 5.14) as representative of ancient writers who denied an OT background to the quote.
38. Moritz, *Profound Mystery*, 100.
39. Lunde and Dunne, "Isaiah in Ephesians 5," 99–101.
40. Childs, *Isaiah*, 190–91.
41. Cf. Baugh, *Ephesians*, 435.

exhortation of Eph 5:18–19 to be filled with the Spirit and to speak or sing spiritual psalms, hymns, and songs.

The next verses in Isaiah (60:1–2) then proclaim: "Arise, shine, for your light has come . . . the LORD will arise upon you, and his glory will appear over you." The impact of the coming of God's glorious light is that God's people themselves become a beacon to draw the nations in. "Nations shall come to your light, and kings to the brightness of your dawn" (Isa 60:3). The ingathering of the nations in the eschaton takes place through the agency of the redeemed and illuminated people of God. This then clarifies the statement in Eph 5:8 "now in the Lord you are light. Live as children of light." To live as light is to be a beacon of God's glory for the whole world, certainly through ethical behavior, but also through their newfound hope and salvation centered in Christ (5:14b). Barth notes that far from being restricted to an intellectual apprehension of truth, illumination here implies ontological, ethical, existential, and cultic transformation.[42] All those who have thus been illumined themselves become a source of illumination for others.[43] Isaiah 60 continues to a climax in 60:19–22 where God's light and glory outshine the sun and moon, and God's people are righteous, secure, and prosperous in the land. As background to the exhortations in Eph 4:17—5:20, this vision illustrates the ultimate fruit of living in Christ's light (Eph 5:9).

9.5 Portrayal of Humanity and the World in Relation to God's Mission

The negative portrayal of nonbelieving gentiles is described as alienated from God, with attendant characteristics of futile thought, hard-heartedness, and darkened understanding (4:17–18). In this state, they are unable to walk worthily of God (4:1; 5:15), or to fulfill their proper ends in God (4:17–18).[44] This portrait recalls 2:1–5 with its analysis of the spiritually dead state of the recipients pre-conversion, as they followed the ruler of the power of the air. It is reminiscent of Jewish polemic against pagan idolatry, which is explicitly identified in 5:5 as the cause behind greed and attendant moral misdeeds (5:3–5; cf. Wis 14:27). In Isaiah's critique of idolatry, the idolater is mocked for being deceived and foolish for putting their hope in a wooden carved idol which is blind, unthinking, and

---

42. Barth, *Ephesians 4–6*, 599–600.

43. Cf. Moritz, *Profound Mystery*, 104, 115; Yoder Neufeld, *Ephesians*, 235–36 (who also detects echoes of Num 6:24–26 and Isa 42:6–7).

44. Fowl, *Ephesians*, 147.

without a heart (44:8–20). The senselessness of the idol reflects the senselessness of those who worship it.

Barth sees the indictment of the gentiles as arising firstly from idolatry, since in ignoring the true God, humanity becomes worthless (cf. Jer 2:5). Secondly, that idolatry results in immoral, selfish deeds (Eph 4:19; 5:3–5; cf. Rom 1:24–29). Finally, it is a portrait of life when renewal in mind and spirit (Eph 4:23) has not progressed appropriately.[45] It is written for believers as motivation for them to turn away from the futility of their old way of life, by presenting the ways in which it deviates from God's ideal for renewed life as modeled and taught by Christ and enabled by the Spirit (4:20, 30; 5:2, 18).[46]

The key theological insight of the passage is that apart from Christ, the human mind (νοῦς 4:17, 23) will be ensnared in futile, corrupt, and self-serving thoughts that result in impure actions that cannot please God because the fundamental disposition of one's life excludes God and his mission of personal, communal, and cosmic renewal.[47]

9.6 Evidence of a Missional Context in the Problems, Crises or Issues Addressed

At the surface level, the problems and issues addressed by the passage are community-damaging behaviors (e.g. 4:25, 28, 29), out of step with God's ideal for his renewed people. The vices cataloged here are similar to other NT and Jewish vice-lists (e.g. Rom 1:29–31; 13:13; Gal 5:19–21; Col 3:8–12; 1 Pet 4:3; 1QS4). Their presence in Ephesians therefore may not reflect a particular situation affecting the recipients, but a generic issue affecting all Christian communities, namely the struggle to adopt distinctively Christian ethics whilst continuing to live in a predominantly non-Christian culture. MacDonald sees the concern for unity among believers in 4:25, 29 as evidence that the author was responding to a serious threat to community life, a risk of assimilation. She characterizes Eph 4:17—5:20 (by comparison with Col 4:5) as more intensely world-rejecting and desirous of protecting community boundaries from evil.[48] While this is a plausible reconstruction, it ignores the letter's overriding concern that the whole cosmos be brought into submission to Christ, and for the church, as Christ's body, to fill the world

---

45. Barth, *Ephesians 4–6*, 526–29.

46. Cf. Best, "Two Types," 140–46, 155, who notes that contrasting life before and after conversion was common in NT texts (e.g. Rom 6:12–14; 1 Pet 1:18) and in Jewish writings (e.g. Jub. 22:16–18; 1QS 4:9–14).

47. Arnold, *Ephesians*, 291–92.

48. MacDonald, *Colossians and Ephesians*, 320–22; Muddiman, *Ephesians*, 245.

(1:10, 20–23). Therefore, any world-rejection is not the ultimate goal, but is limited to what is necessary to enable believers to develop and maintain Christian identity in their society, on the path towards eventually filling and transforming society with God's presence and ways.

Best argues that, viewed objectively, gentile life was not so deplorable as the depiction suggests, but that in the eyes of converts looking backwards, their prior life apart from Christ was steeped in various sins. The primary function of the bleak portrayal is to make the letter's recipients less likely to fall back into old ways.[49] Rikard Roitto offers a more sophisticated analysis drawing on social identity theory. He argues that contrasting the recipients with outsiders strengthens their feelings that group membership is meaningful and valuable.[50] The function of 4:17–31 is to urge the recipients to conform their behavior to the desired prototypical behavior of the author, and to reject the outgroup behavior of nonbelieving gentiles.[51] While there are valid insights from the psychological and social theory of Roitto, these tend towards circular reasoning. The dynamics of social identity formation are identified in the text, but contrary or broader dynamics are neglected, especially the light imagery, discussed in §9.7, below, which suggests greater engagement with the surrounding society than Roitto's construction suggests is occurring.

Best's repeated refrain that Ephesians is concerned with the internal life of congregations and has no interest in mission is largely based on the paraenetic material of 4:17—6:9.[52] At this juncture, we can assess the validity of his position. Best's view that the ethical material of Ephesians, with its focus on conduct of believers towards each other, as individuals and in households, reveals an internal focus is superficial. Biblical ethics are concerned to shape the conduct of the people of God in order to present an attractive witness to the wider world. Wright argues that the holiness code, especially Lev 19, provides a worked example of the priestly mission of God's people to the nations. The concerns of Lev 19 are broadly parallel to Eph 4–6, including economic justice, neighbor love and truth in speech, family relationships, and sexual integrity.[53] Similarly, Martin Salter has argued based on Deuteronomy, Isaiah, Jeremiah, Ezekiel, and Luke-Acts that biblical ethics are missional since when the believing community exercises justice, charity, and worship they bear witness "to the nature and character of God before a

49. Best, "Two Types," 145–46, 155.
50. Roitto, Christ-Believer, 163.
51. Roitto, Christ-Believer, 170.
52. Best, Ephesians, 354, 621, 638.
53. Wright, God's People, 124–27.

watching world."[54] The paraenetic material of Ephesians is concerned with just these things (justice 4:24; 5:9; 6:14; charity 4:2, 15, 16; 5:2; worship 5:18–20). Best's conclusion that because Ephesians is concerned with ethics within the church it is unconcerned with mission betrays an inadequate appreciation of the power and purpose of biblical ethics.

9.7 Character and Mission of God's People in the World

The character of God's people in the world is centered in this passage around their way of living (cf. 4:1), which is to be as recreated image-bearers of God, imitating God's moral virtues (4:24; 5:1). Christ is their standard and teacher of truth (4:20–21); he is the model or prototypical new human. Christ provides the blueprint for the new humanity forged in his death (2:14–15). As an ever-increasing number of humans become part of the church and adopt this pattern of Christ-like humanity, Christ's fullness is dispersed throughout the earth (1:23).

MacDonald sees in the virtue and vice catalog an indication that some in the community of believers were bringing shame (αἰσχρός) on their community (esp. 5:2, 12).[55] Best similarly interprets the references to sexual impropriety in 5:5 as evidence that some in the Christian community had engaged in sexual behavior that breached broader community standards, which would be shameful if exposed.[56] Shame is a publicly judged and felt value, and therefore its mention indicates that the believing community was being observed by their neighbors. The passage may therefore have a subtle missional purpose of seeking to guard or restore the honor of the believing community in the eyes of the broader community. (This goal is only plausible if sufficient elements within the broader gentile society were not as degenerate as portrayed in 4:17–5:18, but would esteem the ethical ideals portrayed in the passage.)

MacDonald sees a further indicator of a missional role for the passage in 5:8–12, where the light-darkness imagery clearly portrays Christians as beacons of tangible ethical conduct, visible to the broader community (esp. 5:8, 11).[57] She concludes that when Christians are visible for their moral way of life, "there is a possible interest in evangelization."[58] While

---

54. Salter, "Missional Ethics," 326.
55. MacDonald, *Colossians and Ephesians*, 310, 315.
56. Best, *Ephesians*, 494–95.
57. MacDonald, *Colossians and Ephesians*, 314–15.
58. MacDonald, *Colossians and Ephesians*, 316.

MacDonald sees Col 4:5 (a parallel text to Eph 5:15–16) as an encouragement to use "every opportunity to evangelize,"[59] she interprets "making the most of the time" (Eph 5:16) to be primarily eschatological in orientation—an exhortation to diligently emulate Christ's moral example, in light of his coming, not in order to convert nonbelievers. MacDonald acknowledges that in Pauline literature *time* (καιρός) is frequently associated with the eschatological urgency of Paul's mission (citing inter alia 2 Cor 6:2), but she sets that meaning aside here, largely because of her conviction that Ephesians is deutero-Pauline.[60]

MacDonald's preference against an evangelistic element in 5:15–16 is less supportable when the context of the intertextual links discussed above is allowed for. Isaiah 60, particularly, envisages God's people, renewed in holiness, becoming a beacon that draws the nations to God. "Making the most of the time" is understood by Barth in the light of Mark 13:10; 2 Pet 3:9; Eph 6:18–19 to particularly necessitate the "spreading of the gospel and the repentance and salvation of men."[61] The mission of God's people in the world as indicated by Eph 5:15–16 encompasses both an ethical witness of doing good works and an evangelistic activity of taking every opportunity to fill the earth with Christ's presence by wisely sharing the gospel with those still in darkness.[62]

Many commentators have noted the light imagery lends itself to a missional understanding of the role of God's people in the world, as per Matt 5:14, "you are the light of the world."[63] In Eph 5:11 the role of the light is not purely as a point of attraction, but to illuminate the misdeeds of unbelieving society (believers are to expose the "unfruitful works of darkness"; cf. John 3:20).[64] Muddiman detects two tendencies in Eph 4–5. Firstly, an inner-ecclesial tendency towards separation from the world and concentration on behaviors within the community (5:3–4, 6–9). This stands in tension with the second, opposite tendency to engage, or even seek to convince and convict (meanings within the semantic range of ἐλέγχω in 5:11) the unbelieving world primarily through their moral behaviors (an "extra-ecclesial" focus). Muddiman sees the author as pursuing a strategy of moving his audience

---

59. MacDonald, *Colossians and Ephesians*, 317.

60. MacDonald, *Colossians and Ephesians*, 317.

61. Barth, *Ephesians 4–6*, 579; see also Lincoln, *Ephesians*, 342.

62. Arnold, *Ephesians*, 347.

63. Muddiman, *Ephesians*, 237; Barth, *Ephesians 1–3*, 596–98, 604 (at 596 he notes Phil 2:15; Prov 4:18; 1 Thess 4:12; Col 4:5; 1 Pet 2:9, 12).

64. Lincoln, *Ephesians*, 330; Schnackenburg, *Ephesians*, 226.

from an inner-ecclesial to an extra-ecclesial focus.[65] This we would label as a missional goal. Barth notes the potential of the light imagery to evoke the concept of the church's mission to the world. However, he rejects the conclusion that the church's mission is to become "the divinely appointed police force of the world . . . censuring [and] convicting" according to the standards of God's laws.[66] Barth accordingly interprets this passage as predominantly focused on internal church behavior, while still acknowledging that Ephesians more broadly is concerned with mission to nonbelievers.

The passage contains both an inward concern for holiness and appropriate conduct in the renewed community of God's people, and an indirect missional function of displaying the moral attractiveness of God's design for human community. While we can agree with Barth that the church is not here exhorted to denounce the world for not being the church, that does not negate a subtle influence on the world of passively witnessing to the benefits of living in accordance with God's standards. The role is consistent with other NT passages in which it is the ethical behavior of believers rather than their proselytizing speech that is the means of participating in God's mission in the world.[67]

At this juncture, we can also assess MacDonald's claim that Ephesians is more strongly introversionist than other Pauline epistles. This claim is largely based on a sociological theory of sects by Bryan Wilson, and comparisons of Ephesians with the Qumran literature.[68] Her claim is that the community addressed in Ephesians is advised to set itself apart from and escape the everyday (evil) world.[69] Some passages (2:1–3; 4:17–20; 6:10–20) aim to reinforce the boundaries of the community as against the outside nonbelieving world. The identity of believers is narrated as being "in Christ" and exalted into heavenly realms (1:3, 20; 2:4–7). MacDonald claims the recipients of Ephesians are not explicitly encouraged to dialogue with outsiders (contrasting Eph 5:15–16 with Col 4:5–6). She does, however, recognize a tension "typical of a conversionist response to the world . . . Texts that call for world rejection are found in a work that also displays great interest in universal mission (e.g., Eph 3:8–13; 6:19–20)."[70] With this nuance, MacDonald is not making a claim that Ephesians displays no interest in mission

65. Muddiman, *Ephesians*, 237, 239–40.

66. Barth, *Ephesians 4–6*, 597.

67. Cf. Dickson, *Mission-Commitment*, 262–92, discussing 1 Thess 4:11–12; Phil 4:5; Col 4:5; Titus 2:3–10; 3:1–8.

68. E.g. Perkins, *Ephesians*, 29–30, 103; Esler, *First Christians*, 70–91; Wilson, *Sectarianism*, 23–24, 36–41.

69. MacDonald, *Colossians and Ephesians*, 21.

70. MacDonald, *Colossians and Ephesians*, 238.

(or using her terminology, "universal salvation"), just that it is less interested than the other Pauline letters.[71]

The missional reading developed in this project calls into question MacDonald's conclusions. Firstly, her conception of mission seems too restrictive. Although never defined, at one point mission is set in parallel to: "church expansion and . . . dialogue between believers and nonbelievers."[72] The analysis above indicates, by contrast, that the *missio Dei*, as portrayed in Ephesians encompasses all of God's gracious actions to overcome alienation, division, and other communal manifestations of sin in order that the cosmos is renewed and brought into unified submission under Christ's lordship. Secondly, the supposed introversionist turn is a sociological inference in most cases. Virtually the only verse with an explicit exhortation to turn away from the world is 5:7, "Therefore do not be associated with them [the disobedient]." MacDonald says that the only similarly strong verse in the Pauline corpus is 2 Cor 6:14–7:1, which she labels as an interpolation, and then ignores.[73] But MacDonald's reading of Eph 5:7 as referring to nonbelievers flies against the majority scholarly position that it is referring to errant church members.[74] In fact, 1 Cor 5:9–10 is highly pertinent. There, believers are encouraged to shun hypocritical believers, not nonbelievers. The issue is condoning and participating in immorality, not contact with the broader world (as Eph 5:11 clearly envisages).[75] Ephesians does envisage ongoing contact with nonbelievers at 4:25, 28; 6:5–7. MacDonald's assessment of Ephesians as introversionist is too heavily reliant on a selective set of texts read in the light of sociological theory, and a narrow conception of mission.

9.8 Conclusion

Ephesians 4:17—5:20 is much more than a generic Christian version of the Jewish *two ways* paraenetic tradition. God's purpose is to create a new humanity in God's image, modeled on Christ (4:13, 24), especially in his loving self-sacrifice and forgiveness. As God's Spirit fills the church for wise, grateful, and reverent conduct, God's presence fills the church and through it, permeates the world. Christ illuminates believers especially in their ethical witness to a darkened world, inviting sinners to come to the light of

71. MacDonald, *Colossians and Ephesians*, 238.
72. MacDonald, *Colossians and Ephesians*, 21.
73. MacDonald, *Colossians and Ephesians*, 321.
74. Barth, *Ephesians 4–6*, 566–67; Best, *Ephesians*, 486.
75. Baugh, *Ephesians*, 428; Hoehner, *Ephesians*, 668–69.

salvation (5:13-14). The passage is Trinitarian in scope as God, Christ, and the Spirit are all active in the moral transformation of believers for the sake of their missional life in the world.

There is a rich intertextuality in the passage, supporting the new creation motif (Eph 4:24; Deut 32:4; Ps 144:17 LXX). A number of OT allusions, especially Zech 8:16 in Eph 4:25, and Isa 26:19 and 60:1-2 in Eph 5:14 have contexts where God's restoration of his people leads to gentile pilgrimage to God or worship of God, and so are strongly missional. To live as light (Eph 5:8) is to be beacons of God's glory for the whole world, certainly through ethical behavior (Isa 60), but also through their newfound hope and salvation centered in Christ. Truth-speaking (4:25) likely includes gospel proclamation (cf. 1:13; 4:21) by which those in darkness come to experience the blessings of salvation. The negative portrayal of humanity apart from Christ is tied particularly to the issue of idolatry (4:19; 5:3-5), which is a root cause of immorality as well as alienation from God, since idolaters are blind and deceived by their false priorities (cf. Isa 44).

The social context addressed by Eph 4-5 seems to be behaviors that undermine community (such as anger and lying) and traits that would frustrate God's missional purposes for the church and the world (such as greed, unforgiveness, or debauchery). Finally, this passage supports the importance of an ethical witness to the gospel through the speech and actions of the believing community. In particular, "making the most of the time" should be understood on the analogy of 2 Pet 3:9 and Eph 6:18-19 to involve extending Paul's mission and making efforts to wisely share the gospel with those still in darkness.

10

Ephesians 5:21—6:9

10.1 Introduction

THE HOUSEHOLD CODE OF Ephesians has been the subject of considerable research and debate, especially regarding the motivations behind its utilization of existing household codes known from classical Greek and Hellenistic Jewish texts, and modifications thereof.[1] Especially in the section addressing husbands and wives, there is found theologically rich material that gives insights into the *missio Dei* and the character and actions of Christ. In addition to a quotation from Gen 2:24, the passage also contains echoes of and allusions to a variety of OT texts, whose original context and function help to illuminate the ethic being advocated in the household code. We will evaluate a variety of proposals regarding the apologetic function and missional setting of the code, and also consider how the household code portrays the believing household as a microcosm of God's new society. The code portrays a Christian household, and is silent on the issue of humanity and the world in relation to God's mission, so this will not be discussed.

10.2 Portrayal of God's Intentions, Actions, and Purposes (the *missio Dei*)

As with previous material in Eph 4–5, the household code indicates that God's mission includes reshaping everyday relationships such that sinful behaviors are abandoned, and behaviors pleasing to God are adopted. This passage

---

1. Hering, *Haustafeln*, 9–60.

continues to express how believers are to walk worthily of their calling (4:1). Verse 21 is a hinge verse, carrying forward the idea of being filled with the Spirit (5:18), expressed in singing, thankfulness, and submission; while foreshadowing submission based on reverence (fear) of Christ as the principal ethic governing the three pairs of relationships in the household code that follows. "Submitting to one another is understood as central to a way of life that sets believers apart from the Gentiles (cf. 4:17)."[2] The household code therefore has as a goal the creation of a visibly distinctive behavioral ethic, which nonbelievers would be able to observe and evaluate. While not evangelistic in any overt sense, the family life of believers was to be a public witness to the impact the lordship of Christ had over all of life.[3]

The material on husband-wife relations contains a theologically rich section (5:23–30) in which the relationship of Christ to the church becomes a model for husbands and wives. This section reveals a number of elements of the *missio Dei*: that Christ is the Savior of the church (5:23); that Christ loved and gave himself up for the church (5:25); that Christ cleansed, sanctified (ἁγιάσῃ), and perfected the church for himself (5:26–27); and that Christ nourishes and cares for the church (5:29). Christ's role as the initiator of these actions for the church is emphasized through repetition (Christ as the subject vv. 24, 25, 29, or using pronouns vv. 25, 26). Also prominent is the ultimate purpose of God's mission (introduced with ἵνα, v. 26): to create a sanctified (ἅγιος), glorious (ἔνδοξος), blemish-free (ἄμωμος) people for himself. In each of these adjectives we see an implicit contrast with humanity's current state outside of Christ: unholy, ignominious, and blameworthy.

Sanctification is elaborated to have taken place "by cleansing (καθαρίσας) her with the washing of water by the word" (v. 26). The aorist particle καθαρίσας, cleansing, indicates not a prior action but a contemporaneous action with the main verb ἁγιάζω. The imagery of v. 26 is clearly baptismal (cf. 1 Cor 6:11).[4] The following phrase ἐν ῥήματι, *by the word*, is ambiguous. Best takes it as a reference to the baptismal formula "in the name of Christ" spoken at the time of baptism, while a number of commentators prefer to see it as a reference to the proclamation of the gospel (consistent with the use of ῥῆμα at Eph 6:17; cf. Rom 10:17 and Eph 1:13 where λόγος is used).[5] This latter view

2. MacDonald, *Colossians and Ephesians*, 325.

3. Yoder Neufeld, *Ephesians*, 284.

4. Lincoln, *Ephesians*, 375; Best, *Ephesians*, 542–43; MacDonald, *Colossians and Ephesians*, 328.

5. Best, *Ephesians*, 542–44; those who see it referring to the proclaimed gospel include Caird, *Paul's Letters*, 89; Lincoln, *Ephesians*, 376; Hoehner, *Ephesians*, 755; Thielman, *Ephesians*, 385; Arnold, *Ephesians*, 400–401. Cf. 1 Pet 1:25, τοῦτο δέ ἐστιν τὸ ῥῆμα τὸ εὐαγγελισθὲν εἰς ὑμᾶς "that *word* is the good news that was announced to you."

is preferable since NT baptismal formulas generally include ἐν τῷ ὀνόματι "in the name" of Christ or into Christ (Acts 2:38; 1 Cor 1:13; Rom 6:3; Gal 3:27), but such a construction is absent in Eph 5.

The church is also the beneficiary of Christ's ongoing care and provision, so that God's mission is understood to be the ongoing sustenance and rejuvenation of human society within the world (v. 29).[6] A further element of God's mission is implied in 5:32, the "mystery" that is Christ and the church. In 1:9–10 the mystery is God's plan to unite all things in Christ. In 3:6 the mystery is the reconciliation of Jews and gentiles in the church. Here in 5:32, the mystery concerns the unity of husband and wife in parallel to the unity of Christ and the church. Taken together, the mystery encompasses God's plan to be reconciled, or reunited, with sinful humanity through the saving work of Christ.[7]

10.3 Portrayal of God's Person and Character

This passage gives a prominent place to Christ as the model for self-sacrificial, loving behavior for husbands in 5:25–33. The concentration of familial language in 5:25–33 conveys a sense of intimacy linked to the caring quality of Christ's actions for the church, which balances the more hierarchical, authoritarian language that predominates in the advice for wives in 5:22–24 ("be subject to," "head"), and children and slaves in 6:1–9 ("obey," "honor"). The caring quality of Christ's action is particularly prominent in 5:29 where an analogy between a man's care of his own body is made with Christ's care of his body the church: "he nourishes and tenderly cares for it."[8]

The impartial character of God, committed to justice for all (slaves as well as free persons), is reflected in 6:9, which states that with God, "there is no partiality." This principle is significant for mission since no member of the Christian household is without worth in God's eyes, and God's mission encompasses justice for all humanity. Moreover, the Ephesian household code accords greater worth to slaves, children, and wives than was theirs according to the prevailing social and legal standards of the first century.[9] God's mission promotes justice for those in society who are more vulnerable due to tradition or sinful structures such as slavery.

---

6. Arnold, *Ephesians*, 386.
7. MacDonald, *Colossians and Ephesians*, 351.
8. Arnold, *Ephesians*, 400.
9. Lincoln, *Ephesians*, 409, 424–25; cf. Talbert, *Ephesians and Colossians*, 139.

10.4 Intertextuality—Literary and Thematic Links to the Wider Biblical Narrative

The passage contains quotations from Gen 2:24 at Eph 5:31 and Exod 20:12 at Eph 6:2–3. There is also an echo from Deut 10:17 at Eph 6:9. Some scholars see an allusion to Ezek 16:1–7 at Eph 5:26. The three intertextual links to the Pentateuch anchor the household code in creation, exodus, and the covenantal framework by which Israel lived. These literary linkages will be discussed in turn.

10.4.1 Genesis 2:24

The quotation at Eph 5:31 comes from Gen 2:24, "For this reason a man will leave his father and mother and be joined to his wife, and the two will become one flesh." This quotation underpins the author's argument that husbands are to love and care for their wives as they would their own body. The "one flesh" idea of Gen 2:24 therefore proves the author's point that wives are one body with their husband, and analogously, Christ is one with his body the church. The missional significance of a reference to Gen 2 in this context is that caring household relationships are rooted in God's creational design. Abuse and neglect are symptoms of the fall. Christ has inaugurated a new creation (cf. Eph 2:14–16; 4:22–24).[10] A mutually caring marriage relationship, it can be inferred, becomes a public witness to the goodness of God's design for all marriage relationships in society, and an implicit invitation for nonbelievers to consider how the lordship of Christ positively impacts household and intrachurch relationships, bringing greater unity and closeness.[11]

10.4.2 Exodus 20:12

At Eph 6:2–3, the LXX of Exod 20:12 (rather than Deut 5:16) is quoted virtually verbatim (with only a minor change of form and position of the verb γίνομαι, and the interjection of the comment at v. 2b, "this is the first commandment with a promise").[12] Exodus 20:12: τίμα τὸν πατέρα σου καὶ τὴν μητέρα, ἵνα εὖ σοι γένηται, καὶ ἵνα μακροχρόνιος γένῃ ἐπὶ τῆς γῆς. Eph 6:2–3: τίμα τὸν πατέρα σου καὶ τὴν μητέρα, ἥτις ἐστὶν ἐντολὴ πρώτη ἐν ἐπαγγελίᾳ, 3

---

10. Thielman, "Ephesians," 828.
11. Cf. Goheen, *Light to the Nations*, 185–86.
12. Moritz, *Profound Mystery*, 154–55; Hoehner, *Ephesians*, 788.

ἵνα εὖ σοι γένηται καὶ ἔσῃ μακροχρόνιος ἐπὶ τῆς γῆς. "Honor your father and mother"—this is the first commandment with a promise: "so that it may be well with you and you may live long on the earth."

The explicit quotation of the first commandment in the second table of the Ten Commandments is a clear indication that the ethics governing the Christian household (and all human relationships) are grounded in Torah. Christ's lordship had not abolished the law but enabled its fulfillment (cf. Matt 5:17–18). The mission of the church, to fill the world with a witness to God's wisdom and Christ's presence (Eph 1:23; 3:10), includes providing concrete lived examples of Torah in action—healthy human relationships founded on love and honor. The honor owed to God by believers is manifest in the honor shown within the household.[13]

Muddiman sees an allusion to Gen 3:16 ("your desire shall be for your husband, and he shall rule over you") in Eph 5:22, "Wives, be subject to your husbands as you are to the Lord."[14] By contrast, Barth claims that the lack of a quotation of Gen 3:16 is proof that Paul was not seeking to establish male authoritarian headship in Christian marriage, and that his approach to marriage derives from before the fall (Gen 2) rather than after it (Gen 3).[15] The lack of any comment in Eph 5 about the fall and any particular association of Eve or women with sin supports the conclusion that the understanding of marriage being advanced in Eph 5:22–31 reflects a new creation, rather than an outworking of the curse of Gen 3:16. The missional impact of marriage as portrayed in Eph 5:22–31 is therefore not in its continuation of patterns of hierarchy and male domination (as per Stephen Miletic's characterization of some readings of Eph 5:22–33), but in the attractiveness of husbands displaying *agape* love to their wives, being committed to their well-being ahead of their own desire or comfort. Wives can respond to a husband's selfless love with a reciprocal expression of discipleship.[16]

10.4.3 Deuteronomy 10:17

Another verse that echoes an OT text is Eph 6:9, "both of you have the same Master in heaven, and with him there is no partiality." This echoes Deut 10:17, "the Lord your God . . . is not partial and takes no bribe," and 2 Chr 19:7, "let the fear of the Lord be upon you; take care what you do, for there is no perversion of justice with the Lord our God, or partiality, or taking of bribes." In

---

13. Thielman, "Ephesians," 829.
14. Muddiman, *Ephesians*, 259.
15. Barth, *Ephesians 4-6*, 715, 732.
16. Miletic, *One Flesh*, 118–20.

Deut 10, the following verse (v. 18) emphasizes God's commitment to justice, especially for the orphan, widow and stranger. Verses 19–21 remind Israel of their own rescue from slavery in Egypt as a reason for them to be committed to justice for the vulnerable. Eph 6:9, with Deut 10 as intertext, therefore helps believers understand the importance in God's mission of the church being a source and champion of justice, especially for any economically or socially vulnerable individuals and groups.

10.4.4 Ezekiel 16:1–7

Ezekiel 16 contains a lengthy allegory in which Israel is portrayed firstly as an exposed infant rescued by God (vv. 1–7), and then as the unfaithful bride of God (vv. 8–63). In Ezek 16:9 God says he "bathed you with water and washed off the blood from you, and anointed you with oil." According to a number of commentators, Eph 5:26 "cleansing her with the washing of water" echoes or alludes to Ezek 16:9.[17] Arnold gives five points of correlation: (a) the covenant as marriage bond; (b) God initiating the marriage with an undeserving, unclean people; (c) God's action of cleansing his people; (d) a two-stage cleansing comprising an initial act and a final eschatological perfection; and (e) God's persistent faithfulness leading ultimately to the bride's glorification.[18] J. Paul Sampley sees three elements of particular importance: (a) the great love of Christ for the church; (b) Christ sanctifying the church through washing of water; and (c) the goal of the church to be presented ἔνδοξος, *without blemish*.[19] These thematic correspondences are only one indicator of an allusion. Hays's other tests will enable a fuller evaluation of the possible intertextual link.

The *volume* of the verbal correspondence is low. Only one word in Eph 5:26 ἵνα αὐτὴν ἁγιάσῃ καθαρίσας τῷ λουτρῷ τοῦ ὕδατος ἐν ῥήματι "in order to make her holy by cleansing her with the washing of *water* by the word" is exactly paralleled in Ezek 16:9 (LXX), namely water (ὕδωρ). There is conceptual equivalence between τῷ λουτρῷ "the washing" (Eph) and ἔλουσά σε "washing you" (Ezek).[20] The marriage imagery in both texts strengthens the

---

17. Lincoln, *Ephesians*, 375; Sampley, "Two Shall Become One," 38–43; MacDonald, *Colossians and Ephesians*, 328–29; Barth, "Traditions in Ephesians," 4, 11.

18. Arnold, *Ephesians*, 385–86.

19. Sampley, "Two Shall Become One," 35.

20. However, there are thirty other occurrences in the LXX of "washing with water" using a combination of the roots υδωρ and λουω, mostly concentrated in Leviticus and Numbers (e.g. Lev 15:10, 11, 13, 16, 18, 21, 22, 27; 16:4, 24, 26, 28; Num 19:7, 19). The cultic action of washing with water is therefore a prevalent OT figure. The further connection between Eph 5 and Ezek 16 is the marriage motif.

volume of conceptual parallelism. Ezekiel was certainly *available* to the author of Ephesians, with Ezekiel texts alluded to at least a dozen times in the Pauline corpus (e.g. Ezek 16:63 in Rom 6:21; Ezek 36–37 in Eph 2, discussed above).[21] The criterion of *recurrence* is not satisfied since Ezek 16:9 is not clearly alluded to elsewhere in the Pauline corpus.

In favor of seeing *thematic coherence* are the points noted by Arnold and Sampley above. Against seeing thematic coherence is the fact that the predominant focus of Ezek 16 is on the unfaithfulness of Israel, whereas Eph 5 does not portray the church as unfaithful. An allusion to the covenantal relationship between Israel and God pictured in marital terms would be a *historically plausible* interpretation of Eph 5, since covenantal imagery is explicit in Eph 1, and Paul's explicit line of argument is to see human marriage as analogous to the church and Christ relationship. There is no precritical evidence of seeing Ezek 16 as a precursor text to Eph 5:26. While a number of commentators note the possible relevance of Ezek 16 as background, very few explicitly claim the author is making a deliberate allusion, and so the *history of interpretation* provides only weak support for an intentional allusion. Hays's final test of *satisfaction* invites the interpreter to judge whether a proposed intertextual reading illuminates the surrounding discourse.[22] Overall, it may be concluded that while there is a likelihood that Eph 5:22–31 draws on the OT theme of Israel as God's bride by covenant, of which Ezek 16 is one witness, the more specific claim made by Lincoln, Arnold, and Sampley that Eph 5:26 alludes to the bridal bath of Ezek 16:9 may be an interpretive overreach. Ephesians 5 does not draw on the concept of unfaithfulness, which is the dominant concern of Ezek 16, and there are ample texts in Leviticus which speak of "washing with water." These provide a sufficient background for the metaphor of God purifying his people from sin as an aspect of his covenantal relationship with them (e.g. Lev 16:4, 24).

10.5 Evidence of a Missional Context in the Problems, Crises or Issues Addressed

A number of commentators discuss the idea that the Ephesian household code has an apologetic function. Muddiman states that "the adoption and adaptation of the household code offered reassurance that the Christian movement posed no immediate practical threat to the *status quo* . . . and did not therefore warrant suppression or harassment."[23] MacDonald ar-

21. UBS5, 878–79.
22. Hays, *Echoes of Scripture*, 31–32.
23. Muddiman, *Ephesians*, 278; cf. Lincoln, *Ephesians*, 397.

gued that believers (especially slaves and women) who rejected traditional gods may have prompted criticism of first-century Christian groups.[24] The Pauline adoption of household codes was therefore "an attempt to stabilize relations with outsiders."[25] Lisa Belz states:

> household codes are a form of apologetic literature written to assure Roman authorities that the persons writing them, as well as those either to whom they are addressed or whom they describe, are upstanding and loyal members of the empire, in full support of its system of order imposed through structured, hierarchical relationships where all know their place in subordination to higher-ups. In other words, household codes served to indicate a group's conformity to official imperial "morality," as understood by Roman tradition and upheld by Roman law.[26]

Similar comments are found in Lincoln and James Dunn, who all draw parallels to Ephesians from David Balch's analysis of the household code in 1 Peter.[27] Another account of the apologetic function of the household codes was developed by Elisabeth Schüssler Fiorenza. She argued that the earliest Christian vision was a "discipleship of equals practiced in the house church [which] attracted especially slaves and women to Christianity but also caused tensions and conflicts with the dominant cultural ethos of the patriarchal household."[28] The household codes of the NT function to soften the inherited harshness of patriarchy, but nevertheless represented an accommodation to the "politeuma of Rome and its ancestral customs."[29]

An increasing number of scholars have questioned the apologetic thesis, at least as it applies to the household code in Ephesians. While there are explicit comments connecting the household conduct of believers to unbelievers in 1 Pet 3:1, 15 (and Col 4:5, 6 comes shortly after the Colossian household code), the Ephesian household code is not framed by reference to unbelieving household members or surrounding society.[30] Daniel Darko argued that the code in Eph 5:21—6:9 continues the wisdom-folly contrasts of 4:17—5:21, whereby the church is differentiated from surrounding

---

24. MacDonald, *Pauline Churches*, 121.

25. MacDonald, *Pauline Churches*, 109.

26. Belz, "Household Relations," 229.

27. Lincoln, *Ephesians*, 360; Dunn, "Household Rules," 43–64; Balch, *Let Wives Be Submissive*, 81–116.

28. Schüssler Fiorenza, *In Memory of Her*, 251; see also Yoder Neufeld, *Ephesians*, 279–80.

29. Schüssler Fiorenza, *In Memory of Her*, 262.

30. Cf. Moritz, *Profound Mystery*, 166.

society. It has an intragroup concern to promote mutuality among members and has no explicit references to outsiders or the reputation of the church in society. Darko concludes, "the view that the *Haustafel* is intended to have integrative function in Ephesians lacks evidence."[31] Having rejected the apologetic thesis, Darko then fails to offer a compelling alternative explanation for the function of the household code in Ephesians. In Darko's analysis, the code is simply conventional moral philosophy, with a heightened christological basis and motivation for its acceptance.[32] Darko's dependence on social identity theory results in him elevating social description above analysis (be that social, ideological, or theological analysis). Darko fails to adequately account for the impact of the christological distinctives on the Ephesian household code.

A stronger theological account of the function of the household codes is found in Talbert, who states: "In 1:10 God's plan for the fullness of time... is the establishment of cosmic unity and peace... the Christian household's unity and harmony are sought as yet another expression of the summing up of all things through Christ."[33] Talbert's approach upholds the intragroup function of the household code as an exhortation to mutual submission and respect, which results in peace, while still allowing for these distinctive household dynamics to represent a witness to the surrounding culture. The Christian household, as empowered by the Spirit, could voluntarily cultivate unity and harmony rather than having these imposed from above by imperial powers or through fear of spiritual forces.

The household code in Ephesians is therefore an effective missional strategy, not by advocating accommodation to prevailing cultural patterns, but by publicly displaying the healing of sin-damaged familial relationships.[34] The quote from Gen 2:24 alerts readers to the reconciling and restorative power of Christ in the realm of personal relationships. What was intended in the first creation yet lost in the fall, has now become possible once more for believers through Christ's self-sacrifice which models agapic love and the power of the Spirit to transform marriage. The issue being addressed is therefore human relationships that have been distorted and damaged by sinful power structures (be they harsh patriarchy in the household, the Artemis cult, magical rituals, or Roman imperial political and cultural domination). Ephesians 5:21—6:9 presents a vision of

---

31. Darko, *No Longer Living*, 107 (and see 71–105 for his supporting argument).

32. Darko, *No Longer Living*, 106–7.

33. Talbert, *Ephesians and Colossians*, 147–48, citing Sampley, "Two Shall Become One," 96.

34. Cf. Witherington, *Philemon*, 321.

household relationships that are attractive to nonbelievers because they are characterized by mutuality, respect, love, and harmony, rather than fear, dysfunction, or abuse.

10.6 Character and Mission of God's People in the World

Gehring notes that in Ephesians "the church" refers to the universal body of Christ (3:10, 21; 4:4–6; 5:22, 25, 27, 32), which despite this global referent, in its local manifestation always met in homes, that is, in house churches.[35] Accordingly, the household code represents a vision for relationships between all members of the church as a prototypical new society (cf. Eph 2:19).[36] In this new society, the overarching principle is mutual submission and acknowledgment of Christ as Lord in all areas of life (5:21, 22, 25; 6:1, 4–9).[37] Similarly, Yoder Neufeld notes that in the Aristotelean tradition the family is a microcosm of the societal macrocosm. Therefore, the behaviors shaping a Christian household would influence society more generally.[38] We see from these scholars that this passage envisages a role for humanity in which all relationships are renewed and recast by the lordship of Christ, resulting in greater mutual love and service. The goal towards which humanity is moving is enunciated in 5:27; Christ is forming for himself a sanctified (ἅγιος), glorious (ἔνδοξος), blemish-free (ἄμωμος) people. Humanity, when constituted as God's family, is intended to reflect a unity and mutuality of love and service that originates from God himself (cf. 2:19; 3:15; 4:13).[39]

10.7 Conclusion

The Ephesian household code sets all household relationships as subject to the lordship of Christ (5:21, 22, 25; 6:1, 5, 9) and framed by an overarching exhortation to mutual submission (5:21). God's mission is understood to be the renewal of human society within the world through the reformation of the household, now characterized by the self-giving love and care modeled by Christ, which creates unity. Christ is particularly portrayed as the initiator

---

35. Gehring, *House Church*, 257–58.
36. Stott, *Message of Ephesians*, 244; Sampley, "Two Shall Become One," 149.
37. Eph 5:21, in which the fear of the Lord is "the overarching theological touchstone for regulating [Haustafeln] relations," Hering, *Haustafeln*, 136.
38. Yoder Neufeld, *Ephesians*, 275–76.
39. Sampley, "Two Shall Become One," 149–50; 162.

and means of the church's sanctification and purification (5:26–27). God's mission is marked by his commitment to justice and impartiality, endowing vulnerable members of the household with greater dignity and worth than they had experienced under the prevailing culture.

The intertextual links within the passage draw on a creation text (Gen 2:24), the fifth commandment (Exod 20:12), and Deut 10:17 to support the portrayal of the believing household as the realization of God's original design for human society. The household is to be marked by unity, intergenerational obedience to Torah as God's path to prosperity, as well as justice for the vulnerable. The evidence does not support seeing an allusion to Ezek 16 in Eph 5:26. Rather, the broader OT background is the more generic concept of Israel as God's bride by covenant, which aligns with the way in which the church is portrayed in Eph 5.

The household code does not necessarily reflect an apologetic strategy of social assimilation, as proposed by Muddiman, or stabilization as against the disruption of women and slaves finding freedom through faith, as proposed by MacDonald. Instead, the household code represents an outworking of the summation of all things in Christ announced in 1:10. The unity, harmony, mutuality, care, and respect at work in the believing household was a non-overt display of the potential of the gospel to positively transform human relationships and institutions that were otherwise tainted by sinful abuses.

11

Ephesians 6:10–24

11.1 Introduction

EPHESIANS 6:10-24 CONCLUDES AT least the parenetic section of the letter (4:1–6:20), if not the whole letter.¹ Lincoln, Moritz, Yoder Neufeld, and Jean Aletti view it as a fitting culmination to the whole letter, reiterating key themes by way of a vivid military metaphor.² These themes include the power of God (1:19-20; 2:6; 6:10); the sharing of believers in the triumph of Christ (4:7-11; 6:13); truth (1:13; 4:15, 21, 24, 25; 5:9; 6:14); and salvation (1:13; 2:5, 8; 6:17).³ The passage may be divided into an introductory command and rationale (6:10-13); the detailed metaphor for six virtues (6:14-17); a call to persevering prayer (6:18-20); and a concluding commendation and prayer (6:21-24). We will explore in turn its contribution to understanding the *missio Dei*, the character of God, its missional meaning in the light of intertextual links, humanity and the world, the passage's missional context, the character and mission of God's people, and finally its portrayal of Paul as missionary.

---

1. Bruce, *Epistles*, 241 is an example of the former view.

2. Lincoln, *Ephesians*, 432; Moritz, *Profound Mystery*, 181–83; Yoder Neufeld, *Put on the Armour*, 110; Aletti, *Épître aux Éphésiens*, 305.

3. Lincoln, *Ephesians*, 432; Moritz, *Profound Mystery*, 181; Thielman, "Ephesians," 830.

11.2 Portrayal of God's Intentions, Actions, and Purposes (the *missio Dei*)

The key insight of this passage concerning the *missio Dei* is that God strengthens and equips his people to be intentionally involved in a spiritual struggle against evil spiritual forces, specifically through the gifts of salvation, God's word, faith, and righteousness. Faith and righteousness are also character virtues to be actively cultivated in the life of believers.

This passage begins with either τοῦ λοιποῦ (genitive *from now on*) or τὸ λοιπόν (accusative, *finally*). The genitive is textually better supported particularly in Alexandrian texts ($\mathfrak{P}^{46}$ ℵ* N* A B I and a number of minuscules) compared with the accusative which is predominantly supported by Western and Byzantine texts (ℵ² D F G K L P Ψ).[4] The genitive is the harder reading since the temporal sense of the genitive (future action) seems inappropriate given the recipients are already engaged in a spiritual battle. The accusative likely arose to harmonize this text with the normal Pauline usage of τὸ λοιπόν in 1 Cor 7:29, Phil 3:1, 4:8, and 2 Thess 3:1. Internal evidence therefore also supports the genitive. Accepting the genitive is the stronger reading: does it bear a logical or temporal meaning? The majority of commentators and English translations adopt a logical sense, *finally*, as suggested in some grammars and BDAG.[5] However, Barth argues that the genitive's temporal sense, *for the remaining time*, should be reflected in translation as the readers are in the final stage of salvation history, in which conflict with evil spiritual powers is heightened.[6] There is no precedent in *TLG* for the genitive to bear the meaning *finally*, so the temporal meaning should be preferred, which also heightens the urgency of the appeal to steadfastness in this concluding exhortation.

This passage confirms the idea present earlier in Ephesians that evil spiritual forces oppose God's mission (6:12; cf. 2:2). Nevertheless, God's power is greater than that of his opponents, and that power is made available to believers so that they can participate in his mission in the world (6:10, 13).

The first action of God is indicated through the passive imperative ἐνδυναμοῦσθε, *be strengthened* (cf. 3:16 where Paul prayed the recipients would be strengthened; Phil 4:13).[7] The realm in which that strengthening

---

4. NA28, 601.

5. See references in Best, *Ephesians*, 589; BDAG, s.v. λοιπός, ή, όν, 3.a; Hoehner, *Ephesians*, 819-20; Lincoln, *Ephesians*, 441; translations that read "finally" include NRSV, NIV, NASB, ESV, CSB.

6. Barth, *Ephesians 4–6*, 759; Baugh, *Ephesians*, 533-34; Thielman, *Ephesians*, 417.

7. Hoehner, *Ephesians*, 820.

occurs is then specified by a prepositional phrase ἐν κυρίῳ καὶ ἐν τῷ κράτει τῆς ἰσχύος αὐτοῦ "in the Lord and in the strength of his power." The Lord is understood from context by the majority of interpreters as the Lord Jesus Christ (5:20; 6:23, 24).[8] Being *in Christ* is therefore the precondition to accessing God's resources for the spiritual conflict.[9] The specific way in which believers are strengthened is then clarified in 6:11 using the military notion of armor (6:11). Τὴν πανοπλίαν τοῦ θεοῦ, "the whole armor of God," indicates both the comprehensiveness of the equipping ("the *whole* armor," πανοπλία indicating every piece of equipment) and the source of the armor, which is God (τοῦ θεοῦ genitive of source, although a minority of commentators see an additional nuance—a genitive of possession, "God's own armor").[10]

God's intention is that in the spiritual struggle against evil, his people will prevail. Vocabulary from the ιστημι root (*stand*) occurs four times: στῆναι *to stand* (aorist infinitive, 6:11, 13); στῆτε *stand* (aorist imperative, 6:14); ἀντιστῆναι *stand against, resist* (aorist infinitive 6:13). While στῆναι and στῆτε have a range of possible meanings, the military metaphor as context in Eph 6:10–17 together with the usage of the unambiguous ἀντιστῆναι makes it clear that the words collectively reinforce the primary sense of *resisting, prevailing against* or *withstanding* an enemy in battle.[11]

More than resisting evil, as will become clear in the light of intertextual links (see below, §11.4), vv. 15, 17, 18, 19 call believers to actively participate in the apostolic mission of prayer, life witness, and proclamation. In so doing, believers further the *missio Dei*.

11.3 Portrayal of God's Person and Character

The passage portrays God as the Divine Warrior, bringing together a number of characteristics of God that link to earlier passages in Ephesians as well as the broader biblical portrait of God.[12] Verse 10 begins by affirming that the Lord is a source of power which strengthens (ἐν τῷ κράτει τῆς ἰσχύος αὐτοῦ "in the strength of his power"). Verses 11 and 13 then expand the characterization of God to show that it is God who enables his people to stand against

---

8. E.g. Hoehner, *Ephesians*, 821; Johnson, *Ephesians*, 230; Lincoln, *Ephesians*, 441–42.

9. Arnold, *Ephesians*, 443.

10. Hoehner, *Ephesians*, 823. Lincoln and Yoder Neufeld propose reading the genitive as possessive: Lincoln, *Ephesians*, 442; Yoder Neufeld, *Put on the Armour*, 293.

11. Lincoln, *Ephesians*, 442; Barth, *Ephesians 4–6*, 761–63; BDAG, s.v. ἀνθίστημι, s.v. ἵστημι.

12. Cross, *Studies in Ephesians*, 29–30, cited in Barth, *Ephesians 4–6*, 799, n. 220.

the devil by equipping them with spiritual armor (v. 11, 13). God's person is characterized by or is the source of truth (4:21; 6:14), righteousness (4:24; 6:14), and peace (1:2; 2:14; 6:15). The letter is concluded by a grace in 6:23, "Peace...and love with faith, from God the Father and the Lord Jesus Christ." This grace specifies God the Father and the Lord Jesus Christ as the source of peace, love, and faith (cf. 1:2). These combined characteristics of God indicate that God's mission is not to promote conflict, but to establish his kingdom values of peace, love, faith, truth and righteousness, initially in his people, and then through them, the broader cosmos.

Both Lincoln and Arnold detect similar Trinitarian elements in the passage. Lincoln, who has the more detailed description, notes that God is the equipper of his people, particularly through his armor and word (vv. 11, 13-18). "The Lord Jesus Christ" (vv. 23, 24) is portrayed by reference to his power (v. 10). Believers are empowered because they exist in a dynamic relationship with Christ, who is Lord of all, but especially who is the head of the church community (6:23; cf. 1:22; 4:15). Finally, the Spirit is mentioned in connection to the word, which is "the sword of the Spirit" in v. 17. The Spirit makes effective the word of God in the lives of those who hear it (cf. Isa 55:11). The Spirit also prompts and directs the prayers of believers (6:18).[13] This analysis is sound, and accords with the particular emphases attributed to God as the source of blessings for believers in 1:3-6, Christ as head of the body in 4:12-16, and the empowering Spirit in 3:16 and 5:18.

11.4 Intertextuality—Literary and Thematic Links to the Wider Biblical Narrative

Scholars have detected a range of literary and thematic linkages connecting Eph 6:10-17 with Josh 5; Isa 11:4-5; 40:26; 52:7; 59:17; Wis 5:17-20; 1 Thess 5:8. All of these texts except Josh 5 contain Divine Warrior imagery. Without a doubt the dominant precursor text is Isa 59:17, and so we will briefly explore the nature of the other suggested intertexts, before examining the major influence of Isa 59. We may note in passing that while it is popular to find suggestions that Paul penned Eph 6 while reflecting on a Roman soldier guarding him during his imprisonment, the linkages with the OT represent a far better context than Roman military equipment.[14]

---

13. Lincoln, *Ephesians*, 105; Arnold, *Ephesians*, 474, 494.
14. Yoder Neufeld, *Put on the Armour*, 131; Lincoln, *Ephesians*, 435-36.

11.4.1 Joshua, Wisdom of Solomon 5, 1 Thessalonians 5

Baugh notes thematic parallels and distinctions between Paul and Joshua. Eph 6:10-20 is framed as advice for the people of God embarking on a military/spiritual campaign. He notes the exhortations to be strong (Josh 1:6-9; 10:25; Eph 6:10); and the significance of Paul as the leader of the gentile mission (Eph 3:8; Rom 11:13) as a parallel to Joshua as God's commissioned and spiritually enabled leader (Deut 31:6-7; Josh 5:13-15). There is a significant difference in mode of operation, however, since Joshua conquered by military might, while Paul proclaims the gospel of peace, supported by faithful prayer (Eph 2:14-17; 6:15, 18-20).[15]

Andreas Lindemann claims that Eph 6 only alludes to Isa 59 as mediated through the tradition seen in Wis 5:17-20.[16] Wisdom of Solomon, however, most probably dates from the first century CE. It is clearly influenced by Isa 59. The vocabulary, however, is somewhat unique, "he will put on righteousness as a breastplate, and wear impartial justice as a helmet (κόρυς); he will take holiness as an invincible shield (ἀσπίς), and sharpen stern wrath for a sword (ῥομφαία)" (Wis 5:18-20). The pairing of justice with helmet, holiness with shield, and wrath with sword is not found in either Isa 59 or Eph 6. Furthermore, the terms employed for helmet (κόρυς), shield (ἀσπίς), and sword (ῥομφαία) are also distinctive and unparalleled in Isaiah or Ephesians.[17] Therefore it is quite unlikely that Wis 5 is a precursor text to Eph 6.[18]

First Thessalonians 5:8 mentions two items of armor, the breastplate and helmet, associated with three virtues faith, love, and hope, the latter being tied particularly to salvation. In common with Eph 6:10-17, 1 Thess 5:8 emphasizes the eschatological nature of the believer's life in order to elicit commitment to virtuous living for the sake of the collective life and witness of the believing community (1 Thess 5:6, 11). Since Eph 6 develops a more elaborate panoply with additional items of armor and virtues, it most likely arises from Isa 59 rather than 1 Thess 5:8.

---

15. Baugh, *Ephesians*, 526-27.
16. Lindemann, *Aufhebung*, 65; cf. Moritz, *Profound Mystery*, 191.
17. Baugh, *Ephesians*, 528.
18. Hoehner, *Ephesians*, 838 and cf. references cited in n. 3.

11.4.2 Isaiah 11:4–5

Thielman sees the mention of the word of God as a means of God's judgment in Isa 11:4–5 echoed in Eph 6:17.[19] Isaiah 11:4 states πατάξει γῆν τῷ λόγῳ τοῦ στόματος αὐτοῦ καὶ ἐν πνεύματι διὰ χειλέων ἀνελεῖ ἀσεβῆ ("he will strike the land with the word of his mouth, and with breath through his lips he will destroy ungodly things"). Λόγος is thus parallel to ῥῆμα in Eph 6:17. Furthermore, Isa 11:5 then includes two Divine Warrior images: righteousness (δικαιοσύνη LXX) and truth (ἀλήθεια LXX) as belts around the waist (ὀσφῦς LXX) (cf. Eph 6:13, 16 where righteousness [as a breastplate], and a belt of truth around the waist are mentioned). Isaiah 11:1–16 explores the nature of the messianic reign first introduced in Isa 7:10–25. God will deal with the injustice pervading the land through his messiah, who will come and restore justice through military action.[20] There is, accordingly, not only verbal but thematic congruence with Eph 6. The *history of interpretation* supports a reference to Isa 11:4–5.[21] Hays's test of *recurrence* is also satisfied, since Isa 11:2 is alluded to at Eph 1:17; Isa 11:4 at 2 Thess 2:8; and Isa 11:10 at Rom 15:2.

The missional significance of an allusion to Isa 11 at Eph 6 is that the Isaiah passage portrays the messianic age as one in which "the earth will be full of the knowledge of the Lord," (Isa 11:9) and the root of Jesse stands "as a signal to the peoples; the nations shall inquire of him." (11:10). By implication, therefore, the appearance of the Divine Warrior is not merely with the goal of purifying God's own people, but extending knowledge of the Lord to fill the earth, being visible to all nations. This supports the interpretation of the armor as not merely defensive, or passive, but as public virtues and actions meant to attract the attention of those beyond the community of faith.

11.4.3 Isaiah 40:26

Robert Wild suggests that Isa 40:26, where κράτος (power) and ἰσχὺς (strength) are linked, may have been in the author's mind when writing Eph 6:10.[22] Scholarly support for this proposal, however, is lacking. A few commentators list Isa 40:26 as an illustrative parallel to Eph 1:19 and 3:15, where power and strength are combined, but none of these commentators

---

19. Thielman, "Ephesians," 831.

20. Childs, *Isaiah*, 102–3.

21. Lincoln, *Ephesians*, 448; Yoder Neufeld, *Ephesians*, 299–300; Arnold, *Ephesians*, 436.

22. Wild, "Warrior and Prisoner," 287.

mention it as background for 6:10.[23] Isaiah 40 is an anti-idolatry polemic which promises God's strength in support of his faithful people. It is thematically related to Eph 6:10–20, but without stronger verbal parallels, it is too slender a basis for claiming an allusion.

11.4.4 Isaiah 52:7

The author of Ephesians has already alluded to Isa 52:7 at 2:17.[24] The verbal parallels between Isa 52:7 and Eph 6:15 consist of three common elements: feet, good news proclamation/gospel, and peace.

> Isa 52:6–7 (LXX): πάρειμι ὡς ὥρα ἐπὶ τῶν ὀρέων, ὡς πόδες εὐαγγελιζομένου ἀκοὴν εἰρήνης, ὡς εὐαγγελιζόμενος ἀγαθά, ὅτι ἀκουστὴν ποιήσω τὴν σωτηρίαν σου λέγων Σιων Βασιλεύσει σου ὁ θεός, "I am present as an hour [season] upon the mountains, as the *feet of one who brings the good news of peace*, as the *one who brings the good news* of good things; for I will make your salvation heard, saying, 'O Zion, your God will reign!'" (LES)

> Eph 6:15: καὶ ὑποδησάμενοι τοὺς πόδας ἐν ἑτοιμασίᾳ τοῦ εὐαγγελίου τῆς εἰρήνης, "and, as shoes for your *feet*, having put on the readiness given by the *gospel* of *peace*." (ESV)

The context of Isa 52 also has elements that appear in Eph 6:10–20, as follows:

Isa 52:1	Eph 6:11, 14
ἐνδύω put on (twice)	put on (ἐνδύω) "the whole armor of God," "the breastplate"
Isa 52:1	Eph 6:10
strength "put on your strength (ἰσχύς), O Zion"	"the strength (ἰσχύς) of his power"

---

23. Arnold, *Ephesians*, 110, 209; Best, *Ephesians*, 337; Hoehner, *Ephesians*, 270; a rare mention in support of Wild's proposal is found in Arnold, *Ephesians, Power and Magic*, 108.

24. Thielman, "Ephesians," 817.

Isa 52:6	Eph 6:13
ἐν τῇ ἡμέρᾳ ἐκείνῃ "on that day"	ἐν τῇ ἡμέρᾳ τῇ πονηρᾷ "on that [evil] day"
Isa 52:7, 10	Eph 6:17
σωτηρία salvation	"helmet of salvation" σωτηρία

Table 7: Parallel Terms in Isaiah 52 and Ephesians 6

The extent of the verbal parallels both in the verses and their contexts supports the conclusion that Eph 6:15 represents an intentional allusion (Hays's test of *volume*). The other elements in Hays's tests are also satisfied. The *availability* of Isaiah 52 is seen, for example, in the citation of Isa 52:5 at Rom 2:24. *Recurrence* is satisfied since Isa 52:7 is quoted at Rom 10:15, and alluded to at Eph 2:17. The history of modern interpretation supports the recognition of an allusion.[25] *Thematic coherence* is established because of the prominence of God as Divine Warrior at Isa 52:10, 12 and in Eph 6:10–17, in addition to the specific coherence of feet and peace. It is also *historically plausible* for the author of Ephesians to have alluded to Isa 52, as this would reinforce the Divine Warrior theme that is central to Eph 6.

The key elements of Isa 52:6–7 are a prominent role for the messenger, proclamation of salvation, and God's sovereignty and victory. In Rom 10:15, the citation of Isa 52:7 underpins Paul's logic that gospel messengers are needed in order that salvation can be universally proclaimed. Ephesians 6:15 emphasizes readiness (i.e. the activity of the messenger) and the content of the proclamation (the gospel of peace). A minority of translations (e.g. NRSV and GNB) and interpreters such as Gnilka and Muddiman see the readiness as readiness to proclaim the gospel.[26] However, the majority of translations and interpreters view the phrase as indicating believers are readied to stand firm because of the gospel.[27] The genitive τοῦ εὐαγγελίου in 6:15 is then an objective one, which Winger explains as "the Christian is prepared for battle by *receiving* the Gospel from Christ."[28] In the light of both Isa 52 and Rom 10, readiness is more likely to indicate a readiness to proclaim, rather than a readiness to receive the gospel.

---

25. Barth, *Ephesians 4–6*, 770; Gnilka, *Epheserbrief*, 311; Muddiman, *Ephesians*, 291; Robinson, *Ephesians*, 215; Yoder Neufeld, *Ephesians*, 301.

26. Gnilka, *Epheserbrief*, 311–12; Arnold, *Ephesians*, 455; Witherington, *Philemon*, 352–54; Oepke, "ὑποδέω (ὑπόδημα, σανδάλιον)," 312; Schlier, *Brief*, 296.

27. E.g. Lincoln, *Ephesians*, 448–49; Best, *Ephesians*, 599–600; Hoehner, *Ephesians*, 843–44.

28. Winger, *Ephesians*, 713, italics in original.

In addition to strengthening the case for reading ἑτοιμασία as readiness to proclaim the gospel, the missional significance of the allusion to Isa 52:7 is that it also potentially illuminates the nature of the principalities and powers, and the nature of the church's conflict with them. The plight narrated in Isa 52:3–10 is the exile and oppression of Israel at the hands of pagan powers, and the attendant blaspheming of the Lord's name among the nations. The good news is that God is in no way silent, impotent, or willing to allow this to continue. Not only Israel but the whole earth will be confronted with the knowledge of God's sovereignty and salvation. In the light of this background, it is reasonable to draw a link between the spiritual "powers and principalities" of Eph 6 with pagan nations and their idols. Taking up the armor of God, therefore, is not an individualistic exercise in purely personal piety, but should be understood as a communal response to worldviews and ideologies that deny Christ as Lord. The church engages in the spiritual battle envisaged by Eph 6 both through bold proclamation of the gospel, and through the critiquing and unmasking of the enslaving and destructive elements of human structures that are opposed to Christian living and worship.[29]

Moritz objects to Arnold's interpretation that ἑτοιμασίᾳ conveys an offensive military action on the grounds that sandals would be inappropriate for such action, in comparison to soldier's half-boots (*caliga*).[30] This objection is spurious, since the verb ὑποδέω can apply to any form of footwear, not just sandals and Eph 6:15 is silent on the form of footwear.[31] Moritz's second objection is that attacking spiritual powers by proclaiming the gospel to them is incomprehensible. This too depends on a misreading. The proclamation of the gospel envisaged is to other humans, which results in the growth of the church and a consequent loss to the number of people under the control of Satan.[32]

---

29. Cf. Wink, *Naming the Powers*, 11–12, 85–86; Talbert, *Ephesians and Colossians*, 167–69 provides a helpful summary of approaches to understanding the powers including as literal ontological evil beings through to human existential struggles, and political or ideological structures.

30. Moritz, *Profound Mystery*, 200.

31. *LSJ*, s.v. ὑποδέω, 1879.

32. Cf. Arnold, *Ephesians*, 455.

11.4.5 Isaiah 59–60

Allusions to Isaiah occur in every chapter of Ephesians except Eph 3. One particular passage in Isaiah (59:1—60:6) appears to have been particularly influential in shaping aspects of the argument in Eph 5 and 6.

Isaiah 59:17 is clearly alluded to in Eph 6:14 where the phrase ἐνδυσάμενοι τὸν θώρακα τῆς δικαιοσύνης "put on the breastplate of righteousness" is only slightly different from Isaiah 59:17 LXX, ἐνεδύσατο δικαιοσύνην ὡς θώρακα. Similarly, in Eph 6:17 τὴν περικεφαλαίαν τοῦ σωτηρίου "helmet of salvation" adds only a definite article to Isa 59:17 LXX, περικεφαλαίαν σωτηρίου. This indicates that Hays's test of *volume* is met.

In addition to the specific allusion of Eph 6:14 to Isa 59:17, there is a broader engagement with Isa 59–60 in this part of Ephesians. As noted above in §9.4.6, Isaiah 60:1, "Arise, shine; for your light has come, and the glory of the LORD has risen upon you" (NRSV) is alluded to in Eph 5:14, "Sleeper, awake! Rise from the dead, and Christ will shine on you." Ephesians 5:14 also alludes to earlier passages in Isaiah (26:19; 51:17; and especially 52:1, "Awake, awake, put on your strength, O Zion! Put on your beautiful garments, O Jerusalem, the holy city . . .").

11.4.5.1 OLD TESTAMENT CONTEXT

Isaiah 59:1-8 is the prophet's indictment of Israel's sins. Verses 9–15a are a communal complaint, with elements of confession. Verses 15b–20 are a theophany introducing God as Divine Warrior, who comes in judgment (v. 18) and finally to redeem the repentant (v. 20).[33] Isaiah 60 then looks forward to an era in which God's glory is manifest in Israel (vv. 1–2, 7), and the nations are drawn centripetally to Israel's light (vv. 3–4), bringing tribute and joining in the praise of Yahweh (vv. 5–6). The story of Isaiah 59–60 is therefore one of transformation from darkness to light, injustice to justice, judgment to salvation, shame to glory—all because of God's intervention as Divine Warrior, which ushers in a new era of salvation open to many.

John Oswalt interprets this section of Isaiah as having a clear orientation towards universal witness. The new era in which God's people are cleansed and refined, enables them to finally fulfill the vocation envisaged for them in Isa 2:2–3 (where the nations stream to Jerusalem in order to learn God's ways, cf. Isa 49:6). Commenting on 59:21, Oswalt says Israel will be "a clean vehicle for the Spirit of God to speak through to reveal himself to

---

33. Childs, *Isaiah*, 484.

the watching world."³⁴ God's Spirit will be upon them and God's words will be put in their mouths, so that God's glory rises in Israel and the nations are drawn to that glory (60:1–3).

11.4.5.2 NT Context and Thematic Coherence

The key negative vocabulary and concepts found in Isa 59–60 as descriptors of Israel: darkness (59:8; 60:2), sin/transgression (59:12, 20), injustice (59:8, 9, 11, 14, 15), absence of peace (59:8), lying (59:13) are regularly encountered throughout Ephesians to portray the former way of life of the recipients: darkness (2:1; 4:18; 5:8, 11; 6:12), trespasses (1:7); injustice (2:3; 4:19 obliquely); hostility (2:14, 16); and lying, trickery, and deceit (4:14, 29; 5:4, 6).

The contrasting positive traits that are associated with God as Divine Warrior and the new era he ushers in are also mirrored between Isaiah and Ephesians: light (Isa 59:9; 60:1–2; Eph 1:18; 5:8, 9, 13, 14); salvation (Isa 59:11, 17; Eph 1:13; 2:5, 8; 6:17); justice, righteousness (Isa 59:9, 14; Eph 4:24; 6:14); peace (Isa 59:8; Eph 2:14, 15, 17; 6:15); and truth (Isa 59:15; Eph 1:13; 4:15, 21, 25; 6:14). The extent and quantity of these conceptual and lexical parallels indicate a strong probability that the author of Ephesians was consciously drawing on Isa 59–60 in these chapters.

Hays's test of *availability* is certainly satisfied since Isaiah is quoted in Pauline literature over twenty times, and alluded to approximately fifty times.³⁵ A connection between Eph 6:10–20 and Isa 59:17 is noted in both ancient and modern works on Ephesians (*history of interpretation*).³⁶ The extensive verbal linkages also demonstrate *thematic coherence*. Studies by Yoder Neufeld and Owens provide further support for thematic coherence. They argue that the Divine Warrior motif shapes not just Eph 6:10–20 but is an integrating motif for the whole letter.³⁷

A further criterion noted by Hays is *recurrence*—Paul cites or alludes to Isa 59:7–8 in Rom 3:15–17, Isa 59:20–21 in Rom 11:26–27, and Isa 59:17 in 1 Thess 5:8.³⁸ Paul's usage outside of Ephesians indicates that Pauline communities would be familiar with the broader context evoked by the precursor text (Isa 59–60), not just the verses alluded to (Isa 59:14,

---

34. Oswalt, *Isaiah 40–66*, 527, 531.

35. UBS5, 861–62, 874–76.

36. E.g. Barth, *Ephesians 4–6*, 768, 775; Best, *Ephesians*, 598, 602; Hoehner, *Ephesians*, 850; Lincoln, *Ephesians*, 448–50; Schnackenburg, *Ephesians*, 277–79; cf. Moritz, *Profound Mystery*, 190–206; for an ancient work see, e.g. Chrysostom, *Hom. Eph.* XXIV.

37. Yoder Neufeld, *Put on the Armour*, 11; Owens, "Spiritual Warfare," 88.

38. Hübner, *Vetus Testamentum*, 54, 182, 564.

17). As noted above in §9.4.6, Isa 26:19, 51:17, 52:1, and 60:1 are alluded to in Eph 5:14.

The allusion is *historically plausible* since allusions to Isa 59–60 in Eph 6:13–17 strengthen and effectively conclude the author's focus on character formation evident in the preceding chapters of Ephesians (Eph 4:17—6:9, esp. 4:24). Moreover, the vocabulary of truth, faith, righteousness, and peace occurs in varying combinations in other Pauline letters (e.g. 2 Cor 6:7; Gal 5:22; 2 Tim 2:22), often with these virtues being linked to the Christian's witness to those beyond the existing community of faith (e.g. 2 Cor 6:2–3; 2 Tim 2:21–26).

Having considered Hays's criteria, we can conclude that the weight of evidence shows that the Eph 6:10–20 allusion to Isa 59–60 was not an isolated intertextual link, but a metaleptic trope consistent with the development of Paul's argument about the nature and role of his audience as participants in God's mission in the world. As such, the virtues associated with the panoply (truth, righteousness, peace, faith, and salvation) are deliberately set in contrast to the negative traits afflicting Israel in exile before God's intervention. These negative traits are employed to depict the state of the gentile audience of Ephesians before their conversion. The impact of the broader context of Isa 59–60 is therefore to encourage the Christian readers of Ephesians to see themselves as the beneficiaries of God's gracious saving intervention, and through the exhortation to "take up the whole armor of God" as the new agents of God's saving action in the world. There is creative transformation of the object of salvation from Israel alone (Isa 59:1–21) to all nations (Isa 60:3–6), a transformation that shapes Paul's ministry (Eph 3:1, 6, 8; 6:19), and by implication the ministry of the letter's recipients too (4:7–24).

The missional significance of the allusions to Isaiah is that the precursor passage looks to a time when the people of God become a light attracting the nations to acknowledge and praise Yahweh. The central figure in Isa 59–60 is God as Divine Warrior. God acts in judgment on Israel and the nations' unrighteousness, and ushers in the new age when Israel becomes a clean vessel proclaiming God's glory. At this time the nations actively seek God and join in universal praise of God, even as God's chosen people enjoy a privileged position (59:19; 60:6).

The missional themes in the precursor text have ramifications for other elements in Eph 6:10–20. A long-standing interpretive debate concerns the phrase in 6:17, "take . . . the sword of the Spirit, which is the word of God." Scholarly opinion is divided between those who see the word of God functioning defensively to strengthen the faith of the individual believer (e.g.

Hoehner, Bruce, and Best[39]) and those who see this imagery as promoting the proclamation of the gospel to nonbelievers (e.g. Barth, Lincoln, Roitto, and Schnackenburg[40]). Having established Isa 59-60 as a precursor text, we should give significant weight to Isa 59:21 in the interpretation of Eph 6:17. Isaiah 59:21 looks forward to the time when God will give his Spirit and word to his cleansed people so that they may be a light to attract the nations. Accordingly, Eph 6:17 more likely connotes an active speaking of God's words by the bearer of God's armor than a mere passive use of Scripture to bolster personal faith.

A further interpretive implication of the link to Isaiah regards the question of whether Eph 6:14-17 is a list of divine gifts or character virtues.[41] The former approach construes truth, righteousness, faith, peace, and salvation as objective benefits of God's grace which strengthen the individual believer when they are received through cognitive assent; they have no necessary ethical impact. Thus they would be the objective truth of the gospel, righteousness as God's gift to believers, saving faith, and so forth. By contrast, if the list represents character virtues that are to be cultivated, then the list is an exhortation to individual believers and the church collectively to manifest its faith through behavior that is righteous (just), truthful, and fosters peace, salvation, and faith. Israel's exile was caused, according to Isa 58-59, by the hypocritical stance of its people who were outwardly pious yet actually unjust and ungodly. What was needed was integrity of belief, worship, and social action (e.g. Isa 58:6-13). Therefore, in the light of this context it seems best to understand the panoply of Eph 6 as a call to receive the spiritual gifts of salvation, righteousness, and faith, *and* to actively cultivate the subjective virtues that manifest them communally. Too many commentators have adopted an either/or approach rather than seeing the need for both gift and virtue.[42]

11.4.5.3 Conclusion

The wider contexts of the Isaianic passages alluded to in Eph 6:10-20 consistently envisage a new age in which the nations come to acknowledge or

---

39. Best, *Ephesians*, 604; Hoehner, *Ephesians*, 853; Bruce, *Epistles*, 409-10.

40. Barth, *Ephesians 4-6*, 777, 800; Lincoln, *Ephesians*, 451; Roitto, *Christ-Believer*, 284-88; Schnackenburg, *Ephesians*, 280.

41. Cf. Moritz, *Profound Mystery*, 201-5 and the footnotes for representative exponents of both positions.

42. Lincoln, *Ephesians*, 457 is one of the few commentators to see the panoply as both gift and virtues.

praise the glory of Yahweh; an outcome which occurs when God's people are redeemed from their political and spiritual bondage and become heralds of God's gracious saving actions to Israel and the whole earth. This context is particularly significant as it sharpens the intent of the exhortations in Eph 6. The armor of God is not merely a metaphor to illustrate the objective elements of salvation and so bolster the faith of believers, but God's equipment supplied to assist believers corporately to manifest and proclaim God's salvation and glory to the nations. The usage of plural verbs and pronouns in this passage indicates that the recipients collectively rather than individually bear the obligation to proclaim the gospel. While the majority of commentators on Ephesians have observed the individual linkages to verses in Isaiah, they have failed to see the consistency of missional themes that emerge from an analysis of the context of the precursor texts. The intertextual analysis of this passage broadens our appreciation for the way in which OT Scriptures were intended to shape the beliefs and actions of first-century Christian communities.[43]

11.5 Portrayal of Humanity and the World in Relation to God's Mission

Consistently with Eph 2:1–5, Eph 6:11–12 portrays humanity as living subject to the malignant influence of the devil and a range of evil spiritual forces. The devil is presented, as elsewhere in the NT, as the primary spiritual entity opposed to God and actively deceiving or enslaving humanity (cf. Eph 4:27; 2 Cor 2:11; 4:4; 1 Thess 2:18; 1 Pet 5:8; Rev 12).

Following the mention of the devil, a series of four appellations are used to identify the forces arrayed against believers: "principalities," "authorities" (cf. 1:21; 3:10), "cosmic powers of this present darkness," and "spiritual forces of evil in the heavenly places." Best adopts a demythologizing interpretation, whereby evil spiritual powers are equated with "the pressures of society."[44] Bultmann saw the powers as internal existential

---

43. The metaleptic effects of Isa 59–60 as intertext of Eph 6:10–20 presume the kind of readerly competence argued for by Hays, *Conversion of the Imagination*, 49. More pertinently for Ephesians, Moritz concludes that the use of OT traditions in the letter are extensive and sophisticated, *Profound Mystery*, 214–19. If the original recipients of the letter were residents in and around Ephesus (see below, chapter 12), then they had the benefit of Paul living and teaching there for three years (Acts 20:31). That surely would have resulted in awareness of and sensitivity to the OT precursor texts that were routinely employed in discussion.

44. Best, *Ephesians*, 207.

struggles experienced by humans.⁴⁵ Barth allows for both a literal and structural meaning: "intangible spiritual entities and concrete historical, social, or psychic structures or institutions of all created things and all created life."⁴⁶ Wink, addressing modern Western readers, argues that the devil's influence can come through the immorality and self-centered sinfulness characteristic of pagan society (4:22, 25–31; 5:3–8), or through structures such as political empire, social class, commerce, and even religion.⁴⁷ To discount entirely the reality of spiritual beings, as Hübner does,⁴⁸ is a reflection of his particular Western materialist worldview. In the light of more recent contributions from African and Asian perspectives, it is better to affirm that many parts of the global church uphold a literal meaning for the powers, since it is consistent with the worldview of Scripture and their contemporary experience.⁴⁹

Rather than setting literal, moral, and structural interpretations in conflict with each other, it is more consistent with Pauline theology to affirm a comprehensive view of evil, which can manifest itself in individual morality, in the structures of society, and in the direct oppressive actions of ontologically real spiritual beings working to frustrate the mission of God and his people.

11.6 Evidence of a Missional Context in the Problems, Crises or Issues Addressed

The major concern of this passage is that the recipients of the letter stand against evil spiritual forces. No mention is made, however, of the kind of spirit possession so prominent in Jesus's ministry as portrayed in the Synoptic Gospels. This suggests that the spiritual conflict envisaged here in Eph 6 is not the overt battleground of exorcisms but normally revolves around other manifestations and activities of evil spiritual forces in the lives of people.⁵⁰ The elements of spiritual armor cited (truth, righteousness, the gospel, faith, salvation, the word of God) emphasize the elements of God's action in salvation for the benefit of believers, and so the struggle certainly incorporates the full appreciation of and belief in God's saving

---

45. Bultmann, *Theology*, 1:259, cited in Talbert, *Ephesians and Colossians*, 168.
46. Barth, *Ephesians 4–6*, 800–801.
47. Wink, *Naming the Powers*, 85.
48. Hübner, *Philemon*, 267–68.
49. Asumang, "Powers of Darkness"; Wendland and Hachibamba, "Potentates," 341–63; Wintle and Gnanakan, *Ephesians*, 49–50, 204–6.
50. Cf. Witherington, *Philemon*, 352.

acts for believers. The missional context related to that goal is therefore one of contested beliefs, or doubts felt by the recipients. Believers are exhorted to stand against the "wiles" (μεθοδεία) of the devil (6:11). While not expanded in this passage, the devil's schemes would include the earlier-mentioned actions of enslaving humanity and keeping them in a spiritually dead state (2:1–5). The author's positive prayers for the recipients emphasize the importance of grasping the truth of the gospel (cf. 1:18; 3:9, 18), which implies a risk that some would fail to do so. This portrait is consistent with 4:14 where it is people who act craftily to hamper the work of the church (κυβείᾳ τῶν ἀνθρώπων, ἐν πανουργίᾳ πρὸς τὴν μεθοδείαν τῆς πλάνης "by people's trickery, by their craftiness in deceitful scheming"). The composite picture, then, is that the believers addressed by the letter were not yet secure in the cognitive dimensions of their faith. They had not yet fully grasped and intellectually committed to the faith Paul proclaimed. Rhetorically, the armor of God therefore serves as a vivid way in which to emphasize the importance of remaining anchored in the foundational beliefs of Paul's proclaimed gospel. However, the intertextual analysis suggests more than an intellectual battle is in view.

The spiritual conflict passage comes at the conclusion to the parenetic section of the letter. Character formation is a vitally important activity for the author of Ephesians. This is explicitly stated in Eph 4 where the author links the former life of ignorant darkness in alienation from God with immoral behaviors (vv. 17–19), and then moves to argue that the objective truth of Jesus should be manifested in virtuous behaviors (vv. 20–32). The missional context is therefore one in which identity and character formation go hand in hand with the behavioral outworking of God's saving initiative to establish believers in a gracious, forgiving, loving community that is a positive counterpoint to the wiles of the devil (6:11; cf. 4:14, 24, 27). Ephesians 6:10–18 is in many ways an expansion of 4:24, "clothe yourselves with the new self, created according to the likeness of God in true righteousness and holiness."[51]

Ephesians is therefore oriented towards public manifestations of behavior that counteract the dominant community-destroying tendencies of evil, whether that evil presents itself in the form of evil spirits and personal temptations to sin, or as structural evil. The church engages in spiritual conflict by having a comprehensive understanding of the gospel as God's means to rescue individuals from sin and spiritual darkness and to transform society through confronting injustices and unmasking the destructive patterns of ideologies, institutions, and empires. All this takes place in a setting of

---

51. Arnold, *Ephesians*, 475.

eschatological tension between salvation which is already available in Christ, and a yet-future day of final evil (6:13).

Paul's autobiographical comments in vv. 18-20 also support a missional context. He uses the self-descriptor "ambassador" to emphasize his calling to proclaim the gospel. Paul is presented as a role model for believers, since the power of the gospel he proclaims cannot be silenced by the dominant culture despite drawing on its legal and political resources to oppose God's servant.

11.7 Portrayal of the Character and Mission of God's People in the World

It was noted above in §11.4.5.2 that, in the light of the allusions to Isaiah, the readiness of the gospel in Eph 6:15 likely connotes proclamation of the gospel, and that the sword of the Spirit, the word of God, also includes an offensive sense. In further support of this interpretation is the usage of ῥῆμα for word rather than the more common λόγος in 6:17. The use of ῥῆμα particularly connotes the spoken word, which in context (vv. 15, 19) is clearly the proclamation of the gospel by which those under the sway of evil powers are enlightened and transferred from the realm of spiritual death to life (1:13; 2:1-7; cf. Rom 10:18). The mission of God's people includes the speaking of God's word, the gospel, as an offensive weapon to deliver captives out of Satan's realm as they hear and believe that proclaimed good news.[52]

As concluded above (in §11.4.4), Eph 6:15 exhorts the church corporately to be active in gospel proclamation. Particularly in the light of the differentiation of ministries in 4:11, O'Brien's characterization of Eph 6:15-17 as the Pauline Great Commission that lays on "each and every believer" an individual obligation to evangelize is slightly overstated.[53] A more measured position is that every believer is to support the church's lived and spoken witness to the gospel in accordance with God's provision and empowering. The emphasis is, as Gorman characterizes it, on an incarnational witness and impact in the world, a participatory embodiment of the gospel of peace.[54]

While there is some diversity of opinion concerning the individual believer's responsibility to be active in gospel proclamation, there is no ambiguity in the role played by Paul. The author uses the word (δεῖ, *must* 6:20) to describe Paul's compulsion to proclaim the gospel boldly, in a clear reflection of his understanding of Paul's role in God's mission (cf. 1 Cor 9:16, "woe

---

52. Fee, *Empowering Presence*, 728-29; Lincoln, *Ephesians*, 451.
53. O'Brien, *Gospel and Mission*, 124-25.
54. Gorman, *Becoming the Gospel*, 205-6.

to me if I do not proclaim the gospel!"). But more broadly, the recipients of the letter are also enlisted in the task of supporting gospel proclamation through prayer for the apostle: "Pray also for me, so that when I speak, a message may be given to me to make known with boldness the mystery of the gospel" (6:19). Barth states, "The church is co-responsible for Paul's mission among unbelievers and participates in it by her intercession."[55]

Thielman provides a succinct summation of the message of this passage for God's people. Standing against the devil is one aspect of how believers contribute to the ultimate unification of all things in Christ. Believers:

> must constantly receive both salvation and the Spirit's application of the gospel to their lives. In addition, they must constantly and devotedly pray for themselves, for other Christians, and especially for Paul in his difficult circumstances.[56]

As Thielman observes in his final sentence, prayer is of vital importance in the mission of God's people. Roitto explains that prayer is the method by which believers are to put on the armor of God, that is, to receive God's empowerment.[57] Similarly, Arnold notes that vv. 18–20 flow in structural continuity from the head verb στῆτε *stand* in v. 14 by means of the present participle (προσευχόμενοι "[keep on] praying"), v. 18.[58] Prayer is a means by which believers come to know God initially (1:17), grow in knowledge of God's mission and their place in it (1:18–19), increasingly apprehend the benefits of salvation they have received by faith (3:18–19), and are empowered to live holy lives and participate in God's mission (3:16–17; 6:18–20). Prayer is therefore a fitting note on which to end the body of the letter.

11.8 Portrayal of Paul and His Involvement in God's Mission

The portrait of Paul that emerges in 6:18–20 is one of a dedicated apostle, committed (indeed under divine compulsion) to proclaim the gospel boldly and widely. He is motivated by his calling as an apostle, which he refers to as serving as an "ambassador in chains" (πρεσβεύω ἐν ἁλύσει). This terminology of ambassadorship, also used in 2 Cor 5:20, highlights the honor associated with Paul's role of gospel proclamation in God's mission and by his present imprisonment; yet it is ironically paired with his

---

55. Barth, *Ephesians 4–6*, 784, and cf. 807–8.
56. Thielman, *Ephesians*, 414.
57. Roitto, *Christ-Believer*, 249.
58. Arnold, *Ephesians, Power and Magic*, 112; cf. Best, *Ephesians*, 604–5.

imprisonment, which would limit any ambassador in the performance of their duties.[59] Paul is presented as a model missionary, since he speaks as a representative of God, announcing the gospel mystery of reconciliation between God and all humanity (Jew and gentile), that has been revealed to him and its promulgation particularly entrusted to him. His whole life course has been shaped by the gospel—in planting and encouraging churches and in suffering for Christ as a consequence.[60]

This material (vv. 18–20) flows directly on from the metaphor of the armor of God, suggesting that Paul's struggle in prayer is a facet of the spiritual battle in which believers are exhorted to engage. Proclamation of the gospel and the expansion of the church through mission is intimately tied to the consistent and deliberate prayers of all believers. Ephesians 6:18 begins with, "Pray in the Spirit at all times . . . for all the saints" and progresses directly to 6:19, "pray also for me . . . to make known with boldness the mystery of the gospel." Prayer for all the saints flows without interruption into prayer for Paul's proclamation of the gospel as an apostle.[61] Carson argues that the integrated nature of the exhortations to prayer in 6:18–19 imply a reciprocal effect for all believers flowing from Paul's request for prayer in the area of proclamation:

> part of what believers should be praying for when they pray for all the saints is a certain holy boldness in their own witness. If even the apostle Paul, who can insist that he is not ashamed of the gospel (Rom. 1:16), discloses his need for God's help in declaring the mystery of the gospel fearlessly, how much more do the rest of us need such help?[62]

The concluding section of Ephesians therefore incorporates an encouragement that all believers are to be involved in the proclamation of the gospel through prayer and their own action in response to Paul's example.

Paul exemplifies a whole-life commitment to the gospel. His willingness to suffer for the sake of the continued proclamation of the gospel models perseverance despite suffering in order that God's mission may continue. Ephesians therefore ends, like Acts, with an image of the gospel going forth and the church growing despite chains physically restraining the apostle. Apostolicity is thus inherently a matter of missional action and missional mindset that is not deterred by suffering or spiritual opposition. God's

---

59. Baugh, *Ephesians*, 560–61.
60. Barth, *Ephesians 4–6*, 781–82.
61. Carson, "Paul's Mission," 181.
62. Carson, "Paul's Mission," 182; see also Lincoln, *Ephesians*, 455.

people are summoned by Paul to continue his apostolic mission despite his absence, imprisonment, or eventual death.

11.9 Conclusion

Ephesians 6:10–20 portrays the *missio Dei* as involving a spiritual struggle against evil powers and principalities. God has equipped believers to prevail in this struggle. They are to be involved in the struggle intentionally, empowered through the objective benefits of salvation bestowed by God of faith, truth, righteousness, and peace. Additionally, as believers appropriate these gifts they are meant to be manifest as character virtues counteracting the community and life-destroying tendencies of evil that operate at both the personal level and through human political, economic, and cultural structures. The image of God as Divine Warrior stands in the background to vv. 14–17, informing our understanding of God's power and priorities, as well as the task with which believers have been entrusted. Lincoln and Arnold both note the Trinitarian elements evident in the passage, with God, Christ, and the Spirit variously involved in providing and activating power in the believer's life for the struggle.

The passage is rich in intertextual allusions, particularly to Isa 11, 52, 57, and 59–60. These Isaianic passages envisage the eschaton as a time when God's salvation and glory will be made manifest to all nations. Humanity outside of Christ is portrayed as under the dominion of Satan. The "powers and principalities" is a particularly rich concept for understanding the scope of human alienation from God, since evil is not only manifest in personal temptations or overt spiritual oppression but is present in sinful structures that operate in human politics, economics, and society.

The missional context envisaged by the passage is that of contested worldviews where believers need to be convinced of the truth and power of the gospel as against the majority belief structures where spiritual beings held power to cause harm or bring benefit. Moreover, mature understanding is meant to manifest itself in virtuous living that demonstrates the positive impacts on individuals and communities of commitment to Christ. The people of God are to witness to the gospel in word and deed, in the empowerment provided by God. The passage enjoins believers to be consistently praying for the spread of the gospel. Paul is portrayed as the model missionary in his commitment to gospel proclamation despite suffering, undertaken with the fellowship and prayer of the believing community.

12

Missional Context of Ephesians

12.1 Introduction

HAVING WORKED METHODICALLY THROUGH the data of the letter itself with our missional hermeneutic lens, we are now in a position to explore two issues that involve a macro-level appraisal of the letter's message, namely, the context (this chapter) and purpose of the letter (chapter 13, below). Scholarly reconstructions of a NT letter's context are always generated primarily from the data of the letter itself. While commentaries routinely include discussion of the circumstances that prompted the author to write Ephesians in their introduction, in the present study this discussion has been deferred until after the discussion of each passage, in order not to prematurely restrict or distort the insights that would emerge regarding the context of the letter's original recipients.

The occasion for the letter is not explicitly stated in the text in the same way as other Pauline letters (e.g. 1 Cor 1:11; Gal 1:6–7). It is "the least situational" of all Pauline letters.[1] These textual characteristics cause Lincoln to deny the possibility of discerning directly the original historical setting of the letter, and instead he chooses to focus on the "rhetorical situation" of the "implied readers and author."[2] In the following analysis, we will proceed on the basis that the rhetorical setting of the letter does provide adequate indication of its historical setting.[3] It is inaccurate to claim that Ephesians is

---

1. Arnold, *Ephesians*, 41.

2. Lincoln, *Ephesians*, lxxiv.

3. Lona, *Eschatologie* , 430–41; cf. Stamps, "Rhetorical Situation," 193–210, cited in Starling, *Not My People*, 168.

entirely without context and occasion,[4] since it adopts themes, vocabulary, and reasoning that are distinct from other Pauline letters (including Colossians, to which it bears a clear relationship). These particularities reflect conscious emphases of the author.[5] Thus, the prayer reports of 1:15–23 and 3:14–21 imply a need for the letter's recipients to grow in knowledge and to be reassured by God's power that is for them as against forces opposing them. The concern with unity and reconciliation in Eph 2 was theologically and socially significant for the original recipients. We will therefore persist with investigation of the occasion and life-setting of the letter, focusing on whether it addresses a particular missional context, and is comprehensible as a product of God's mission.

Several of the earliest manuscripts of Ephesians omit ἐν Ἐφέσῳ from 1:1 ($\mathfrak{P}^{46}$ ℵ* B* 424^c 1739).[6] Despite this seeming obstacle to definitively ascertaining the letter's original destination, there are sufficient internal and historical indicators for most commentators to retain a connection to Ephesus or at least Western Asia Minor. Muddiman, Hoehner, Thielman, and Arnold all uphold Ephesus as the most likely destination.[7] Lincoln opts for communities in and around the Lycus Valley (Colosse, Hierapolis and Laodicea), while Best and Sellin nominate Asia Minor as the letter's destination.[8] The internal factor supporting the connection to Ephesus is the mention of Tychicus (6:21). The literary and historical factors include the connection with Colossians, the manuscript and patristic traditions associating it with Ephesus or Laodicea, and sometimes judgments about the cultural milieu of the letter aligning with the culture and ethos of Asia Minor.[9] (It is noteworthy that the majority of scholarly works on the history, religion, and culture of Ephesus in the first century in relation to Christianity exclude Ephesians from their sources. Those who specify the reason for this exclusion do so because of the scholarly doubts about the provenance and destination of the letter.[10])

---

4. Cf. Best, *Ephesians*, 74–75, citing Beker, *Heirs of Paul*, 68–71.

5. Moritz, "Reasons for Ephesians," 8–14; Immendörfer, *Ephesians and Artemis*, 307–12.

6. Metzger, *Textual Commentary*, 532.

7. Muddiman, *Ephesians*, 35; Hoehner, *Ephesians*, 77; Arnold, *Ephesians*, 29–41; Thielman, *Ephesians*, 15–16.

8. Lincoln, *Ephesians*, lxxxii–lxxxiii (Western Asia Minor, esp. Hierapolis and Laodicea); Best, *Ephesians*, 2–6 (tentatively Asia Minor); Sellin, *Brief*, 56–57 (Asia Minor, perhaps Lycus Valley).

9. Cf. Arnold, *Ephesians*, 23–29.

10. Detailed by Immendörfer, *Ephesians and Artemis*, 44–49 including, inter alia, the following works: Thiessen, *Christen in Ephesus*, 350; Trebilco, *Early Christians*, 94;

The dating of the letter is essentially a choice between 60–62 CE, in the final years of Paul's life, during a Roman imprisonment, or if it is a pseudonymous work, 80–90 CE, a generation after Paul's death.[11] In both timeframes the political, religious, and cultural environment of Western Asia Minor is essentially similar. A date after 90 CE is unlikely, since the letter begins to be quoted and alluded to by early first-century patristic authors including Ignatius and Polycarp.[12]

12.2 Summary of Missional Context Observations from Preceding Chapters

During the course of reading each passage of Ephesians, a section has been devoted to discussing the missional context of the passage, that is, the particular problems, crises, or issues addressed by the text. In order to build a sound basis for drawing those comments together, below is a summary of each passage's possible missional context.

Ephesians 1:1–14. The positive affirmations that the recipients are chosen and blessed by God effectively counters any feelings of "insecurity and insignificance in the face of the claims of syncretistic mystery religions or cosmic forces."[13] For Christ-believers who have moved away from the dominant cults and belief systems, there would certainly be a sense of social and psychological isolation and vulnerability.

Ephesians 1:15–23. The first prayer report of the letter emphasizes the superior power available to the letter's recipients, as against all other rulers or authorities (1:21). The context is one in which the recipients need reassurance and persuasion that God's power available to them in Christ is superior to that available through other channels of spiritual power (be they pagan deities or magic).

Ephesians 2:1–10. The context of this passage is humanity's spiritual bondage by "the ruler of the power of the air." When the powers are understood as ontologically real beings, the missional context is the desperate plight of nonbelievers, which creates a strong impetus for believers to evangelize nonbelievers with the goal of leading them to salvation. When the powers are understood as political, ideological, social, or historical forces of domination, dehumanization and control, the missional context is one in which the church embodies and witnesses to God's greater glory and power to give

---

Murphy-O'Connor, *St. Paul's Ephesus*, 231; Tellbe, *Christ-Believers*, 17, 54.

11. E.g. Hoehner, *Ephesians*, 96 (60–62 CE); Best, *Ephesians*, 45 (80–90 CE).
12. Best, *Ephesians*, 15–16.
13. Lincoln, *Ephesians*, 44.

(rather than degrade) life. The strong affirmation of God's grace as the basis of salvation also indicates a missional context in which some people were pursuing a moralistic or religious works-based righteousness.

Ephesians 2:11–22. This passage implies a missional context in which predominantly gentile churches were marked by ignorance of the Jewish roots of their faith, by disunity, and an inadequate response to God's Spirit in their midst. This failure to grasp the nature and significance of their corporate identity meant that God's intention for them to be a new humanity, manifesting and progressively filling the world with his glory and reconciliation was being frustrated. The temple language well suits the context of Ephesus, where the temple of Artemis together with her cult dominated life in the city and province of Asia.

Ephesians 3:1–13. Uncertainty about the validity and divine authority of the Pauline gentile mission was prompted by Paul's imprisonment or death. Coupled with the minority status of Pauline churches in a largely unbelieving world, this uncertainty led to insecurity and a lack of confidence in God's purposes for the church. These purposes include witnessing to God's wisdom before the "heavenly powers and authorities" by continuing to bring gentiles to faith in Christ, building God's new society of reconciliation, forgiveness, new life and unity, and so diminishing Satan's power over humanity.

Ephesians 3:14–21. This prayer consolidates the thrust of the first half of the letter, emphasizing strengthening in faith, love, and knowledge. It is aimed at recipients who were lacking assurance and confidence to participate in God's purposes for the church in the world, the practical steps towards which become the focus in the following paraenesis.

Ephesians 4:1–16. The leading exhortation to recipients to walk worthily of their calling indicates a danger of *unworthy* walking. In context, unworthy walking may include disunity, failure to grow through mutual service, or failing to continue apostolic pioneering and evangelism ministries. Finally, the warning about false teaching, in common with all communities addressed by NT writers, indicates the presence of philosophical, religious and cultural patterns of thought inimical to the apostolic faith passed on through the ministries of 4:11.

Ephesians 4:17—5:20. The missional context of this virtue-vice list is a strong dominant culture, still exerting psychological pressure on converts to Christ to engage in behaviors that are contrary to the community-building virtues being promoted. Reinforcing community identity would protect the community from assimilation to a non-Christian norm.

Ephesians 5:21—6:9. The missional context of the household code in Ephesians is not a simplistic desire to accommodate the Christian movement to prevailing culture. Rather, the codes foster mutuality, respect, love, and harmony within household relationships where members are "in Christ." The context is one of relationships that have been distorted by sin and the social manifestations of sin evident in the powers of patriarchy, Roman culture and law, and local religious traditions. A healthy Christian household is a witness to nonbelieving neighbors of the healing power of the gospel.

Ephesians 6:10–24. The armor of God equips believers for two complementary struggles. Firstly, a cognitive growth in understanding and appropriation of their salvation as against the doubts and deceits of a world under Satan's influence. Secondly, the missional context of the church's struggle is one in which community-destroying manifestations of evil such as personal temptations to sin and structural injustices and evils are ever-present. The church fights these through individual virtues and by fostering communities in which grace, forgiveness, and love transform society. The closing autobiographical comments of Paul as ambassador in chains remind the recipients that even the legal and political might of the Roman Empire cannot silence God's servants from proclaiming the gospel.

The recurrent elements in this summary are: insecurity (1:1–14, 15–23; 3:1–13, 14–21; 6:10–24); pressure from or fear of spiritual powers (1:1–14, 15–23; 2:1–10; 3:1–13; 6:10–24); a community in danger of cultural assimilation or compromise (1:15–23; 2:1–10; 3:1–13; 4:1–16; 4:17—5:20; 5:21—6:9; 6:10–24); and inadequate Christian knowledge and identity formation (1:1–14; 2:1–22; 3:14–21; 4:1–16; 4:17—6:24). As Wright argues, the fact that the NT writers addressed a multiplicity of challenges, including the struggle of believers to form and maintain their identity as against "competing religious claims and worldviews that surrounded them" is evidence that the books of the NT are products of mission.[14]

12.3 Historical Context of Ephesus and Asia Minor

Having surveyed the primary evidence from Ephesians itself, we now turn to the historical context of Ephesus and Asia Minor. The particular research question is whether the rhetorical life-setting of Ephesians aligns in particular elements with the setting of Ephesus and Western Asia Minor (such that a generalized setting or connection to other cities in the Roman Empire is less likely).

---

14. Wright, *Mission of God*, 49.

12.3.1 Artemis Cult

The religious and social life in Ephesus in this period has been documented in considerable detail by numerous researchers. Oster has detailed the variety of cults and religions present in Ephesus, but confirmed the Artemis cult as by far the dominant force in the city.[15] Oster declared that Artemis was a deity particularly venerated because of her power over fate and the supernatural realm, seen through her titles (e.g. βασιλιηῒς κόσμου "Queen of the cosmos," οὐράνιος θεός Ἄρτεμις Ἐφεσία "heavenly goddess Artemis Ephesia") and visually depicted by the astrological symbols featured around the neck of Artemis cult statues.[16] Numerous inscriptions from Ephesus address a thanksgiving (εὐχαριστω) formula to Artemis in response to answered prayers.[17] These characteristics associated with Artemis provide a very fitting backdrop to Eph 1:1–13, with its thanksgiving to God and pronouncement of God's sovereignty over fate.

Guy Rogers similarly highlighted the significance of Artemis, not only in Ephesus, but throughout the empire as one of the most widely worshipped deities of the time. The history of the Artemis cult in Ephesus had begun with her being promoted by Lysimachus in 294 BCE as a goddess of salvation (assisting his military victory at that time).[18] By the late first century CE, the celebration of the mysteries included processions, music, libations, drinking, and dance.[19] These cultic activities, together with Artemis's reputation as a protector goddess, capable of healing and rescuing from plague is attested in a second-century CE inscription probably originally from the town or region around Sardis, in Lydia.[20] Elements of walking (a related idea to processing), not getting drunk on wine, and making music are prominent parts of the particularly Christian behaviors advocated in Ephesians (2:2, 10; 4:1, 17; 5:2, 8, 15, 18–20), though these are by no means behaviors unique to Ephesus and so in themselves do not establish the letter's historical context.

---

15. Oster, "Religious Centre," 1661–728.

16. Oster, "Religious Centre," 1724; Moritz, *Profound Mystery*, 212 also refers to Rochberg-Halton, "Babylonian Contribution," 51–62 in support of the influence of astrology in Western Asia Minor.

17. Oster, "Religious Centre," 1723–25.

18. Rogers, *Mysteries of Artemis*, 6–7, 26, 79, 85.

19. Rogers, *Mysteries of Artemis*, 128–29.

20. Graf, "Oracle Against Pestilence," 267–79; cf. Faraone and Obbink, *Magika Hiera*, 112–13 discuss an inscription connecting Artemis with healing of migraine.

12.3.2 Magic

Apart from the cult of Artemis, Ephesus also had a connection with the widespread practice of magic in the ancient world (indeed, David Aune characterizes the first centuries of the Christian era as a time when magic increased in popularity throughout the Roman Empire).[21] The presence of magic in Ephesus is reflected in Acts 19:11–20, where the sons of Sceva attempt to invoke the name of Jesus in a magical exorcism, an episode that concludes with former practitioners of magic burning a collection of magical scrolls of high value.[22] The *Ephesia grammata* were six magical words, utilized in curses, spells, and for protection of their bearer when incorporated on amulets or in charms.[23] While not necessarily originating in Ephesus, the *Ephesia grammata* came to be associated unambiguously with Ephesus in ancient literature.[24] Having surveyed the data of Acts and a number of pertinent magical papyri, Guy Williams concludes: "the historical setting of Paul's mission in Ephesus was one characterized by exorcisms, magical rivalry, and violent controversy regarding idolatry."[25]

A second, more specific question is whether the goddess Artemis was particularly associated with magic. Arnold answered this question in his published thesis with a firm yes, claiming she was "a goddess of the underworld and intimately linked with magical practices."[26] He based this conclusion on a link between Artemis and Hecate (goddess of magic and the underworld) in magical papyri, the existence of the *Ephesia grammata*, and inscriptions from magical amulets mentioning Artemis.[27] Rick Strelan objected to Arnold's reading of the evidence and claimed Artemis was not a goddess of magic, that residents of Ephesus did not characteristically *fear* Artemis, death, or magic, and the Greek Magical Papyri upon which much of Arnold's claims depend are Egyptian (not Asian), date from a later period, and do not unambiguously connect Artemis and magic.[28]

James Harrison has recently revisited this debate referring to inscriptional and papyrological evidence not utilized by Arnold or Strelan. He

21. Aune, "Magic," 1519.
22. Porter, "Magic in Acts," 119–21.
23. Faraone and Obbink, *Magika Hiera*, 121–22; Immendörfer, *Ephesians and Artemis*, 112–15.
24. Faraone and Obbink, *Magika Hiera*, citing Menander, Plutarch, Pausanius, Anaxilas.
25. Williams, "Paul's Beast Fight," 52–53.
26. Arnold, *Ephesians, Power and Magic*, 168.
27. Arnold, *Ephesians, Power and Magic*, 22–24.
28. Strelan, *Paul*, 83–88, 158–60.

concluded that both Arnold and Strelan lack a balanced use of the evidence, and that both their positions go beyond the evidence. The claim that Artemis was particularly associated with magic cannot be firmly established on existing evidence. Nevertheless, "Arnold is definitely correct in proposing that there is a polemic against magic in Ephesians."[29]

Putting aside the weakly substantiated link between Artemis and magic, the question remains whether Ephesians addresses recipients situated in a particularly magic-oriented society. Indicators for a positive answer are quite numerous: (a) the phrasing of references to named powers (Eph 1:21 "far above every name that is named"), suggests an allusion to the magical practice of calling on particular deities, demons, or other spiritual beings in the formulation of spells and curses;[30] (b) the repeated references to God and Christ's superior power (e.g. 1:19-21; 3:7, 16, 20; 6:10);[31] (c) Ignatius, *Eph.* 19 discusses the incarnation of Christ as causing the destruction of all kinds of magic and bondage to evil, suggesting that the original Ephesian audience of Ignatius's letter had a familiarity or concern with magic in their circumstances (and Ignatius's other letters to different destinations do not mention magic); (d) the narrative of Acts 19:11-19 which highlights magical and miraculous events at Ephesus, which may be a deliberate Lukan reflection of local religious color;[32] (e) the plausible interpretation of 1 Cor 15:32 (Paul's fight with wild beasts in Ephesus) as a reference to the evil spirits he encountered through opposing magic and idolatry in the city;[33] (f) the *Ephesia grammata* magical words;[34] and (g) multiple inscriptions from Ephesus reflect magical beliefs and practices and divination.[35] Cumulatively, these factors leave little doubt that Ephesus was a city in which magical practices were prevalent, and that Ephesians contains numerous elements that would be relevant in such a life-setting.

A significant assumption in Arnold's thesis was that the recipients of Ephesians lived in fear of the spiritual forces around them.[36] Strelan rightly

---

29. Harrison, "Artemis Triumphs," 46 and 39-45 for evaluation of Arnold's and Stelan's works.

30. Sellin, *Brief*, 143; Immendörfer, *Ephesians and Artemis*, 230-32; Best, *Ephesians*, 177-79; Arnold, *Ephesians, Power and Magic*, 24.

31. Arnold, *Ephesians, Power and Magic*, 70-85.

32. Schwindt, *Weltbild*, 75-87.

33. Williams, "Paul's Beast Fight."

34. Arnold, *Ephesians, Power and Magic*, 14-16; Schwindt, *Weltbild*, 77-78.

35. Schwindt, *Weltbild*, 79.

36. Arnold, *Ephesians, Power and Magic*, 18, 27, 41, 47, 50, 51, 56, 58, 121-23; Arnold, *Powers of Darkness*, 285-86; cf. Lona, *Eschatologie*, 438-39; Schwindt, *Weltbild*, 42; Moritz, *Profound Mystery*, 19-21.

objected that expressions of fear are not routinely found in the primary sources, and that the people of the first century approached the deities with confidence rather than fear.[37] It may be that Arnold's characterization of Artemis as demonic and fearful owes more to Christian polemicists of later centuries rather than the situation in the first century.[38]

The case for Ephesians to be understood as a letter addressing a specific setting in which spiritual powers were perceived to be prevalent has been substantially strengthened recently by two major works. Firstly, Rainer Schwindt has drawn on apocryphal and pseudepigraphic writings, the Qumran literature, Philo, Josephus, patristic writers, rabbinic sources, classical Greek and Roman works, Gnostic writings, inscriptions from Ephesus, and the magical papyri in order to present a survey of the belief systems of Hellenistic cultures of the first century, focused on cosmology and beliefs about demons and powers. In the light of this detailed work, Schwindt undertakes a sustained comparison of elements within Ephesians that are elucidated by the primary sources he has surveyed; these include the world as God's creation, the demonic powers (1:21; 2:2; 3:10; 6:11, 12), Christology (especially the concept of πλήρωμα *fullness*), and the church as a dynamic cosmic reality, revealing God's wisdom. The breadth of primary sources Schwindt draws on means that his picture of the worldview of the Hellenistic world is not location specific. He is therefore reticent to draw firm conclusions about setting. Nevertheless, he highlights the Artemis Ephesia cult with its many elements of cosmic dominion which Ephesians particularly addresses in chapters 1, 2, 3 and 6.[39]

Most recently, Michael Immendörfer has analyzed the substantial collections of inscriptions from Ephesus, together with ancient literary works that mention Artemis Ephesia in order to test whether Ephesians, "contains similarities with the local situation in Ephesus, especially with regard to the cult of the city goddess Artemis."[40] His findings are too extensive to convey fully here. However, two key indicators that Ephesians does indeed reflect ancient Ephesus as its setting are as follows: (a) 30 percent of the thirty-five hapax legomena of Ephesians are words repeatedly found in Ephesian inscriptions (e.g. βέλος *dart*, ἐπιφαύσκω *shine upon*, κληρόω *choose by lot*, κοσμοκράτωρ *ruler of the world*, μέγεθος *greatness*);[41] and (b) there are verbal and conceptual parallels between the Artemis cult and Ephesians around

37. Strelan, *Paul*, 83, 93.
38. Strelan, *Paul*, 85.
39. Schwindt, *Weltbild*, 512, and more generally, 351–99, 498–512.
40. Immendörfer, *Ephesians and Artemis*, 3.
41. Immendörfer, *Ephesians and Artemis*, 307–8, 333–34.

the following themes: temple building, sacrifices, wealth and inheritance, honorific titles, thanksgiving, armor, arrows, citizenship, covenant, nurture, fruitfulness/fertility, identity, purity, mystery, sung praises, and wine/debauchery.[42] Not every aspect of Immendörfer's case is compelling. For example, Immendörfer follows Knibbe in claiming Artemis was viewed as a protector of the dead based on the practice of making sacrifices and the route of the cult procession past tombs on festival days.[43] There is insufficient evidence of the activities undertaken during a procession to link it with sacrificing on behalf of the dead or conveying divine power to the dead, as suggested by Knibbe. Despite occasional weaknesses, the cumulative weight of the parallels highlighted by Immendörfer increase the probability that the cult of Artemis and the city of Ephesus may have constituted the setting against which Ephesians was composed.

12.3.3 Imperial Context

Having considered both magic and the Artemis cult as background to the letter, a third element of the historical setting also warrants attention: the Roman Empire. A handful of studies have attempted to read Ephesians in the light of imperial language and culture. Nijay Gupta and Fredrick Long have rebutted the presumption that Ephesians adopts an accommodationist stance towards the dominant culture (e.g. in the household code), by showing that Ephesians employs a language of resistance to the claims of imperial power, instead exalting Christ as the true Lord and the church as an alternative political entity.[44] Harry Maier argues, as another example, that Ephesians uses concepts of civic harmony and reciprocity (e.g. 4:1) to draw:

> its audience into an orbit of political and civic ideals shared by its Greco-Roman contemporaries, where honours, dedication and allegiance in response to benefaction were basic elements of cultural and political transaction.[45]

Holland Hendrix has proposed that Eph 1:3–14 fits the genre of an honorific decree.[46] Harrison characterizes Eph 1:3–14 as employing the civic benefaction language of Ephesian inscriptions in order to "implicitly

---

42. Immendörfer, *Ephesians and Artemis*, 179–278 and summary table at 301.
43. Knibbe "Via Sacra Ephesiaca," 144; Immendörfer, *Ephesians and Artemis*, 167–68.
44. Gupta and Long, "Politics of Ephesians," 112–36.
45. Maier, *Picturing Paul*, 107.
46. Hendrix, "Form and Ethos," 3–15.

[critique] the city's propaganda about the Roman ruler, its gods, its benefactors, and its priests."[47] Eberhard Faust has interpreted Eph 2:11–22 in the light of Hellenistic speeches in praise of the emperor, and also proposed that Jewish nationalism was perceived by some gentile citizens of the empire as a threat to the *pax Romana*.[48]

While Maier adduces considerable literary, iconographic, and numismatic evidence illustrating the concept of *homonoia* (concord) as helpful background to Eph 2:11–20 and 4:1–3, the picture that emerges of civic life does not exclusively reflect the circumstances of Ephesus but could be found throughout the Roman Empire. The political power and cultural dynamics of dominion, benefaction, reconciliation, and unity are certainly evident as components in the life-setting of the letter. Accordingly, they contribute to a composite picture of the setting of the letter where the recipients were facing pressure to conform to the values and loyalties of the dominant culture and the ruling empire. There is, however, nothing particularly unique in the imperial perspective that reveals a particular crisis or circumstance facing the recipients of the letter.

12.4 Conclusion

This chapter has sought to relate insights from our missional reading of Ephesians to the possible historical context of the letter. This exercise is necessarily tentative since our discussions of the missional context for Ephesians have used mirror-reading and many elements of life in Ephesus in the first century would also be true in other cities in the Greco-Roman world. Nevertheless, there are some remarkable parallels between elements of Ephesians and historical particularities of the Artemis cult, magic, and the inscriptions of Ephesus. Accordingly, Ephesians is best understood as a contextualized response for Christ-believing residents of Western Asia Minor (including Ephesus) in the late first century CE. They were largely gentile converts to Christ, an insecure minority, feeling the weight of cultural pressure to conform to existing patterns of interpersonal and communal behaviors, shaped as they were by life under the Roman Empire, the dominant Artemis cult, the pervasive presence of magic, and a belief in spiritual beings able to help or harm individuals, families, and communities. Against this context, the mission of God is to establish Christ as Lord of the entire cosmos (comprising both earth

47. Harrison and Welborn, *Ephesus*, 292.

48. Faust, *Pax Christi*, 280–324, citing Philo, *Legat.* 143–7, as an example of Hellenistic encomium.

and the heavens), through the church, which is Christ's body, expanding his presence throughout the earth, a vanguard of a renewed creation and restored community in which the destructive personal, interpersonal, and structural effects of sin are exposed and overcome.

Viewed in this way, Ephesians is a perfect exemplar of the fourth stream of missional hermeneutics identified by Hunsberger.[49] The author of Ephesians skillfully drew upon Pentateuchal and prophetic texts and a mature Pauline theological perspective to shape the letter's recipients for participation in the *missio Dei* as it was unfolding in a new eschatological era. The author addressed the perennial challenges of idolatry, community injustice, and cultural compromise faced by God's people in the OT era, and applied them with the interpretive matrix of the gospel to Christ-followers facing similar struggles in their contemporary existence. In contrast to the OT people of God, the gospel yields new means of empowerment through the Spirit, a new basis for reconciliation through Christ's death, and a new relationship with God portrayed using familial, political, and architectural images of intimacy and access.[50]

---

49. Hunsberger, "Proposals," 316–17; see above, §1.6.6. This project has employed a stream two missional hermeneutic, but our conclusions support Brownson's claim that NT authors read the OT scriptures in a stream four manner, Brownson, *Speaking the Truth*, 39–41.

50. Cf. Brownson, *Speaking the Truth*, 39–41.

13

The Purpose of Ephesians

13.1 Introduction

ON THE BASIS OF an inductive study of the contents of Ephesians viewed through a missional hermeneutics lens, we are now able to apply the implications of that reading to the issue of the letter's occasion and purpose. The hypothesis advanced in this project is that Ephesians is a missional document, written to inform, encourage, and shape its recipients for participation in the *missio Dei*. In this chapter we will evaluate whether a missional purpose for the letter better accounts for the data than existing non-missional proposals.

As noted in the introduction (§1.1), a number of prominent scholars claim that Ephesians has little interest in mission, and that its purpose is to strengthen the internal life of Christian communities. For example, Best states that the letter contains much "about the church and yet [there is an] absence of discussion about its place and that of its members in the external world."[1] MacDonald claims that in Ephesians believers "are urged . . . to turn into the church and away from the nonbelieving world. Despite an awareness of the goal of church expansion and the importance of universal mission, Ephesians displays very little interest in dialogue between believers and non-believers."[2] In the light of the missional reading of Ephesians offered above, these claims can now be better assessed. Before doing so, however, we will set the scene with a review of existing scholarly proposals concerning the purpose of the letter.

1. Best, *Ephesians*, 64, see also 74, 638.
2. MacDonald, *Colossians and Ephesians*, 21.

13.2 Review of Existing Proposals

The range of scholarly proposals for the purpose of Ephesians is wide. It has been viewed as an introduction to Paul's letters, a response to Gnosticism, an attempt to strengthen the institutional church after the death of Paul, a catechism for new believers, a liturgical work such as a baptismal homily, a plea for unity between gentile and Jewish Christians, an encouragement for Christians experiencing persecution, and as an attempt to strengthen believers to withstand the spiritual and cultural pressures from their pagan surroundings (especially the Artemis cult). In the last two decades or so, a consensus position has emerged that the purpose of the letter is identity formation. While the majority of these proposals relate to one or more elements in the text, they often also depend on presumptions about the dating and religious and cultural setting of the letter, which are more speculative. After surveying existing proposals, we will explore the extent to which a missional perspective can bring clarity to the question of the letter's purpose.

13.2.1 An Introduction to Paul's Letters

Edgar Goodspeed proposed that Ephesians was a preface added to a collection of Paul's letters late in the first century. Its purpose was to introduce readers unfamiliar with Paul's letters to key themes in Pauline thought.[3] Goodspeed's theory lacks evidence that Ephesians ever stood at the head of a collection of Pauline letters, and has been rejected. Nevertheless, the idea that Ephesians represents a compendium of Pauline thought, or a parting "spiritual testament" penned by Paul not long before his death has surfaced periodically during the last century.[4]

13.2.2 A Circular Letter

The lack of a destination in Eph 1:1 in early manuscripts, the paucity of personal references compared with other Pauline letters, and the supposed generalized nature of the letter's contents has given rise to the theory that Ephesians was a circular letter, intended to meet the needs of a number of

---

3. Goodspeed, *Key to Ephesians*, xiv–xvi; Goodspeed, *Introduction*, 222–23, citing works by Jülicher and Weiss.

4. Sanders, *Studies in Ephesians*, 16 (spiritual testament); Bruce, *Epistles*, 229–46 (compendium); Robinson, *Ephesians*, 10 (non-controversial exposition of positive truth).

congregations in Asia Minor.[5] The circular letter theory does not in itself constitute a purpose, merely the vehicle through which one or more particular or general purposes are expressed, and signals a skepticism that there is a particular occasion being addressed.

13.2.3 A Response to Gnostic Heresy

Ephesians includes a number of words that are prominent in later gnostic writings, including πλήρωμα (1:10, 23; 3:19; 4:10, 13; 5:18), μυστήριον (1:9; 3:3, 4, 9; 5:32; 6:19), and σοφία (1:8, 17; 3:10). This focus prompted scholars following a history of religions approach to hypothesize that Ephesians was interacting in some way with Gnostic or proto-Gnostic thought.[6] Current scholarly opinion is that second-century and later Gnostic writings drew vocabulary and concepts from Ephesians, rather than the other way around.[7] Ephesians' use of this vocabulary arises from the OT, not Gnosticism.[8] The purpose of Ephesians was not to refute Gnosticism.

In a variation on this interpretation, Moritz proposed that Ephesians was a rewriting of Colossians for an audience in which Jewish Christians were more numerous than gentile Christians, and that the author was attempting to counter "Torah mysticism."[9] Moritz's proposal has not been accepted because of the near-universal scholarly conclusion that Ephesians is addressed to a majority or almost exclusively gentile audience (note especially, 2:11; 3:1; 4:17).

13.2.4 An Introduction to Pauline Jewish Christian Thought for a Gentile Audience Unfamiliar with Paul

C. Leslie Mitton argued that the author aimed to introduce key Pauline concepts, translated from their Jewish particularity into more generic religious language for a new generation of gentile believers. Thus, Jewish terms such as law and justification are reinterpreted, and the unity of the

---

5. Dahl, "Proömium," 315–34; Schlier, *Brief*, 24–25; Schnackenburg, *Ephesians*, 29; Witherington, *Philemon*, 215–19.

6. Dahl, "Ephesians," 455; Evans, "Meaning of Πλήρωμα," 263–64; Pokorný, *Brief*, 443–46; Schlier, *Brief*, 20–22.

7. As is explicitly claimed by Irenaeus, *Haer.* 1.8.4.

8. Hoehner, *Ephesians*, 301–4.

9. Moritz, *Profound Mystery*, 11–12.

now predominantly gentile church is emphasized.[10] While plausible, this proposal fails to account for the unique elements of Ephesians, such as the opening *berakah*, the presentation of Christ as "our peace" (2:11–22), and the spiritual conflict passage (6:10–20); elements which are significant in the overall message of the letter.

13.2.5 An Appeal for Unity

Henry Chadwick proposed that Ephesians sought to foster the unity of humankind through a united church. In order to attain that unity, the chief barrier to be overcome was Jewish-gentile division. Accordingly, the letter represents an appeal to gentile converts to accept the Jewish heritage of their new religion. By connecting gentiles with the ancient roots of Christianity in Judaism, the new religion was also legitimized in the eyes of broader society.[11] Chadwick also explicitly links Ephesians with a missional goal. First-generation Christian expectations of an imminent Parousia were replaced with the hope of God bringing about global salvation through the steady growth of the church towards perfection. The pursuit of this goal required future generations of believers to be taught appropriate behavior and to be witnesses to the faith.[12] Hoehner has fairly criticized Chadwick's reconstruction on the grounds that there is insufficient evidence in the letter of gentile believers being urged to accept Jewish believers.[13] Nevertheless, Chadwick's attempt to set the letter in the context of the witness of the church within society can be affirmed based on our missional analysis. Schnackenburg similarly identified the purpose of Ephesians as fostering unity and a distinctive Christian way of life as against their pagan context.[14]

13.2.6 Establishing the Institutional Church

Käsemann and Lindemann also believed Ephesians arose in a context where gentile Christians had come to despise Jewish Christianity. Furthermore, the ecclesiological focus of Ephesians marks a shift from early Christianity

---

10. Mitton, *Ephesians*, 30–31, 260–65.
11. Chadwick, "Absicht," 145–53; cf. Martin, "Epistle," 300; and Barnard, "Unity in Christ," 167–71 both argue that Jewish-gentile tensions are addressed by Ephesians.
12. Chadwick, "Absicht," 148–49.
13. Hoehner, *Ephesians*, 99.
14. Schnackenburg, *Ephesians*, 28, 34.

to "early Catholicism."[15] The death of the apostles led to the need to establish the institutional church as the focus of salvation, once the charismatic leadership of the apostles in faith formation and mission ended along with a diminishment of eschatological expectations. Käsemann also suggested that the changes impacted mission: "Intra-church problems press to the fore and cause, at the same time, the idea of mission to recede."[16] This characterization of the situation behind Ephesians is not supported by the text. There is no mention or promotion of institutional church leadership such as an overseer/bishop (ἐπίσκοπος). There is also a continued expectation of *charismatic* (Spirit-enabled) gifting in ministries and church life (Eph 4:11; 5:18–20).[17] Further, the missional reading developed above demonstrates that mission has not in the least receded from view.

13.2.7 *A Liturgical Work Connected with Baptism*

John Kirby argued that Ephesians was a homily specifically written for the occasion of baptism, or as catechesis for baptism candidates. He affirms with Schille that Ephesians incorporates prayers, doxology, hymnic material, and exhortation, and is therefore suited to liturgical use.[18] Martin Kitchen also viewed the letter as essentially a liturgical text.[19] While there are elements including prayers, hymns, and doxology, a purpose of *liturgical use* is inadequate, since most NT letters contain these in some measure. Many scholars have also highlighted that a major flaw with Kirby's thesis is that baptism is mentioned only once (at 4:5), which is inexplicable if the letter was intended to explain baptism or be read on the occasion of baptism.[20]

13.2.8 *A Response to Persecution*

Lindemann hypothesized that under the Domitian persecution of 96 CE, Christians needed consolation and encouragement. Drawing especially on Eph 6:10–20, the letter functions to reassure such believers of the power

---

15. Käsemann, "Ephesians and Acts," 290; Lindemann, *Aufhebung*.
16. Käsemann, "Ephesians and Acts," 296.
17. Cf. Muddiman, *Ephesians*, 14.
18. Kirby, *Ephesians*, 5–7, 165–68, citing Schille, *Frühchristliche*; Lincoln, *Paradise Now*, 135–36 also characterizes Ephesians as a "liturgical homily" connected with baptism.
19. Kitchen, *Ephesians*, 11–14.
20. E.g. Lincoln, *Ephesians*, lxxix.

and victory of Christ.[21] A variation on this view is that held by Allen Verhey, who sees that the Jewish rebellion of 66 CE created conditions of both political and ethnic hostility. After the fall of the temple, with a break between synagogue and Christian communities looming, and the *pax Romana* crumbling, Ephesians announces the good news and the requirements of the *pax Dei*. The key passage to set this purpose for the letter is 2:14–18.[22] Although Ephesians does contain much that would be of comfort and encouragement for those experiencing persecution, there is little in the text itself to suggest the recipients were suffering. Vocabulary associated with suffering in other NT letters (e.g. θλῖψις or διωγμός in 2 Cor 12:10, 1 Thess 1:6, and 2 Thess 1:4) is simply absent from Ephesians (except in 3:13 referring exclusively to Paul).

13.2.9 A Resource to Strengthen Believers in the Face of Pagan Spiritual and Cultural Pressures

Of the proposals surveyed so far, only those relating to Gnosticism and persecution gave particular attention to the cosmology of the letter or to the spiritual warfare section (6:11–17) in understanding the context of the writer or recipients. Arnold, responding to this deficiency, advanced the hypothesis that Ephesians was a contextualized response to the magic, astrology, and mystery cults associated with the Artemis cult in Ephesus. Converts were fearful of oppressive spiritual powers and may have been tempted to syncretistically maintain some methods of obtaining protection and spiritual blessing that were common in first-century Ephesus. Against this fear and tendency, Ephesians aims to reassure converts of the superior power and efficacy of Christ as against every other power in heaven or earth.[23]

Arnold's study has found only partial acceptance within the scholarly community. A number of commentaries now acknowledge that the cult of Artemis, magic, and a fear of supernatural powers may constitute a relevant background to Ephesians.[24] However, Arnold overstated the demonic, magical, and fearful characterizations of Artemis and her cult.[25] Arnold's recon-

---

21. Lindemann, "Adressaten," 242–43.

22. Verhey, *Great Reversal*, 123–26; cf. Verhey and Harvard, *Ephesians*, 27–29.

23. Arnold, *Ephesians, Power and Magic*, 167–72; cf. Kreitzer, *Ephesians*, sees the pagan background as the cult of Demeter, and the setting as Hierapolis.

24. E.g. Best, *Ephesians*, 33; Pokorný, *Brief*, 39; Schnelle, *History and Theology*, 122; Sellin, *Brief*, 60–61; Thielman, *Ephesians*, 28.

25. Strelan, *Paul*, 83–85, 155–62, and cf. discussion above at §12.3.1.

struction is unbalanced to the extent that it fails to account adequately for other elements of the letter such as ethics and ecclesiology.[26]

Recent studies by Schwindt, Harrison, and Immendörfer have nuanced the interpretation of primary data in this area, and now present a more balanced and better-supported argument that Ephesians does indeed reflect and respond to the spiritual activity, magic, and the Artemis cult which dominated life in and around Ephesus.[27] Immendörfer concludes that Ephesians' purpose is to convince its recipients that all the benefits they had previously associated with Artemis (blessing, protection, power, and belonging) are provided in exceeding measure by Christ, whose sacrifice, cleansing, and temple building eclipses that of Artemis.[28]

13.2.10 Identity Formation

An article by Hendrix which explored Ephesians in the light of client-benefactor dynamics in the ancient world highlighted the importance of social-scientific analyses for determining the purpose of Ephesians. Drawing from this field of study, Hendrix concludes:

> Ephesians is a prescription of reality. The author adapts a pervasive social reality, the benefactor-beneficiary phenomenon, and through his adaptation prescribes a new network of benefaction. What is achieved is a powerful reinforcement of Christian identity and cohesion. Christians are those who honor their divine benefactor through moral behavior, animated by love as expressed in mutual benefit.[29]

Hendrix pinpoints identity reinforcement as a key outcome of the rhetoric of Ephesians.

One of the first major commentaries to similarly focus on identity formation as a major purpose for Ephesians was Lincoln in 1990. He saw Ephesians as a pseudonymous letter concerned to address a crisis of confidence and cohesion caused by the death of Paul. This general letter aimed to strengthen recipients' *identity* in Christ by explaining salvation, the nature of

---

26. Muddiman, *Ephesians*, 15; Lincoln, *Ephesians*, lxxxi; Hoehner, *Ephesians*, 101; Schnackenburg, *Ephesians*, 33.

27. Schwindt, *Weltbild*, 134, 303-9; Harrison, "Artemis Triumphs," 37-47; Immendörfer, *Ephesians and Artemis*, 327; Arnold, *Ephesians*, 33-34 provides his own rebuttal of Strelan's objections.

28. Immendörfer, *Ephesians and Artemis*, 321.

29. Hendrix, "Form and Ethos," 10.

the church, and providing guidelines to foster "more consistent living in such areas as speech, sexuality, and household relationships."[30]

A similar conclusion was reached by Elna Mouton who analyzed Ephesians' rhetorical situation as distinct from its historical setting and claimed that the author's purpose was to offer readers "a radically new self-understanding, a new identity awareness, leading to a new ethos, new attitudes and actions."[31] This new identity is framed particularly with regard to the religious and social status of gentile Christians as against Jewish Christians (Eph 2).[32] More recently Mouton has extended her analysis to consider the impact on Christian identity formation of the church's location in the Roman Empire (while not neglecting the church seen in continuity with the story of Israel).[33]

MacDonald has also based her research on Ephesians around social-scientific perspectives. She states: "The document is deeply concerned with the identity of the *ekklesia* and, although it is often on an ideological rather than a social plane, one senses an attempt throughout to articulate this identity in relation to Jews and Gentiles in the Roman world."[34] Yee also sees Jewish-gentile relations as a central concern of Ephesians. He argues that the author aims to deconstruct Jewish ethnocentrism, establishing the reasons for gentiles formerly being excluded from Israel, but now incorporated in a renewed and enlarged Israel. With this understanding, gentile believers can appreciate their true identity.[35]

Another social-scientific approach is found in Minna Shkul, who describes Ephesians as a work of, "social entrepreneurship—deliberate shaping of ideological beliefs and social orientations."[36] The letter serves as a "legitimating discourse . . . that explains the communality of the group and their difference from others and legitimates their distinctiveness as reasonable, correct and worthy of commitment."[37] More specifically, the text overcomes the weak and unstable social identity of the recipients by providing:

> a compelling explanation for the community, its role as God's people and distinctiveness from others. Secondly, the writer sought to firmly establish Christ-followership among other

30. Lincoln, *Ephesians*, lxxxi.
31. Mouton, *Reading Ethically*, 163.
32. Mouton, *Reading Ethically*, 110.
33. Mouton, "Ascended Far Above," 1–9.
34. MacDonald, "Politics of Identity," 420.
35. Yee, *Ethnic Reconciliation*, 219–21.
36. Shkul, *Reading Ephesians*, 12.
37. Shkul, *Reading Ephesians*, 13.

ethnicities, providing cultural models for worshipping Israel's God and "Christ." This is seen as the resocialization of the non-Israelites so that they would internalize the story of Israel's god and the symbolic universe it requires, rejecting their cultural origins that contrasted with Israelite understanding of holiness.[38]

A final approach is offered by Roitto, who draws on social identity theory and cognitive psychology to analyze Ephesians as a document navigating in-group/out-group identity through characterization of prototypical versus deviant behavior. The purpose of Ephesians is to firstly persuade the recipients to accept the author's interpretation of their past, present, and future identity in relation to gentile society, Israel, and Christ; and then to promote prototypical behaviors (modeled by Paul such as love, holiness, Spirit-controlled speech, and mutual submission) and so strengthen in-group identification and cohesion.[39]

The collective weight of these social-scientific studies has influenced the authors of recent commentaries, such that Talbert, Thielman, Fowl, and Windsor all name identity formation as the predominant (though not only) purpose that prompted the writing of Ephesians.[40]

13.2.11 Summary

Scholars who postulated specific conflicts, heresies, or threats to the church have failed to convince the broader scholarly community. Accordingly, Gnosticism, Jewish-gentile tension, disunity, baptismal instruction, or persecution as the occasion for the letter can be rejected. The remaining options present variations on the idea of faith or identity formation. In the next section we will assess whether a missional perspective assists us to better express the overarching purpose of Ephesians.

13.3 Ephesians as a Missional Document

If we discard those proposals which have fallen out of favor or only ever been entertained by a minority of scholars, we are left with a set of three broad purposes for Ephesians: (a) an appeal for unity; (b) a resource to

---

38. Shkul, *Reading Ephesians*, 241.

39. Roitto, *Christ-Believer*, 162–71; an earlier, less developed use of social-identity theory to reach similar conclusions was presented by Darko, *No Longer Living*.

40. Talbert, *Ephesians and Colossians*, 12–14; Thielman, *Ephesians*, 24; Fowl, *Ephesians*, 30; Windsor, *Reading Ephesians*, 70.

strengthen believers in the face of pagan spiritual and cultural pressures; and (c) identity formation.

A missional hermeneutic invites us to see the *missio Dei* as a common thread and background rationale for why these purposes were significant. The greatest weakness with many current scholarly appraisals of Ephesians is their failure to provide a comprehensive account for why the document (as a whole) was written, rather than providing a hypothesis concerning one element of the document. To identify one of the dominant themes in the text is not the same as determining why the author felt that theme needed emphasis, or how that theme contributes to a unified final document. Conspicuous in their absence from most theories is an account of why Pauline biographical material is so prominent, and an explanation of the link between the doctrinal (indicative) material of Eph 1–3 and the ethical (imperative) material of Eph 4–6. The missional reading pursued in the present study provides a defensible account of these features while also explaining the stress on unity and identity formation.

We have argued that the *berakah* of 1:3–14 is not abstract praise but that it sensitizes the recipients to their particular role as forerunner beneficiaries of God's salvation who are blessed in order to be agents of the cosmic reconciliation that is now underway. The prayer of 1:15–23 continues to emphasize the significance of the church. As members of the church grow in knowledge of God's purposes and access God's power, they are to contribute to the progressive filling of the world with Christ's dominion. The gracious reconciliation effected by God through Christ as "our peace" and the imagery of the church as temple has a number of distinct implications: the church is to be an inclusive, growing, ethically distinctive, unified conduit spreading God's presence in the world (2:11–22). The following passage (3:1–13) grounds the ongoing gentile mission (of which the letter recipients are a part) in Paul's authority and divine commissioning. The witness of the church to the powers (3:10) is an intrinsic aspect of their existence, flowing from their status as recipients of God's reconciling action (Eph 1–2) and leading into their behaviors as a distinctive community in the world (Eph 4–6).

This summary of Eph 1–3 indicates that the raison d'être of the church is participation in the *missio Dei*. Ephesians 1–3 therefore provides the rationale, context, and goal for the paraenesis of Eph 4–6.[41] The communal behavior of the recipient congregations is to flow out of their changed status with respect to the gentile world from which they have been rescued (2:1–10). The key verses linking identity and behavior are 2:10 and 4:1; the letter's recipients have been created for good works, which are the worthy

---

41. A point that has previously been argued by Ciampa, "*Missio Dei.*"

walk to which they have been called. Awareness of this link has not been entirely absent from the scholarly literature. Pokorný, for example, recognized that the concentration upon ethics in Ephesians did not necessarily mean the church had turned inwards and had no regard for witness to the pagan world. Indeed, the church exists in an eschatological tension between an exclusivity shaped by the demands of holiness and a universal openness for the sake of mission. He states, "The Church as the 'fullness' of the Lord of all creation is neither identical with Christ nor with the world. It gives everyone access to God (3:10–12), but precisely for the sake of its mission it has to be different from its environment."[42]

The relationship of theology to ethics (or indicative to imperative) in Ephesians arises from mission. Ephesians 4:1–3 functions as a thesis statement for the following ethical material, beginning with the logical conjunction οὖν *therefore*. In the light of salvation history, that is God's mission, believers are to walk worthily of God's action in their lives. That the continuing goal is missional is seen then in 4:11–13. Christ equips believers with gifts of church founding, proclamation, and evangelism (apostles, prophets, evangelists) in order that all believers actively participate in the mission of God resulting in unity, maturity, and growth.[43]

We further observe that the function of the biographical comment about Paul's ministry (3:1–13) and the prayers in 1:15–23 and 3:14–19 is to motivate the recipients to continue Paul's apostolic mission to the gentiles, confident in God's empowerment, God's sovereignty over salvation history, and the legitimacy of the mission despite Paul's imprisonment and sufferings.

13.3.1 The Theme of Unity in the Light of Mission

The letter's theme of unity (4:3–6) is also grounded in the *missio Dei*. As detailed in 2:1–22, the status of those outside of Christ is death, alienation, and exclusion. The allusions to Gen 3 connect Eph 2 to a broader biblical theology of sin and redemption in which humanity's plight is answered by Christ's reconciling work on the cross. Christ brings formerly estranged people into fellowship with God and each other. The unity within the church is thus an indispensable expression of the fruit of God's saving mission.

Social-scientific analyses of the letter remain stuck in the sociological horizon of Jewish-gentile relations and the conundrum that there are few indicators of actual community tension or division on ethnic grounds. A

---

42. Pokorný, *Brief*, 33, my translation.
43. Darko, *No Longer Living*, 29.

missional reading helps us see that the Jewish-gentile discussion so prominent in Eph 2 serves more to explain the course of salvation history than to address an acute conflict in the recipient communities. Christ-believers, whatever their ethnic, religious, or geographic background, are all swept up in the new reconciled community which is the church, the foretaste of God's renewed universal human eschatological society which will ultimately fill all things.[44] The church is to pursue and promote unity because in so doing it provides a witness to humanity outside Christ, who live daily with symptoms of the disunity, alienation, and exclusion caused by sin (cf. 4:17; 5:8).

13.3.2 Strengthening Believers to Face Pagan Spiritual and Cultural Pressures

In his work on Ephesians, Arnold explicitly identified spiritual conflict (6:10–20) as an expression of the church's mission. He states:

> The military imagery describes both the task of mission and the divine enabling power for fulfilling the task. The author depicts the mission in the context of spiritual warfare to heighten the expectation of the readers for encountering demonic opposition and their need to continue the mission with the power God will supply."[45]

In his commentary, Arnold clarifies how Ephesians functions as a response to the threat of spiritual powers. Drawing on the narrative of Acts 19:13–20, Arnold describes a setting for the recipients of the letter as one where people routinely used amulets, charms, and invocations as a means of gaining spiritual power in the area of illness and daily struggles.[46] One purpose of Ephesians is accordingly to assure believers that they "can resist the supernatural powers because they have been co-resurrected and have co-ascended with Christ (2:6), and on that basis, they can 'be strong in the Lord' (6:10)."[47]

The spiritual resources provided to believers to empower holy living are also specified in 1:15–23; 3:16–19; 4:7, 20–24, 30; 5:1, 18. Ephesians repeatedly emphasizes the role of the Holy Spirit and fellowship amongst believers as means by which they are equipped to withstand the cultural patterns

---

44. Gorman, *Becoming the Gospel*, 192.
45. Arnold, *Ephesians, Power and Magic*, 144–45.
46. Arnold, *Ephesians*, 34.
47. Arnold, *Ephesians*, 45.

of behavior that had previously dominated their lives.[48] We therefore see in Ephesians a multipronged missional strategy of countering idolatry conceived both as demonic forces and as cultural pressures that would undercut believers' devotion to the absolute lordship of Christ.[49] The stark language of 2:1–10, 3:10, and the polemic against pagan lifestyle in 4:17—5:20 make sense as a missional response to the pervasive threat of idolatry.

13.3.3 Identity Formation and Mission

Finally, we can consider identity formation in the light of the broader missional currents flowing through Ephesians. Social identity theory provides numerous insights into the means by which community identities are shaped through a rhetorical text like Ephesians. They answer the *how*, but the contribution social identity theory makes to the *why* of theological texts is less convincing. For example, Roitto states that the goals of forming group ideals and beliefs are to bolster self-esteem and maximize cognitive distinctiveness (by which group members feel participation in the group is meaningful and useful).[50] While this is reasonable as a description of what may be occurring at the individual psychological level, such goals do not adequately address the reality of divine action in and beyond the believing community. Theological description is needed at that point.

The theological goal of identity formation is multifaceted, comprising an individual ethic of holiness in thought and deed, an intragroup dynamic of mutual love and service, and also an outward-oriented disposition towards nonbelieving society. The missional prayers of Eph 1:15–23 and 3:14–21 touch on this individual and corporate formation with a view to empowerment for mission. We have seen that as individual believers grow in knowledge and appropriation of God's saving actions in their lives, they constitute a new creation, the firstfruits of God's mission to redeem humanity from enslavement to the powers. In the first instance, therefore, identity formation requires a cognitive grasp of the gospel proclaimed by Paul and passed on by evangelists, prophets, and teachers in the context of the recipient communities. That cognitive response is then manifest in the adoption of a lifestyle that demonstrates the shift of allegiance to Christ and a rejection of former ties to other deities and ways of behaving arising from a non-Christian worldview (e.g. 2:1–10; 4:17—5:9; 6:10–17).

---

48. Fee, *Empowering Presence*, 733.
49. Cf. Wright, *Mission of God*, 135–88, esp. 186.
50. Roitto, *Christ-Believer*, 108–11.

Identity formation at the corporate level is a manifestation of how Christ's sacrificial death creates a new humanity, a community in which reconciliation with God is expressed in reconciled interpersonal relationships and a new ethic of mutual love, submission, and service (2:11-22; 4:1-6, 13-16; 5:21—6:9). The new humanity can be a reflection of God's holy and glorious character (cf. Eph 1:4, 6, 12, 14). The household code is theological because the pair relationships are practical demonstrations that Christ's lordship transforms the hostilities and distortions that blight human relationships outside of the community of faith.

Finally, an overarching goal of the identity formation advocated in Ephesians is church growth. This is indicated by a number of verses. In Eph 4, walking worthily of God's calling (v. 1), maintaining unity (v. 3), receiving grace gifts (v. 7), exercising equipping gifts (vv. 11–12), and speaking truth in love (vv. 15, 25) collectively function to further the growth of the church (vv. 12, 15, 16). The growth is not purely maturation of existing members, since the building language used (οἰκοδομή vv. 12, 16) naturally connotes expansion in size (although at 4:29 the connotation is edification).[51] In Eph 5, the character virtues advocated for believers are *light* against the backdrop of the *darkness* that characterizes the behaviors of unbelievers (5:8–15). The missional function of believers as light echoes Matt 5:14–16 (and cf. John 12:46; Acts 26:17–18; 2 Cor 4:4–6). In Eph 6:10–20 the virtues symbolized by the armor of God are largely defensive, but viewed as a comprehensive identity, they include the elements of gospel proclamation (v. 15) and Spirit-enabled use of God's word (v. 17). Prayer is an indispensable component of believers' identity, and it is to be concerned with gospel proclamation (6:18–20).

In brief, the formation of identity as a goal is by no means restricted to providing the psychological benefits of self-esteem and cognitive distinctiveness, but it enables the church to collectively participate in God's mission through their renewed relationships, behaviors, beliefs, and words. As Fowl succinctly states: "[Ephesians insists] that Christians live together in a manner worthy of their calling so that they might bear witness to the world at large."[52]

---

51. Dickson, *Mission-Commitment*, 328, citing van Swigchem, *Het missionair karakter*, 108, 259.

52. Fowl, *Ephesians*, 30.

13.4 Conclusion

Although in recent decades scholars have largely settled on identity formation as the primary purpose underlying Ephesians, a missional reading provides further depth to the discussion about purpose. The outworking of the *missio Dei* provides the common thread linking the doctrinal and paraenetic material in Ephesians. The furtherance of the church's mission is the underlying rationale for pursuing unity since it is in the reconciled fellowship of the church that the powers are shown to have failed in their attempts to divide and enslave humanity. A missional reading enables us to see that the prayers and the account of Paul's gentile mission motivate believers to continue that mission, confident in its divine origin, legitimacy, and facilitation. A missional reading also accounts for the emphasis on conflict with spiritual powers, and the prominent role given to the Holy Spirit as the enabler of the godly behaviors that are promoted in contrast to the former way of life of the gentile recipients. Identity formation is not merely a sociological phenomenon with psychological benefits, but an outworking of God's purposes to transform individuals, church communities, and through them progressively impact the whole world. The purpose of Ephesians is to communicate and exhort participation in the multifaceted *missio Dei*. The letter itself is therefore an instrument of the *missio Dei*.

14

Conclusion

14.1 The Research Question

THIS PROJECT SET OUT to explore whether Ephesians can fairly be characterized as a missional document. It disputed Best's assertion that Ephesians has no interest in mission, and MacDonald's characterization of the letter as reflecting an "introversionist" turn in Pauline communities after the death of the apostle.[1] A review of existing literature on mission in Ephesians by biblical scholars and missiologists revealed that the letter has not been analyzed consistently or comprehensively with regard to its perspective on mission. Using missional hermeneutics as the interpretive approach, every passage in Ephesians has been analyzed for its portrayal of the *missio Dei*, the characterization of God, intertextual links to mission in the wider biblical narrative, the portrayal of humanity and the world in relation to God's mission, evidence for a missional context, the character and mission of God's people, and the portrayal of Paul and his involvement in mission. This analysis has redressed the lack of consistent or comprehensive consideration of mission in Ephesians. Following this inductive analysis, the context and purpose of Ephesians was evaluated to test whether a missional reading accounted for the data of the letter as well as or better than existing proposals. It now remains to summarize and synthesize the findings in each of the focal areas in the missional hermeneutics framework, before presenting a final evaluation.

---

1. E.g. Best, *Ephesians*, 4, 56; MacDonald, *Colossians and Ephesians*, 223, 260, 264, 265. Their positions were evaluated at §§9.6 and 9.7, above.

14.2 Summary of Arguments

14.2.1 Focus 1: *The Portrayal of God's Intentions, Actions, and Purposes for the World and Humanity (the missio Dei)*

The *missio Dei*, as celebrated in Eph 1:3–14, is God's action prompted by love to choose, redeem, adopt, and sanctify for himself a holy people, who are the firstfruits of his inheritance, sealed by the Spirit until the eschaton, at which time a reconciled and unified cosmos will exist to the praise of his glory. Christ's resurrection is the central moment in God's mission, demonstrating God's victory over death and the establishment of his universal reign through the risen and enthroned Christ (1:20–23). The church is instrumental in manifesting Christ's reign, since it is his body in the world, progressively expanding the sphere of Christ's redemptive presence (1:22–23). As believers are filled with knowledge of God's will and receive God's power to participate in his mission, they experience the fullness of God as his glory is increasingly manifest in and through them (3:16–21).

Sinful humanity is the unmeritorious recipient of God's gracious actions. Those now *in Christ* have had their status changed from under wrath to under grace, and from death to life; and this change constitutes a witness or demonstration to the whole world and all spiritual powers that God's redemptive mission has succeeded (2:1–10).

God acts in mission as a builder. He is building a new humanity, a restored Davidic kingdom, a restored community and a world-filling, living temple made up of an ever-increasing number of believers (2:14–21). The church is both the fruit and a vehicle of God's mission in the world. As gentiles join believing Jews as equal beneficiaries of salvation, the resultant community characterized by unity, inclusion, and reconciliation continues the process of Christ filling the cosmos with his lordship, thereby defeating the darkness, death, and destruction which the powers represent (3:6, 10). Therefore, God's mission encompasses all creation, not just humanity.

The paraenetic material of Eph 4–6 continues to elaborate the *missio Dei*. God's purpose is to foster unity in the church and ultimately the world as a reflection of God's own unity (4:4–6). God also intends the church to grow in maturity and impact through the exercise and cultivation of ministry gifts (4:11–16). God's Spirit empowers believers to live holy, distinct lives marked by reconciliation, forgiveness, mutuality, love, and praise (5:18—6:9). God as Divine Warrior equips believers to stand firm in virtue and in the truths of the gospel, against the spiritual powers that oppose God and his mission (6:10–20).

14.2.2 Focus 2: The Portrayal of God's Person and Character

Ephesians 1 stresses God's sovereignty, love, and initiative in providing a path of salvation for humanity. Christ is the focal point for God's saving actions, revealing God's purposes, being the source of blessing for all who are *in him*, and reigning as the true sovereign over the whole cosmos. The Spirit is portrayed as the eschatological seal guaranteeing the adoption and security of believers as God's inheritance (1:13; 4:30).

Ephesians 2 emphasizes God's loving kindness towards all humanity, and Christ's identity as "our peace"—the reconciler of humanity with God and the one in whom all divided and alienated human groups can find reconciliation. God's Spirit is active in revealing God's will and the grace of salvation to apostles and prophets (3:5), and in strengthening believers to apprehend fully Christ's work in and for them (2:18; 3:16).

In Eph 3, God is particularly portrayed as Father (3:14–15), evoking notions of relationality and the covenantal love that was expressed in the exodus and was a promised feature of the new exodus. God is filling the world through the church. That is, God is neither distant nor detached from creation, but is immanent in his holy love that desires to see all created things brought into restored fellowship with him (1:23; 3:19; 4:10). Ephesians 4 then elaborates how the church is equipped to communicate and extend God's presence in the world—primarily through ministries of proclamation and edification (4:11–16).

God's relationships, grounded in love (5:2), are paradigmatic for human society and relationships. God's character is righteous and holy (4:24); characteristics which are intended to be manifest in believers' lives. God's mission involves humanity being renewed in God's likeness, and not grieving God's Spirit (4:30) by acting (or particularly speaking) in community destructive ways (5:18). Christ's light both illuminates believers and transforms the world through them (5:11–14). Christ is the model for the self-sacrificial loving behavior of husbands (5:25–33), while God's impartiality and justice are the ground for social justice in work relationships (6:9). Finally, God is portrayed as the Divine Warrior, whose virtues including truth and righteousness are given to believers to empower them for their spiritual struggle as God's people (6:10–17).

Ephesians presents a multifaceted portrait of God who is lovingly and determinedly at work in the world for the sake of his own glory, to redeem all humanity and all creation from the destructive patterns of life engendered by sin and the domination of the devil.

14.2.3 Focus 3: Missional Intertextuality

Five passages in Ephesians have been identified that intentionally evoke the context of OT precursor texts through allusion, and so creatively extend the meaning that results in the Ephesians text: Eph 1:3–14; 2:1–10, 11–22; 5:7–14; 6:10–17. These texts each contain a strongly missional image or theme.

In 1 Chr 16:8 (alluded to in Eph 1:3–14) the hearers are exhorted to "make known his deeds among the peoples," while in 1 Chr 16:24 the charge is to "declare his glory among the nations, his marvelous works among all the peoples." Enjoyment of God's blessings should always yield a broader witness to those outside God's covenant community.

Ezekiel 36:23 (alluded to in Eph 2) explicitly proclaims that when God cleanses Israel from idolatry and unfaithfulness, that act of sanctification is a witness to the gentiles: "the nations shall know that I am the LORD . . . when through you I display my holiness before their eyes." The vision of the valley of dry bones (Ezek 37) and two sticks concludes with a further reiteration of how God's saving actions are to become a revelation for gentiles: "Then the nations shall know that I the LORD sanctify Israel, when my sanctuary is among them forevermore" (Ezek 37:28).

Lastly, in Isa 59–60 (alluded to in Eph 5:7–14; 6:10–17) the coming of God as Divine Warrior signals a moment of global recognition of God's power (Isa 59:19) and a pilgrimage of gentiles and their rulers bearing tribute as they come towards God's light now manifest in the restored people of God (Isa 60:3, 10, 14, 16).

These five passages which function as metaleptic tropes consistently draw on precursor texts in which God's actions for his people result in witness to the gentiles of God's power, glory, and salvation.

In addition to the passages above, there are twenty-one quotations or allusions which, while not metaleptic, contain significant themes that reinforce the key missional themes in Ephesians. The recurrent themes in the OT precursor texts are: God's people chosen to live distinctively holy lives governed by God's laws (in view of or as a witness to the nations) (Eph 1; 4:25–26; 5:14; Deut 7; Ps 4:5; Isa 26); God who judges covenant unfaithfulness, injustice, and idolatry (Eph 4:30; Isa 63); God who redeems his people from slavery, sin, and exile; God who brings healing and peace after judgment (Eph 2:13–17; Isa 9; 57); knowledge of God, his salvation and his glory being extended worldwide (Eph 1:17; 2:13–17; Isa 11; 52:10); a new creation (Eph 1:22; Ps 8:6); and a gentile pilgrimage or turning to God in the eschatological (messianic) age (Eph 4:25; Zech 8:16). From these intertexts, it is clear that God's people play a mediatorial role to the nations—revealing to the wider world God, his glory, salvation, peace, justice, blessings, and patterns of life.

14.2.4 Focus 4: Portrayal of Humanity and the World in Relation to God's Mission

Ephesians conceives of all humanity, the whole created world, indeed the whole cosmos (inclusive of all spiritual entities and the physical world), as the sphere of God's mission (1:10, 20–22). God's plan is *cosmic* reconciliation. Ephesians 2 portrays humanity's plight outside of Christ: they are dead *in the sphere* of their sins and dead *because* of sins (2:1–5). Humanity lives under wrath, enslaved by the "the ruler of the power of the air," i.e., the devil (2:2; cf. 4:27; 6:11). In Eph 4 and 6, the devil's influence can come through the immorality and self-centered sinfulness characteristic of pagan society (4:22, 25–31; 5:3–8), or through structures such as political empire, social class, commerce, and even religion, according to interpreters. In both cases, the consequences for humanity are estrangement from God and the corruption of human social existence, division and mutual antipathy (2:11–19; cf. 4:14, 17–22).

God's mission is to bring about a thoroughgoing reconciliation (vertical and horizontal), encompassing humanity in relation to God, humanity in relation to itself (2:13–22), and humanity in relation to the created world (1:10; 3:10; 6:3). The believing community is a new creation (2:10, 15), united across previous ethnic and religious divides, now living in God-ordained good works. God's mission results in the ethical transformation of humanity.

14.2.5 Focus 5: The Missional Context of Ephesians

Ephesians reflects an identifiable set of problems and issues that prompted the letter. These issues are: insecurity (1:1–14, 15–23; 3:1–13, 14–21; 6:10–24); pressure from or fear of spiritual powers (1:1–14, 15–23; 2:1–10; 3:1–13; 6:10–24); a community in danger of cultural assimilation or compromise (1:15–23; 2:1–10; 3:1–13; 4:1–16; 4:17—5:20; 5:21—6:9; 6:10–24); and inadequate Christian knowledge and identity formation (1:1–14; 2:1–22; 3:14–21; 4:1–16; 4:17—6:24).

The historical characteristics of Ephesus in the first century CE that are most pertinent to our analysis are the dominance of the Artemis cult, the pervasive presence of magic and the influence of imperial Roman politics and culture. Seen against this backdrop, Ephesians is best understood as a contextualized letter written to Christ-believing residents of Ephesus and Western Asia Minor in the late first century CE. They were largely gentile converts to Christ, an insecure minority, feeling the weight of cultural pressure to conform to existing patterns of interpersonal and communal behaviors. Ephesians is framed with sensitivity to address this context and proclaims that God's mission will see Christ established as Lord of the entire cosmos (comprising both earth and the heavens). The descriptions of the spiritual realities of life in Eph 2 and the futility and destructiveness of life outside of Christ portrayed in Eph 4–5, heightens the readers' awareness of their missional context and the seriousness of the call to walk worthily of their calling.

14.2.6 Focus 6: The Character and Mission of God's People in the World

God's people are chosen to live "to the praise of his glory" (1:6, 12, 14). This refrain in the opening *berakah* of the letter effectively captures a central aspect of mission according to Ephesians: that the lifestyle of believers is to be a public witness to God's glorious work in them and in the world. Believers have been graciously chosen, blessed, sanctified, adopted, redeemed, forgiven, enlightened, and sealed with God's Spirit (1:3–14). These benefits are not intended to produce pride (2:9), still less are they intended to result in the believing community turning away from their nonbelieving neighbors (4:25, 29; 5:15–16); rather, they are bestowed in order that believers become firstfruits (1:10–12) in a larger, global movement of reconciliation as all people and all heavenly powers come to acknowledge Christ's lordship (1:10, 22–23).

The identity of God's people as a temple dwelling place for God is significant since multiple OT texts identified the temple as the focal point for God's revelation to the whole world, and prayers directed towards the temple by gentiles would be heard (e.g. 3 Kgdms 8:41–43 LXX; Ps 33:21–22; Ezek 37:28). Now that the believing multiethnic community is a living temple, an organic growing dwelling place for God, the geographical limits of a single physical temple are overcome. Consequently, God's presence can progressively fill the earth, providing a universal witness to God's glory and the foundational sacrifice of Jesus by which all people may be forgiven and come to be included in God's household (Eph 2:11–22).

God's people are *empowered* by God (1:19; 3:16, 20; 6:10) to understand and therefore conduct themselves consistently with God's purposes (his mission) in the world (5:17). The repeated calls for them to walk worthily of their calling, by doing good works, living in love and unity, and displaying godly virtues (2:10; 4:1; 5:2, 5, 15; 6:14–16), achieve the goal of the believing community presenting a compelling witness to the cosmos (3:10) of the wisdom of God's actions in salvation history (3:6, 11–12). The light-darkness imagery of 5:8–12 (with intertextual links to Isa 60) also supports the goal of believers presenting an ethical witness to the gospel through their lifestyle.

The church is furthermore gifted by Christ for ongoing growth and witness, particularly as apostles and evangelists verbally proclaim the gospel by which nonbelievers may come to faith. This externally oriented ministry is complemented by the work of prophets, pastors, and teachers whose roles strengthen believers in faith and equip them for ministry (4:7–16). Believers are also exhorted to make the most of the time (5:15–16), a phrase which plausibly endorses evangelistic speech. A further basis for encouraging evangelism is met in 6:15, 17, where believers are encouraged to be ready with the gospel and to wield the proclaimed word ($ῥῆμα$) of God. God's people are to be steadfast in prayer, both for Paul, as a model apostle engaged in gospel proclamation and missional church planting, and for "all the saints" as they collectively participate in God's mission in the world (6:18–20).

14.2.7 Focus 7: Portrayal of the Apostle Paul

Paul is portrayed in Ephesians as a missionary wholeheartedly committed to the gospel which not only significantly transformed his own life, but also constitutes God's means for the transformation of the world (6:19–20). Paul's consciousness of his own unworthiness underlines his appreciation of God's grace to sinners (3:8). God's grace is never given to be received selfishly, but it is given in order that it then be passed on to the many (3:7–9). Paul is one who, as a steward of the mission ($οἰκονομία$, 3:2), proclaims the gospel and makes known the mystery of God's saving mission ($οἰκονομία$, 1:10; 3:9) to the whole world (3:10). Paul's imprisonment is not a defeat or indicator of the impotence or shamefulness of God's mission. Rather, it serves to highlight that God's servants (as ambassadors) will face suffering as they faithfully participate in God's mission in the world (3:13; 6:18–20). Paul is also a role model in missional prayer. His desire is that God's people are so compelled by the vastness of God's gracious gift of love, that they will be empowered for a transformed life and effective witness to God's glory (3:14–21; 6:18–20).

14.3 Evaluation

The preceding summary has highlighted the consistent and comprehensive concern for mission that is evident in every part of Ephesians. The author of Ephesians portrays God's actions and intentions as driven by an eternal plan to bring all humanity and all creation into reconciled submission under Christ's lordship. God's character is inherently missional. God's mission is the rationale for the existence of the church, which is never portrayed as existing for its own sake, or as a social institution only concerned about self-preservation. Rather, the church is the manifestation of God's saving purposes in the world. It has a revelatory, exemplary, and proclamatory role with regard to the world which would be frustrated entirely if it turned inwards and disregarded the wider world which is God's sphere of concern. Mission can legitimately involve both centripetal and centrifugal movements. The people of God gather in order to be encouraged and equipped to engage in outward-focused mission.[2] The portrait of Paul as the paradigmatic missionary apostle to the gentiles is not set exclusively in the past. Instead, as a living, present-tense ambassador, the apostle addresses a community of believers whom he wishes to inform and energize for their own missional task.

The intertextual links that enrich the message of Ephesians are also dominated by passages in which the universality of God's dominion in the world is evident and the futility or error of idolatry is denounced. The role of God's people in these texts is to declare God's sovereignty, salvation, and glory before all the nations, as well as to live holy lives exemplifying the blessings of living under God's covenant. Many of the texts alluded to in Ephesians foreshadow an eschatological gentile pilgrimage or turning to God. It seems warranted to speak about Ephesians employing a deliberate *missional intertextuality*. This observation suggests an area for further research; that is, whether Ephesians' missional appeal to OT texts is consistent with other Pauline letters, or is a unique feature of Ephesians.

With regard to the purpose of Ephesians, we have seen that a missional reading enables the themes of unity, spiritual conflict, and identity formation to be accommodated within an overarching framework of mission. Unity strengthens the church's witness. God informs and empowers his people for the spiritual conflict of ethical living and the battle against the destructive and divisive lies of ideological, cultural, and religious powers opposed to Christ's lordship. Identity formation is pursued in order that God's transformative power reaches individuals and church communities,

---

2. Gorman, *Becoming the Gospel*, 18–20.

and through them progressively impacts the whole world. Mission provides a coherent and comprehensive account of the purpose of the letter. Ephesians is a missional document, written to inform, encourage, and shape its recipients for participation in the *missio Dei*.

As a case study in missional hermeneutics, the present work has confirmed the utility of the approach. When used as an interpretive framework, the resulting portrait of mission goes well beyond the valid but incomplete themes identified in missiological works that mention Ephesians (such as reconciliation, spiritual warfare, prayer, or spiritual gifts). A missionally focused study of intertextuality highlights the hopes of universal redemption and gentile blessing in key OT precursor texts. The intertextual analysis confirms that mission is a metanarrative uniting the broader canon of Scripture.

14.4 Contribution to Scholarship

The present study has contributed to biblical studies and missiological scholarship most prominently in four particular areas. Firstly, it has overcome the lack of a comprehensive and consistent analysis of mission in Ephesians in existing literature. We have developed a missional reading of Ephesians that is more comprehensive, nuanced, and structured than any previous work in the field. Secondly, the claims that Ephesians is an inward-focused or introversionist document have been roundly rebutted. Thirdly, the intertextual analysis has broken new ground by highlighting the prominence of missional themes such as an ethical and verbal witness to the nations in the immediate contexts of virtually all the OT allusions and quotations in Ephesians. Fourthly, the present study has confirmed the utility of missional hermeneutics as an approach that yields fresh perspectives on disputed issues in biblical scholarship such as the purpose of NT letters.

14.5 Conclusion

The present study was prompted by the observation that numerous biblical scholars either neglected mission as a theme within Ephesians (e.g. Hoehner, Thielman), or explicitly denied that the author had any interest in mission (most notably Fischer, Best, and MacDonald). Contrary to these scholars, this research has demonstrated that the letter to the Ephesians displays a consistent and coherent concern for mission.

The portrayal of mission that emerges in Ephesians is richer and far deeper and wider than the portrait offered by missiologists based on the limited set of verses and passages most frequently cited from the letter. We see the *missio Dei* elucidated in every pericope, touching every aspect of the letter's concerns from the *berakah*'s panorama of salvation history, to the function of the church as mediator of God's grace, love, forgiveness, and reconciliation to the surrounding world through its prayer, ethical witness, and through the verbal proclamation of apostles and evangelists. Ephesians reveals the character and distinctive roles of the missional God. Ephesians creatively draws on varied OT texts and themes to strengthen the portrayal of God's people as witnesses and mediators of God's glory and grace to the nations. Ephesians closes with encouragements to stand firm in the truths of salvation, godly virtues, prayer, and commitment to the apostolic ministry of gospel proclamation modeled by Paul. From start to finish, Ephesians effectively exhorts its readers to understand, support, and participate in God's mission to rescue humanity and all creation from the damage and distortion of sin, and so bring about a renewed creation filled with God's glorious fullness.

Bibliography

Adai, Jacob. *Der Heilige Geist als Gegenwart Gottes: in den einzelnen Christen, in der Kirche und in der Welt: Studien zur Pneumatologie des Epheserbriefes*. Regensburger Studien zur Theologie. Frankfurt am Main: Peter Lang, 1985.
Aletti, Jean Noël. *Saint Paul, Épître aux Éphésiens*. Paris: Gabalda, 2001.
Altink, Willem. "1 Chronicles 16:8–36 as Literary Source for Revelation 14:6–7." *AUSS* 22, no. 2 (1984) 187–96.
Arnold, Clinton E. *Ephesians*. ZECNT. Grand Rapids: Zondervan, 2010.
———. *Ephesians, Power and Magic: The Concept of Power in Ephesians in Light of Its Historical Setting*. SNTSMS 63. Cambridge: Cambridge University Press, 1989.
———. *Powers of Darkness: Principalities and Powers in Paul's Letters*. Downers Grove, IL: InterVarsity, 1992.
Asumang, Annang. "Powers of Darkness: An Evaluation of Three Hermeneutical Approaches to the Evil Powers in Ephesians." *Conspectus: The Journal of the South African Theological Seminary* 5 (2008) 1–19.
Aune, David E. "Magic in Early Christianity." In *ANRW* 23.1:1507–57. Part 2, *Principat* 23.1, edited by Hildegard Temporini and Wolfgang Haase. Berlin: de Gruyter, 1980.
———. *Revelation 6–16*. WBC. Nashville: Thomas Nelson, 1998.
Bader-Saye, Scott. *Church and Israel after Christendom: The Politics of Election*. Eugene, OR: Wipf & Stock, 2005.
Balch, David L. *Let Wives Be Submissive: The Domestic Code in 1 Peter*. SBLMS 26. Chico, CA: Scholars, 1981.
Barker, Margaret. *Temple Theology: An Introduction*. London: SPCK, 2004.
Barnard, Jody A. "Unity in Christ: The Purpose of Ephesians." *ExpTim* 120, no. 4 (2009) 167–71.
Barr, James. *The Semantics of Biblical Language*. London: Oxford University Press, 1961.
Barram, Michael. "The Bible, Mission, and Social Location: Toward a Missional Hermeneutic." *Interpretation* 61, no. 1 (2007) 42–58.

———. "'Located' Questions for a Missional Hermeneutic." *The Gospel and Our Culture Network*, November 1, 2006. http://www.gocn.org/ resources/articles/located-questions-missional-hermeneutic.

———. *Mission and Moral Reflection in Paul.* StBibLit 75. New York: Peter Lang, 2006.

Barrett, Lois Y., ed. *Treasure in Clay Jars: Patterns in Missional Faithfulness.* Grand Rapids: Eerdmans, 2004.

Barth, Markus. *The Broken Wall: A Study of the Epistle to the Ephesians.* London: Judson, 1959.

———. "Conversion and Conversation: Israel and the Church in Paul's Epistle to the Ephesians." *Interpretation* 17, no. 1 (1963) 3–24.

———. *Ephesians 4–6.* AB. New Haven: Yale University Press, 1974.

———. *Ephesians: Introduction, Translation, and Commentary on Chapters 1–3.* AB. Garden City: Doubleday, 1974.

———. "Traditions in Ephesians." *NTS* 30 (1984) 3–25.

Bartholomew, Craig G. "A Manifesto for Theological Interpretation." In *A Manifesto for Theological Interpretation*, edited by Craig G. Bartholomew and Heath A. Thomas, 1–25. Grand Rapids: Baker Academic, 2016.

Bauckham, Richard. *Bible and Mission: Christian Witness in a Postmodern World.* Easneye Lectures. Grand Rapids: Baker Academic, 2003.

———. "Biblical Theology and the Problem of Monotheism." In *Out of Egypt: Biblical Theology and Biblical Interpretation*, edited by Craig Bartholomew, 187–232. Carlisle: Paternoster, 2004.

Baugh, Steve M. *Ephesians: Evangelical Exegetical Commentary.* Bellingham, WA: Lexham, 2015.

Baulès, Robert. *L'insondable Richesse du Christ: Étude des thèmes de l'Épître aux Éphésiens.* Lectio Divina 66. Paris: Cerf, 1971.

Beale, G. K. "The Conversion of the Imagination: Paul as Interpreter of Israel's Scripture." *JETS* 50, no. 1 (2007) 190–94.

———. *Handbook on the New Testament Use of the Old Testament: Exegesis and Interpretation.* Grand Rapids: Baker Academic, 2012.

———. *The Temple and the Church's Mission: A Biblical Theology of the Dwelling Place of God.* NSBT. Downers Grove, IL: InterVarsity, 2004.

Beale, G. K., and D. A. Carson, eds. *Commentary on the New Testament Use of the Old Testament.* Grand Rapids: Baker Academic, 2007.

Beale, G. K., and Benjamin L. Gladd. *Hidden But Now Revealed: A Biblical Theology of Mystery.* Nottingham: InterVarsity, 2014.

Beale, G. K., and Mitchell Kim. *God Dwells Among Us: Expanding Eden to the Ends of the Earth.* Downers Grove, IL: InterVarsity, 2014.

Beeby, H. D. *Canon and Mission.* Christian Mission and Modern Culture. Harrisburg, PA: Trinity, 1999.

———. "A Missional Approach to Renewed Interpretation." In *Renewing Biblical Interpretation*, edited by Craig Bartholomew, Colin Greene, and Karl Möller, 268–83. Carlisle: Paternoster, 2000.

Beetham, Christopher A. *Echoes of Scripture in the Letter of Paul to the Colossians.* BibInt 96. Leiden: Brill, 2008.

Beker, Johan C. *Heirs of Paul: Paul's Legacy in the New Testament and in the Church Today.* Minneapolis: Fortress, 1991.

Belz, Lisa Marie. "Proper Household Relations in Whose Basileia? Examining Ephesians' Subtle Revisions to the Household Code of Colossians." *Conversations with the Biblical World* 34 (2014) 226–49.
Berkhof, Hendrikus. *Christ and the Powers*. Translated by J. H. Yoder. 2nd ed. Scottdale, PA: Herald, 1977.
Best, Ernest. *Ephesians*. ICC. London: T. & T. Clark, 1998.
———. "Ephesians 2.11–22: A Christian View of Judaism." In *Text as Pretext: Essays in Honour of Robert Davidson*, edited by Robert P. Carroll and Robert Davidson, 47–60. JSOT 138. Sheffield: JSOT, 1992.
———. "Ministry in Ephesians." *IBS* 15 (1993) 146–66.
———. "Recipients and Title of the Letter to the Ephesians: Why and When the Designation 'Ephesians'?" In *ANRW* 25.4:3247–79. Part 2, *Principat* 25.4, edited by Hildegard Temporini and Wolfgang Haase. Berlin: de Gruyter, 1987.
———. "Two Types of Existence." In *Essays on Ephesians*, 139–55. Edinburgh: T. & T. Clark, 1997.
Billington, Antony, ed. *Mission and Meaning: Essays Presented to Peter Cotterell*. Carlisle: Paternoster, 1995.
Bird, Jennifer G. "The Letter to the Ephesians." In *A Postcolonial Commentary on the New Testament Writings*, edited by Fernando F. Segovia and R. S. Sugirtharajah, 265–80. The Bible and Postcolonialism 13. London: T. & T. Clark, 2009.
Bird, Michael F. *Crossing Over Sea and Land: Jewish Missionary Activity in the Second Temple Period*. Peabody: Hendrickson, 2010.
Blackburn, W. Ross. *The God Who Makes Himself Known: The Missionary Heart of the Book of Exodus*. NSBT. London: Apollos, 2012.
Blenkinsopp, Joseph. *Ezekiel*. IBC. Louisville: John Knox, 1990.
Bloesch, Donald G. *The Holy Spirit: Works and Gifts*. Downers Grove, IL: InterVarsity, 2000.
Bolt, Peter G., et al., eds. *The Gospel to the Nations: Perspectives on Paul's Mission: In Honour of Peter T. O'Brien*. Leicester: Apollos, 2000.
Bosch, David J. "Reflections on Biblical Models of Mission." In *Toward the Twenty-First Century in Christian Mission: Essays in Honor of Gerald H. Anderson*, edited by James M. Phillips and Robert T. Coote, 175–93. Grand Rapids: Eerdmans, 1993.
———. *Transforming Mission: Paradigm Shifts in Theology of Mission*. Maryknoll, NY: Orbis, 1991.
———. *Witness to the World: The Christian Mission in Theological Perspective*. London: Marshall, Morgan & Scott, 1980.
Braaten, Carl E. "The Triune God: The Source and Model of Christian Unity and Mission." *Missiology* 18, no. 4 (1990) 415–27.
Brannan, Rick, et al., eds. *The Lexham English Septuagint*. Bellingham, WA: Lexham, 2012.
Brannon, M. Jeff. *The Heavenlies in Ephesians: A Lexical, Exegetical, and Conceptual Analysis*. LNTS 447. London: T. & T. Clark, 2011.
Breed, Gert. "'n Kritiese blik op *missio Dei* in die lig van Efesiërs." *In Die Skriflig (Online)* 48, no. 2 (2014). http://www.indieskriflig.org.za/index.php/skriflig/article/view/1707/2589.
Brown, Colin, ed. *New International Dictionary of New Testament Theology*. 4 vols. Grand Rapids: Zondervan, 1975–1985.

Brown, Jeannine K. "Metalepsis." In *Exploring Intertextuality: Diverse Strategies for New Testament Interpretation of Texts*, edited by B. J. Oropeza and Steve Moyise, 29–41. Eugene, OR: Wipf & Stock, 2016.

Brownson, James V. *Speaking the Truth in Love: New Testament Resources for a Missional Hermeneutic*. Christian Mission and Modern Culture. Harrisburg: Trinity, 1998.

———."Speaking the Truth in Love: Elements of a Missional Hermeneutic." *International Review of Mission* 83, no. 330 (1994) 479–504.

Bruce, F. F. *The Epistles to the Colossians, to Philemon, and to the Ephesians*. NICNT. Grand Rapids: Eerdmans, 1984.

Burke, Trevor J., and Brian S. Rosner, eds. *Paul as Missionary: Identity, Activity, Theology, and Practice*. LNTS 420. London: T. & T. Clark, 2011.

Busch, Peter. *Magie in neutestamentliche Zeit*. Göttingen: Vandenhoeck & Ruprecht, 2006.

Butler, Trent C. "Forgotten Passage from a Forgotten Era (1 Chr 16:8–36)." *VT* 28, no. 2 (1978) 142–50.

Caird, George Bradford. *Paul's Letters from Prison: Ephesians, Philippians, Colossians, Philemon*. Oxford: Oxford University Press, 1976.

———. *Principalities and Powers: A Study in Pauline Theology*. Oxford: Clarendon, 1956.

Campbell, Constantine R. *Basics of Verbal Aspect in Biblical Greek*. Grand Rapids: Zondervan, 2008.

Campbell, William S. "Unity and Diversity in the Church: Transformed Identities and the Peace of Christ in Ephesians." *Transformation* 25, no. 1 (2008) 15–31.

Caragounis, Chrys C. *The Ephesian Mysterion: Meaning and Content*. Lund: CWK Gleerup, 1977.

Carleton Paget, James. "Jewish Proselytism at the Time of Christian Origins: Chimera or Reality?" *JSNT* 62 (1996) 65–103.

Carr, Wesley. *Angels and Principalities: The Background, Meaning, and Development of the Pauline Phrase* Hai Archai Kai Hai Exousiai. SNTSMS 42. Cambridge: Cambridge University Press, 1981.

Carson, Donald A. "Paul's Mission and Prayer." In *The Gospel to the Nations: Perspectives on Paul's Mission: In Honour of Peter T. O'Brien*, edited by Peter G. Bolt and Mark Donald Thompson, 175–84. Leicester: Apollos, 2000.

Chadwick, Henry. "Die Absicht des Epheserbriefes." *ZNW* 51, nos. 3–4 (1960) 145–53.

Childs, Brevard S. *Isaiah*. OTL. Louisville: Westminster John Knox, 2001.

Ciampa, Roy E. "*Missio Dei* and *Imitatio Dei* in Ephesians." In *New Testament Theology in Light of the Church's Mission: Essays in Honor of I. Howard Marshall*, edited by Jon C. Laansma, Grant R. Osborne, and Ray Van Neste, 229–43. Eugene, OR: Cascade, 2011.

Ciampa, Roy E., and Brian S. Rosner. *The First Letter to the Corinthians*. PNTC. Grand Rapids: Eerdmans, 2010.

Clark, Andrew C. "Apostleship: Evidence from the New Testament and Early Christian Literature." *Vox Evangelica* 19 (1989) 49–82.

Cohick, Lynn H. *Ephesians: A New Covenant Commentary*. New Covenant Commentary Series. Eugene, OR: Cascade, 2010.

Commission on Faith and Order. *The Nature and Mission of the Church: A Stage on the Way to a Common Statement*. Faith and Order Paper. Geneva: World Council of Churches, 2005. https://www.oikoumene.org/en/resources/documents/

commissions/faith-and-order/i-unity-the-church-and-its-mission/the-nature-and-mission-of-the-church-a-stage-on-the-way-to-a-common-statement.
Cozart, Richard M. *This Present Triumph: An Investigation into the Significance of the Promise of a New Exodus of Israel in the Letter to the Ephesians.* Eugene, OR: Wipf & Stock, 2013.
Cross, Frank Leslie. *Studies in Ephesians.* London: Mowbray, 1956.
Culpepper, Hugo H. "Ephesians: A Manifesto for the Mission of the Church." *Review and Expositor* 76, no. 4 (1979) 553–58.
Dahl, Nils Alstrup. "Benediction and Congratulation." In *Studies in Ephesians: Introductory Questions, Text- and Edition-Critical Issues, Interpretation of Texts and Themes,* edited by David Hellholm, Vemund Blomkvist, and Tord Fornberg, 279–313. Tübingen: Mohr Siebeck, 2000.
———. "Cosmic Dimensions and Religious Knowledge (Eph 3:18)." In *Studies in Ephesians: Introductory Questions, Text- and Edition-Critical Issues, Interpretation of Texts and Themes,* edited by David Hellholm, Vemund Blomkvist, and Tord Fornberg, 365–88. Tübingen: Mohr Siebeck, 2000.
———. "Das Proömium des Epheserbriefes." In *Studies in Ephesians: Introductory Questions, Text- and Edition-Critical Issues, Interpretation of Texts and Themes,* edited by David Hellholm, Vemund Blomkvist, and Tord Fornberg, 315–34. Tübingen: Mohr Siebeck, 2000.
———. "Einleitungsfragen zum Epheserbrief." In *Studies in Ephesians: Introductory Questions, Text- and Edition-Critical Issues, Interpretation of Texts and Themes,* edited by David Hellholm, Vemund Blomkvist, and Tord Fornberg, 3–106. Tübingen: Mohr Siebeck, 2000.
———. "Ephesians and Qumran." In *Studies in Ephesians: Introductory Questions, Text- and Edition-Critical Issues, Interpretation of Texts and Themes,* edited by David Hellholm, Vemund Blomkvist, and Tord Fornberg, 107–44. Tübingen: Mohr Siebeck, 2000.
———. "Gentile, Christians, and Israelites in the Epistles to the Ephesians." *HTR* 79, nos. 1–3 (1986) 31–39.
———. "Interpreting Ephesians: Then and Now." *Currents in Theology and Mission* 5, no. 3 (1978) 133–43.
———. "The Letter to the Ephesians: Its Fictional and Real Setting." In *Studies in Ephesians: Introductory Questions, Text- and Edition-Critical Issues, Interpretation of Texts and Themes,* edited by David Hellholm, Vemund Blomkvist, and Tord Fornberg, 451–59. Tübingen: Mohr Siebeck, 2000.
———. *Studies in Ephesians: Introductory Questions, Text- and Edition-Critical Issues, Interpretation of Texts and Themes,* edited by David Hellholm, Vemund Blomkvist, and Tord Fornberg. Tübingen: Mohr Siebeck, 2000.
Danker, Frederick W., et al. *A Greek-English Lexicon of the New Testament and Other Early Christian Literature.* 3rd ed. Chicago: University of Chicago Press, 2000.
Darko, Daniel K. *No Longer Living as the Gentiles: Differentiation and Shared Ethical Values in Ephesians 4.17—6.9.* LNTS 375. London: T. & T. Clark, 2008.
Davy, Timothy J. "The Book of Job and the Mission of God: An Application of a Missional Hermeneutic to the Book of Job." PhD diss., University of Gloucestershire, 2014. http://eprints.glos.ac.uk/2271/.
De Boer, Martinus. "Images of Paul in the Post-Apostolic Period." *CBQ* 42, no. 3 (1980) 359–80.

DeClaisse-Walford, Nancy, et al. *The Book of Psalms*. NICOT. Grand Rapids: Eerdmans, 2014.
Demarest, Gary W. *1, 2 Thessalonians, 1, 2 Timothy, Titus*. Preacher's Commentary 32. Nashville: Thomas Nelson, 1984.
Dickson, John P. *Mission-Commitment in Ancient Judaism and in the Pauline Communities: The Shape, Extent and Background of Early Christian Mission*. WUNT II 159. Tübingen: Mohr Siebeck, 2003.
Dodd, C. H. *According to the Scriptures: The Sub-Structure of New Testament Theology*. London: Nisbet, 1952.
———. *The Old Testament in the New*. Philadelphia: Fortress, 1963.
Donaldson, Terence L. *Paul and the Gentiles: Remapping the Apostle's Convictional World*. Minneapolis: Fortress, 1997.
Dunn, James D. G. "The Household Rules in the New Testament." In *The Family in Theological Perspective*, edited by Stephen C. Barton, 43–64. Edinburgh: T. & T. Clark, 1996.
———. *The Theology of Paul the Apostle*. Grand Rapids: Eerdmans, 1998.
Dunning, Benjamin. "Strangers and Aliens No Longer: Negotiating Identity and Difference in Ephesians 2." *HTR* 99, no. 1 (2006) 1–16.
Edwards, M. J., ed. *Galatians, Ephesians, Philippians*. ACCS 8. Downers Grove, IL: InterVarsity, 2005.
Ehorn, Seth M. "The Use of Psalm 68(67).19 in Ephesians 4.8: A History of Research." *CurBR* 12, no. 1 (2013) 96–120.
Ellis, E. Earle. *Paul's Use of the Old Testament*. Grand Rapids: Baker, 1981.
Engen, Charles Van, and Dean Gilliland, eds. *The Good News of The Kingdom: Mission Theology for the Third Millennium*. Maryknoll, NY: Orbis, 1993.
Esler, Philip F. *The First Christians in their Social Worlds: Social-Scientific Approaches to New Testament Interpretation*. London: Routledge, 1994.
Evans, Craig A. "The Meaning of πλήρωμα in Nag Hammadi." *Biblica* (1984) 259–65.
Faraone, Christopher A., and Dirk Obbink, eds. *Magika Hiera: Ancient Greek Magic and Religion*. New York: Oxford University Press, 1991.
Faust, Eberhard. *Pax Christi et Pax Caesaris: Religionsgeschichtliche, traditionsgeschichtliche und sozialgeschichtliche Studien zum Ephesebrief*. Göttingen: Vandenhoeck & Ruprecht, 1993.
Fee, Gordon D. *God's Empowering Presence: The Holy Spirit in the Letters of Paul*. Peabody, MA: Hendrickson, 1994.
Filbeck, David. *Yes, God of the Gentiles Too: The Missionary Message of the Old Testament*. Wheaton: Billy Graham Center, 1994.
Fischer, Karl Martin. *Tendenz und Absicht des Epheserbriefes*. Göttingen: Vandenhoeck & Ruprecht, 1973.
Flemming, Dean E. *Recovering the Full Mission of God: A Biblical Perspective on Being, Doing, and Telling*. Downers Grove, IL: InterVarsity Academic, 2013.
———. *Why Mission?* Nashville: Abingdon, 2015.
Flett, John G. "Missio Dei: A Trinitarian Envisioning of a Non-Trinitarian Theme." *Missiology* 37, no. 1 (2009) 5–18.
———. *The Witness of God: The Trinity, Missio Dei, Karl Barth, and the Nature of Christian Community*. Grand Rapids: Eerdmans, 2010.
Forbes, Christopher. "Paul's Principalities and Powers: Demythologizing Apocalyptic?" *JSNT* 82 (2001) 61–88.

Foster, Robert L. "'A Temple in the Lord Filled to the Fullness of God': Context and Intertextuality (Eph. 3:19)." *NovT* 49, no. 1 (2007) 85-96.

Fouts, David M. "בנה bnh 1215." In *New International Dictionary of Old Testament Theology and Exegesis*, edited by Willem A. VanGemeren, 1:677-81. Grand Rapids: Zondervan, 1997.

Fowl, Stephen E. *Ephesians: A Commentary*. NTL. Louisville: Westminster John Knox, 2012.

García Martínez, Florentino, and Eibert J. C. Tigchelaar, eds. *The Dead Sea Scrolls: Study Edition*. 2 vols. Leiden: Brill, 1997.

Gardner, J. F. *The Roman Household: A Sourcebook*. New York: Routledge, 1991.

Gärtner, Bertil E. *The Temple and the Community in Qumran and the New Testament: A Comparative Study in the Temple Symbolism of the Qumran Texts and the New Testament*. SNTSMS 1. Cambridge: Cambridge University Press, 1965.

Gatumu, Kabiro wa. *The Pauline Concept of Supernatural Powers: A Reading from the African Worldview*. Milton Keynes: Paternoster, 2008.

Gehring, Roger W. *House Church and Mission: The Importance of Household Structures in Early Christianity*. Peabody, MA: Hendrickson, 2004.

Gentry, Peter John, and Stephen J. Wellum. *Kingdom Through Covenant: A Biblical-Theological Understanding of the Covenants*. Wheaton, IL: Crossway, 2012.

George, Sherron Kay. *Better Together: The Future of Presbyterian Mission*. Louisville, KY: Geneva, 2010.

———. "God's Holistic Mission: Fullness of Parts, Participants, and Places." *Missiology* 41, no. 3 (2013) 286-99.

———. "'Joined and Knit Together . . . Each Part Working Properly': A Missiological Reflection on Practices of God's Holistic Mission in Ephesians." *Missiology* 37, no. 3 (2009) 397-409.

Georges, Jayson. *The 3D Gospel: Ministry in Guilt, Shame and Fear Cultures*. N.p.: Ingram, 2014.

Gese, Michael. *Das Vermachtnis des Apostels: Die Rezeption der paulinischen Theologie im Epheserbrief*. WUNT 99. Tübingen: Mohr Siebeck, 1997.

Gilliland, Dean. *Pauline Theology and Mission Practice*. Grand Rapids: Baker, 1983.

Glasser, Arthur F., et al. *Announcing the Kingdom: The Story of God's Mission in the Bible*. Grand Rapids: Baker Academic, 2003.

Gnilka, Joachim. "Das Paulusbild im Kolosser—und Epheserbrief." In *Kontinuität und Einheit* (Festschrift F. Mußner), edited by Paul-Gerhard Müller and Werner Stenger, 179-93. Freiburg: Herder, 1981.

———. *Der Epheserbrief*. Freiburg: Herder, 1977.

Goetzmann, "House, Build, Manage, Steward." In *New International Dictionary of New Testament Theology*, edited by Colin Brown, 2:247-56. Rev. ed. Grand Rapids: Zondervan, 1986.

Goheen, Michael W. *A Light to the Nations: The Missional Church and the Biblical Story*. Grand Rapids: Baker Academic, 2011.

———. "Bible and Mission: Missiology and Biblical Scholarship in Dialogue." In *Christian Mission: Old Testament Foundations and New Testament Developments*, edited by Stanley E. Porter and Cynthia Long Westfall, 204-35. McMaster New Testament Studies. Eugene, OR: Pickwick, 2011.

———. "Continuing Steps Towards a Missional Hermeneutic." *Fideles* 3 (2008) 49-99.

———. *Introducing Christian Mission Today: Scripture, History, Issues.* Downers Grove, IL: InterVarsity, 2014.
Goheen, Michael W., ed. *Reading the Bible Missionally.* Grand Rapids: Eerdmans, 2016.
Goheen, Michael W., and Christopher J. H. Wright. "Mission and Theological Interpretation." In *A Manifesto for Theological Interpretation*, edited by Craig G. Bartholomew and Heath A. Thomas, 171–96. Grand Rapids: Baker Academic, 2016.
Gombis, Timothy G. "Being the Fullness of God in Christ by the Spirit: Ephesians 5:18 in Its Epistolary Setting." *TynBul* 53, no. 2 (2002) 259–71.
———. "Cosmic Lordship and Divine Gift-Giving: Psalm 68 in Ephesians 4:8." *NovT* 47, no. 4 (2005) 367–80.
———. *The Drama of Ephesians: Participating in the Triumph of God.* Downers Grove, IL: InterVarsity Academic, 2010.
———. "Ephesians 2 as a Narrative of Divine Warfare." *JSNT* 26, no. 4 (2004) 403–18.
———. "Ephesians 3:2–13: Pointless Digression, or Epitome of the Triumph of God in Christ?" *WTJ* 66 (2004) 313–23.
———. "A Radically New Humanity: The Function of the Haustafel in Ephesians." *JETS* 48, no. 2 (2005) 317–30.
Goodman, Martin. *Mission and Conversion: Proselytizing in the Religious History of the Roman Empire.* Oxford: Clarendon, 1994.
Goodspeed, Edgar J. *An Introduction to the New Testament.* Chicago: University of Chicago Press, 1937.
———. *The Key to Ephesians.* Chicago: University of Chicago Press, 1956.
Gorman, Michael J. *Becoming the Gospel: Paul, Participation, and Mission.* Grand Rapids: Eerdmans, 2015.
———. *Reading Paul.* Milton Keynes: Paternoster, 2008.
Gosnell, Peter W. "Networks and Exchanges: Ephesians 4:7–16 and Community Function of Teachers." *BTB* 30, no. 4 (2000) 135–43.
Graf, Fritz. "An Oracle Against Pestilence from a Western Anatolian Town." *ZPE* 92 (1992) 267–79.
Graham, Glen H. *An Exegetical Summary of Ephesians.* 2nd ed. Dallas: SIL International, 2008.
Grams, Rollin Gene, et al., eds. *Bible and Mission: A Conversation Between Biblical Studies and Missiology.* Schwarzenfeld: Neufeld, 2008.
Greever, Joshua Matthew. "The New Covenant in Ephesians." PhD diss., Southern Baptist Theological Seminary, 2014.
Grindheim, Sigurd. "What the OT Prophets Did Not Know: The Mystery of the Church in Eph 3, 2–13." *Biblica* 84, no. 4 (2003) 531–53.
Guder, Darrell L. *Called to Witness: Doing Missional Theology.* Gospel and Our Culture Series. Grand Rapids: Eerdmans, 2015.
———. "Missional Hermeneutics: The Missional Authority of Scripture—Interpreting Scripture as Missional Formation." *Mission Focus: Annual Review* 15 (2007) 106–21.
———. *Unlikely Ambassadors: Clay Jar Christians in God's Service.* Louisville, KY: Office of the General Assembly, Presbyterian Church USA, 2002.
Guder, Darrell L., and Lois Barrett, eds. *Missional Church: A Vision for the Sending of the Church in North America.* Grand Rapids: Eerdmans, 1998.

Gupta, Nijay K. "Mirror-Reading Moral Issues in Paul's Letters." *JSNT* 34, no. 4 (2012) 361–81.

———. "Towards a Set of Principles for Identifying and Interpreting Metaphors in Paul: προσαγωγη (Romans 5:2) as a Test Case." *ResQ* 51, no. 3 (2009) 169–81.

Gupta, Nijay K., and Fredrick J. Long. "The Politics of Ephesians and the Empire: Accommodation or Resistance?" *JGRChJ* 7 (2010) 112–36.

Hafemann, Scott. "'Because of Weakness' [Galatians 4:13]: The Role of Suffering in the Mission of Paul." In *The Gospel to the Nations: Perspectives on Paul's Mission: In Honour of Peter T. O'Brien*, edited by Peter G. Bolt and Mark D. Thompson, 131–46. Downers Grove, IL: InterVarsity, 2000.

———. "The Role of Suffering in the Mission of Paul." In *The Mission of the Early Church to Jews and Gentiles*, edited by Jostein Ådna and Hans Kvalbein, 165–84. WUNT 127. Tübingen: Mohr Siebeck, 2000.

Hahn, Ferdinand. *Mission in the New Testament*. London: SCM, 1965.

Harris, W. Hall, III. *The Descent of Christ: Ephesians 4:7–11 and Traditional Hebrew Imagery*. Leiden: Brill, 1996.

Harrison, James R. "§8 Artemis Triumphs over a Sorcerer's Evil Art." In *New Documents Illustrating Early Christianity*, edited by Greg H. R. Horsley and Stephen Llewelyn, 10 (2012) 37–47. North Ryde, NSW: The Ancient History Documentary Research Centre, Macquarie University.

———. "An Epigraphic Portrait of Ephesus and Its Villages." In *The First Urban Churches 3: Ephesus*, edited by James R. Harrison and L. L. Welborn, 1–67. WGRWSup 9. Atlanta: SBL, 2018.

Harrison, James R., and L. L. Welborn, eds. *The First Urban Churches 3: Ephesus*. WGRWSup 9. Atlanta: SBL, 2018.

Hartenstein, Karl. "Theologische Besinnung." In *Mission Zwischen Gestern Und Morgen*, edited by Walter Freytag, 51–72. Stuttgart: Evangelische Missionsverlag, 1952.

Hay, David M. *Glory at the Right Hand: Psalm 110 in Early Christianity*. Nashville: Abingdon, 1973.

Hayes, Elizabeth R. "The Influence of Ezekiel 37 on 2 Corinthians 6:14—7:1." In *The Book of Ezekiel and Its Influence*, edited by H. J. de Jonge and Johannes Tromp, 123–36. Aldershot: Ashgate, 2007.

Hays, Richard B. *The Conversion of the Imagination: Paul as Interpreter of Israel's Scripture*. Grand Rapids: Eerdmans, 2005.

———. *Echoes of Scripture in the Letters of Paul*. New Haven: Yale University Press, 1989.

Hedlund, Roger E. *The Mission of the Church in the World: A Biblical Theology*. Grand Rapids: Baker, 1991.

Heil, John Paul. *Ephesians: Empowerment to Walk in Love for the Unity of All in Christ*. Atlanta: SBL, 2007.

Hendrix, Holland. "On the Form and Ethos of Ephesians." *USQR* 42, no. 4 (1988) 3–15.

Hengel, Martin. *Between Jesus and Paul: Studies in the Earliest History of Christianity*. Eugene, OR: Wipf & Stock, 1983.

Hering, James P. *The Colossian and Ephesian Haustafeln in Theological Context: An Analysis of Their Origins, Relationship, and Message*. AUS 260. New York: Peter Lang, 2007.

Hill, C. E. "Paul's Understanding of Christ's Kingdom in 1 Corinthians 15:20–28." *NovT* 30, no. 4 (1988) 297–320.

Hirsch, Alan. *The Forgotten Ways: Reactivating Apostolic Movements*. 2nd ed. Grand Rapids: Brazos, 2016.
Hoehner, Harold W. *Ephesians: An Exegetical Commentary*. Leicester: Baker, 2002.
Horsley, G. H. R. "The Inscriptions of Ephesos and the New Testament." *NovT* 34, no. 2 (1992) 105–68.
Howard, J. E. "The Wall Broken: An Interpretation of Ephesians 2:11–22." In *Biblical Interpretation: Principles and Practices*, edited by F. F. Kearley, E. P. Myers, and T. D. Hadley, 296–306. Grand Rapids: Baker, 1996.
Howell, Don N., Jr. "Mission in Paul's Epistles: Genesis, Pattern, and Dynamics." In *Mission in the New Testament: An Evangelical Approach*, edited by William J. Larkin and Joel F. Williams, 63–91. American Society of Missiology 27. Maryknoll, NY: Orbis, 1998.
Hubbard, Moyer V. *New Creation in Paul's Letters and Thought*. Cambridge: Cambridge University Press, 2002.
Hübner, Hans. *An Philemon, an die Kolosser, an die Epheser*. Tübingen: Mohr Siebeck, 1997.
———. *Vetus Testamentum in Novo*. Vol. 2. Göttingen: Vandenhoeck & Ruprecht, 1996.
Hulst, A. R. "בנה Bnh to Build." In *Theological Lexicon of the Old Testament*, edited by Ernst Jenni and Claus Westermann, 1:245–46. Translated by Mark E. Biddle. Peabody, MA: Hendrickson, 1997.
Hunsberger, George R. "Mapping the Missional Hermeneutics Conversation." In *Reading the Bible Missionally*, edited by Michael W. Goheen, 45–67. Grand Rapids: Eerdmans, 2016.
———. "Missional Bible Study Questions." *The Gospel and Our Culture Newsletter* 11, no. 3 (1999) 7.
———. "Proposals for a Missional Hermeneutic: Mapping a Conversation." *Missiology* 39, no. 3 (2011) 309–21.
Immendörfer, Michael. *Ephesians and Artemis: The Cult of the Great Goddess of Ephesus as the Epistle's Context*. WUNT II 436. Tübingen: Mohr Siebeck, 2017.
Jeal, Roy R. *Integrating Theology and Ethics in Ephesians: The Ethos of Communication*. Lewiston, NY: Mellen, 2000.
Jeremias, Joachim. "Ἀκρογωνιαῖος." In *TDNT* 1:792.
———. *Jesus' Promise to the Nations*. London: SCM, 1958.
Johnson, Andy R. *Apostolic Function in 21st Century Missions*. Pasadena: William Carey Library, 2009.
Johnson, Edna. *A Semantic and Structural Analysis of Ephesians*. Dallas: SIL International, 2008.
Jolivet, Ira. "The Ethical Instructions in Ephesians as the Unwritten Statutes and Ordinances of God's New Temple in Ezekiel." *ResQ* 48, no. 4 (2006) 193–210.
Kähler, Martin. *Schriften zur Christologie und Mission: Gesamtausgabe der Schriften zur Mission*. Munich: Kaiser, 1953.
Kalimi, Isaac. *The Retelling of Chronicles in Jewish Tradition and Literature: A Historical Journey*. Winona Lake, IN: Eisenbrauns, 2009.
Käsemann, Ernst. "Ephesians and Acts." In *Studies in Luke-Acts*, edited by Leander E. Keck and J. Louis Martyn, 288–97. London: SPCK, 1968.

Katongole, Emmanuel. "Mission and the Ephesian Moment of World Christianity: Pilgrimages of Pain and Hope and the Economics of Eating Together." *Mission Studies* 29, no. 2 (2012) 183–200.
Keener, Craig. "Paul and Spiritual Warfare." In *Paul's Missionary Methods: In His Time and Ours*, edited by Robert L. Plummer and John Mark Terry, 107–23. Downers Grove, IL: InterVarsity Press Academic, 2012.
Kertelge, Karl, and Norbert Brox. *Mission im Neuen Testament*. Freiburg: Herder, 1982.
Kirby, John C. *Ephesians, Baptism and Pentecost: An Inquiry into the Structure and Purpose of the Epistle to the Ephesians*. Montreal: McGill University Press, 1968.
Kirk, J. Andrew. *What Is Mission? Theological Explorations*. London: Darton, Longman & Todd, 1999.
Kitchen, Martin. *Ephesians*. London: Routledge, 1994.
Kittel, Gerhard, and Gerhard Friedrich, eds. *Theological Dictionary of the New Testament*. Translated by Geoffrey W. Bromiley. 10 vols. Grand Rapids: Eerdmans, 1964–1976.
Klauck, Hans Josef. *The Religious Context of Early Christianity: A Guide to Graeco-Roman Religions*. Translated by Brian McNeil. Edinburgh: T. & T. Clark, 2000.
Klein, Ralph W., and Thomas Krüger. *1 Chronicles: A Commentary*. Hermeneia. Minneapolis: Fortress, 2006.
Klein, William W. *The Book of Ephesians: An Annotated Bibliography*. New York: Garland, 1996.
Kleinig, John W. *The Lord's Song: The Basis, Function, and Significance of Choral Music in Chronicles*. JSOTSup 156. Sheffield: JSOT, 1993.
Klopfenstein, M. A. "כזב *Kzb* to Lie." In *Theological Lexicon of the Old Testament*, edited by Ernst Jenni and Claus Westermann, translated by Mark E. Biddle, 2:608. Peabody, MA: Hendrickson, 1997.
Knapp, Robert C. *The Dawn of Christianity: People and Gods in a Time of Magic and Miracles*. Cambridge, MA: Harvard, 2017.
Koester, Helmut, ed. *Ephesos, Metropolis of Asia: An Interdisciplinary Approach to Its Archaeology, Religion, and Culture*. HTS 41. Valley Forge, PA: Trinity, 1995.
Komolafe, Sunday Babajide. "Christ, Church, and the Cosmos: A Missiological Reading of Paul's Epistle to the Ephesians." *Missiology* 35, no. 3 (2007) 273–86.
Kreitzer, Larry Joseph. *The Epistle to the Ephesians*. London: Epworth, 1997.
———. *Hierapolis in the Heavens: Studies in the Letter to the Ephesians*. London: T. & T. Clark, 2007.
———. "The Messianic Man of Peace as Temple Builder: Solomonic Imagery in Ephesians 2:13–22." In *Temple and Worship in Biblical Israel*, edited by John Day, 484–509. London: T. & T. Clark, 2005.
Kruse, Colin G. "Apostle, Apostleship." In *Dictionary of Later New Testament and Its Development*, edited by R. P. Martin and P. H. Davids, 76–82. Downers Grove, IL: InterVarsity, 1997.
———. "Ministry in the Wake of Paul's Mission." In *The Gospel to the Nations: Perspectives on Paul's Mission: In Honour of Peter T. O'Brien*, edited by Peter G. Bolt and Mark Donald Thompson, 205–20. Leicester: Apollos, 2000.
———. "Servant, Service." In *Dictionary of Paul and His Letters*, edited by G. F. Hawthorne, R. P. Martin, and D. G. Reid, 869–71. Downers Grove, IL: InterVarsity, 1993.

Kuhn, Karl Georg. "The Epistle to the Ephesians in the Light of the Qumran Texts." In *Paul and Qumran*, edited by J. Murphy-O'Connor, 115–31. London: Chapman, 1968.

Kuruvilla, Abraham. *Ephesians: A Theological Commentary for Preachers*. Eugene, OR: Cascade, 2015.

Laansma, Jon, et al., eds. *New Testament Theology in Light of the Church's Mission: Essays in Honor of I. Howard Marshall*. Eugene, OR: Cascade, 2011.

Labahn, Michael, and L. J. Lietaert Peerbolte, eds. *A Kind of Magic: Understanding Magic in the New Testament and Its Religious Environment*. LNTS 306. London: T. & T. Clark, 2007.

Lane, A. N. S., ed. *The Unseen World: Christian Reflections on Angels, Demons and the Heavenly Realm*. Grand Rapids: Baker, 1996.

Larkin, William J., and Joel F. Williams, eds. *Mission in the New Testament: An Evangelical Approach*. American Society of Missiology 27. Maryknoll, NY: Orbis, 1998.

Lausanne Committee for World Evangelization. "Reconciliation as the Mission of God." *A New Vision, a New Heart, a Renewed Call*. Lausanne Occasional Papers 51. Pattaya, Thailand, 2004. https://www.lausanne.org/content/lop/lop-51-reconciliation-as-the-mission-of-god.

Lausanne Movement. "Deliver Us From Evil—Consultation Statement." Nairobi, Kenya: Lausanne, 2000. https://www.lausanne.org/content/statement/deliver-us-from-evil-consultation-statement.

Lawless, Charles. "Spiritual Warfare and Missions." *Missiology: An Introduction to the Foundations, History, and Strategies of World Missions*, edited by John Mark Terry, 539–54. 2nd ed. Nashville: B&H, 2015.

Liddell, Henry George, and Robert Scott. *A Greek-English Lexicon*, edited by H. S. Jones. 9th ed. Oxford: Clarendon, 1996.

Lincicum, David. "Mirror-Reading a Pseudepigraphal Letter." *NovT* 59, no. 2 (2017) 171–93.

Lincoln, Andrew T. *Ephesians*. WBC. Nashville: Thomas Nelson, 1990.

———. *Paradise Now and Not Yet: Studies in the Role of the Heavenly Dimension in Paul's Thought with Special Reference to His Eschatology*. Cambridge: Cambridge University Press, 1981.

———. "The Use of the OT in Ephesians." *JSNT* 4, no. 14 (1982) 16–57.

Lincoln, Andrew T., and Alexander J. M. Wedderburn. *The Theology of the Later Pauline Letters*. Cambridge: Cambridge University Press, 1993.

Lindemann, Andreas. "Bemerkungen zu den Adressaten und zum Anlass des Epheserbriefes." *ZNW* 67, nos. 3–4 (1976) 235–51.

———. *Der Epheserbrief*. ZBK. Zürich: Theologischer Verlag, 1985.

———. *Die Aufhebung der Zeit: Geschichtsverständnis und Eschatologie im Epheserbrief*. Gütersloh: Gütersloher Verlagshaus Mohn, 1975.

Little, Christopher R. *Mission in the Way of Paul: Biblical Mission for the Church in the Twenty-First Century*. StBibLit 80. New York: Peter Lang, 2005.

Llewelyn, S., James Harrison, and E. Bridge, eds. *New Documents Illustrating Early Christianity: Volume 10: Greek and Other Inscriptions and Papyri Published 1988–1992*. Grand Rapids: Eerdmans, 2012.

Lona, Horacio E. *Die Eschatologie im Kolosser- und Epheserbrief*. Würzburg: Echter, 1984.

Longman, Tremper, and Daniel G. Reid. *God Is a Warrior*. SOTBT. Grand Rapids: Zondervan, 1995.

Lotter, George, and van Aarde, Timothy. "A Rediscovery of the Priesthood of Believers in Ephesians 4:1–16 and Its Relevance for the *Missio Dei* and a Biblical Missional Ecumenism." *In Die Skriflig (Online)* 51, no. 2 (2017) 1–10. http://dx.doi.org/10.4102/ids.v51i2.2251.

Louw, J. P., and Eugene A. Nida, eds. *Greek-English Lexicon of the New Testament: Based on Semantic Domains*. New York: United Bible Societies, 1988.

Lucas, Alec J. "Assessing Stanley E. Porter's Objections to Richard B. Hays's Notion of Metalepsis." *CBQ* 76, no. 1 (2014) 93–111.

Lunde, Jonathan, and John Anthony Dunne. "Paul's Creative and Contextual Use of Isaiah in Ephesians 5:14." *JETS* 55, no. 1 (2012) 87–110.

———. "Paul's Creative and Contextual Use of Psalm 68 in Ephesians 4:8." *WTJ* 74, no. 1 (2012) 99–117.

Lynch, M. "Zion's Warrior and the Nations: Isaiah 59:15b—63:6 in Isaiah's Zion Traditions." *CBQ* 70, no. 2 (2008) 244–63.

MacDonald, Margaret Y. *Colossians and Ephesians*. Sacra Pagina. Collegeville, MN: Liturgical, 2000.

———. *The Pauline Churches: A Socio-Historical Study of Institutionalization in the Pauline and Deutero-Pauline Writings*. Cambridge: Cambridge University Press, 1988.

———. "The Politics of Identity in Ephesians." *JSNT* 26, no. 4 (2004) 419–44.

Maclean, Jennifer. "Ephesians and the Problem of Colossians: Interpretation of Texts and Traditions in Eph 1:1—2:10." PhD diss., Harvard, 1995.

Maier, Harry O. *Picturing Paul in Empire: Imperial Image, Text and Persuasion in Colossians, Ephesians and the Pastoral Epistles*. London: Bloomsbury T. & T. Clark, 2013.

Malina, Bruce J. Review of *Naming the Powers: The Language of Power in the New Testament*, by Walter Wink. *USQR* 40, no. 3 (1985) 73–76.

Malone, Andrew S. *God's Mediators: A Biblical Theology of Priesthood*. NSBT. London: Apollos, 2017.

Marshall, I. Howard. "Acts." In *Commentary on the New Testament Use of the Old Testament*, edited by G. K. Beale and D. A. Carson, 513–606. Grand Rapids: Baker Academic, 2007.

———. *New Testament Theology: Many Witnesses, One Gospel*. Downers Grove, IL: InterVarsity, 2004.

Martin, Ralph P. "An Epistle in Search of a Life-Setting." *ExpTim* 79 (1967) 296–302.

———. *Ephesians, Colossians and Philemon*. IBC. Atlanta: John Knox, 1991.

———. *Reconciliation: A Study in Paul's Theology*. Atlanta: John Knox, 1981.

Martin-Achard, Robert. *A Light to the Nations: A Study of the Old Testament Conception of Israel's Mission to the World*. Edinburgh: Oliver & Boyd, 1962.

Mascarenhas, Theodore. *The Missionary Function of Israel in Psalms 67, 96 and 117*. Lanham, MD: University Press of America, 2005.

Massey, John. "The Missionary Mandate of God's Nature." In *Missiology: An Introduction to the Foundations, History, and Strategies of World Missions*, edited by John Mark Terry, 87–98. 2nd ed. Nashville: B&H, 2015.

Mbennah, E. D. "The Goal of Maturity in Ephesians 4:13–16." *Acta Theologica* 36, no. 1 (2016) 110–32.

McKelvey, R. J. *The New Temple: The Church in the New Testament.* London: Oxford University Press, 1969.

McKinzie, Greg. "Missional Hermeneutics as Theological Interpretation." *Journal of Theological Interpretation* 11, no. 2 (2017) 157–79.

McKnight, Scot. *A Light Among the Gentiles: Jewish Missionary Activity in the Second Temple Period.* Minneapolis: Fortress, 1991.

McNair Scott, Benjamin G. *Apostles Today: Making Sense of Contemporary Charismatic Apostolates: A Historical and Theological Appraisal.* Eugene, OR: Pickwick, 2014.

Merkle, Benjamin L. *Ephesians.* EGGNT. Nashville: B&H Academic, 2016.

Merklein, Helmut. *Christus und die Kirche: die theologische Grundstruktur des Epheserbriefes nach Eph 2,11–18.* Stuttgart: KBW, 1973.

———. *Das kirchliche Amt nach dem Epheserbrief.* Munich: Kosel, 1973.

Metzger, Bruce M. *A Textual Commentary on the Greek New Testament.* 2nd ed. London: United Bible Societies, 1994.

Meyer, Regina Pacis. *Kirche und Mission im Epheserbrief.* SBS 86. Stuttgart: Katholisches Bibelwerk, 1977.

Miletic, Stephen Francis. *"One Flesh": Eph 5.22–24, 5:31 Marriage and the New Creation.* Rome: Editrice Pontificio Istituto Biblico, 1988.

Minear, Paul Sevier, ed. "The Vocation to Invisible Powers: Ephesians 3:8–10." In *To Die and to Live*, 89–106. New York: Seabury, 1977.

Mitton, C. Leslie. *The Epistle to the Ephesians: Its Authorship, Origin and Purpose.* Oxford: Clarendon, 1951.

Moore, Michael S. "Ephesians 2:14–16: A History of Recent Interpretation." *EvQ* 54, no. 3 (1982) 163–68.

Moritz, Thorsten. *A Profound Mystery: The Use of the Old Testament in Ephesians.* NovTSup 85. Leiden: Brill, 1996.

———. "The Psalms in Ephesians and Colossians." In *The Psalms in the New Testament*, edited by Steve Moyise and Maarten J. J. Menken, 181–95. NTSI. London: T. & T. Clark, 2004.

———. "Reasons for Ephesians." *Evangel* 14, no. 1 (1996) 8–14.

Morris, Leon. *Expository Reflections on the Letter to the Ephesians.* Grand Rapids: Baker, 1994.

Motyer, J. A. *The Prophecy of Isaiah.* Leicester: InterVarsity, 1993.

Mouton, Elna. "'Ascended Far Above All the Heavens': Rhetorical Functioning of Psalm 68:18 in Ephesians 4:8–10?" *HTS Teologiese Studies/ Theological Studies* 70, no. 1 (2014) 1–9.

———. *Reading a New Testament Document Ethically.* Atlanta: SBL, 2002.

Moyise, Steve. *Evoking Scripture: Seeing the Old Testament in the New.* London: T. & T. Clark, 2008.

———. "Intertextuality and Biblical Studies: A Review." *Verbum et Ecclesia* 23, no. 2 (2002).

———. *Paul and Scripture.* Grand Rapids: Baker Academic, 2010.

Moyise, Steve, and Maarten J. J. Menken, eds. *Isaiah in the New Testament.* The New Testament and the Scriptures of Israel. London: T. & T. Clark, 2005.

———. *The Psalms in the New Testament.* The New Testament and the Scriptures of Israel. London: T. & T. Clark, 2004.

Muddiman, John. *A Commentary on the Epistle to the Ephesians.* BNTC. London: Continuum, 2001.

Murphy, Edward F. *Spiritual Gifts and the Great Commission*. South Pasadena: Mandate, 1975.

Murphy-O'Connor, J. *St. Paul's Ephesus: Texts and Archaeology*. Collegeville, MN: Liturgical, 2008.

Mussner, Franz. "Contributions Made by Qumran to the Understanding of the Epistle to the Ephesians." In *Paul and Qumran*, edited by J. Murphy-O'Connor, 159–78. London: Chapman, 1968.

Nestle, Eberhard, et al., eds. *Novum Testamentum Graece: Based on the Work of Eberhard and Erwin Nestle*. 28th ed. Stuttgart: Deutsche Bibelgesellschaft, 2012.

Newman, Carey C. *Paul's Glory-Christology: Tradition and Rhetoric*. NovTSup 69. Leiden: Brill, 1992.

Nissen, Johannes. *New Testament and Mission: Historical and Hermeneutical Perspectives*. 4th ed. Frankfurt am Main: Peter Lang, 2007.

O'Brien, Peter T. *Gospel and Mission in the Writings of Paul: An Exegetical and Theological Analysis*. Grand Rapids: Baker, 1995.

———. "Principalities and Powers and Their Relationship to Structures." *Evangelical Review of Theology* 6, no. 1 (1982) 50–61.

Oepke, Albrecht. "Ὑποδέω (Ὑπόδημα, Σανδάλιον)." In *TDNT* 5:310–15.

Okoye, James Chukwuma. *Israel and the Nations: A Mission Theology of the Old Testament*. American Society of Missiology Series 39. Maryknoll, NY: Orbis, 2006.

Oropeza, B. J., and Steve Moyise. *Exploring Intertextuality: Diverse Strategies for New Testament Interpretation of Texts*. Eugene, OR: Wipf & Stock, 2016.

Oster, Richard E. "The Ephesian Artemis as an Opponent of Early Christianity." *JAC* 19 (1976) 24–44.

———. "Ephesus as a Religious Centre Under the Principate, I. Paganism Before Constantine." In *ANRW* 18.3:1661–1728. Part 2, *Principat*, 18.3, edited by Hildegard Temporini and Wolfgang Haase. Berlin: de Gruyter, 1990.

Oswalt, John N. *The Book of Isaiah Chapters 40–66*. NICOT. Grand Rapids: Eerdmans, 1998.

Ott, Craig, ed. *The Mission of the Church: Five Views in Conversation*. Grand Rapids: Baker, 2016.

Ott, Craig, et al. *Encountering Theology of Mission: Biblical Foundations, Historical Developments, and Contemporary Issues*. Encountering Mission. Grand Rapids: Baker Academic, 2010.

Owens, Mark D. *As It Was in the Beginning: An Intertextual Analysis of New Creation in Galatians, 2 Corinthians and Ephesians*. Eugene, OR: Wipf & Stock, 2015.

———. "Spiritual Warfare and the Church's Mission According to Ephesians 6:10–17." *TynBul* 67, no. 1 (2016) 87–103.

Pate, C. Marvin. *Communities of the Last Days: The Dead Sea Scrolls*. Leicester: Apollos, 2000.

Patzia, Arthur G. *Ephesians, Colossians, Philemon*. NIBC. Carlisle: Paternoster, 1990.

Perkins, Pheme. *Ephesians*. ANTC. Nashville: Abingdon, 1997.

Peters, George W. *A Biblical Theology of Missions*. Chicago: Moody, 1972.

Peterson, David. "The New Temple: Christology and Ecclesiology in Ephesians and 1 Peter." In *Heaven on Earth*, edited by T. Desmond Alexander and Simon J. Gathercole, 161–76. Carlisle: Paternoster, 2004.

Petrenko, Ester A. G. D. *Created in Christ Jesus for Good Works: The Integration of Soteriology and Ethics in Ephesians*. Milton Keynes: Paternoster, 2011.

Plummer, Robert L. *Paul's Understanding of the Church's Mission: Did the Apostle Paul Expect the Early Christian Communities to Evangelize?* Milton Keynes: Paternoster, 2006.

Pokorný, Petr. *Der Brief des Paulus an die Epheser.* Leipzig: Evangelische Verlagsanstalt, 1993.

———. "Epheserbrief und Gnostische Mysterien." *ZNW* 53 (1962) 160–94.

Porter, Stanley E. "Allusions and Echoes." In *As It Is Written: Studying Paul's Use of Scripture*, edited by Stanley E. Porter and Christopher D. Stanley, 29–40. Leiden: Brill, 2008.

———. *Hearing the Old Testament in the New Testament.* Grand Rapids: Eerdmans, 2006.

———. "Magic in the Book of Acts." In *A Kind of Magic: Understanding Magic in the New Testament and Its Religious Environment*, edited by Michael Labahn and L. J. Lietaert Peerbolte, 107–21. LNTS 306. London: T. & T. Clark, 2007.

———. *Verbal Aspect in the Greek of the New Testament, with Reference to Tense and Mood.* New York: Peter Lang, 1989.

Porter, Stanley E., and Cynthia Long Westfall, eds. *Christian Mission: Old Testament Foundations and New Testament Developments.* McMaster New Testament Studies. Eugene, OR: Pickwick, 2011.

Qualls, Paula Fontana, and John D. W. Watts. "Isaiah in Ephesians." *RevExp* 93, no. 2 (1996) 249–59.

Rader, William Harry. *The Church and Racial Hostility: A History of Interpretation of Ephesians 2, 11–22.* Tübingen: Mohr, 1978.

Redford, Shawn B. *Missiological Hermeneutics: Biblical Interpretation for the Global Church.* ASM Monographs 11. Eugene, OR: Pickwick, 2012.

Regev, Eyal. "Community as Temple: Revisiting Cultic Metaphors in Qumran and the New Testament." *BBR* 28, no. 4 (2018) 604–31.

Reumann, John. "*OIKONOMIA*='Covenant': Terms for Heilsgeschichte in Early Christian Usage." *NovT* 3, no. 4 (1959) 282–92.

Reynier, Chantal. *L'épître aux Éphésiens.* N.p., CERF, 2004.

Robertson, A. Ewen. "The Distinctive Missiology of the New Churches: An Analysis and Evaluation." *JEPTA* 35, no. 2 (2015) 144–61.

Robinson, J. A. *St Paul's Epistle to the Ephesians.* 2nd ed. London: MacMillan, 1904.

Roels, Edwin D. *God's Mission: The Epistle to the Ephesians in Mission Perspective.* Grand Rapids: Eerdmans, 1962.

Rogers, Guy MacLean. *The Mysteries of Artemis of Ephesos: Cult, Polis, and Change in the Graeco-Roman World.* Synkrisis. New Haven: Yale University Press, 2012.

Roitto, Rikard. *Behaving as a Christ-Believer: A Cognitive Perspective on Identity and Behavior Norms in Ephesians.* Winona Lake, IN: Eisenbrauns, 2011.

Rommen, Edward, ed. *Spiritual Power and Missions: Raising the Issues.* EMS 3. Pasadena: William Carey Library, 1995.

Rosner, Brian S. "Biblical Theology." In *New Dictionary of Biblical Theology*, edited by T. Desmond Alexander and Brian S. Rosner, 3–11. Leicester: InterVarsity, 2000.

———. *Greed as Idolatry: The Origin and Meaning of a Pauline Metaphor.* Grand Rapids: Eerdmans, 2007.

———. "The Missionary Character of 1 Corinthians." In *New Testament Theology in Light of the Church's Mission: Essays in Honor of I. Howard Marshall*, edited by Jon

C. Laansma, Grant R. Osborne, and Ray Van Neste, 181–96. Eugene, OR: Cascade, 2011.
Russell, Brian D. *(Re)Aligning with God: Reading Scripture for Church and World.* Eugene, OR: Cascade, 2016.
Salter, Martin C. "An Exegetical Definition of Missional Ethics." PhD diss., Aberdeen, 2017.
Sampley, J. Paul. *"And the Two Shall Become One Flesh": A Study of Traditions in Ephesians 5:21–33.* SNTSMS 16. Cambridge: Cambridge University Press, 1971.
Sanders, J. N. *Studies in Ephesians.* London: Mowbray, 1956.
Schille, G. *Frühchristliche Hymnen.* Berlin: Evangelische Verlagsanstalt, 1965.
Schlier, Heinrich. "ἀνακεφαλαιόομαι." In *TDNT* 3:681–82.
———. *Christus und die Kirche im Epheserbrief.* Tübingen: Mohr Siebeck, 1930.
———. *Der Brief an die Epheser: Ein Kommentar.* Dusseldorf: Patmos, 1957.
———. *Principalities and Powers in the New Testament.* Freiburg: Herder, 1961.
Schnabel, Eckhard J. *Early Christian Mission.* 2 vols. Downers Grove, IL: InterVarsity, 2004.
———. *Paul the Missionary: Realities, Strategies and Methods.* Downers Grove, IL: InterVarsity Academic, 2008.
Schnackenburg, Rudolf. *Epistle to the Ephesians: A Commentary.* London: T. & T. Clark, 1991.
Schnelle, Udo. *The History and Theology of the New Testament Writings.* Translated by M. Eugene Boring. London: SCM, 1998.
Schreiner, Thomas R. *New Testament Theology: Magnifying God in Christ.* Grand Rapids: Baker, 2008.
Schrenk, Gottlob. "Εὐδοκέω, Εὐδοκία." In *TDNT* 2:738–51.
———. "Πατήρ, Πατρῷος, Πατριά, Ἀπάτωρ, Πατρικός." In *TDNT* 5:945–1022.
Schüssler Fiorenza, Elisabeth. *In Memory of Her: A Feminist Theological Reconstruction of Christian Origins.* New York: Crossroad, 1983.
Schweizer, Eduard. "The Church as the Missionary Body of Christ." *NTS* 8 (1961) 1–11.
Schwindt, Rainer. *Das Weltbild des Epheserbriefes: Eine Religionsgeschichtlich-Exegetische Studie.* WUNT I 148. Tübingen: Mohr Siebeck, 2002.
Scroggs, Robin. "Put on the Armour of God: The Divine Warrior from Isaiah to Ephesians." *CBQ* 61, no. 3 (1999) 600–601.
Seifrid, Mark A. "Romans." In *Commentary on the New Testament Use of the Old Testament*, edited by G. K. Beale and D. A. Carson, 607–94. Grand Rapids: Baker Academic, 2007.
Sellin, Gerhard. "Adresse und Intention des Epheserbriefes." In *Paulus, Apostel Jesu Christi: Festschrift fur Gunter Klein zum 70. Geburtstag*, edited by Günter Klein and Michael Trowitzsch, 171–86. Tübingen: Mohr Siebeck, 1998.
———. *Der Brief an die Epheser.* KEK. Göttingen: Vandenhoeck & Ruprecht, 2008.
———. *Studien zu Paulus und zum Epheserbrief.* Göttingen: Vandenhoeck & Ruprecht, 2009.
Senior, Donald, and Carroll Stuhlmueller. *The Biblical Foundations for Mission.* London: SCM, 1983.
Sherwood, Aaron. "Paul's Imprisonment as the Glory of the *Ethnē*: A Discourse Analysis of Ephesians 3:1–13." *BBR* 221 (2012) 97–112.
Shipp, R Mark. "'Remember His Covenant Forever': A Study of the Chronicler's Use of the Psalms." *ResQ* 35, no. 1 (1993) 29–39.

Shkul, Minna. *Reading Ephesians: Exploring Social Entrepreneurship in the Text*. London: T. & T. Clark, 2009.
Silva, Moisés. "εὐαγγέλιον." In *New International Dictionary of New Testament Theology and Exegesis*, edited by Moisés Silva, 2:306–313. 2nd ed. Grand Rapids: Zondervan, 2014.
Smith, Daniel Lynwood. "The Uses of 'New Exodus' in New Testament Scholarship: Preparing a Way through the Wilderness." *CurBR* 14, no. 2 (2016) 207–43.
Smith, Julien. *Christ the Ideal King: Cultural Context, Rhetorical Strategy, and the Power of Divine Monarchy in Ephesians*. WUNT II 313. Tübingen: Mohr Siebeck, 2011.
Stamps, Dennis L. "Rethinking the Rhetorical Situation: The Entextualization of the Situation in New Testament Epistles." In *Rhetoric and the New Testament: Essays from the 1992 Heidelberg Conference*, edited by Stanley E. Porter and Thomas H. Olbricht, 193–210. Sheffield: JSOT, 1993.
Stanley, Christopher D. *Arguing with Scripture: The Rhetoric of Quotations in the Letters of Paul*. New York: T. & T. Clark, 2004.
———. *Paul and Scripture: Extending the Conversation*. Atlanta: SBL, 2012.
Starling, David I. "Ephesians and the Hermeneutics of the New Exodus." In *Reverberations of the Exodus in Scripture*, edited by R. Michael Fox, 139–59. Eugene, OR: Pickwick, 2014.
———. *Not My People: Gentiles as Exiles in Pauline Hermeneutics*. BZNW. Berlin: de Gruyter, 2011.
Stetzer, Ed. "The Missional Church." In *Missiology: An Introduction to the Foundations, History, and Strategies of World Missions*, edited by John Mark Terry, 99–110. 2nd ed. Nashville: B&H, 2015.
Stirling, Andrew Mark. "Transformation and Growth: The Davidic Temple Builder in Ephesians." PhD diss., St Andrews, 2012.
Stott, John R. W. *The Message of Ephesians: God's New Society*. 2nd ed. BST. Leicester: InterVarsity, 1981.
Strack, Hermann L. and Paul Billerbeck. *Kommentar zum Neuen Testament aus Talmud und Midrasch*. 6 vols. Munich: Beck, 1922–1961.
Strelan, Rick. *Paul, Artemis, and the Jews in Ephesus*. Berlin: de Gruyter, 1996.
Stroope, Michael W. *Transcending Mission: The Eclipse of a Modern Tradition*. London: Apollos, 2017.
Stuhlmacher, Peter. *Biblical Theology of the New Testament*. Translated by Daniel P. Bailey. Grand Rapids: Eerdmans, 2018.
———. "'Er Ist Unser Friede' (Eph 2,14)." In *Neues Testament Und Kirche: Für Rudolf Schnackenburg*, edited by Joachim Gnilka, 337–58. Freiburg: Herder, 1974.
———. "'He Is Our Peace' (Eph 2:14). On the Exegesis and Significance of Eph 2:14–18." In *Reconciliation, Law and Righteousness: Essays in Biblical Theology*, 182–200. Translated by E. R. Kalin. Philadelphia, PA: Fortress, 1986.
Suh, Robert H. "One New Humanity in Christ: The Use of Ezekiel 37 in Ephesians 2." PhD diss., Southern Baptist Theological Seminary, 2006.
———. "The Use of Ezekiel 37 in Ephesians 2." *JETS* 50, no. 4 (2007) 715–33.
Swartley, Willard M. *Covenant of Peace: The Missing Peace in New Testament Theology and Ethics*. Grand Rapids: Eerdmans, 2006.
Swigchem, Douwe van. *Het missionair karakter van de Christelijke gemeente volgens de brieven van Paulus en Petrus*. Kampen: Kok, 1955.
Taber, Charles R. "Missiology and the Bible." *Missiology* 11, no. 2 (1983) 229–45.

Tachau, Peter. *"Einst" und "jetzt" im Neuen Testament: Beobachtungen zu einem urchristlichen Predigtschema in der neutestamentlichen Briefliteratur und zu seiner Vorgeschichte*. Göttingen: Vandenhoeck & Ruprecht, 1972.
Talbert, Charles H. *Ephesians and Colossians*. Paideia Commentaries on the New Testament. Grand Rapids: Baker Academic, 2007.
Tellbe, Mikael. *Christ-Believers in Ephesus: A Textual Analysis of Early Christian Identity Formation in a Local Perspective*. WUNT 242. Tübingen: Mohr Siebeck, 2009.
Temporini, Hildegard, and Wolfgang Haase, eds. *Aufstieg und Niedergang der römischen Welt: Geschichte und Kultur Roms im Spiegel der neueren Forschung*. Part 2, *Principat*. Berlin: de Gruyter, 1972-.
Tennent, Timothy C. *Invitation to World Missions: A Trinitarian Missiology for the Twenty-First Century*. Grand Rapids: Kregel, 2010.
Terry, John Mark, ed. *Missiology: An Introduction to the Foundations, History, and Strategies of World Missions*. 2nd ed. Nashville: B&H, 2015.
Thielman, Frank S. *Ephesians*. BECNT. Grand Rapids: Baker Academic, 2010.
———. "Ephesians." In *Commentary on the New Testament Use of the Old Testament*, edited by G. K. Beale and D. A. Carson, 813–34. Grand Rapids: Baker Academic, 2007.
Thiessen, Werner. *Christen in Ephesus: Die historische und theologische Situation in vorpaulinischer und paulinischer Zeit und zur Zeit der Apostelgeschichte und der Pastoralbriefe*. Tübingen: Francke, 1995.
Thompson, J. A. *1, 2 Chronicles*. NAC 9. Nashville: Broadman & Holman, 1994.
Thomson, Ian H. *Chiasmus in the Pauline Letters*. JSNTSup 111. Sheffield: Sheffield Academic, 1995.
Throntveit, Mark A. "Songs in a New Key: The Psalmic Structure of the Chronicler's Hymn (1 Chr 16:8-36)." In *God So Near: Essays on Old Testament Theology in Honor of Patrick D. Miller*, edited by Brent A. Strawn and Nancy R. Bowen, 153–70. Winona Lake, IN: Eisenbrauns, 2003.
Tidball, Derek J. "Social Setting of Mission Churches." In *Dictionary of Paul and His Letters*, edited by G. F. Hawthorne and R. P. Martin, 883–92. Downers Grove, IL: InterVarsity, 1993.
Towner, P. H. "Households and Household Codes." In *Dictionary of Paul and His Letters*, edited by Gerald F. Hawthorne and Ralph P. Martin, 417–19. Downers Grove, IL: InterVarsity, 1993.
Trebilco, Paul R. *The Early Christians in Ephesus from Paul to Ignatius*. Grand Rapids: Eerdmans, 2004.
Turner, Geoffrey. "Paul and the Old Testament: His Legacy and Ours." *New Blackfriars* 91, no. 1032 (2010) 128–41.
Turner, Max. "Mission and Meaning in Terms of 'Unity' in Ephesians." In *Mission and Meaning: Essays Presented to Peter Cotterell*, edited by Antony Billington, 138–66. Carlisle: Paternoster, 1995.
———. "Spiritual Gifts and Spiritual Formation in 1 Corinthians and Ephesians." *JPT* 22 (2013) 187–205.
Unger, Merrill F. *Zechariah: Prophet of God's Glory*. Grand Rapids: Zondervan, 1963.
Van Aarde, Timothy A. "The Missional Church Structure and the Priesthood of All Believers (Ephesians 4:7-16) in the Light of the Inward and Outward Function of the Church." *Verbum et Ecclesia* 38, no. 1 (2017) 1–9.

———. "The Relation of God's Mission and the Mission of the Church in Ephesians." *Missionalia* 44, no. 3 (2016) 284–300.
———. "The Use of Οἰκονομία for Missions in Ephesians." *Verbum et Ecclesia* 37, no. 1 (2016) 1–10.
———. "The Use of Οἰκονομία for the Missional Plan and Purpose of God in Ephesians 1:3–14." *Missionalia* 43, no. 1 (2015) 45–62.
Van Engen, Charles Edward. "Toward a Theology of Mission Partnerships." *Missiology* 29, no. 1 (2001) 11–44.
Van Roon, Aart. *The Authenticity of Ephesians*. Leiden: Brill, 1974.
VanGemeren, Willem A., ed. *New International Dictionary of Old Testament Theology and Exegesis*. 5 vols. Grand Rapids: Zondervan, 1997.
Vanhoozer, Kevin J. "Introduction: What Is Theological Interpretation of the Bible?" In *Dictionary for Theological Interpretation of the Bible*, edited by Kevin J. Vanhoozer, 19–25. Grand Rapids: Baker Academic, 2005.
Verhey, Allen. *The Great Reversal: Ethics and the New Testament*. Grand Rapids: Eerdmans, 1984.
Verhey, Allen, and Joseph S. Harvard. *Ephesians*. Louisville: Westminster John Knox, 2011.
Von Rad, Gerhard. "Εἰρήνη, Εἰρηνεύω, Εἰρηνικός, Εἰρηνοποιός, Εἰρηνοποιέω." In *TDNT* 2:402–6.
Wagner, J. Ross. *Heralds of the Good News: Isaiah and Paul in Concert in the Letter to the Romans*. NovTSup 101. Boston: Brill, 2003.
Wallace, Howard N. "What Chronicles Has to Say about Psalms." In *The Chronicler as Author: Studies in Text and Texture*, edited by M. Patrick Graham and Steven L. McKenzie, 267–91. JSOTSup 263. Sheffield: Sheffield Academic, 1999.
Walls, Andrew F. *The Cross-Cultural Process in Christian History: Studies in the Transmission and Appropriation of Faith*. Maryknoll, NY: Orbis, 2002.
Ware, James P. *Paul and the Mission of the Church: Philippians in Ancient Jewish Context*. Grand Rapids: Baker Academic, 2011.
Watts, James W. *Psalm and Story: Inset Hymns in Hebrew Narrative*. JSOTSup 139. Sheffield: JSOT, 1992.
Wendland, Ernst R., and Salimo Hachibamba. "A Central African Perspective on Contextualizing the Ephesian Potentates, Principalities, and Powers." *Missiology* 28, no. 3 (2000) 341–63.
Wenkel, David H. "The 'Breastplate of Righteousness' in Ephesians 6:14: Imputation or Virtue?" *TynBul* 58, no. 2 (2007) 275–87.
Wessels, G. F. "The Eschatology of Colossians and Ephesians." *Neotestamentica* 21, no. 2 (1987) 183–202.
Westcott, Brooke F. *Saint Paul's Epistle to the Ephesians: The Greek Text with Notes and Addenda*. London: Macmillan, 1906.
Westermann, Claus. *Isaiah 40–66: A Commentary*. OTL. London: SCM, 1969.
Wild, Robert A. "The Warrior and the Prisoner: Some Reflections on Ephesians 6:10–20." *CBQ* 46, no. 2 (1984) 284–98.
Wilder, William N. "The Use (or Abuse) of Power in High Places: Gifts Given and Received in Isaiah, Psalm 68, and Ephesians 4:8." *BBR* 202 (2010) 185–99.
Wilk, Florian. *Die Bedeutung des Jesajabuches für Paulus*. Göttingen: Vandenhoeck & Ruprecht, 1998.

Williams, Guy. "An Apocalyptic and Magical Interpretation of Paul's 'Beast Fight' in Ephesus (1 Corinthians 15:32)." *JTS* 57, no. 1 (2006) 42–56.

———. *The Spirit World in the Letters of Paul the Apostle: A Critical Examination of the Role of Spiritual Beings in the Authentic Pauline Epistles*. FRLANT 231. Göttingen: Vandenhoeck & Ruprecht, 2009.

Wilson, Bryan R. *Patterns of Sectarianism*. London: Heinemann, 1967.

Windsor, Lionel J. *Reading Ephesians and Colossians after Supersessionism: Christ's Mission through Israel to the Nations*. Eugene, OR: Cascade, 2017.

Winger, Thomas M. *Ephesians*. Concordia Commentaries. St Louis: Concordia, 2015.

Wink, Walter. *Engaging the Powers: Discernment and Resistance in a World of Domination*. Minneapolis: Fortress, 1992.

———. *Naming the Powers: The Language of Power in the New Testament*. Philadelphia, PA: Fortress, 1984.

Wintle, Brian, and Ken Gnanakan. *Ephesians*. Asia Bible Commentary. Singapore: Asia Theological Association, 2006.

Witherington, Ben, III. *The Letters to Philemon, the Colossians, and the Ephesians: A Socio-Rhetorical Commentary on the Captivity Epistles*. Grand Rapids: Eerdmans, 2007.

Wright, Christopher J. H. *The Mission of God's People: A Biblical Theology of the Church's Mission*. Grand Rapids: Zondervan, 2010.

———. *The Mission of God: Unlocking the Bible's Grand Narrative*. Nottingham: InterVarsity, 2006.

———. "'Prophet to the Nations': Missional Reflections on the Book of Jeremiah." In *A God of Faithfulness: Essays in Honour of J. Gordon McConville on His 60th Birthday*, edited by Jamie A. Grant, Alison Lo, and Gordon Wenham, 112–29. New York: Bloomsbury, 2011.

———. "Reading the Old Testament Missionally." In *Reading the Bible Missionally*, edited by Michael W. Goheen, 107–23. Grand Rapids: Eerdmans, 2016.

Wright, Gerald D. "The Purpose of Missions." In *Missiology: An Introduction to the Foundations, History, and Strategies of World Missions*, edited by John Mark Terry, 19–30. 2nd ed. Nashville: B&H, 2015.

Wright, N. T. *Bringing the Church to the World: Renewing the Church to Confront the Paganism Entrenched in Western Culture*. Minneapolis: Bethany House, 1993.

———. "The Letter to the Ephesians." *Theology in Scotland* 20, no. 2 (2013) 5–32.

———. *Paul and the Faithfulness of God*. COQG 4. Minneapolis: Fortress, 2013.

———. "Reading the New Testament Missionally." In *Reading the Bible Missionally*, edited by Michael W. Goheen, 175–93. Grand Rapids: Eerdmans, 2016.

Yee, Tet-Lim N. *Jews, Gentiles and Ethnic Reconciliation: Paul's Jewish Identity and Ephesians*. Cambridge: Cambridge University Press, 2005.

Yoder Neufeld, Thomas R. *Ephesians*. BBC. Scottdale, PA: Herald, 2001.

———. *"Put on the Armour of God": The Divine Warrior from Isaiah to Ephesians*. JSNTSup 140. Sheffield: Sheffield Academic, 1997.

Yuckman, Colin H. "An Ulterior Gospel: The Mission of Critical Hermeneutics and the Critical Hermeneutics of Mission." Paper presented at the Annual Meeting of SBL-AAR, Philadelphia, November 19, 2005. http://www.ibrarian.net/navon/ paper/ An_Ulterior_Gospel.pdf?paperid=3439877.

www.ingramcontent.com/pod-product-compliance
Lightning Source LLC
Chambersburg PA
CBHW071237230426
43668CB00011B/1483